Beatles gear

by ANDY BABIUK

foreword by MARK LEWISOHN

edited by TONY BACON

BEATLES GEAR

Andy Babiuk

A BACKBEAT BOOK

First edition 2001

Published by Backbeat Books

600 Harrison Street,

San Francisco, CA94107

www.backbeatbooks.com

An imprint of The Music Player Network United
Entertainment Media Inc.

Published for Backbeat Books by Outline Press Ltd,
115J Cleveland Street, London W1T 6PU, England.
www.backbeatuk.com

ISBN 0-87930-662-9

Art Director: Nigel Osborne

Design: Paul Cooper

Editors: Tony Bacon, Paul Quinn

Production: Phil Richardson

Origination by Global Colour (Malaysia)

Print by Tien Wah (Singapore)

01 02 03 04 05 5 4 3 2

FOREWORD

I have to make a confession. Though I know I have a reputation of being an "expert" on The Beatles, there has always been a gaping omission in my knowledge, one major aspect of their lives and careers that has remained beyond my grasp: the musical equipment they used.

After I wrote *The Beatles Recording Sessions* I received hundreds of letters from readers, mostly asking some very specific questions. Among these correspondents were scores of fans who hunger for musical equipment data. They asked me intricate questions about the knob on this Beatles guitar or the make of that amp, and I always had to reply that I had no idea about any of it. I have never been a musician; beyond noting that John loved his Rickenbackers and Paul his Hofner violin bass, that George came back from America with a 12-string and Ringo played Ludwig – OK, I do know a few more details beyond this – I had never sought to acquire further information.

And yet The Beatles were musicians who cared deeply for and had great knowledge about their musical instruments. They knew what they liked and why they liked it, and could talk the musicians' talk in the clubs and in the studios. *Beatles Gear: All The Fab Four's Instruments, From Stage To Studio* s an authoritative guide to The Beatles' equipment, with all the evocative names – Vox and Gibson and Leslie and Elpico – making appearances along the way, correctly placed in The Beatles' timeline.

Facts, mundanely reported, can become very boring very quickly; discernibly interpreted and imaginatively presented, however, they can tell a strong story. Andy Babiuk shows himself to be both a persistent researcher and a writer of clarity. The result is a book about a narrow path that permits a broader vista, offering another glimpse, in its way significant, into the Beatles mechanism – that once-in-several-lifetimes combination of hubris, chutzpah and a musical invention literally unparalleled in the modern era.

Mark Lewisohn

Hertfordshire, England, July 2001

**"He was playing one
of these guitars
guaranteed not to
crack, you know?
Not a very good one.
But he was making a
very good job of it
and I remember being
quite impressed."**

PAUL McCARTNEY RECALLS HIS FIRST MEETING WITH JOHN LENNON

1956

"I STARTED WITH BANJO WHEN I WAS 15," SAID JOHN LENNON, "WHEN MY MOTHER TAUGHT ME SOME BANJO CHORDS."[1] WAS THIS THE BEGINNING OF THE MOST POPULAR AND INFLUENTIAL MUSICAL GROUP OF ALL TIME? BUT FIRST, WE MUST TRAVEL BACK IN TIME TO LIVERPOOL, ENGLAND, TO OCTOBER 9TH 1940.

John Winston Lennon was born to Julia and Freddie Lennon at the city's Oxford Street Maternity Hospital. Freddie, a merchant seaman, was away. He would spend most of his time at sea, and rarely saw his son. At first Julia was left alone to bring up John, but soon she began living a more carefree life, dating other men, and increasingly left John to be looked after by her sister, Mary Elizabeth "Mimi" Smith. By the age of five John had moved in with Aunt Mimi at Mendips, a house on Menlove Avenue in a pleasant area of Liverpool.

John attended the nearby Quarry Bank Grammar School, where he showed little interest in schoolwork. In an early display of artistic gifts he spent more time on his own creative projects, including a book he called *The Daily Howl*, which he would fill with drawings and humorous stories.

Lennon's first musical instrument was the harmonica. He later recalled, "I can remember why I took it up in the first place: I must have picked one up very cheap. [Mimi] used to take in students and one of them had a mouth organ and said he'd buy me one if I could learn a tune by the next morning. So I learned about two. I was somewhere between eight and 12 at the time – in short pants, anyway. Another time, I was travelling to Edinburgh on my own to see my Auntie, and I played the mouth organ all the way up on the bus. The driver liked it and told me to meet him at a place in Edinburgh the next morning, and he gave me a good mouth organ."[2]

While living with Aunt Mimi at Mendips, Lennon would often visit his mother's home. During one of these visits, probably in 1955, Julia taught him some basic chords on her banjo, and Lennon's interest in playing a stringed instrument was underway. Lennon's teenage influences included 1950s movies such as *Blackboard Jungle* and *The Wild One* and role models like James Dean, Elvis Presley and, perhaps most significantly, the British skiffle star Lonnie Donegan. By 1956 skiffle, a crude form of homemade popular music, was all the rage with British teenagers. It was popularised by Donegan's hit recording of Leadbelly's 'Rock Island Line', which peaked at number eight in the UK charts in the opening months of 1956, although the music's roots were in the jazz, folk-blues and country-blues of American players like Big Bill Broonzy, Woody Guthrie and others.

Forming a skiffle group was relatively easy. The formula was simple and inexpensive, using cheap folk guitars, a metal washboard, a tea-chest with broomstick "neck" and single string for a bass, a drummer (if you were lucky), and any other instruments that would fit the format, from banjo to piano. Just about anything would do. Teenagers all over Britain were picking up instruments and getting groups together to play this basic new music.

Lennon was a restless 16-year-old when skiffle hit, and along with his schoolmate Pete Shotton they started their own group. At first they were called The Black Jacks, but soon became The Quarry Men – as at first all the members went to Quarry Bank Grammar. The group started to play at parties and church dances. The first line-up consisted of Lennon on guitar, Shotton on washboard, Eric Griffiths on guitar, Rod Davis on banjo, Colin Hanton on drums, and Bill Smith on the tea-chest bass. Smith was later replaced by Ivan Vaughan, then Nigel Whalley, and finally Len Garry.

John Lennon, African guitar player

The band's equipment was primitive, but that was one of skiffle's requirements. Lennon's guitar was a Gallotone Champion, which he ordered from a newspaper ad. There is a much-repeated story that Aunt Mimi bought Lennon his first guitar for £17, but that is not true. Mimi did later buy Lennon a guitar that involved her parting with £17, but it was not his first.

Lennon's biographer Ray Coleman described[3] how Lennon first tried to coax his aunt and then his mother into buying him a guitar. Mimi wouldn't because she thought it would affect his studies. Undeterred, Lennon ordered a guitar and had it sent to Julia's address, figuring that way he would run less risk of being scolded by Mimi. This was the Gallotone Champion. In 1964 Lennon recalled, "I was about 14 when I got my first guitar. It was a beat-up old Spanish model which cost about ten quid. It was advertised in *Reveille* magazine as 'guaranteed not to split'."[4] The Gallotone Champion flat-top acoustic guitar was crudely constructed, about three-quarter size compared to a regular model, and made from laminated woods, unlike the solid material employed for better instruments.

The South African-based Gallo company had been started when Eric Gallo opened his Brunswick record shop in Johannesburg in 1926, but gradually Gallo began to expand as they took on the South African distribution and manufacturing for big labels such as Decca and CBS, and in 1946 became Gallo (Africa) Ltd. Various subsidiary businesses began, and in the late 1930s Gallo set up a small factory next to their Johannesburg premises to build Singer-brand guitars, banjos, ukuleles and mandolins. Around 1946 the instrument factory was moved to a larger, more modern facility in Jacobs, an industrial suburb of Durban. At about the same time the company changed the name of its record imprint to Gallotone, and after a complaint from the Singer sewing machine company the instrument brandname was also changed. For more than two decades Gallo built stringed instruments for the South African market and conducted a large export business. The operation shut down in about 1969, although Gallo continues in the music and video business today.

Inevitably, Gallo's guitars found their way to Britain, where they were marketed through a number of outlets to supply the demand for cheap beginners' instruments. The Champion was the cheapest Gallotone; around 1955 it was being offered at a wholesale price of £2/10/-. This means it probably would have retailed in the UK for around £6 (about $17 then, and in the region of £90 or $125 when translated into today's buying power). The general sound and playability of the Champion reflected its low price. Inside the soundhole was a label that did indeed claim: "GUARANTEED NOT TO SPLIT", and some versions added: "Specially manufactured to withstand all climatic conditions." Even, presumably, the heat of the South African sun. Like many budget guitars of the day, it was probably torture to play. But none of this hindered Lennon's ambition.

"When I was young I played the guitar like a banjo, with the sixth string hanging loose," Lennon remembered later. "I always thought Lonnie and Elvis were great, and all I ever wanted to do was to vamp," he said, meaning to play simple chords to accompany songs. "I got some banjo things off OK, [and later] George and Paul came along and taught me other things. My first guitar cost me £10, advertised in the paper. Why did I get it? Oh, the usual kid's desire to get up on stage, I suppose. And also my mother said she could play any stringed instrument. She did teach me a bit."[5]

Former Quarry Men banjo-player Rod Davis also disagrees with the story that Mimi bought Lennon his first guitar for £17. "The very first guitars that I remember John and Eric Griffiths having were almost identical, and I don't think they would have cost more than £5. Eric's was a lighter coloured wood, John's more of a brownish-red. My recollection is that John got a mail-order guitar from one of the newspapers. It had a treble clef on the headstock, between the machine-heads. The strings weren't attached to the bridge; they went over the bridge and to a tailpiece."

Davis points out that a cheap first guitar was unlikely to cost as much as £17 – which would be the equivalent in today's money of about £250, or $350. "That was an awful lot in those days," he says. "Even a few years later, in 1960, when I first started work before I went to university, I was only getting £5 a week, and that was a lot of money. So £17 would have been a bloody fortune for a guitar." Davis says that the strings they used were mostly Cathedral-brand banjo strings and all roundwound, in other words with round wire wrapped around the central core, as opposed to flatwound strings which have a flatter, smoother surface. "Flatwounds were available," he says, "but they were a lot more expensive – and we were at the bottom of the market."

He recalls that Lennon thrashed his Gallotone guitar and frequently broke strings. "So then he'd take my banjo and play that, and I would have the job of re-stringing his guitar ready for the next number. I frequently held that guitar and put strings on it for him. In fact, he would play it so furiously that he'd take the skin off his index finger and spray blood into his guitar. So somewhere somebody's got a guitar with brown stains inside, under the soundhole – which is John's old guitar."[6]

A Gallotone Champion was sold for a considerable sum in 1999 by Sotheby's as Lennon's original guitar. The auction catalogue related that in the 1980s Aunt Mimi had donated this restored instrument – in a trunk with various other items – to a Liverpool charity that asked her for articles owned by Lennon. Among other items with the guitar in the sale was a typed and undated letter signed "Mimi", agreeing to the request.

"I must admit I didn't know these things still existed until John asked me to sort out his bits and pieces from the old days and send them on to [New York]," the letter states. "The poor old guitar was in such a state when I found it I had it professionally repaired." The auctioned guitar had indeed been restored, including a completely new paint finish, and (presumably done at the same time) a plaque added to the headstock reading: "Remember You'll Never Earn Your Living By It". The sale catalogue says the plaque referred back "to a remark [Mimi] is reported to have made out of exasperation with the hours John spent practising rather than studying".

The letter specified that there was to be no publicity associated with the donation. A handwritten addition to the letter by "Maggie", the addressee, suggests hanging on to the trunk "till I hear back from Olive Mount", referring to a local centre for disabled children. The guitar apparently stayed at Olive Mount and was played by the children there. Subsequently, the father of one of these children who came into possession of the guitar put the instrument up for auction in 1999. A percentage of the sale proceeds was donated to the Olive Mount Learning Disabilities Directorate in Liverpool.

Mimi was interviewed by *The Liverpool Echo* in December 1981 on the first anniversary of Lennon's murder. The paper said the Beatle never forgot Liverpool. "The empty drawers and attic at Aunt Mimi's bungalow are a testimony to that. They used to be full of mementos and souvenirs from the past that Mimi had hoarded for years ... John's first school report, his early paintings, poems, songs, and even his old school tie."[7] A guitar is not mentioned.

Lennon had despatched May Pang from his new home in New York to England in the 1970s to bring back some of these treasured items, including a Rickenbacker guitar and various keepsakes from his schooldays.[8] But evidently no Gallotone. Would a musician in nostalgic mood not want to have his first guitar – if it still existed? The letter allows for this. "[The restored guitar] was to have been a big surprise for John, I can't bring myself to look at it now, it's just too painful." This line would place the letter after Lennon's murder in December 1980. So the donation would have taken place some time in 1981. Mimi herself died in 1991.

All these assumptions hinge on the authenticity of a letter. It's also unfortunate that a restored guitar cannot be visually compared with the few original pictures of the instrument in action with Lennon. And as we shall learn in the next chapter, in the late 1950s Lennon was without a guitar when an early group of his went to Manchester for an audition. It is quite possible that the guitar sold by Sotheby's is Lennon's Gallotone – but equally there is no absolute proof.

Rod Davis wrote about the guitar after the sale, telling of the auction house's request for him to authenticate the instrument. He had been able to do this, he reported, because of that old memory of Lennon cutting his finger while playing the Gallotone and spraying blood inside, onto and around the guitar's label. "I looked inside for the bloodstains," wrote Davis. "Yes, they were clearly there when you knew what to look for." Davis deemed the Gallotone an "extraordinary find", and concluded, "Now I have one less guitar to look for when trawling the junk shops."[9]

Davis told this author of a mysterious guitar that he recalls Lennon playing prior to that first mail-order Gallotone. Quarry Men guitarist Eric Griffiths also recalls such an instrument. "I don't know where John got his, I can't even remember where I got mine, but we had guitars prior to that mail-order one," says Griffiths. "In the early days, the first guitars we both had were very, very cheap, and I think second-hand. I'm almost certain that would have been his original – and then he sent away for the mail-order one. I think he just felt he wanted to improve on that guitar, and so did I. I changed mine relatively soon after we started, too. The mahogany colour of his mail-order guitar wasn't much different to his first."[10]

Lennon himself cleared up the mystery of this "first" guitar in a later interview. "I used to borrow a guitar at first," he said. "I couldn't play, but a pal of mine had one and it fascinated me. Eventually my mother bought me one from one of these mail-order firms – I suppose it was a bit crummy when you think about it, but I played it all the time and I got a lot of practice. After a while we formed The Quarry Men."[11] Unfortunately there are no other details or pictures of this mysterious unnamed acoustic guitar, and no one recalls from whom Lennon borrowed it.

Davis says that when he joined The Quarry Men he used a Windsor Whirle Victor Supremus banjo. Arthur O Windsor had been a big Birmingham-based maker of banjos who'd stayed in business until 1940; Davis's instrument was probably made in the 1920s. Davis had an uncle who played violin and musical saw in a danceband in Wales. "Just after the skiffle craze had started, I was trying to find something to play. We discovered that my uncle's brother-in-law, who played in the same band, was selling a guitar and a banjo, but by the time we got around to it, he'd already sold the guitar. I occasionally wonder what would have happened if he hadn't sold that guitar.

Davis trooped off to north Wales one Sunday and bought the banjo. The following day he bumped into Eric Griffiths at Quarry Bank Grammar. "I said, 'Hey Eric, I got a banjo yesterday.' And he said, 'Oh, great. Do you want to be in a skiffle group?' I said yes, and asked who else was in it. He

I USED TO BORROW A GUITAR AT FIRST. I COULDN'T PLAY, BUT A PAL OF MINE HAD ONE AND IT FASCINATED ME.

John Lennon

Late-1950s string pack from Quarry
Men banjoist Rod Davis's instrument
case, with handwritten banjo tuning
used for the band's guitars. The banjo
magazine was left at Mendips, John's
childhood home, after his Aunt Mimi
moved out.

told me Shotton was playing washboard, some other guy – Bill Smith – is on the tea-chest, and it's
him and Lennon with guitars.

"So that's how I got into The Quarry Men, just by having an instrument," says Davis. "Very
quickly they showed me the three chords, or however many it was, and Eric would shout 'C, F, G7th'
at me. I've still got the banjo tutor I bought to help me get a bit further." Davis says the book taught
him to start playing "inversions", a technical term for altered renderings of chords. "But Lennon
complained that he wouldn't have me playing inversions," laughs Davis. "He didn't like that. It was
too bloody fancy."[12]

In tune with The Quarry Men

Lennon and Griffiths were the guitarists in the new group. Lennon used his Gallotone, Griffiths an
inexpensive archtop instrument possibly made by the Dutch manufacturer Egmond. This non-
cutaway, full-size, hollow-body guitar was distinctive thanks to its unusual cat's-eye-shape f-holes.

The two Quarry Men guitarists did not use the standard guitar tuning of E-A-
D-G-B-E, mainly because their guitar-playing education was less than orthodox.
Griffiths explains how he and Lennon visited someone in nearby Hunts Cross who
advertised guitar lessons. "We only went twice, because the chap wanted to teach
guitar properly, whereas we wanted instant music. So we gave up on that. But John's
mother had played the banjo, so she re-tuned our guitars to banjo tuning and
taught us banjo chords, maybe three or four at the most. And that was it: instant
guitar playing."

Griffiths says they adopted a five-string-banjo tuning. "Lennon and I used this

A Gallotone Champion (main guitar) as John's guitar would have looked. The second example (right) is the Gallotone sold at auction as John's guitar.

Two flyers (far right) from the 1960s issued by the South African Gallotone music company, including the Champion model as played by John.

for some time, until probably a couple of months after Paul McCartney joined. So far as I recall we played the correct banjo chords for the songs instead of guitar chords."[13] Lennon remembered later: "The trouble was that half [the banjo chords were Julia's] own invention and sounded diabolical. Also, when I played them on my guitar I only tuned five strings, and everybody used to laugh when they saw my sixth string flapping about."[14]

Some accounts of The Quarry Men's music-making have Lennon and Griffiths travelling to see someone just to get their guitars tuned. Griffiths corrects this, insisting that he and Lennon tuned their own guitars. Recently, Davis found an original pack of their favourite Cathedral strings in his banjo case, a leftover from his Quarry Men days. This most interesting relic has a handwritten note on the back revealing a banjo "C tuning" of G-C-G-B-D. Only these five notes are written down, confirming Lennon's recollection that five of the guitar's six strings would be tuned, leaving the sixth un-tuned and "flapping about".

Tea-chest bass, washboard and drums

The tea-chest bass was skiffle's inexpensive replacement for the traditional upright double-bass. Rod Davis recalls several versions of the group's tea-chest. "One of them was painted black, and again had the treble clef on it, plus a couple of notes. There was another covered in white wallpaper with brown lines on it – we had some paper left over from our lounge, and I remember my mum wallpapering the tea-chest. With a piece of string and a broomstick handle, it worked very well. You could get quite a good range of notes out of it."[15]

Pete Shotton played the washboard in The Quarry Men, with thimbles on his fingers to scrape the ribbed board and produce a steady, percussive scratch, filling out the rhythm section. The Quarry Men's drummer was Colin Hanton. A drum kit was rare in skiffle groups, mainly because drums cost so much more than a guitar. Hanton's kit was a John Grey Broadway outfit, part of a line of budget-price drums made by British instrument manufacturer and distributor Rose-Morris. Hanton purchased the kit at Hessy's music store in Liverpool – a shop that would become an important source of Beatle equipment in the coming years. "There was a small bass drum," says Hanton of his Broadway kit, "a floor tom, a tom tom, a snare drum, a cymbal, and that was it. No hi-hat. The heads were made of calfskin. It was finished in white lacquer paint – going on orange now," he laughs.

The Quarry Men decided it would be good to have their name on the front of the bass-drum

I ONLY TUNED FIVE STRINGS, AND EVERYBODY USED TO LAUGH WHEN THEY SAW MY SIXTH STRING FLAPPING ABOUT.

John Lennon, recalling his banjo-influenced early guitar playing head. "At first I had my name on it in black," says Hanton, "which I did myself. But my friend Charles Roberts was an apprentice printer, and he made me a nameplate out of a circular piece of paper which fitted over the bass-drum head. It was in florescent orange with black lettering, very professional. In the top left corner it had 'Colin Hanton' and then 'The Quarry Men Skiffle Group' across the middle in a sort of fancy longhand style. It was brilliant, actually. What a pity it's lost."[16]

One of the first Quarry Men performances was on Saturday June 22nd 1957 at a street party in Rosebery Street, Liverpool 8. The Quarry Men played on the back of a flat-bed coal lorry. The show was arranged by Hanton's printer friend Charles Roberts, and the group's line-up for the performance was Lennon on his Gallotone flat-top guitar, Griffiths on his Egmond archtop, Len Garry on tea-chest bass, Pete Shotton on washboard, Rod Davis on his Windsor banjo, and Colin Hanton on the Broadway drum set. Lennon recalled, "We didn't get paid. We played at blokes' parties after that, or weddings, perhaps got a few bob. Mostly we just played for fun."[17]

Lennon meets McCartney

Undoubtedly the most important gig The Quarry Men ever played was at St Peter's Church Garden Fete, in Woolton, near the River Mersey. It was at this historic performance on July 6th 1957 that a 15-year-old Paul McCartney first saw Lennon and his Quarry Men perform. Years later, McCartney naturally remembered the day. "I had a mate at school ... Ivan Vaughan. We were born on exactly the same date in Liverpool, so we were great mates. One day he said, 'Do you want to come to the Woolton Village Fete?' I said, 'Why?' and he said, 'Well, I've got some friends and they'll be there.' That was where he was from, Woolton. And I said, 'Yeah, well, alright.' So we went along one Saturday..."[18]

The Quarry Men pictured at the now-famous church fete performance in the summer of 1957. Left to right: Eric Griffiths with his Egmond guitar; Colin Hanton on Broadway drum kit; Rod Davis with Windsor Whirle banjo; John Lennon on Gallotone Champion guitar; Pete Shotton scratching the washboard; and Len Garry on tea-chest bass.

Lennon too recalled that day. "There was a friend of mine called Ivan who lived at the back of my house, and he went to the same school as Paul McCartney, the Liverpool Institute ... It was through Ivan that I first met Paul. Seems that he knew Paul was always dickering about in music and thought he would be a good lad to be in the group. So one day when we were playing at Woolton, he brought him along. The Quarry Men were playing on a raised platform and there was a good crowd because it was a warm, sunny day. I'd been kingpin up till then. I was the singer and the leader. But now I thought: if I take him on, what will happen? He was good. He also looked like Elvis."

Lennon knew that he had to make an important decision about adding a new person to the group. Should he get in someone new who was better than the existing people, or maintain his position by not making a change and keeping the weaker members? He decided he had to get McCartney in and make his group stronger. "Paul had bought a trumpet," Lennon remembered, "and had this wild theory that he'd actually learn how to play the oldie 'When The Saints Go Marching In'. He just blew away as hard as he could, drowning out everything we were trying to do. He thought he was doing a great job on the tune – but we didn't recognise any of it."[19]

Varying accounts of McCartney meeting Lennon have been detailed in a number of books – some may even have influenced the recollections of those actually there at the time. Most agree that McCartney played Eddie Cochran's 'Twenty Flight Rock' and Gene Vincent's 'Be-Bop-A-Lula' for Lennon and his band. It remains uncertain what guitar McCartney used – an issue complicated by McCartney's left-handedness. Whose guitar did he play? Did he bring his own, or did he invert Lennon's? From the drastically differing accounts given by the five members of The Quarry Men present on the day, no certain answers can be given.

Hanton recalls little about McCartney playing a guitar. Davis doesn't remember much either, but says that if someone had played 'Twenty Flight Rock' impeccably in front of him he'd certainly have remembered. "I think I must have gone to the toilet when this great moment happened,"[20] he laughs.

Shotton doesn't think McCartney had his guitar with him. "Why would he bring his guitar? He didn't come to play. I think Paul said, 'Well, I could play the guitar,' and John said, 'Well go ahead and play this one.' So Paul, being left-handed, took all the strings off and put them back the other way around, and then played 'Twenty Flight Rock' or whatever it was. Then when he'd done all that, John got the guitar back and it was strung left-handed – but John had seen where all the notes were and he left it that way to learn ... John was hungry for information on how to play guitar – he couldn't play very well, he didn't know how to play chords, and Paul came along and knew all that."[21]

Griffiths doesn't think Paul played a guitar that day. "And I definitely don't think Paul switched John's strings around. Being a guitar player, I think I would have been aware of that. I was around all of the time, and I certainly don't think that happened."[22] Tea-chest bass player Len Garry's recollection is that Ivan Vaughan persuaded McCartney to ride his bike home from the Garden Fete and get his guitar, having told McCartney there would be a jam session before the evening show.

Perhaps McCartney himself can remember? Recently, he gave this account. "I went back ... in the mid-day interval that they had, to the church hall, and they were having a few beers. I was a little bit young for that, because John was one-and-a-half years older than me. But they were just hanging out, and someone had a guitar. At some point I thought, 'well, I've got to have a go on this'. What I used to have to do was turn it upside down, being left-handed – no one would ever let me change the strings ... And because I'd done this rather a lot with my mates' guitars, I could play a couple of songs upside down – providing they only had three chords. So I played 'Twenty Flight Rock', and the great thing was I knew all the words to it – and this was true status. Anyone who knew all the words to a thing was quids in. I remember John looking at me, like, wow, this guy's got something here."[23]

The debate will no doubt continue between the five surviving Quarry Men about what actually happened on the day Lennon met McCartney. What was important was that McCartney obviously left a lasting impression on Lennon with his ability to play guitar using "real" guitar chords in a standard guitar tuning, and his knowledge of the lyrics to 'Be-Bop-A-Lula' and 'Twenty Flight Rock'. Two weeks later Shotton by chance ran into McCartney while riding his bike in Woolton. Shotton said, "By the way ... John and I have been talking it over and we both agreed we'd like to ask you if you want to join the group."[24] McCartney said yes.

A trumpet for a Zenith

Lennon always thought McCartney was more advanced musically, writing songs that usually had more chords, probably as a result of his dad having been something of a musician. Lennon's songs were at first based on the simple banjo chords (he called them "funny chords") his mother had taught him. "Paul told me the chords I had been playing weren't real chords," said Lennon. "And his dad said they weren't even banjo chords, though I think they were. Paul had a good guitar at the time. It cost about £14. He got it in exchange for a trumpet his dad had given him. When we first started playing together I learned some chords from Paul – and of course he taught me left-handed shapes. So I was playing a sort of upside-down version of the correct thing, if you can work that one out."[25]

McCartney's guitar at this time was a six-string Zenith Model 17, an archtop non-cutaway acoustic with f-holes. Boosey & Hawkes, a leading British manufacturer and distributor of musical instruments, marketed Zenith guitars in the UK. They were made in Germany and what was then Czechoslovakia. The Model 17 was made by German company Framus. The Zenith brand must have been reasonably popular in Liverpool at the time – Gerry Marsden, later of Gerry & The Pacemakers, had a skiffle group at the time and also owned one. "That was my first guitar, a Zenith," he says. "It actually played quite good."[26]

Probably the nearest equivalent for playability and sound among American-made instruments of the time would have been one of the cheaper laminated-wood archtop guitars by Harmony. But even if musicians could afford them, American instruments were not available in Britain at that time. A UK government embargo on foreign imports had been in place since 1951 and would not be lifted until 1959. So budding musicians in those days had to rely on European-made guitars of sometimes questionable quality.

I COULD PLAY A COUPLE OF SONGS UPSIDE DOWN – PROVIDED THEY ONLY HAD THREE CHORDS.

Paul McCartney

Programme for the church fete at which the Quarry Men played, and the auspicious occasion where John Lennon first met Paul McCartney.

GARDEN FETE
ST. PETER'S CHURCH FIELD

WOOLTON PARISH CHURCH   Rector: M. Pryce Jones

Saturday, 6th July, 1957
at 3 p.m.

ADMISSION BY PROGRAMME
CHILDREN 3d.

PROCEEDS IN AID OF CHURCH FUNDS.

PROGRAMME

STALLS   —   SIDESHOWS   —   ICE CREAM   —   LEMONADE

Teas and Refreshments in large Marquee situated behind the hut.

2-00 p.m. PROCESSION leaves Church Road, via Allerton Road, Kings Drive, Hunt's Cross Avenue; returning to the Church Field. Led by the Band of the Cheshire Yeomanry. Street Collection by the Youth Club during the procession.

3-00 p.m. CROWNING OF THE ROSE QUEEN (Miss Sally Wright) by Mrs. THELWALL JONES.

3-10 p.m. FANCY DRESS PARADE.
Class 1. Under 7 years.
Class 2. 7 to 12 years.
Class 3. Over 12 years.
Entrants to report to Miss P. Fuller at the Church Hall before the procession.

3-30 p.m. MUSICAL SELECTIONS by the Band of the to Cheshire (Earl of Chester) Yeomanry. Band-
5-00p.m. master: H. Abraham.
(By permission of Lt.-Col. G. C. V. Churton, M.C., M.B.E.)

4-15 p.m. THE QUARRY MEN SKIFFLE GROUP.

5-15 p.m. DISPLAY by the city of Liverpool Police Dogs. By kind permission of the Chief Constable and Watch Committee.

5-45 p.m. THE QUARRY MEN SKIFFLE GROUP.

8-0 p.m.   GRAND DANCE in the CHURCH HALL

GEORGE EDWARDS BAND also The Quarry Men Skiffle Group

TICKETS 2/-

REFRESHMENTS AT MODERATE PRICES.

The 1950s Slim Whitman ad from
Melody Maker that helped Paul realise
a guitar could in fact be strung and
played left-handed.

McCartney traded a trumpet for the Zenith, which retailed for 14 guineas (£14.70, about $40 then; around £215 or $300 in today's money). McCartney explained that his father had first bought him the trumpet. "I tried to play [it] and learned 'The Saints' and a couple of things, but my lip was going funny, and I realised I wouldn't be able to sing while I was playing a trumpet. I liked singing. So I traded that in for [the Zenith], which was a right-handed one."[27]

In another interview, McCartney recalls being about 15 when he got the trumpet. "It was kind of a heroic instrument at that time, *The Man With The Golden Arm* and all that. I liked it, and [my father had] been a trumpet player so he showed me a bit. But I realised I couldn't sing with it ... so I asked him if he wouldn't mind if I traded it in for a guitar. He said fine. He was very understanding, an amateur musician himself – he'd had a little band called Jim Mac's Band, in the 1920s.

"So I went down and got a Zenith guitar, which I've still got around somewhere. Quite nice, and I learned on that. My biggest problem – and I realised this when I got it home – was that it was right-handed and I was left-handed, and I didn't know what you did about that, there were no rule books, nobody talked about being left-handed. So I tried it this way and I couldn't get any rhythm because it was the wrong hand doing it. And then I saw a picture of Slim Whitman in *NME* or *Melody Maker*, one of the early musical papers ... and I noticed how he had the guitar on the wrong way around ... And I found out he was left-handed – so I thought, that's good, you can have it the other way 'round.

"Then I changed the strings around. I never could change the nut, I wasn't a tech ... The sixth string always had a fat hole, where the first string would have to go – we'd chop a little bit of a match off, stick that in there, and that would lift the nut enough. And then you had to hollow out a bit of the nut to get the bass string in, because that kept slipping out. So you did your own technical work. High precision! A very do-it-yourself affair. But it eventually worked, and it would hold all the strings, that was the main thing ... if you clouted it, it would just come off."[28]

As well as his Zenith, McCartney also brought a new style of

playing to The Quarry Men. Lennon later explained how he had to revise his banjo-oriented playing. "I thought it was the correct way to play, but after a while I discovered it wasn't and I had to start learning all over again."[29]

But there were changes afoot in The Quarry Men line-up: Davis and Shotton left – Davis says it was probably late July/early August in his case. McCartney first appeared with The Quarry Men on October 18th 1957 at the New Clubmoor Hall in Norris Green, Liverpool, by which time the group had begun taking a greater interest in rock'n'roll, rather than skiffle. The Lennon & McCartney partnership was born.

Lennon still played his Gallotone Champion guitar, McCartney had his new Zenith archtop guitar, Griffiths his Egmond guitar, Len Garry the tea-chest bass, and Hanton his Broadway drum set. McCartney recalls: "I went in as lead guitarist, because I wasn't bad on guitar. When I wasn't on-stage I was even better, but when I got up on stage my fingers all went stiff and found themselves underneath the strings instead of on top of them. So I vowed that first night it was the end of my career as the lead guitar player."[30] That autumn Lennon had enrolled in the Liverpool College Of Art, allowing him time to keep his music and his band alive. The Quarry Men continued playing scattered performances around Liverpool throughout 1957.

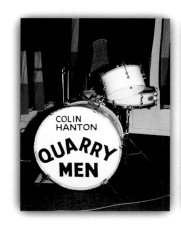  

Recent pictures of Quarry Men equipment, left to right: Colin Hanton's original Broadway drum kit with newly-painted drum head; Rod Davis with his original Windsor Whirle Victor Supremus banjo; and Davis with a reproduction of one of the band's tea-chest basses.

A Zenith model 17 (main guitar) like Paul's original (though his had a pickguard), and an Egmond instrument similar to the one played by Eric Griffiths in The Quarry Men.

"**It's funny how little things can change your whole life. Don't ask me why he chose a guitar instead of a mouth organ or something. They certainly weren't popular at the time.**"

GEORGE HARRISON, ON HIS FIRST GUITAR, BOUGHT FOR HIM BY HIS DAD

1958

THERE WERE SEVERAL CHANGES TO THE QUARRY MEN'S LINE-UP IN 1958. AFTER PAUL McCARTNEY JOINED, AND BANJO PLAYER ROD DAVIS LEFT, THEY ENLISTED A PIANIST, JOHN 'DUFF' LOWE. "JOHN AND PAUL DECIDED THEY WANTED A PIANO PLAYER," SAYS LOWE, "SO THEY ASKED ME. THEN GEORGE HARRISON CAME ALONG."

George had known Paul for some time, Lowe explains. "John let George in about the same time I joined. Skiffle was really falling apart. Len Garry had left, too, so the tea-chest bass and the washboard were gone. All we were left with was Colin the drummer, John, Paul, George, and me. So it was no longer a skiffle band, it was definitely country and rock then."

Duff Lowe's performances with The Quarry Men were sporadic. Some characterise his role as more like sitting in once in a while. Lowe himself says his disappearance before the end of some gigs was simply so that he could catch the last bus. "Remember," he emphasises, "in those days parents were more strict. If you didn't get home, there was hell to pay. So you made sure you got home. But looking back, we weren't taking it seriously. None of us knew what was going to happen. It was just a giggle and having a good time. It was a new thing. Anyone could get into a band if you could play something. It was a hip thing, you know?"[1]

Harrison had started playing guitar at an early age. His first instrument was an inexpensive secondhand acoustic. He later remembered: "When I was about 12 or 13, I heard there was a guy who went to the junior school I went to, and he was selling this guitar. Cost me £3/10/- ... Just a little cheap acoustic guitar, but I didn't really know what to do with it. I noticed where the neck fitted on the box it had a big bolt through it, holding it on. I thought, 'Oh, that's interesting.' I unscrewed it, and the neck fell off. And I was so embarrassed, I couldn't get it back together, so I hid it in the cupboard for a while. Later my brother fixed it. Then there was this big skiffle craze happening for a while in England – which was Lonnie Donegan. He set all them kids on the road. Everybody was in a skiffle group. Some gave up, but the ones who didn't give up became [the bands] of the early 1960s ... We all just got started on that. You only needed two chords ... And I think that is basically where I've always been at. I'm just a skiffler, you know? Now I do posh skiffle. That's all it is."[2]

George's first guitar

Harrison's first guitar was a Dutch-made Egmond instrument, distributed in the UK by Rosetti. The guitar is currently on display at the Rock & Roll Hall Of Fame Museum in Cleveland, Ohio. Egmond's main factory was at Best, just north of Eindhoven in The Netherlands, and it produced low-cost, low-quality guitars for many European players. They were imported exclusively into the UK by Rosetti, who used their own name on many Egmond products. Harrison acquired his Egmond some time in 1955 or 1956. It was a primitive beginner-instrument – but of course that didn't stop him persevering with guitar playing.

"I started learning to play the guitar when I was 13," Harrison recounted a few years later, "on an old Spanish model which my dad picked up for fifty bob [£2.50]. It's funny how little things can change your whole life. Don't ask me why he chose a guitar instead of a mouth organ or something. They certainly weren't popular at the time. Anyway, I learned my first basic chords on it."[3]

Harrison was friends with McCartney prior to his arrival in The Quarry Men. "I met John and George round about the same time," says McCartney. "George used to get on the bus one stop after mine. We were round about the same age, [and] it was probably his haircut or something [that made me think] he's a bit groovy. He had what we used to call a bit of a Tony Curtis, greased back, you know? So I'd think, well, he's probably all right to talk to. We got chatting on the bus, and he had an interest in guitars like I did, and music. Turned out he was going to try to make a little solid-body Hawaiian [guitar] – which was a good place to start, you didn't have to get into the hollow body or anything, which was very difficult. We kind of hung out and became good friends. He did that Hawaiian thing and it wasn't bad. Real high action, of course."[4]

The 15-year-old Harrison's first encounter with his friend's group was at the Morgue Skiffle Cellar, as Quarry Men drummer Colin Hanton explains. "We went to an unofficial club in Liverpool called The Morgue," he remembers. "I found out in later years the reason nobody knew about it was because it was in the basement of a disused building, and gatherings in a disused building were illegal – so it wasn't advertised.

"I think Rory Storm & The Hurricanes had something to do with the club, and we were invited

This Hofner President (main guitar) is exactly like the one George used in The Quarry Men and which he later traded for an electric model with a member of The Swinging Blue Jeans. The other instrument here is an Egmond similar to George's first guitar.

along one weekday evening to play. We met George Harrison there. Whether it was pre-arranged or not I don't know, but I remember George was there. There was a long corridor in this place, with changing rooms at one end and the playing room at the other, and George played something like a guitar boogie for us.

"On the Saturday following, late afternoon, I was going out to the bus stop, and the band's manager at the time, Nigel Wally, came pedalling around the corner on his push bike. He said, 'I've been up with John and Paul and they want George Harrison in the group and they want Eric Griffiths out.' Eric was the third guitarist at the time. I said it didn't make a lot of sense to me, but John and Paul ran the thing: if they wanted someone in they could have them in, if they wanted someone out, they can have that too. And that was it. George was in, Eric was out."[5]

It was McCartney who persuaded Lennon to hear Harrison audition – on a bus. McCartney told Lennon he had a mate who was a really good guitarist, but Lennon seemed unimpressed until it was mentioned that this potential guitarist could manage 'Raunchy'. This piece – a big instrumental hit in the UK for saxophonist Bill Justis at the time, and Ernie Freeman had put a guitar version in the US charts – was one of the group's favourites, so Lennon was persuaded to host an audition.

"I remember we ended up on the top deck of an empty late-night bus," McCartney recalled. "It was just us there, and I was saying, 'Go on, George, you get your guitar out. Go on. You show him.'

Then he got it out ... Sure enough, note perfect, 'Raunchy'. You're in!"[6] Lennon's memories of Harrison joining were much the same. "Paul introduced me to George, and Paul and I had to make the decision whether to let George in. I listened to George play, and I said, 'Play "Raunchy",' ... and I let him in. That was the three of us, then. The rest of the group was thrown out gradually. It just happened like that: instead of going for an individual thing, we went for the strongest format, and for equals."[7]

George in his early teens playing his first guitar, a cheap acoustic flat-top made by Egmond in The Netherlands.

The first President and early electronic experiments

With Harrison in The Quarry Men the group now included three members of the future Beatles. Harrison's guitar was a Hofner President he'd acquired before joining. Hofner had been set up way back in the 1880s by Karl Höfner in Schoenbach, Germany, at first to make violins, cellos and double-basses. Guitars appeared in 1925, by which time Karl's sons Josef and Walter had joined their father, and the business had grown considerably. After World War II the Höfner family moved to Erlangen, and began production again in 1949, two years later relocating to Bubenreuth. Archtop guitars were added to the catalogue during the early 1950s. Electric models were soon introduced to address the growing market in Germany, and included smaller semi-hollow models with a single-cutaway shape something like that of a Gibson Les Paul.

Hofner guitars appeared in the UK in 1953, thanks to importer Selmer who commissioned acoustic archtop models made specifically to their requirements,

with UK-only model names such as Golden Hofner, Committee, President and Senator. Electric single-pickup Club 40 and two-pickup Club 50 in Hofner's semi-hollow single-cutaway style were added to Selmer's line in 1955. Harrison's sunburst acoustic President was one of the better models in the Hofner line, and cost 32 guineas (£33.60, or $90 then; around £475 or $670 in today's money).

Harrison said later, "I got what they call a cello-style, f-hole, single-cutaway called a Hofner, which is like the German version of a Gibson. I got a pickup and stuck it on."[8] Up to this point The Quarry Men had used only acoustic instruments, with no amplification other than the simple microphones used for singing at gigs. About the time Harrison joined, the group began to play around with amplifying their instruments. John Lowe recalls, "They were trying to experiment with pickups that you could buy and stick on the guitar. These units had two prongs that you would put down the neck and bolt in place. You got a sort of electric sound – otherwise you just wouldn't be heard. If you listen to The Quarry Men recordings [on *Anthology 1*] of 'In Spite Of All The Danger' and 'That'll Be The Day' the guitars sound amplified, not acoustic."[9]

McCartney too remembered the group's early games with amplification. "I've still got my first amp. I think I bought it from Currys, the electrical shop. Nobody could afford electric guitars, they were very expensive. So what you would buy was a pickup and an amp, and you'd put your pickup on your acoustic. I got this green amp called an Elpico, which was great. It was really built for some bygone era, where there were mikes and gramophones. It was probably the cheapest I could find, you know? Not being a cheapskate, but I didn't have that much money, and our family wasn't rolling in it, so I couldn't really hit my dad for it. I've still got it, and it's brilliant."[10]

The Elpico brandname came from the initial letters – L P Co – of the manufacturer, Lee Products Co, which was based in north-west London. Lee made a number of small units designed for amplifying musical instruments, vocal microphones and record-players. At the time McCartney bought his Elpico AC-55 model, UK distributors included Beare & Sons, Rosetti, and Boosey & Hawkes. The retail price would have been £24/3/- (£24.15, about $68 then; around £330 or $460 in today's money). The Quarry Men now consisted of Lennon on his Gallotone Champion guitar, McCartney on his Zenith, Harrison on his Hofner President, Hanton on his Broadway drum set, and John 'Duff' Lowe on piano.

Getting it recorded

By the middle of 1958 The Quarry Men had set out to make their first semi-professional recording. After putting their money together, the band headed for 38 Kensington, Liverpool 7, where Percy Phillips had a primitive tape-recording facility set up in his home, advertised as PF Phillips Professional Tape & Disk Recording Service. He offered minimal recording equipment, but enough to get the job done. There was a Vortexion portable reel-to-reel tape recorder, an MSS portable disc-cutting machine, an amplifier and four-way microphone mixer, and just three microphones, by Reslo, HMV and AKG.

At Phillips makeshift home studio in the early summer of 1958 The Quarry Men recorded a 78rpm 10-inch acetate disc of Buddy Holly's 'That'll Be The Day' and an original composition by Harrison and McCartney called 'In Spite Of All The Danger', both sung by Lennon. The session featured Lennon, McCartney and Harrison on guitars, John Lowe on piano, and Colin Hanton on drums. There was no bass guitar. These historic recordings can be heard on *Anthology 1*.

Some accounts of the session suggest that the recording was made on tape first and then cut to a lacquer acetate disc. John Lowe maintains that they recorded it direct to disc. "For three reasons," he explains. "First, it would have cost us more to have gone to tape first. Second, on 'In Spite Of All Danger' in particular there are mistakes where John comes in late with the vocals. If we were running tape I think we would have gone back to put it right. And third, I can well remember Percy Phillips waving his hands at us to say, 'You've got to finish now lads,' because we were getting to the centre of the disc. If we'd been recording to tape first, he'd have said we were going too long and that we would have to re-record it shorter."[11]

The Quarry Men continued to play live dates throughout 1958. One of the only documents of these performances is a photograph taken on December 20th 1958 at the wedding reception of Harrison's brother, Harry. It shows McCartney with his Zenith guitar and Harrison with his Hofner President. Lennon is present, but with no instrument visible. It was also during this period that

NOBODY COULD AFFORD ELECTRIC GUITARS ... YOU WOULD BUY A PICKUP AND AN AMP, AND PUT YOUR PICKUP ON YOUR ACOUSTIC.

Paul McCartney

Lennon and McCartney began to write songs together, some of which would later become Beatle songs, including 'Love Me Do', 'The One After 909', 'Hello Little Girl' and 'When I'm 64'.

A night at the Casbah

The Quarry Men stayed together into 1959… but with no particular direction. Drummer Colin Hanton was the next to leave. After a performance in the early part of the year in Prescot, out towards St Helens, Hanton had fallen into a vicious argument with the other members of the group. That night on his way home Hanton decided to leave, and never played with them again.

The Quarry Men would perform without a drummer after Hanton's departure, as McCartney recalls. "We used to have three guitars, it was just John, me and George, and we used to say to people, 'We don't need a drummer, the rhythm's in the guitars, man.' When they used to book us they'd say, 'You haven't got a drummer?' And we'd say, 'The rhythm's in the guitars.'"[12] Drummerless, the group started to drift apart and eventually all but disbanded. Harrison started to play with another band called The Les Stewart Quartet, which also included guitarist Ken Brown.

The summer of 1959 brought the opening of a new Liverpool hang-out, the Casbah Coffee Club in Hayman's Green, West Derby. It was a teenager's social club that boasted live music, and was run by Mona Best. The Les Stewart Quartet was scheduled to perform on the opening night, August 29th 1959. Mona Best's son Pete – who would soon be a Beatle – recalls the events that led up to the first night at the Casbah. "The original line-up of the Les Stewart Quartet that should have opened the club broke up a couple of weeks before," he says. "Mo, my mother, had already promised Ken Brown the gig with the Quartet.

"It was going to be a residency, and residencies in those days were like gold-dust. So Ken and George Harrison came down and saw Mo to explain their position. George said not to worry too much because he happened to know a couple of guys he used to play with – who turned out to be John Lennon and Paul McCartney. So they all came down the next day, and Mo, George and Ken introduced them to one another. It was the first time Ken had met them.

"They put the deal to John and Paul, who said, 'Yeah, we're going for it. Sounds great – our own club. We've got a residency!' Then Mo asked what they were going to call themselves. And John said, 'Well, I had a band called The Quarry Men. How does that sound?' She said that sounded great. So they took the stage on the opening night as a four-piece, with no drummer."[13] The revitalised Quarry Men continued after that opening night at the Casbah, playing every Saturday through to October.

Aunt Mimi puts down £17 for a Hofner

With the extended Casbah engagement providing some welcome cash, Lennon and Harrison both acquired new Hofner Club 40 electric guitars. These were small, semi-hollow-body German-made electric guitars, commissioned and imported to Britain by Selmer.

Lennon purchased his Club 40 just one day before the first Casbah performance. A hire-purchase receipt from Hessy's Music shop dated August 28th 1959 details a "Club 40 Hofner guitar" sold to John Lennon of 25 Menlove Avenue, Woolton, Liverpool, with Lennon described as a "student". The guarantor of the loan is noted as Mary Elizabeth Smith – better known to John, of course, as Aunt Mimi. She placed a deposit of £17 for the new Hofner on that Friday in August. Total cash price was £28/7/-, but hire-purchase pushed that up to £30/9/- (£30.45, about $85 then; around £400 or $560 in today's money). The document shows not only the date that Lennon acquired his Club 40, but finally puts to rest the story that Mimi bought Lennon his "first guitar" for £17.

Author Ray Coleman has described how Lennon kept working on Aunt Mimi to buy him "a real guitar". Mimi recalled, "I wasn't too ready to provide it because I thought he should be getting on with his school work a little more seriously. But he kept on and on: 'Let me get it out of my system, Mimi.' I said: 'All right, get it out of your system'." One morning, wrote Coleman, she took Lennon along to Hessy's musical instrument shop, off Whitechapel. Mimi continued: "There were guitars hanging all around the room and John didn't know which one to choose for the best. Finally, he pointed to one and the man took it down, and he played it and said, 'I'll have that one.' What I do remember is John nodding his head to me, and me paying the £17 there and then for it. He was as happy as could be on the bus home."[14]

Aunt Mimi pictured at Mendips, the house in Liverpool where she brought up John.

The receipt from Hessy's music store for John's original Hofner Club 40 guitar. The document shows that Aunt Mimi was the guarantor for the hire-purchase deal, and paid a £17 deposit.

ROCK 'N' ROLL   SKIFFLE

The Quarry Men

                MANAGER
OPEN FOR ENGAGEMENTS   GATEACRE 1715

George swapped his Hofner President for a Club 40 owned by Ray Ennis of The Swinging Blue Jeans. Ennis is pictured here with the group (second from bottom left) playing the Club 40.

This new discovery of the Hessy's receipt shows that Mimi's famous £17 was a deposit only, and that this guitar she started to pay for was not in fact his first – that was the Gallotone acoustic – although it probably does qualify as his first "real" instrument.

Harrison, who had also acquired a Hofner Club 40 guitar, remembered a few years later, "My first electric job [was] a big Hofner President. But I soon got fed up with it and did a straight swap for a Club 40. I thought it was the most fantastic guitar ever."[15]

Harrison said he swapped his Hofner President with one of The Swinging Blue Jeans to acquire his Club 40. Ray Ennis of that band remembers the trade. "The Club 40 that George got was originally mine," he confirms. "We had our residency on Tuesdays at the Cavern, and I remember we did the swap there. I swapped it for his acoustic Hofner, which was sunburst, with f-holes. I haven't got it now – because at the time, who thought The Beatles would be so famous? In those early days we used to get fed up with guitars very quickly, so we'd swap and change a lot."[16]

A more obscure guitar from around this period is mentioned by Lennon in an early-1960s interview. "After a few months of chord-learning I decided to buy a model which I think was called a Martin Coletti," said Lennon. "But a short time later both George and I saw a Hofner Club 40 and we both thought it was the end."[17]

Unfortunately there are no photographs to substantiate Lennon owning or playing a Martin Coletti guitar. The only evidence of the guitar is what Lennon himself mentioned in this one interview. Considering what he said more carefully, it's possible to infer that he'd "decided" to buy the guitar... but didn't actually get around to the purchase, preferring the electric Hofner.

A pair of Hofner Club 40s similar to those played by John and George. John's was like the main guitar, with a rectangular control panel and vertical headstock logo, while George's had the early-style round panel and horizontal logo.

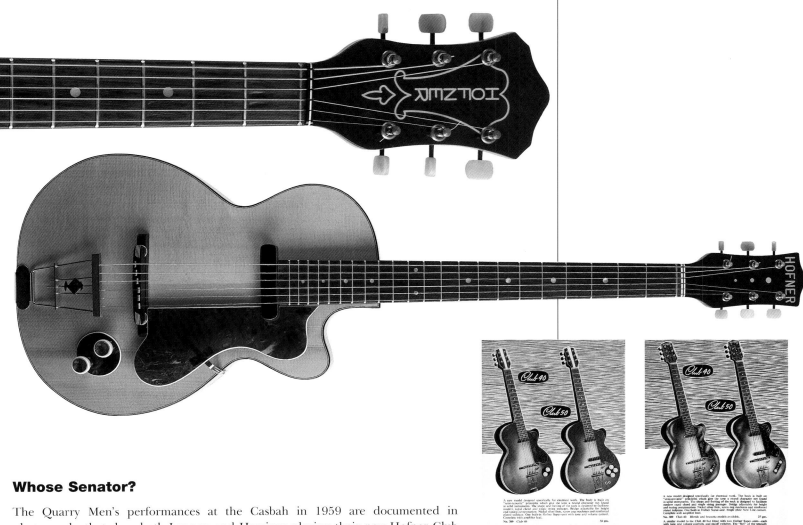

Whose Senator?

The Quarry Men's performances at the Casbah in 1959 are documented in photographs that show both Lennon and Harrison playing their new Hofner Club 40 electric guitars. McCartney is pictured with his Zenith guitar that has a pickup attached, and in this same photograph Ken Brown can be seen with a blonde-finish Hofner Senator model guitar.

In more recent years a guitar similar to Ken Brown's turned up at a 1992 auction as "John Lennon's Hofner … Senator", offered with a letter of authenticity from George Harrison which in part read that "the Hofner is one of the first guitars of John's going back to the early days in Liverpool (1960-ish)".[18] Lennon was never pictured playing this guitar, nor did he ever mention such a Hofner in interviews about his original guitars. Generally, Lennon accurately recalled his succession of instruments – but never once mentioned a Hofner Senator. And it is difficult to imagine why Lennon would have gone back to playing an archtop acoustic instrument after owning a Hofner Club 40 electric.

Yet there are pictures of Ken Brown playing a Hofner Senator with the same type of finish. Perhaps the auctioned Hofner may have been Ken Brown's? Perhaps Harrison's memory of this guitar may have been confused with what Lennon described as his Martin Coletti? But there are no

Two catalogues issued by Selmer, the company that distributed Hofner guitars in the UK in the 1950s, showing the two different Club model styles.

facts to support the idea that the blonde Hofner Senator offered at auction ever belonged to or was played by John Lennon.

Cool cats?

Ken Brown's involvement with The Quarry Men turned out to be brief, lasting only for the six-week stretch of shows at the Casbah during 1959. Brown wrote of his experiences in a fanzine published six years later. "Sometimes I could kick myself – hard." he began. "I could still be one of The Beatles, earning thousands of pounds a week, instead of living in a caravan." He explained how he accompanied John, Paul and George the first time they played together at the Casbah. "We shared everything – our music, and the £3 a night we used to earn in those far-off days in 1959."

Brown recalled how he used to play with Harrison in the Les Stewart Quartet, practising for hours at the Lowlands Club, Hayman's Green. Harrison's girlfriend Ruth suggested seeing Mrs Best, who promised that the Quartet could play at her Casbah club's opening – as mentioned above, in Pete Best's recollection. On the Saturday in question Brown went to Les Stewart's house. Harrison sat in the lounge, his Hofner guitar across his lap, and idly plucked at the strings. "The atmosphere," wrote Brown, "seemed a bit tense. 'What's up?' I asked. George looked down at his guitar, and said nothing. So I turned to Les. He looked daggers. 'You've been missing practice,' he said. 'I know,' I replied, 'but only so's we can have somewhere to play – I've spent hours working up the club.' 'You've been getting paid for it,' challenged Les. 'No I haven't'. 'Well, I'm not going to play there,' said Les, as our argument got steadily more heated. I turned to George. 'Look,' I said, 'the club opens tonight. We've spent months waiting for this – you're not backing out, too?'

"George thought for a moment. Then he told me that he would go on with me, so we left Les at his house. As we were walking down the road, I turned to George and said: 'We can't let Mrs Best down now. Let's try and get a group together ourselves. Do you know anyone?' 'There's two mates I sometimes play with out at Speke,' ventured George. 'OK, let's ask them,' I said, and George went off on the bus, joining me two hours later at the Casbah with his two mates – John Lennon and Paul McCartney."

This was the first time Brown had met John and Paul. He said they'd each be paid 15 bob a night (15 shillings, or 75p, about $2 then; around £10 or $14 in today's money). "We went down great," wrote Brown in that 1960s fanzine, "particularly when Paul sang 'Long Tall Sally'. Our most popular numbers were John and Paul's vocals – I was the rhythm guitarist. John's pet solo was 'Three Cool Cats', which he used to growl into the mike. John was always very quiet. He was a lonely youngster."

During one of the following Saturday sessions at the Casbah, Brown suddenly felt a crippling pain in his leg. He could barely stand, but insisted on doing something. Mona Best asked him to take money on the door. "Just as everyone was going home, I was sitting in the club when Paul came back down the steps. 'Hey, Ken, what's all this?' he said. 'What?' I asked him. 'Mrs Best says she's paying you, even though you didn't play with us tonight.' 'That's up to her,' I replied as Paul bounded back up the stairs, still arguing over it with Mrs Best. They all came downstairs to me. 'We think your 15 bob should be divided between us, as you didn't play tonight,' said Paul. 'That's up to Mrs Best,' I said as the argument continued. By this time, we were all shouting. And Mrs Best insisted on paying me the 15 bob. 'All right, that's it then,' shouted Paul, and they stormed off down the drive towards West Derby village, shouting that they would never play at the Casbah again. That wasn't the last time they played at the Casbah – though we didn't play together again,"[19] concluded Brown.

All seven of the performances by The Quarry Men in 1959 were without a drummer, and if they were questioned about the absence of percussion the group cheerfully continued to use the line about the rhythm being in the guitars. There were certainly enough guitars to provide that rhythm: a Zenith, two Hofner Club 40s, and a Hofner Senator. As for amplifiers, Ken Brown says: "During the period we played together as The Quarry Men at the Casbah, amplification was provided by my Watkins Westminster. If John, Paul or George had their own amps at the time, they weren't used at the Casbah during the period we played there."[20]

Charlie Watkins was an amplifier maker who'd started out in south London earlier in the 1950s, the Westminster being one of his first products. Later, Watkins became better known when his WEM (Watkins Electric Music) PA equipment appeared at many 1960s pop shows.

A picture from the late 1950s of one-time Quarry Men member Ken Brown playing his Hofner Senator guitar.

Talent on show

October 10th marked the last date of The Quarry Men's residency at the Casbah club. With no regular gigs lined up, Lennon, McCartney and Harrison banded together as Johnny & The Moondogs and set their sights on Carroll Levis's talent contest, known as *Mr Star Maker*. Winning the contest would guarantee an appearance on Levis's popular ATV television show *Discoveries*. Two years earlier, as The Quarry Men, they had failed to pass the audition. This time, as Johnny & The Moondogs, they got through the first test and so went on to the finals, which took place in Manchester on Sunday November 15th 1959.

Harrison and McCartney later recalled the event. Harrison said everyone knew that the Levis show was a scam devised to string out the suspense as long as possible, from week to week (and maximise audience numbers). McCartney said he and Harrison and Lennon travelled to Manchester by train from Liverpool, rehearsing on the way. "And only me and George had our guitars," said McCartney. "I think John must have sold his or busted it or something. He didn't have his with him." Harrison noted that this actually looked quite good – with the left-handed McCartney on one side,

George playing his solidbody Futurama guitar live on-stage, "the only thing I could find resembling a Strat". The Resonet logo on the pickguard refers to the guitar's pickup manufacturer. (The picture was taken at a 1961 performance in Hamburg.)

1959

The Hessy's hire-purchase document for George's Futurama (below) dated November 20th 1959 and showing a deposit payment of £10.

right-handed Harrison on the other, and a guitar-less Lennon in the middle. McCartney added: "We were going to do 'Rave On'. So we went, we did it, [John] put his arms around us … It was OK. We didn't win, as usual."[21]

Another couple of young hopefuls entering the Manchester competition were Allan Clarke and Graham Nash. At the time the duo called themselves Ricky & Dane. Nash gives his account of the competition. "Carroll Levis would get in local talent under the guise of an audition and would be able to make money and have a show for which he paid nothing. At that time Allan Clarke and I used to sing together. We auditioned for Levis because if you made it past all the auditions then you got to go to London and perhaps be on television. This was unbelievable...

"So we went to the venue in Manchester and on that one show of completely unknown talent were Allan and I, who later formed The Hollies, a guy named Freddie Garrity, who was later Freddie of Freddie & The Dreamers, an early English rocker called Billy Fury, and Johnny & The Moondogs, this three-piece band from Liverpool who did a Buddy Holly song. I loved them because they were doing Buddy Holly stuff – and we obviously loved Holly because we soon named our band after him. The Moondogs had a raw edge. They looked as if they didn't give a shit about being there."[22]

While it seems Harrison and McCartney had taken their guitars to the contest finals in Manchester, it turns out it wasn't so unusual for Lennon not to have a guitar with him. The number of guitars the trio used varied from gig to gig, as McCartney explained in another recent interview: "There were three of us on guitar at that time, on and off – the nucleus was just three guitars. Sometimes John wouldn't even have his guitar … He nicked a guitar at that audition, so he had a guitar again. But it was mainly three guitars."[23]

While most authorities date this second attempt at the Carroll Levis talent contest to 1959, it's interesting to ask why, if Lennon had a brand new Hofner Club 40 to show off, he did not take it with him to Manchester. Could it be that the incident actually occurred in late 1958?

In any event, the contest went into overtime. Judgement was made by measuring audience

Like the Futurama played by George, this example is without a maker's name on the headstock and has the pickup maker's logo "Resonet" on the pickguard. These Futurama

instruments were made for British importer Selmer by Delicia, based in what was then Czechoslovakia. The picture below shows the Futurama in its original case.

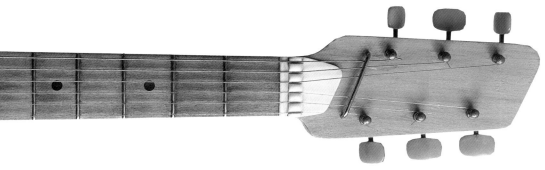

applause when each band made a final appearance. But with no plans of staying overnight and just enough money to get back home, Lennon, McCartney and Harrison had to catch the last train and leave for Liverpool before discovering the outcome. Nonetheless, they probably sensed that they'd failed again.

George gets a Futurama

While the group failed to win the Levis contest, the year finished well for Harrison. Five days after the Moondogs trip to Manchester, he made his way to Frank Hessy's music store to purchase a new guitar, and on November 20th signed a hire-purchase agreement for a Futurama. This instrument was the closest that most guitarists in Britain at the time could get to that holy grail of electric guitars, the Fender Stratocaster. Since late 1958 many keen British guitarists had been ogling the cover of a Buddy Holly record that had a shiny, space-age, three-pickup guitar on the front. George Harrison was one.

"If I'd had my way," Harrison said later, "the Strat would have been my first guitar. I'd seen Buddy Holly's Strat ... on the *Chirping Crickets* album cover, and tried to find one. But in Liverpool in those days the only thing I could find resembling a Strat was a Futurama. It was very difficult to play, [the strings were] about half-an-inch off the fingerboard ... but nevertheless it did look kind of futuristic."[24]

The guitar was made by Delicia, an instrument manufacturer based in Horovice, Czechoslovakia, which produced guitars with a number of brandnames including Neoton and Lignatone. The Futurama had first arrived in Britain around the time Harrison bought his, once again thanks to the shrewd marketing sense of importers Selmer – who also came up with the modern-sounding brandname. The ban on imports of American instruments was still preventing Fender Stratocasters and other Stateside wonders from reaching most British hands.

Delicia's guitar at first had "Grazioso" on the headstock, but Harrison's simply had "Resonet" on the pickguard – the name of the Czech company which supplied Delicia with pickup assemblies. The cheaply-made Futurama, loosely Fender styled, retailed in the UK for 55 guineas (£57.75, about $160 then; around £780 or $1,100 in today's money). Although Harrison later admitted his Futurama was "a dog" to play, he added, "it had a great sound, though, and a real good way of switching in the three pickups and all the combinations."[25] A Fender it was not – but at least it was a solid-body electric guitar.

"People were like: 'My God, what's John playing? We've never seen anything like that before.' Some players asked if he'd had it made specially, and he'd explain that he bought it at a shop."

PETE BEST, ON THE REACTION IN LIVERPOOL WHEN JOHN LENNON BROUGHT HIS NEW RICKENBACKER 325 BACK FROM HAMBURG IN 1960

1960

INTO 1960, AND THREE DISILLUSIONED QUARRY MEN / MOONDOGS WERE DETERMINED TO PERSEVERE, AND TO PUSH FORWARD. AS FATE WOULD HAVE IT, THIS TURNED OUT TO BE A YEAR OF CRUCIAL DEVELOPMENTS FOR LENNON, McCARTNEY AND HARRISON. IT ALL STARTED WHEN LENNON PERSUADED HIS FRIEND FROM ART COLLEGE, STU SUTCLIFFE, TO JOIN THE GROUP AS BASS PLAYER.

As the story goes, Sutcliffe had some of his work displayed at the Walker Art Gallery in Liverpool. One of Sutcliffe's canvases was purchased for £65. At the time this was a large sum of money for a starving artist – it's the equivalent today of about £900 or $1,250. But instead of using the money to further his art career, Sutcliffe was cajoled by his friend Lennon and the other Quarry Men into buying a bass guitar and joining the group.

McCartney recalls the opportunity to add a bass player to the group's line-up when Sutcliffe won his monetary prize. They pointed out to Sutcliffe the terrific coincidence that his prize money would exactly cover the cost of a Hofner bass. Sutcliffe at first insisted that the money was supposed to further his art career. "Well," says McCartney, "we managed to persuade him – over a cappuccino at the Casbah, Pete Best's mum's club in West Derby. We'd kind of helped to make the club, there were painted stripes on the wall and we'd painted a stripe each – very much [like in Cliff Richard's movie] *The Young Ones*. It was a coffee bar, everyone was doing that. It was a nice little hang-out. I remember we were sitting around a table – me, John, Stu, maybe George – and we persuaded Stu to do it. So he bought the giant Hofner, again at Hessy's or Rushworth's in Liverpool, those were the two, depending on who had it in stock, probably Hessy's. You had the little book, paying in each week, like a Christmas club or something.

"The bass dwarfed him a bit, he was a smallish guy. But it looked kind of heroic, he stood a certain way, he had shades, he looked the part ... but he wasn't that good a player. And that was the problem with me and Stu – it was always much reported that we didn't get along. There were two reasons really: one, I was very ambitious for the group, and I didn't actually like anything that might hold us back. Cos there's enough stuff holding you back anyway, without someone in the group who's not that good. Any of our mates could look at the group and spot it, any of the good groups around – Kingsize Taylor & The Dominoes, The Big Three, Faron's Flamingos – any of those guys would just spot it: bass player's not much. You knew that, there was no kidding people from Liverpool, or kids of that age, they don't mess around. It was just: lousy bass player, man. So that was always a little bit of a problem, you know?

"We sometimes used to tell him to turn away when we were doing pictures, because he sometimes wasn't in the same key we were in. We always used to look. I still do. To see if Elvis could play guitar, [checking out the musicians in the movie] *The Girl Can't Help It*, anything. He's doing a D and he's ... yes, it's all right. Whereas [with some] you could tell they couldn't play, it was just a prop. That was one of the things we used to love about guys in the audience. The girls would look at us, the guys would look at the chords. You'd nudge each other: look, eh, this guy down here. He'd be looking deadly serious at you, you could see him copping all the chords."[1]

Liverpool in 1960 was not a place where you could walk into a music shop and find a selection of different bass guitars, much less find affordable ones. American-made Fender and Gibson basses were unavailable in Liverpool at the time, and had only just begun to trickle in to the country after the lifting of an eight-year US import ban. Their prices alone would have made them unobtainable to most. Availability and price – if not quality – favoured the Hofner line, and in this case the German-made hollowbody 500/4 Bass, one of the few electric basses available in Liverpool. It managed a rich bass sound and the neck was playable, even if the overall performance was relatively crude compared to better instruments.

Sutcliffe chose such a Hofner bass, known in the UK by its Selmer catalogue number 333. According to the original hire-purchase receipt that has recently been unearthed, Sutcliffe acquired his bass at Frank Hessy's music store on January 21st. On this original document the bass is described as brunette in colour – it was also offered in blonde – with the serial number 199. And the receipt reveals that Sutcliffe did not pay £65 for the bass. In fact, Sutcliffe put down a deposit of £15 and acquired the instrument on credit, known then as hire purchase. He had to make weekly payments that would add up to a total credit price of £59/15/- (£59.75, about $165 then; around £800 or $1,130 in today's money).

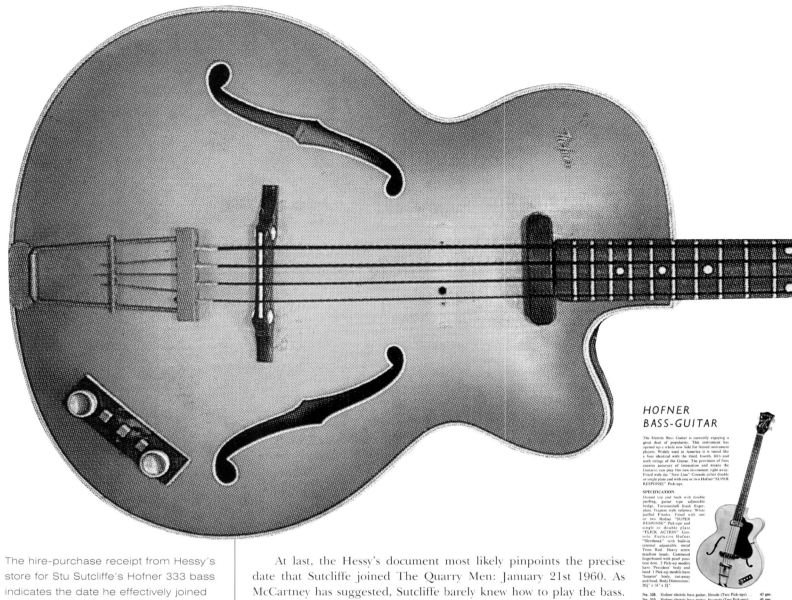

HOFNER BASS-GUITAR

The Electric Bass Guitar is currently enjoying a great deal of popularity. This instrument has opened up a whole new field for fretted instrument players. Widely used in America it is tuned like a bass identical with the third, fourth, fifth and sixth strings of the Guitar. The provision of frets ensures accuracy of intonation and means the Guitarist can play this new instrument right away. Fitted with the "New Line" Console either double or single plate and with one or two Hofner "SUPER RESPONSE" Pick-ups.

SPECIFICATION

Domed top and back with double purfling, guitar type adjustable bridge, Tortoiseshell finish finger-plate, Trapeze style tailpiece. White purfled F-holes. Fitted with one or two Hofner "SUPER RESPONSE" Pick-ups and single or double plate "FLICK ACTION" Console. Exclusive Hofner "Slendneck" with built-in internal adjustable metal Truss Rod. Heavy screw machine heads. Cambered fingerboard with pearl position dots. 2 Pick-up models have "President" body and head. 1 Pick-up models have "Senator" body, cut-away and head. Body Dimensions. 20¼" x 16" x 2⅜".

No. 328.	Hofner electric bass guitar, blonde (Two Pick-ups) ..	43 gns.
No. 333.	Hofner electric bass guitar, brunette (Two Pick-ups) ..	41 gns.
No. 530.	Hofner electric bass guitar, blonde (One Pick-up) ..	34 gns.
No. 531.	Hofner electric bass guitar, brunette (One Pick-up) ..	32 gns.

Cases, see page 30

12

The hire-purchase receipt from Hessy's store for Stu Sutcliffe's Hofner 333 bass indicates the date he effectively joined The Beatles: January 21st 1960. Selmer's Hofner catalogue (right) features a 333 bass.

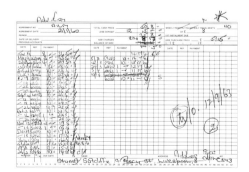

At last, the Hessy's document most likely pinpoints the precise date that Sutcliffe joined The Quarry Men: January 21st 1960. As McCartney has suggested, Sutcliffe barely knew how to play the bass. But the addition to the group of a good-looking guy with an impressive new Hofner bass must have given them a new spark of life. It's important to remember that until this point Lennon, McCartney and Harrison had never worked with a "real" electric bass in their band. The sound of the bass complemented the three-guitar arrangements, and must have provided the band with a palpable lift to their sound. The only element now lacking was a drummer. With Sutcliffe in the group, the band's name was changed from The Quarry Men to the self-consciously mis-spelled "The Beatals", adopting the insect theme started by hero Buddy Holly with his group The Crickets.

The audition

The Beatals would often hang around in the Jacaranda, a Liverpool coffee bar owned by Allan Williams. The music scene was starting to take off in the city, with groups such as Rory Storm & The Hurricanes, Cass & The Cassanovas and Gerry & The Pacemakers springing up from skiffle bands to become fully-fledged rock'n'roll outfits. As a businessman, Williams found a way to cultivate some of this new talent hanging around in his club. He was approached by Larry Parnes, the famous British manager and impresario.

Parnes worked with artists like Marty Wilde and specialised in grooming wild rockers into all-

This is Stu Sutcliffe's Hofner 333, the first bass guitar used in The Beatles, and one that Paul also played before acquiring his own Hofner. By the time the bass was sold at auction, its pickguard had been removed. The 333 is sometimes incorrectly labelled a President Bass, a model name which did not appear until later.

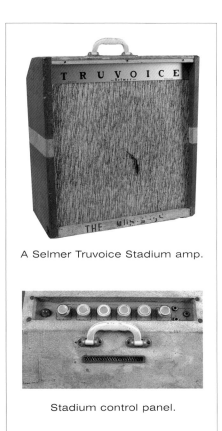

A Selmer Truvoice Stadium amp.

Stadium control panel.

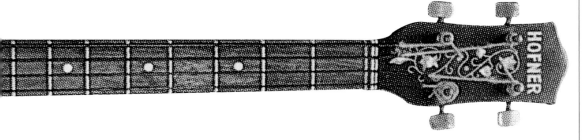

round entertainers. In the middle of 1960 he was in search of backing bands for some of his solo acts: Billy Fury, Johnny Gentle, Tommy Steele, Georgie Fame and others. So it was that on May 10th Williams arranged for Parnes to hold an audition for some of Liverpool's instrumental hopefuls. In attendance with Parnes at the Wyvern Social Club (later Williams's Blue Angel club) was Billy Fury. Cass & The Cassanovas (later The Big Three) were friends with The Beatals, and tried to persuade Williams to let the newly-named group audition for Parnes. But the band needed a drummer. Williams found drummer Tommy Moore and invited The Beatals to the audition.

Unfortunately when it came to the audition Moore was late, and so Cassanovas drummer Johnny Hutchinson had to fill in. Adrian Barber of The Cassanovas recalls the day. "Tommy Moore used to be our drummer. But when we got Hutchinson in, Cass gave Tommy to The Beatles, because they didn't have a drummer – in fact they had problems keeping a drummer. Allan Williams arranged it. All the Liverpool bands went down to the audition – because this was Larry Parnes, man, the big-time promoter! But we all hated him, we hated his acts. He was the epitome of the clichéd British showbiz guy: the mohair coat, always smoking a cigar. They used to call him Larry Parnes Shillings And Pence. But it was a gig, you know? So we all showed up."[2]

Gerry Marsden and his band The Pacemakers were among the many who auditioned for Parnes and Fury that day. "We weren't excited about it," Marsden says. "It was just something to do to pass the time and make a couple of extra quid. That's all it was. There wasn't even a piano, so my pianist had to play the guitar. We just came in and did it, and when we finished Larry Parnes said, 'Well, we'll be in touch,' and all that. That's all it was. Just in and out. I didn't want to be a backing band, really. The Beatles basically got the same reaction – they didn't want to be one of the scousers backing Billy Fury either."[3]

The Beatals had renamed themselves yet again for the audition, this time as The Silver Beetles. They ran through their four-song audition routine, with Lennon playing his Hofner Club 40, Harrison his Futurama, McCartney the Zenith archtop with pickup attached, and Sutcliffe his new Hofner 333 Bass. The Silver Beetles didn't get the prime prize – to be Billy Fury's backing band – but nonetheless netted a job as the band for a seven-date tour of Scotland supporting another of Parnes's charges, singer Johnny Gentle.

With Tommy Moore as their drummer, The Silver Beetles set out on their first set of "professional" shows, starting on May 20th and continuing to the 28th. There is only one known photograph from the tour and it shows Tommy Moore on stage singing, with Harrison playing his Futurama in the background. On these dates McCartney had his Zenith with added pickup, Lennon his Hofner Club 40, and Sutcliffe the Hofner 333 Bass.

This June 1960 hire-purchase receipt for George's Truvoice amp shows that Paul took over the amp a few months later, and that manager Brian Epstein settled the account in 1962.

NOTHING WAS
MIKED UP, APART
FROM THE VOCAL ...
THE SOUND YOU
PRODUCED WAS THE
STAGE SOUND – A
RAW SOUND, AND
VERY POWERHOUSE.
THAT'S WHY I
DEVELOPED THIS
STYLE OF
DRUMMING WHICH
THEY NICKNAMED
THE ATOMIC BEAT.

Pete Best, on The Beatles early

Hamburg dates

The Selmer Truvoice Stadium amplifier

No one knows what kind of amplifiers The Silver Beetles used at the time, but one old theory involves a Selmer Truvoice amplifier. The story is that Lennon and Sutcliffe, who both attended the adjoining Liverpool Institute and Liverpool College of Art, had managed to convince the education authorities that in the name of art and music the school ought to purchase a Truvoice amplifier for the students to use at social functions.

Lennon and Sutcliffe obviously had other intentions for the amplifier, and some say that the two managed a long-term loan of the amp for use with The Silver Beetles. A Selmer Truvoice was considered then as one of the best and biggest amps available in Liverpool. Pictures taken at the Parnes audition reveal The Silver Beetles playing through Selmer Truvoice amplifiers provided for all the bands to use at the audition. These pictures may even have provided the source of the art-college story.

The UK Selmer operation had been started in London by Ben Davis back in 1929, at first to import Selmer Paris instruments. But as we've already seen with Hofner and Futurama, Davis was gradually adding products from other makers to the musical hardware he distributed. Davis's Selmer operation, which lasted to the late 1960s, also began to manufacture items in Britain – including a line of Selmer-branded amplifiers. The all-valve (tube) Selmer Truvoice was a 15-watt amplifier with built-in 10-inch speaker, similar in sound and tone to a Fender Deluxe amp but with a little more volume. It's easy to see why it would have been among the top choices for British bands at the time. But there is no firm evidence for the art college story.

Their first "professional" tour had given the group a fleeting taste of life on the road. And Allan Williams now looked on The Silver Beetles as a real band. Acting effectively as their manager, he began booking the group around Liverpool venues, including his own club, the Jacaranda. But this stint of gigs only lasted a short time, because the group soon found themselves once again without a drummer. Tommy Moore had quit.

Luckily for music, the remaining Silver Beetles had no intention of giving in. On June 14th, the day after Moore's last show with the group at the Jacaranda, Harrison went to Hessy's music store and purchased a Selmer Truvoice amplifier. The original hire-purchase receipts show that Harrison paid a whopping £63 for the amp (some $175 then, and around £850 or $1,200 in today's money). It's clear that Harrison was serious and committed to his group – with or without a drummer.

Drums, or a Rosetti Solid 7 guitar?

The Silver Beatles (with an 'a', as they were now subtly but significantly renamed) continued to play without a drummer. McCartney, in an early demonstration of musical versatility, took over the drums briefly with the group. The arrangement of McCartney on drums, Lennon and Harrison on guitars and Sutcliffe on bass worked out well and probably sounded quite good. But McCartney obviously did not intend to stay in the position permanently. Soon after his 18th birthday in June he decided it was time for a new guitar.

McCartney retired his old Zenith – which he still owns to this day – and on June 30th purchased a Rosetti Solid 7 six-string electric guitar from Hessy's. The Solid 7 was acquired on hire purchase. Despite the rather optimistic name, it wasn't a solidbody guitar. It had a semi-hollow double-cutaway body without f-holes, was fitted with two pickups, and came in a black-to-red sunburst finish. It was produced for UK distributor Rosetti by the Dutch Egmond company, and cost McCartney £21 (about $58 then), making it a relatively inexpensive guitar for the time (around £290 or $400 in today's money). As McCartney would discover, he got what he paid for.

During July another drummer, Norman Chapman, had a shortlived stay in the band, quitting after only a few shows. Yet again Harrison, Lennon and McCartney were drummerless. By that summer, Allan Williams had built a relationship with German club owner Bruno Koschmider who was interested in bringing over British bands to play at his Kaiserkeller and Indra clubs in Hamburg. Williams suggested The Silver Beatles, Cass & The Cassanovas, Gerry & The Pacemakers and a number of other local Liverpool outfits. Soon, Williams approached The Silver Beatles with an offer to play in Hamburg.

The only catch was that Williams demanded the band secure a permanent drummer.

"Mrs Best's little lad", Pete

In a desperate search, The Silver Beatles headed for the West Derby area of town and the Casbah coffee bar. This was the same club that, as The Quarry Men a year earlier, they had vowed never to play again. At the Casbah they found their new drummer. Pete Best, son of club owner Mona, was playing drums there with his band, The Blackjacks. The guitarist in The Blackjacks was no less than ex-Quarry Men strummer Ken Brown. Also on guitar was Chas Newby, who would later have his own brush with The Beatles. The Casbah was hopping, but The Silver Beatles had their eyes on Pete Best and his brand new set of Christmas-present Premier drums, finished in blue mother-of-pearl. It was The Silver Beatles' chance to land a steady drummer.

The Premier Drum Company had been set up in London in 1922 by drummer Albert Della-Porta, making drums under the Premier brandname from 1925. By the early 1930s Premier was a major manufacturer of the early kits with their distinctive metal "console" on which cymbals, drums and other percussion was mounted. A strong export market in the US was developed. During World War II Premier's London factory was destroyed in an air-raid, and production was moved to Leicester in the Midlands. After the war Premier invested in die-casting machinery and quickly re-established their supremacy in the home market. In 1958, barely months after Remo, Premier introduced Everplay plastic drum-heads. At this time Premier also made Krut, Zyn and Super Zyn cymbals.

Best bought his Premier drum set from Rushworth's music store in Liverpool. Mr Swift, who looked after percussion at the store, told him that Premier was the most recognised brand of drums in England at the time, and that they were ideal for his purposes. The store happened to have a Premier kit in stock in marine pearl finish, a very pale blue. The drums seem to have been a mixture of types rather than from one particular Premier kit model, although the cheaper method of clipping fittings to the rim of the bass drum implies model 50 components. Best's kit wasn't from the top of the Premier line, but the drums were certainly good compared to most of the cheaper, lesser-known brands available in Britain in those days.

Unusually, his kit had a large 26-inch bass drum. "That was a lot different to the standard 22-inch bass drums that were around at the time," Best says. "Of course, I didn't know a great deal about the difference at that time. But when I started playing it, that 26-inch bass drum really gave me a thump, a great big bass sound. The kit was a standard four-piece – snare drum, top rack tom, bass drum, and floor tom – in fairly conventional sizes, other than the large bass drum. It also had calfskin heads, though I replaced them later with plastic heads. I got fed up having them re-skinned: soaking them, drying them and all that." Before Best had owned a proper kit and joined groups he'd had a snare drum, and also played around on some bongos. So when Swift told him that some Premier bongos could be ordered in the same stylish finish, Best did not take long to make a decision.

"The first cymbal I had was a Zyn," Best continues, "which was a very big brand at the time. Actually, I put my own rivets in it. I'd bought it from Rushworth's. Later, when I was in Germany, I needed a hi-hat and Zildjian was available, so I got 14-inch Zildjians for hi-hats, which gave a very big, heavy sound. When I needed a crash cymbal, again it was a Zildjian, I think a 20-inch, which had a hell of a boom to it. I loved that! I could make a right noise with that one, finishing up a number. So that's how I ended up with two cymbals and a hi-hat. As for sticks, I tended to go with 5As, they felt comfortable in my hands. I didn't want them too heavy and I didn't want then too light. They were adequate for my purposes."[4]

Best recalled later that his drumming had been improving steadily. "It must have made some impression on Lennon, McCartney and the others," he wrote, "for there was a telephone call for me at the house one afternoon. 'How'd you like to come to Hamburg with The Beatles?' an excited voice asked at the other end of the line. It belonged to Paul McCartney – surprisingly, I often thought later, because John had always struck me as the boss. It was an extremely tempting and exciting offer."[5]

Best says all the bands around at the time were playing a very similar type of music, mainly cover versions of heroes such as Chuck Berry, Little Richard and Gene Vincent. So he would know the basic repertoire required. Best checked with the rest of his group, The Blackjacks, because he didn't intend to leave them in the lurch if he got the new job. But they had no intention of going professional, and said that if Best was successful, they'd be quite happy going back to college. "Once I sorted that out and had talked with my parents, it was a matter of, well … do it. So I phoned Paul back and said, 'Yeah, we're on.' He surprised me and said, 'Oh no, you've got to come down and audition.' And it was like, audition? Who auditioned in those days?"[6]

Rosetti Solid 7 catalogue.

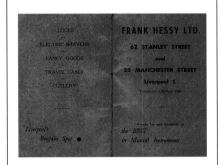

HP book for Paul's Rosetti guitar.

The Beatles packed their gear into this van, seen here being loaded on to the ferry on its way to Hamburg.

Pete would have chosen his Premier drum set and bongos from catalogues like those pictured (right).

It was his lovely blue Premier kit that Best played at the audition for The Beatles on August 12th, at Allan Williams's Wyvern Club. "John Lennon was the only one there when I arrived," Best wrote later. "He played a couple of bars of 'Ramrod' while I beat the skins, until George and Stu turned up and we had a further session. Paul was late, as usual, but once there they all joined in such numbers as 'Shakin' All Over'. We played for about 20 minutes in all and at the end they all reached the same conclusion: 'Yeah! You're in, Pete!' Thus I became the fifth Beatle."[7] Without delay, Best was in the group. A few days later, with the band now renamed The Beatles and the equipment all packed up in Allan Williams's little van, they were off to Germany.

Hamburg first trip – the Indra and Kaiserkeller clubs

On August 17th The Beatles started their engagement at Bruno Koschmider's Indra club on the Grosse Freiheit in Hamburg. Publicity photographs taken on stage at the Indra provide the most detailed record of the first equipment used by the group now officially known as The Beatles. Lennon has his Hofner Club 40 guitar, Harrison his Futurama. Both are plugged into Harrison's new Selmer Truvoice amplifier. McCartney is pictured playing his new right-handed Rosetti Solid 7, strung left-handed and going into his Elpico amplifier. Sutcliffe poses with his Hofner 333 Bass, plugged into a Watkins Westminster amplifier that belonged to Best. Best himself is pictured with his Premier drum set, including the large 26-inch bass drum that would help in the development of his "atomic beat" drum sound. Best also used his Premier bongos with the kit.

It was in Hamburg that The Beatles began to learn about how to function as a proper band. Performing regularly in front of a rough gathering of drunk, heckling Germans quickly taught the group methods to entertain a crowd. Playing from four to six hours every night for some three months certainly helped them develop their own voice and improve their musical skills. "I think that's where we found our style," Harrison recalled later. "We developed our style because of this fella there, he used to say, 'You've got to make a show for the people.' He used to come up every night shouting, 'Mach schau!' ['Do a good stage-act!'] So we used to 'mach schau' … John used to dance around like a gorilla and we'd all knock our heads together … things like that."[8]

The accommodation provided by Koschmider for The Beatles in Hamburg was behind a movie screen at the Bambi-Filmkunsttheater, a small cinema that Koschmider also owned. The conditions were nothing less than deplorable. The impressionable teenagers were thrown into the wild nightlife and decadence of Hamburg's subculture. Their new playground was the Reeperbahn, overflowing with prostitutes, drugs and every kind of excess. The Beatles were transformed from innocent British boys to young men, virtually overnight.

Their performances at the Indra club lasted until October 3rd when, due to a complaint from tenants living above about noise, The Beatles were moved to Koschmider's other venue, the Kaiserkeller. By today's standards, it's hard to believe that The Beatles' little amplifiers and a drum set could provide the appropriate volume, but drummer Best insists they were loud. "Initially we had three amps: a Truvoice, the Elpico and a Watkins – and that was it. John and George were both taking lead breaks, even though George was the dominant lead guitarist. And we had Stu playing bass. To get the volume we needed we had to crank those amplifiers up. Nothing was miked up, apart from the vocal mike. The sound you produced was the stage sound – a raw sound, and very powerhouse. That's why I developed this style of drumming which they nicknamed the atomic beat. The rest of the group were playing at this volume, and I needed something to hang in and hold everything together, in a way to amplify the sound. So I got a great big backbeat, slap bang behind it. I kept working on that style because it fitted in with the stage sound – it was loud and it was powerful. We had to project that sound."[9]

As well as shifting clubs, The Beatles had their contract extended by Koschmider to perform at the Kaiserkeller until December 31st. At the same time there was talk of an additional three months of bookings in West Berlin. For almost two months at the Kaiserkeller the group shared the bill with another Liverpool band, Rory Storm & The Hurricanes. It was there that Lennon, McCartney and Harrison built up a friendship with The Hurricanes' drummer, Ringo Starr.

A lust for gear

During their shows at the Kaiserkeller The Beatles began to acquire new equipment. Most young guitarists dream about and lust over seemingly unobtainable instruments, and the 17-year-old Harrison was no exception. A letter he wrote back home in late October 1960 to his friend Arthur Kelly is packed with information and indicates just how much Harrison thought about guitars. Harrison talked in the letter about another British musician who was playing in Hamburg at the time, Tony Sheridan, saying, "He's now got a Fender guitar and amp like [Buddy Holly's] and I play it well. It also has a vibrato and his bass player has a Fender Bass." Harrison continued, "Look out as I am thinking of getting yet again another new guitar. I may leave solids out of it this time and get an Everly Brother type massive Gibson as they are gear."

Then he gave Kelly some vital information needed to send off for a free Fender catalogue, carefully writing out the Fender company's address in Santa Ana, California. "I might manage a red Fender Stratocaster with gold plating," said Harrison – but added that the guitar he really wanted was made by Gretsch. The valuable document reveals how the group felt about their new drummer, Pete Best. "We have Pete Best, Mrs Best's little lad, with us from Kasbah [sic] fame and he is drumming good." Perhaps Harrison's "with us" implies that the drummer wasn't considered a real member of The Beatles? Maybe this was because most of the group's drummers so far had dropped out. It's almost as if they felt that Best might quit too, just like all the rest.

Coincidentally, this same letter refers to Ringo Starr. Harrison described Rory Storm & The Hurricanes as "crummy" but said that "the only person who is any good in the group is the drummer". Presumably this indicates that Harrison and The Beatles looked favourably on Ringo and probably got on well with him, even at this early stage. He also described a new piece of Beatle equipment. Sutcliffe had bought a "big" Gibson amplifier for £120, reported Harrison, drawing a large amp and a small Sutcliffe alongside to help Kelly comprehend the scale of the monstrous new device. "It has a fabulous tremolo in it and is the Les Paul model." Little did Harrison know that this Gibson amp would soon be his. The tweed-covered Les Paul GA-40 amplifier was a 16-watt all-valve (tube) amp, with tremolo effect and a 12-inch Jensen speaker.

Gibson was a grand old name of the US instrument industry, having originated with its founder Orville Gibson in Michigan in the 1890s. Leading the way over the following decades in the mandolin, banjo and guitar fields, Gibson was one of the pioneers of the electric guitar, pleasing many modern musicians with the early launch of a solidbody model in 1952, endorsed by the famous American guitarist Les Paul. Gibson had made amplifiers since the 1930s, adding the GA-40 to the line at the same time as the Les Paul guitar. Sutcliffe's Les Paul amp was the first piece of American-made equipment to be added to The Beatles' growing arsenal.

John's first Rickenbacker

Lennon was the next Beatle to change his equipment. Harrison recalled years later that the first Rickenbacker guitar he ever saw was during that first Beatles trip to Hamburg. "We went into this shop ... in Hamburg," said Harrison. "John bought that little Rickenbacker that became very well known through the Beatle concerts, with a scaled-down neck. I think he'd just seen an album by Jean Thielemans, who used to be the guitar player in the George Shearing Quintet and had one of those Rickenbackers.

"You have to imagine that in those days, when we were first out of Liverpool, any good American guitar looked sensational to us. We only had beat up, crummy guitars at that stage. We still didn't really have any money to buy them, but I remember that John got that Rickenbacker ... what they call 'on the knocker', you know? [Money] down and the rest when they catch you. I don't know if he ever really paid them off."[10]

This guitar that Lennon acquired in Hamburg would be the

A Watkins Westminster amp (above) like the one used by Stu. This example has the later WEM logo on the front, where Stu's had a Watkins logo.

Paul used an Elpico AC-55 amp like this one on the group's first visit to Hamburg. It was made by the Lee Products Co in north-west London.

The Beatles frontline, live in Hamburg. Left to right: Stu with Hofner 333 bass; John playing his Rickenbacker 325; Paul with the Rosetti Solid 7; and George on his Futurama.

one most associated with him through the years – a 1958 Rickenbacker 325. This legendary guitar would become Lennon's own favourite too. Writer Ray Coleman interviewed Lennon during a tour of the Beatle's new house, Kenwood, in 1965. During the interview Coleman asked Lennon for a list of his prized possessions. "My first Rickenbacker guitar," Lennon replied. "It's a bit hammered now, I just keep it for kicks. I bought it in Germany on the hire purchase. Whatever it cost, it was a hell of a lot of money to me at the time."[11] Lennon was a millionaire by the time of the interview, and had already acquired an abundance of material items. Yet it was the Rickenbacker 325 that he selected above all as his most valued possession.

Lennon would use this Rickenbacker 325 from the moment he got it in 1960 for the next four years exclusively for live shows and on many Beatle recordings. Lennon's first Rickenbacker 325 is revered by most collectors as the holy grail of all Beatle instruments. The guitar is surrounded by stories interwoven with elements of myth, mystery, fact and fiction, and there has been much controversy and debate about it. Very few were produced, and so an original late-1950s Rickenbacker 325 is a rare guitar in any circumstances today, with examples highly sought after.

The Rickenbacker company began life in Los Angeles, California, in the 1920s when Swiss immigrant Adolph Rickenbacker established a tool-and-die operation there. One of his early customers was the nearby National guitar company. A collaboration between some National men and Rickenbacker resulted in the important "Frying Pan" lap-steel guitar of 1931, the first electric guitar with a magnetic pickup, and thus the basis for all modern electric guitars. Rickenbacker guitars continued to appear during the 1930s, mostly electric lap-steels, including some unusual models with bodies made from Bakelite.

The "unpopular" 325 model

After World War II, Adolph Rickenbacker became weary of the business and in 1953 sold it to Francis Cary Hall, who ran the Radio & Television Equipment Co in nearby Santa Ana. Hall soon hired German guitar-maker Roger Rossmeisl to design a series of new instruments to update the Rickenbacker line, including in 1958 the distinctive and stylish semi-hollow "Capri" guitars. The Capri name was soon dropped and the guitars became better known by their 300-series model names. Hall believed that scaled-down versions of the design – designated model numbers 310, 315, 320 and 325 – would make a good addition to the line as they would be easier to handle. But guitar buyers did not embrace the smaller models, and at first they seemed doomed to an early death. These Rickenbacker three-quarter size semi-hollow electric guitars were designed in 1957 and first introduced to the public in January of 1958.

For years the consensus has been that Lennon's first Rickenbacker 325 was manufactured in 1959. But the serial number on the guitar, still owned today by Yoko Ono, is V81. This dates the manufacture of Lennon's Rickenbacker to early 1958, making it one of the first 325 models ever produced. Rickenbacker's production records indicate that 28 examples of model 325 were made in that first year of production, 1958. Twenty were in sunburst finish (which Rickenbacker called autumnglo) and just eight in natural (mapleglo) like Lennon's.

Lennon's 325 had no f-hole in the body, although most of the other 325s manufactured at the time had this feature. The 325 he bought in Hamburg had been photographed at a July 1958 music trade show in the States, the pictures revealing a guitar with only two knobs, one each for volume and tone. There are two distinct cosmetic differences that stand out on Lennon's 325 when it's compared to all other similar Rickenbackers and thus identify it in the trade-show photos. First is the number of screws in the pickguard. At the time Rickenbacker used four screws to hold down the pickguard on to the body, but Lennon's had five, with an extra screw added near the volume knob. The second distinguishing feature concerns the guitar's "Kauffman" vibrato arm. Most Kauffman arms are either straight or have a single, angled bend in them. But the arm on Lennon's 325 had an extremely unusual and distinctive double bend. The 1958 trade show photographs also reveal a distinctive wood grain on the upper bout of the guitar that can easily be matched to later pictures of Lennon's guitar. These early pictures of what became Lennon's guitar also underline how unpopular the model must have been, because this particular example took almost two years to find an owner.

With model 325 poorly received at trade shows, Rickenbacker decided to make some modifications. Back at the Los Angeles factory the company's engineers fitted the 325s with new electronics. With a new complement of two volume and two tone controls, the model now had greater capabilities for variation in sound. The instruments were also fitted with a new set of Art Deco-style knobs, today known as "stove" or "oven" types. Everything else on the 325 remained the same. Rickenbacker no doubt hoped that the changes would help to revive the model's sales potential.

But why did Lennon end up with this odd Rickenbacker 325 model? It may just have been a matter of circumstance, rather than choice. One of the possible stories is recounted by John Hall, son of Francis Hall and current owner of Rickenbacker. "Apparently Lennon had gone into the Steinway store in Hamburg and he wanted a Rickenbacker – that much he knew," says Hall. "He told a sales person there to get him one. Someone from the store came to one of the US trade shows very shortly thereafter, I believe in New York City. My dad thought this was Mr Steinway himself, but I rather doubt that; it was probably a store manager. This guy said to my dad, 'I've got

The choice of professionals and students

1959-1960

𝓕𝓮𝓷𝓭𝓮𝓻 *Fine Electric Instruments*

George advised his friend Arthur Kelly to send away to the States for a real Fender catalogue. This (above) is what he would have received.

a customer that wants one of your guitars, and I'd like to take it back with me.' Well, what model does he want? The guy said he didn't care, just give him anything. And that's how Lennon ended up with the 325, because that's what we had left over from the show. The guy carried it back with him. The reason why John Lennon wanted the Rickenbacker was because one of his favourite artists, Jean 'Toots' Thielemans, was using one of our old 400-series guitars at that time."[12]

Hall's account seems to make sense. Lennon asked a music store in Hamburg to find him a Rickenbacker, but didn't specify a model. Probably Lennon assumed that the German-sounding Rickenbacker must be a German-made guitar, so surely they could find one easily? The store manager was going to a trade show in the US, and so probably bought the least expensive model that Rickenbacker had left at the end of the show (and the most unpopular – hence the price). The manager brought back this Rickenbacker for Lennon, and the Beatle fell in love with the beautifully-made American guitar. It's an interesting story.

However, a recently uncovered document from the Rickenbacker archive details the shipping of three model 325 guitars, including serial number V81, to the Framus company in Germany. Framus was not only an important instrument manufacturer but also an importer and distributor in Germany of various musical equipment, including Rickenbacker products. The document notes that Francis Hall's wife delivered these guitars to the airport, along with 11 other Rickenbackers, for shipment out of the US on October 15th 1958.

So now a different story emerges. Perhaps Lennon simply walked into a music shop in Hamburg in 1960 and by chance found a Rickenbacker there – and, as we now know, one that had been in Germany for some time. "[Toots Thielemans] was the only one we'd ever seen with a Rickenbacker, so when John went in and saw that guitar, he just had to have it and bought it instantly,"[13] Harrison recalled recently. "It was a great looking guitar, and I think in England you had to order them specifically and wait for six months – not just for Rickenbackers, for anything, Fenders, Gibsons ... And I think it [came about] purely because John needed a decent guitar and that one happened to be in the shop and he liked the look of it."[14]

Pete Best too remembers being with Lennon when he purchased the Rickenbacker. "We used to mooch around Hamburg and find these little music stores that were locked away in side streets. We found that there was equipment in Hamburg which you couldn't get in Liverpool. For example, I bought some Zildjian cymbals over there, and you'd get back to Liverpool and people would say, 'Where on earth did you get these?'

"The same thing happened with the guitars. John was looking around, he had his old Hofner Club 40, and we went into this music shop. We were all there together – we used to hunt around in packs, discovering what was available. Just mooching in general, as musicians do. John saw this Rickenbacker, and what actually knocked him out was the short scale of the fingerboard. Whereas before he had to stretch, John found that he could do the same riffs and everything without hardly moving his fingers. He just fell in love with it. He liked the sound. The Rickenbacker was his guitar! That was the one he was in love with and that was the one he came back with and made everyone's head turn in Liverpool. People were like: 'My God, what's John playing? We've never seen anything like that before.' Some players asked if he'd had it made specially, and he'd explain that he bought it at a shop."[15]

"The most beautiful guitar..."

Lennon acquired the Rickenbacker 325 by "ratenzahlung", or credit payments, in Hamburg in November. A Mr Höper who worked at the Steinway store at the time has said[16] that Steinway did not sell Rickenbacker guitars in 1960, and suggests that Lennon bought his guitar somewhere else in Hamburg, possibly at the nearby Musikhaus Rotthoff. Claus-Dieter Rotthoff remembers hanging out as a teenager in his late father's shop on Schanzenstraße at this time. "We were very close to all the clubs, so musicians would often come to us, The Beatles among them. I particularly remember The Beatles because when they showed up they always had a following of nice girls with them. I'm sure John bought his first Rickenbacker guitar at our shop."[17]

Irrespective of which shop he acquired it from, the fact that Lennon ended up with this odd Rickenbacker guitar actually saved the model 325 from almost certain extinction. Instead, it would become one of the most popular and sought-after guitars ever produced by Rickenbacker. In an

WHATEVER IT COST, IT WAS A HELL OF A LOT OF MONEY TO ME AT THE TIME.

John Lennon, on his prized 1958

Rickenbacker 325

The Beatles played at four different clubs in Hamburg: the Indra, the Kaiserkeller (poster below), the Top Ten, and the Star Club.

interview a few years later, Lennon was clearly still in love. "I sold my Hofner," he said, "made a profit on it too ... [the Rickenbacker] is the most beautiful guitar – the action is ridiculously low."[18]

But before Lennon sold his Hofner Club 40, McCartney had managed to borrow it for a spell. In the famous photographs that Astrid Kirchherr took of The Beatles in Hamburg in November 1960 (see page 40), McCartney can be seen holding Lennon's Hofner, re-strung left-handed. Soon after these pictures were taken the Club 40 was indeed sold, as Lennon said. Many guitar collectors lose sleep dreaming of that natural-finish ex-Lennon guitar – which is presumably still out there. Somebody may have a very valuable guitar tucked away somewhere.

There's no evidence of what Lennon paid for his Rickenbacker 325. In the US in 1960 its retail price would have been $269.50 (about £100 then) which would translate to about $1,600 (£1,130) in today's money. Presumably the still relatively poor Lennon got a good deal from the Hamburg shop, which must in turn have been pleased to get rid of something that had been on the wall for some time. A new guitar always deserves a new amplifier – and Lennon decided to spend some more of his hard-earned Deutschmarks. Lennon picked a new Fender Deluxe amp, a tweed-covered, all-valve (tube) 18-watt amplifier with a single 12-inch speaker, making a good match for his new guitar. We'll discover more about the Fender company later on. But Lennon now had what most British musicians wanted and few possessed: an American-made guitar and an American-made amp.

Top Ten club – and problems in Hamburg

By the end of October 1960 the new Top Ten club had opened on the Reeperbahn in Hamburg. It was owned by Peter Eckhorn, who intended to take Bruno Koschmider's lucrative business by winning over the Kaiserkeller's clientele. Eckhorn had booked British singer and guitarist Tony Sheridan to headline at the new club.

The Beatles looked up to Norwich-born Sheridan, who'd already appeared on several of Jack Good's influential British TV rock'n'roll programmes. Between shows at the Kaiserkeller, the group would often visit the Top Ten to watch Sheridan's performances. It wasn't long before they were up on stage at the club, jamming with their new friend. But news of The Beatles performing at the competing Top Ten did not please Koschmider. Using a clause in their contract that prohibited them from performing within a 25 mile radius of the Kaiserkeller, Koschmider served The Beatles with notice of one month's termination of contract, dated November 1st, effectively ordering the band to leave on the 30th.

It was rumoured that Koschmider even tipped off the German authorities about Harrison being under 18 – which made it illegal for him to be in a nightclub after a certain time. Best, however, said that problems arose at first because Allan Williams did not have the correct papers for them to work in Germany. The group was told that they had to register with the "aliens police" – and it was then officially discovered that Harrison was under-age. Best says that as this in effect meant the guitarist couldn't finish the final set with his band, which often had to play until around 2 in the morning, Harrison decided that to stay in Hamburg was pointless, and went home to Liverpool.

The rest of The Beatles stayed, continuing the remainder of their booking at the Kaiserkeller, but still spending most of their free time at Peter Eckhorn's Top Ten club. Eckhorn befriended the group and took them under his wing. Relations with Koschmider deteriorated to the point where The Beatles made a deal with Eckhorn to be the Top Ten's house band, backing Tony Sheridan. Eckhorn also offered them better living quarters, above the club. Perhaps it was because he recognised the raw talent in The Beatles, but whatever his motivation, Eckhorn negotiated a one-month booking at the Top Ten for them the following April.

With the group's new accommodation sorted out, McCartney and Best went back to the deplorable hovel at the Bambi to pack up their belongings and move out. According to Best, this

Two amps similar to those owned by The Beatles. George had a Gibson GA-40 Les Paul (top) and John used a Fender Deluxe.

This famous picture taken by Astrid Kirchherr in Hamburg in 1960 captures The Beatles perfectly. No longer are they the innocent boys from Britain, but a group clearly revelling in the decadent Hamburg lifestyle. The photo also illustrates virtually all the instruments they used at the time (left to right): Pete and a snare drum from his Premier kit; George with the Futurama; John and his Rickenbacker 325; Paul with John's Hofner Club 40 strung left-handed; and Stu cradling the Hofner 333 bass.

Jean "Toots" Thielemans demonstrating guitars at the Rickenbacker display at a 1958 US music trade show. It was Toots playing a Rickenbacker guitar with George Shearing that inspired John to get one. And to complete the circle, the actual Rickenbacker 325 that John bought is just behind Toots's right elbow in this picture.

proved to be difficult. "We had to scrabble our goods and chattels together in the pitch darkness of the windowless dungeons," he wrote later. "In desperation, we invented a novel method of illumination to help us see to pack..." The pair pinned four rubber contraceptives to the frayed wall-covering in the corridor outside their door – and set fire to them. "The condoms spluttered and flickered and gave a vile smell," Best continued, "but at least we had a little light. By the time we made our exit through the pit of the cinema the condoms had almost burned out, having scorched and briefly singed some of the rotting material on the wall."[19]

The fire eventually went out, after they left, but when Koschmider found out he suspected that they meant to burn down his cinema. Promptly, Koschmider had Best and McCartney arrested by the German police on charges of alleged arson. Allowed only to take a few personal belongings and their passports, McCartney and Best were forced to leave their instruments behind at the Top Ten. The authorities soon made the decision to have the two Beatles deported to England. They were flown back to London where they barely had enough money for a train to Liverpool. The Beatles had officially played at the Top Ten for only one night.

By the beginning of December, McCartney, Harrison and Best were all back in Liverpool, with Lennon and Sutcliffe left in Hamburg. On December 10th Lennon set out on his trip home with his two valued possessions. He carried a guitar case with his new Rickenbacker guitar inside, and had his Fender Deluxe tweed amp safely strapped to his back. Sutcliffe, in the meantime, had decided to stay in Hamburg with his new German girlfriend, Astrid Kirchherr.

Regrouping in Liverpool

With the majority of The Beatles back in Liverpool it was time to re-organise. The first course of action was to try to retrieve the equipment left behind in Germany, with Best and his mother Mo taking charge of the task. "The future of The Beatles seemed to concern me more than the others," wrote Best. "It was obvious that there wouldn't be [a future] at all if we didn't make some effort to retrieve the kit we had been forced to leave behind at the Top Ten. John had staggered home with his guitar across his shoulder, but Paul's was still in Hamburg, stranded there with my shining

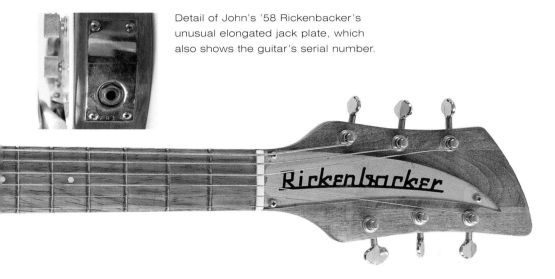

Detail of John's '58 Rickenbacker's unusual elongated jack plate, which also shows the guitar's serial number.

John's original Rickenbacker 325 was his first "real" American-made instrument. The guitar, which he used for the four years of the group's climb to fame, became a virtual extension of his stage persona, and is considered among guitar collectors as one of the most important Beatle instruments. Through the years John made a number of modifications to the guitar. Pictured here as it appears today, the guitar has had its original pickguard changed to a white one, and the body refinished back to a natural colour.

From Rickenbacker's archive, this document includes John's 325 (serial V81) among a batch of guitars shipped from Los Angeles to Rickenbacker's German distributor, Framus.

mother-of-pearl drums, and I wondered if I would ever see them again.

"Mo and I went into action and made some frantic phone-calls to Peter Eckhorn. He was extremely sympathetic and promised to get the stuff back to us by sea as soon as possible. He was a man of his word. Within days he called me to say that the kit had been crated and that the freight invoice would be in the mail. On the day of the ship's arrival in Liverpool, Mo and I booked a taxi – there was no family car at the time – and headed off to the Customs shed at Dingle. The crate was massive and would never fit into a cab, so mother and I set to work on the wharfside and broke it down. Drums, guitar, sound equipment, personal gear – we piled the lot into the taxi and left the debris on the dock. This was the first hurdle cleared, thanks to Peter Eckhorn, and I began to feel a little more optimistic."[20]

Best was reunited with his Premier drum set and McCartney with his Rosetti Solid 7 and Elpico amp. With their equipment in place, this left The Beatles to their next problem. Sutcliffe's decision to stay in Hamburg with Kirchherr left The Beatles without a bass player. The group turned to Best's old bandmate from The Blackjacks, Chas Newby. "Chas was a very versatile guitarist," says Best. "He was left-handed, too, though at the time we didn't pay any notice to that. We had four dates, and Stu had decided to stay over in Hamburg for another two or three weeks. We needed a bass player to stand in, so I asked Chas, who said he'd give it a go. We borrowed a bass off someone for him to play – and then it suddenly became apparent he was left handed. My God, he's playing it upside down! But he knew full well that Stu would be back, and it was only a matter of filling in until he returned."[21]

Newby only performed with The Beatles for four shows, in December. One of these – on the 27th at the Town Hall ballroom in Litherland, north Liverpool – is now recognised as a turning point in the group's career. At this hugely successful show The Beatles played a powerhouse performance, the like of which the stunned teenagers of Liverpool had neither seen nor heard before. Arguably, this concert marked the birth of what would later become identified as Beatlemania.

Best saw the magic unfold in front of him from his vantage point on the drum-stool at the back of the stage as he deployed his "atomic" drum beats. "I didn't realise what was happening at first, because we'd gone out to Germany and developed this powerhouse style. It went down great with the audiences there. Basically, we came back and did the same thing here. It became apparent as I listened to a lot of the bands that the drummers played quite a lightweight style, with a very light bass-drum pattern – if there was any bass-drum pattern – and light cymbals and hi-hat. So when we brought back this sound and image and the power that we had, a lot of the bands and drummers tried to imitate it, because it was going down well with the kids. All of a sudden you found a lot of the drummers in Liverpool increasing their volume and tempo."[22]

After the impact of the Litherland Town Hall performance, promoter Brian Kelly booked The Beatles for 36 shows, to start on January 5th of the new year. But along with this good fortune came more changes. Chas Newby's last performance as The Beatles' bass player was on December 31st at the Casbah. He then left the group and returned to his college studies.

"So it was ... uh-oh, we haven't got a bass player. And everyone sort of turned round and looked at me. I was a bit lumbered with it, really... "

PAUL McCARTNEY, ON RELUCTANLY SWITCHING FROM GUITAR TO BASS.

1961

THE BEATLES STARTED 1961 WITH A LARGE NUMBER OF BOOKINGS... AND A PROBLEM. ON DECEMBER 16TH OF THE PREVIOUS YEAR, IN DESPERATION, HARRISON HAD WRITTEN TO STU SUTCLIFFE AND PLEADED FOR HELP. "COME HOME SOONER," HE SAID. "IT'S NO GOOD WITH PAUL PLAYING BASS, WE'VE DECIDED – THAT IS IF HE HAD SOME KIND OF BASS AND AMP TO PLAY ON!"[1]

So how did McCartney become the bass player who almost wasn't? Harrison explained later: "When we met [Sutcliffe] he couldn't play at all, when he first got a bass. And he learned a few tunes. Occasionally it was a bit embarrassing, if it had a lot of changes to it. But he knew that, too. That's why he was never really at ease being in the band, and that's why he left when we finished the gig in Hamburg – he decided to go back to art college.

"At that point, Paul was still playing the guitar. And I remember saying, 'Well, one of us is going to be the bass player'. And I remember saying. 'It's not me, I'm not doing it'. And John said, 'I'm not doing it either.' [Paul] went for it. He became the bass player from that point on."[2]

"None of us wanted to be the bass player," admits McCartney. "It wasn't the number one job: we wanted to be up front. In our minds, it was the fat guy in the group who nearly always played the bass, and he stood at the back. None of us wanted that; we wanted to be up front singing, looking good, to pull the birds.

"Stu said he was going to stay in Hamburg. He'd met a girl and was going to stay there with her and paint," McCartney continues. "So it was like, uh-oh, we haven't got a bass player. And everyone sort of turned round and looked at me. I was a bit lumbered with it, really – it was like well, it'd better be you, then. I don't think you would have caught John doing it; he would have said: 'No, you're kidding, I've got a nice new Rickenbacker!' I didn't even have a guitar at the time, see, so I couldn't really say, 'But I wanted to be a guitarist.' They'd say, 'Well get a guitar then, that might be a start'."[3]

Although McCartney had been one of the band's original guitar players, he would often fill in on various other instruments when needed. As well as turning his hand to drums in earlier days, in Hamburg McCartney would often play the piano instead of the guitar, or when Sutcliffe was off with Kirchherr, McCartney would fill in on bass, playing Sutcliffe's Hofner 333 bass upside down.

The left-handed McCartney is realistic about the necessity of learning to play the bass upside down. "Well, I had to ... on guitar first of all, and then on bass. You had to, cos guys wouldn't let you change the strings. They said, 'Fuck off, I've just tuned it, I'm not gonna have it detuned and have somebody turn it round' ... No one would let you do that – quite rightly. When John wasn't here I'd pick up his guitar and learn to play it upside down; and John did too, he got pretty good upside down because of me.

"So I used to play Stu's bass upside down, he used to let me use it a little bit, if he didn't come in one night to the club. And eventually he said, 'Well, I'm gonna stay here with Astrid and we're gonna hitch up' ... I'd been playing piano on-stage – quite good for me, gave me a lot of piano practice; couldn't really play, but I learned. So I was quite glad to get back in the front line."[4]

Paul was already showing signs of his musical versatility, and never seemed set on any particular instrument at this time. So it was no surprise when it finally came to filling the bass position, the job fell to McCartney.

The Rosetti and the purloined strings

With his new role as bassman, McCartney had one immediate task: to find an instrument. He resisted the idea of buying a new bass on credit, because this would put him into debt. According to McCartney's original hire-purchase receipt from Hessy's, he had just finished paying for his Rosetti Solid 7 guitar, on January 21st. McCartney explains, "The way I'd been brought up, my dad had always hammered into us to never get in debt, because we weren't that rich."[5]

With this in mind, and little money in his pocket, McCartney decided to use a little ingenuity and transform his Rosetti into a sort of bass guitar. Permanently relieving an innocent piano of a few bass strings, he managed to turn the Solid 7 into a makeshift bass by taking three bass strings from the piano and fitting them on to the guitar. In those days a set of bass strings was expensive. 'Borrowing' a few strings from a piano proved to be much more economical.

McCartney explains, "All these clubs would wonder what had gone wrong with their pianos. We

1961

Tony Sheridan playing with The Beatles at the Top Ten in Hamburg. Sheridan (right) is playing his Martin D-28E electric-acoustic guitar.

had some pliers and it was: 'All right lads, quick it's an A – which is the A?' Dong, dong! And we'd just nick an A-string. You'd be surprised how well they work."[6] McCartney got the idea from Sutcliffe. "Stuart … lent me his bass, and I played bass for a few weeks … He used to have piano strings on it, because you couldn't get bass strings. They were a bit rare, you know, and they cost a lot too, about £2 for one string. So we would cut these big lengths of piano strings from the piano and wind them on the guitar."[7]

The original pickguard and pickup assembly of the Rosetti was removed from the guitar during this transformation, and a new pickup was fitted to the bridge area of the guitar. This new mongrel bass version of the Solid 7 guitar served its purpose. McCartney used it throughout the spring of 1961 for numerous Beatle performances in and around Liverpool.

Another problem that plagued The Beatles at the time was getting decent transportation. With the number of shows they were performing, it was becoming difficult to move their equipment around town. Neil Aspinall, a friend of Best's who sometimes worked at the Casbah club, was hired by the group to transport them and their equipment to the various engagements. Aspinall bought a little old Commer van for £80 and became their driver, roadie and, later, their full-time road manager.

The Cavern

Mona Best's Casbah coffee club had effectively been The Beatles' home gig, but an onslaught of new engagements around Liverpool saw them at a variety of different venues: the Cassanova club, the Aintree Institute and, most importantly, the Cavern. The club, in Mathew Street in central Liverpool, was in a series of cellars below a warehouse, and had been opened by Alan Sytner in 1957 as a jazz-only operation. Ray McFall bought the club from Sytner two years later and began to broaden its musical policy to include the new rock'n'roll, which proved particularly popular at lunchtime performances, attracting many young local workers.

On February 9th 1961 The Beatles performed for the first time at the Cavern, opening for house band The Bluegenes (later renamed The Swinging Blue Jeans). Lennon's original Quarry Men, pre-McCartney, had played at the Cavern jazz club, on August 7th 1957. Les Braid, bass player of the Bluegenes, recalls the '61 gig. "We were playing there from about 1958 as a skiffle group. The Beatles used to play around Liverpool, and of course they played in Hamburg, but the first time they played at night at the Cavern was on our guest night, which I think was on Tuesdays. We'd have all the bands guesting – Gerry & The Pacemakers, The Searchers, Billy J. Kramer – and we had The Beatles on as well.

"The Beatles became very popular and got their own night eventually, on Wednesdays. But they were rough and ready then. Like many other bands we used to rehearse like mad, and we could never understand how such a rough band could be so popular. We thought you had to rehearse and be perfect to be good, but that obviously wasn't the case. "It made you wonder where The Beatles' material and influences and their act came from, because all the other bands were playing sort of Shadows-type stuff, with the smart suits and everything. The Beatles were so different. My first impression was that they were the biggest load of rubbish … but then I became one of the biggest fans."[8] The Cavern was soon The Beatles' new stomping ground, and virtually a home base. As Braid has pointed out, they quickly secured their own night at the club, and played almost 300 performances there during the next two years.

By the end of February Sutcliffe had returned from Hamburg to visit his parents for a few weeks. While at home in Liverpool he sat in with The Beatles on bass. Photographs of the group taken at the Casbah at this time reveal The Beatles with two bass players: Sutcliffe playing his Hofner 333 bass and McCartney using his makeshift three-string Rosetti "bass". Harrison has the Futurama, and Lennon plays his new Rickenbacker.

George on-stage with the band's equipment in Hamburg (left to right): Stu's 333 bass leaning on the Truvoice amp; George holding John's Rickenbacker (with a missing knob), and behind him the club's piano; the Gibson Les Paul amp; Paul's Rosetti Solid 7; George's Futurama; John's Fender Deluxe amp; and Pete's Premier drum kit.

STUART LENT ME HIS BASS ... HE USED TO HAVE PIANO STRINGS ON IT, BECAUSE YOU COULDN'T GET BASS STRINGS

Paul McCartney

Several Liverpudlian bands of the era interviewed for this book went to see The Beatles while Sutcliffe was in the group and remember McCartney with his three-string bass plugged in, but with the other end of the lead (cord) stuffed into his jacket pocket and not plugged into an amp at all. This may explain how the group overcame the sonic problem of two bass players. McCartney himself confirmed the practice when asked about his falling-apart Rosetti. "I used to ... piece it together and plug it in but not plug it in, [that is to say I would] just play it not plugged in."[9]

This line-up did not last long. By mid-March Sutcliffe returned to Hamburg to his girlfriend, and continued to study painting at the city's State High School of Art Instruction.

Hamburg second trip – Top Ten club

The group now had to clear up the mess left behind in Hamburg and prepare for the tentative booking they had made with Peter Eckhorn to play at his Top Ten club in April. Harrison had turned 18, relieving the problems associated with being under-age. But a big hurdle remained with the German authorities concerning the deportation of McCartney and Best. It was Best's mother Mo who had written on behalf of the two musicians, promising their good behaviour and trying to persuade the German government to lift the threat of further deportation.

This time, The Beatles applied for proper work permits that would enable them to perform legally at the Top Ten club. Eckhorn too pleaded with the German immigration department on the group's behalf, going so far as to pay them 158 Deutschmarks to reimburse the cost of McCartney and Best's November deportation flight back to the UK. These efforts evidently worked, because a one-year lifting of the deportation ban was granted. The Beatles negotiated their final deal with Eckhorn and made their way back for their second stay in Hamburg. This time they travelled by train, equipment and all.

On April 1st they started their residency at the Top Ten club on the Reeperbahn in Hamburg, performing with Tony Sheridan. Best explained later that Sheridan was still very much the house

Live at the Top Ten club in Hamburg, and The Beatles are in transition. Paul, whose Rosetti is by now permanently out of action, has switched to piano – but he already owns his new Hofner violin bass guitar (it's in the case by the piano) and it won't be long before he's using it as the band's new bass player.

musician at the club. "We thought we'd have our own show and then back him, but in fact Tony played every set that we played. So we played our numbers and he played his numbers. He liked us backing him because, again, there was this harmony … we used to do [great harmonies] for him."[10]

For the beginning of the group's stay at the Top Ten, Sutcliffe had returned as bass player. The full line-up was Sheridan on his electric-acoustic Martin D-28E flat-top guitar, Lennon playing his Rickenbacker 325 through his Fender Deluxe tweed amp, Harrison with his Futurama through the Selmer Truvoice amp, Best on his Premier drums, and Sutcliffe on his Hofner 333 bass through the Gibson Les Paul amp. With no need for four guitarists in the group, and with his Rosetti guitar converted to bass, McCartney decided to switch to playing piano. His Rosetti was starting to fall apart, probably due to the abnormal stress placed on the guitar's neck by the heavy bass strings he'd put on. McCartney explained, "When I went to Hamburg I had [the Rosetti], a really terrible British guitar with terrible action. It just fell apart on me … just the heat in the club and the sweat made it fall apart. Eventually, I sort of busted it – early rumblings of The Who – in a drunken moment. It was busted somewhere, and it had to go. So I ended up with my back to the audience, playing piano, which was then the only thing I could do unless I could get a new guitar."[11]

In an earlier account, McCartney said he didn't particularly want to be rid of the Rosetti, but didn't have much choice when it got smashed. "I dropped it one day," he recalled in a 1964 interview. "It wasn't a complete write-off, but I didn't think it was worth repairing. So all us – George, Stu, Pete and John, especially John – had a great time smashing it to bits by jumping up and down on it. Bit mad, I suppose. But we had to get rid of our pent-up energy sometimes, and it seemed the obvious thing to do at the time. I couldn't afford to buy a new guitar, so I became the official piano player. No, I didn't know how to play, but I knew a few chords, and the rest of the boys decided that they needed a pianist in the group, so for a few weeks I ruined the Top Ten club piano in Hamburg."[12]

This line-up worked only for a short time, because Sutcliffe made it known that he intended eventually to leave the group and concentrate on his college studies and painting career. With that prospect, McCartney knew he would have to resume his role of bass player.

Best says that Sutcliffe had already made his decision by the time the group came to record with producer Burt Kaempfert for the Polydor label in June. "That solved our problem, because we felt Paul was going to be better recording-wise than Stu. Some people have said that it was already in our minds to kick Stu out, and that's wrong. It was very much a case that we'd asked Paul if he didn't mind covering for Stu at the recording session – and that's as far as we'd taken it. But when Stu announced that he'd be leaving, it relieved us of that sort of embarrassment. It was a case of Stu saying to Paul: you take over the bass or do what you want to do, with my blessing."[13]

Paul's first Hofner violin bass

Sutcliffe's announcement must have helped McCartney make up his mind to start looking for a real bass as a replacement for the smashed Rosetti. "Stu lent me his bass for a week or so,"[14] remembers McCartney. Being left-handed, McCartney had to play Sutcliffe's Hofner 333 Bass upside-down. "Eventually I found a nice little shop in the centre of Hamburg, near a big department store. … I saw this bass in the window, this violin-shaped bass, the Hofner. We'd window-shopped, we'd looked at it. … I thought it looked pretty good. I liked its lightness, too. So I bought it, and I think it was only about £30. It was a good price, anyway, and we were earning reasonable money."[15]

It was on the second floor of the Steinway shop in the centre of Hamburg that McCartney found this solution to his problem: a German-made Hofner 500/1 bass, nicknamed the "violin" bass for its body shape. Günter Höper was one of six salesmen at Steinway at the time. "Paul McCartney bought his Hofner bass from me," says Höper. "As usual in those days, he bought it in instalments. We offered a ten-payment deal, and so we had to set up a contract, for which we needed his passport number. However, Paul had left his passport at the Top Ten club, so I went with him to the club to get the passport and do the deal."[16] Höper says the price of the bass was 287 Deutschmarks.

"I couldn't afford a Fender," McCartney recalled later. "Fenders even then seemed to be about £100. All I could afford really was about £30. Always teetering on the edge of not having much – so I didn't really want to spend that much. So … I found this Hofner violin bass. And to me it seemed like, because I was left-handed, it looked less daft because it was symmetrical. … So I got into that. That became my main bass."[17]

The chances of finding a left-handed Hofner bass on display in a music shop in 1961 was next to impossible. In fact the Hofner was specially ordered for McCartney as a left-hander. Most likely he saw the bass, realised it would look good when played left-handed, and enquired about a custom bass. With Hofner based in Germany it would have been relatively easy to order a left-handed instrument. The major change was to shift the pickguard and the hole for the electronics to the opposite side of the body. The Steinway shop probably saw this as a simple way to achieve a sale.

Tony Sheridan thinks left-handed instruments were not available at all in Hamburg. "This would have been a special order direct from Hofner," he insists. "As there were next to no German rock musicians around, there was no demand for anything much in the way of quality instruments, let alone a left-handed bass. I shouldn't be surprised if Hofner didn't make their first left-handed bass for Paul."[18]

Another piece of evidence that points to McCartney's bass being specially made comes from a 1963 magazine. "[McCartney's] left-handed Hofner bass was specially altered for him in Germany and is *not* available in this country,"[19] ran a report in a British musicians' publication. Best recalls being with McCartney at the time. "He didn't just go into a shop and buy it off the peg, he got it custom made."[20] The Hofner 500/1 violin bass became McCartney's signature instrument. Soon it was unofficially known as the Hofner Beatle Bass and became an important part of the look as well as the sound of The Beatles.

The sound of the Hofner 500/1 is very "round" and rich, with a prominent midrange tone due

IT SEEMED TO ME LIKE, BECAUSE I WAS LEFT-HANDED, IT LOOKED LESS DAFT, BECAUSE IT WAS SYMMETRICAL

Paul McCartney,

on his beloved Hofner violin bass

Stu and George playing at the Top Ten club in Hamburg. Stu is still on bass – but just behind him leans Paul's new violin bass, ready to go.

in part to its hollow body. At times it can be quite bass-heavy if played in the higher register of the neck, a quality that is evident on some later Beatle recordings. Hofner 500/1 basses are lightweight and have a thin, comfortable neck, with a string action that can be set very low. The main disadvantage of these Hofner basses is that they are very fragile. They are not very durable, and are not tolerant to typical musician abuse. In time, most develop neck problems. Many old examples found today have repairs to neck cracks that developed where the body and neck join.

McCartney usually played his Hofner with the Treble switch off and the Bass switch on. The Rhythm/Solo switch he usually selected to Rhythm, which would activate only the forward neck-position pickup, producing the instrument's fullest, richest and most powerful bass tone. Pictures of The Beatles performing at the Top Ten club reveal McCartney with his new Hofner 500/1 violin bass and Sutcliffe, still with the band, playing his Hofner 333 Bass. The arrival of McCartney's new Hofner bass heralds Sutcliffe's imminent departure from the group.

With this instrumental transition there also came a change in The Beatles' amplification. Harrison managed to acquire the outgoing Sutcliffe's Gibson GA-40 Les Paul amplifier, which he used with his Futurama guitar. McCartney needed something larger than his little Elpico amplifier for his new bass and began to use Harrison's more powerful Selmer Truvoice amplifier. Lennon continued to play the Rickenbacker through his Fender Deluxe amp.

During this second trip to Hamburg, Lennon started to have problems with his Rickenbacker. Various pictures from the trip show that the four supplied art deco "oven" knobs had a habit of falling off. The pictures reveal first the lack of a top knob, which was then replaced, and then a bottom knob came off and was in turn replaced. This was the beginning of a series of knob replacements that Lennon's Rickenbacker 325 would experience, and the guitar would later go through a succession of more major changes and transformations.

Paul with his first Hofner 500/1 "violin" bass guitar, acquired during the group's visit to Hamburg in 1961. The bass was specially made for him left-handed.

Tony Sheridan and The Beatles

During their residency at the Top Ten the group played for many hours with Tony Sheridan, and they all lived together above the club. Sheridan claims an early influence on Harrison's choice of guitars, saying that the Beatle guitarist had noticed the Futurama Sheridan often played in the late 1950s during his British TV appearances. "That Futurama wasn't too bad, considering the general quality of instruments – or lack of it – in those days," Sheridan laughs.

During his association with The Beatles in Hamburg Sheridan used a few quite different guitars: an acoustic-electric Martin D-28E, and two Gibson ES-175s, the first with one pickup, the second with two, and both with Bigsby vibrato arms. The 175 was a hollow-body archtop electric model, much revered by jazz players for its fine tone and easy playability. "On stage with The Beatles nightly, for long hours, guitars were passed around quite a bit," Sheridan recalls. "I guess I infected them with my regard for a full sound and quality rather than guitars with a certain image. I used to insist on good guitars. I was into guitars much more. I had a little bit more money, you see, so I could import some good things, like the Gibsons. We used to get our guitars through the Steinway store in Hamburg. It was the only place to go, in the middle of town, and the sole place one could order guitars from the States. It was a very well known place, very respectable, and primarily known for selling pianos."

With the continuing shortage of American-made guitars among British musicians, Sheridan's Gibson ES-175s caused quite a stir. "My 175 – I wish I still had it – was often used by John and George on stage during our collaboration in Hamburg," he says. "It was always nice for them to use a good guitar rather than a rubbish one. I never understood John using this tinny-sounding Rickenbacker. I used to hate the bloody thing! They just didn't sound good – I'd tell him that. But they still liked to play on my Gibson, or even the Martin. When the night got long, in the early wee hours we used to sit on the stage. Sometimes we couldn't stand up any more, just through fatigue and a couple of beers or whatever. We would sit down and play the big guitars and get into a quieter mood – and out of that situation I think they started to write a lot of ballads."[21]

First recording deal

By mid-June, during the Top Ten engagement, The Beatles and Tony Sheridan were approached by Bert Kaempfert, a German orchestra leader and songwriter who had achieved success with an American number-one hit, 'Wonderland By Night'. Kaempfert had offered to make a recording for possible release on the German Polydor label. The group eagerly accepted the recording and publishing deal.

The recording session was held in a makeshift studio in a school auditorium. Best was taken aback: "Studio? We wondered if we'd come to the right place. We had been expecting a recording set-up on the grand scale; after all, Bert was a big name and Polydor an important label, part of the Deutsche Grammophon company. Instead we found ourselves in an unexciting school hall with a massive stage and lots of drapes. The recording equipment was backstage. We were expected to play behind Tony on the stage, as if the whole thing was an outside broadcast. Surely this couldn't be the place where Bert made his own smoochy bestsellers? It was – and he was perfectly satisfied with the conditions."[22]

The recording did not include Sutcliffe, whose departure from the band coincided with the Kaempfert sessions. McCartney played bass. The Beatles recorded a handful of songs backing Tony Sheridan, including 'My Bonnie Lies Over The Ocean' and 'When The Saints Go Marching In' which were released as a single on Polydor. At these same sessions, the group recorded two songs without Sheridan: 'Ain't She Sweet', sung by Lennon, and an original guitar instrumental penned by Lennon and Harrison entitled 'Cry For A Shadow'. Harrison has explained its origins in the group's joking references to The Shadows, the prime British guitar-instrumental band of the time. Shadows-style bands had matching ties and handkerchiefs and smart suits, with lead-guitar players wearing specs to look like Buddy Holly and employing a funny stage-walk while they were playing. The Beatles, by contrast, were leather-clad rockers who favoured Chuck Berry and Little Richard.

"So we used to always joke about the Shadows," said Harrison, "and actually in Hamburg we had to play so long [we would play The Shadows' hit 'Apache']. John and I were just bullshitting one day, and he had this new little Rickenbacker with a funny kind of wobble bar on it. [He started off 'Cry

OUR BEST WORK WAS NEVER RECORDED ... AS SOON AS WE MADE IT ... THE EDGES WERE KNOCKED OFF

John Lennon

By the middle of 1961, the Beatles relationship with their first "manager", Allan Williams, had broken down. Williams, who once claimed "sole direction" for the band (as seen on the card above), had organised many of their early gigs in Liverpool and Hamburg. Before the end of the year, though, the management vacancy would be amply filled.

For a Shadow'] and I just came in, and we made it up right on the spot. Then we started playing it a couple of nights, and it got on a record somehow. But it was really a joke."[23]

The Beatles used the same equipment for the recording session as they did at the Top Ten, but Sheridan says they also played his ES-175. "They used it on some of the recordings. John used it on a couple of rhythm tracks that I wasn't on, 'Cry For A Shadow' and 'Ain't She Sweet'. It sounded good in the studio just through a Fender amp." Polydor released the single of 'My Bonnie' and 'The Saints' in the summer in Germany, credited to Tony Sheridan and the "Beat Brothers" instead of The Beatles. Apparently Polydor felt that "Beatles" sounded too much like a German slang word for penis (possibly "Schniedel").

It could have been a Strat

Best says that Harrison had always looked to the music first over such considerations as "birds and booze" and was forever experimenting with different tones and the improvement of his sound. From all accounts it seems that Harrison thought a lot about guitars – and especially about acquiring new ones. During the group's second stay in Hamburg, Harrison was once again on the look-out for a new guitar.

Had it not been for an incident with a rival band, Harrison may well have played a Fender Stratocaster in the early days of The Beatles. For the second half of the group's engagement in Hamburg they once again shared the stage with fellow Liverpudlians Rory Storm & The Hurricanes. A distinct rivalry had developed between the two outfits.

Harrison was finding his Futurama difficult to play, not least because of its very high "action", a technical term for the height of the strings from the fingerboard. "Nevertheless, it did look kind of futuristic," Harrison recalled recently. "Then when I was in Hamburg I found out that some guy had a Stratocaster for sale, and I arranged that I was going to go first thing the next morning and buy it. I believe it was a white one. And this fellow who was the guitar player in Rory Storm & The Hurricanes … found out about it too, and he got up earlier and went and bought it. By the time I got there it had gone. I was so disappointed it scarred me for life, that experience. I think after that happened I got [my] Gretsch – it was a denial kind of thing."[24]

Johnny Guitar, lead guitarist in Rory Storm & The Hurricanes, remembered arranging to meet The Beatles in Hamburg's Steinway music shop. Storm was going to lend them 1300 Deutschmarks to buy Harrison a Fender. "I asked Rory why he was lending them the money when our own guitarist, Ty Brian, needed one. So when we got there Rory told them he'd changed his mind and we were buying the guitar for Ty. All hell broke loose and Lennon went mad, but Ty held his own, rolling around the floor. They ignored us for a few days after, but it all blew over."[25]

The Beatles finished their engagement at the Top Ten on July 1st and headed back to Liverpool. Now decked out all in black leather, the group resumed their home gigs, frequenting the Cavern and other venues around Liverpool. Photographs taken of them at the Cavern in July show McCartney with his new Hofner bass, Lennon with his Rickenbacker 325, and Harrison still playing his Futurama guitar. But Harrison was clearly ready to make a change.

With the German Stratocaster incident behind him, Harrison set his sights on acquiring a new guitar. As he had written to his friend Arthur Kelly in an earlier letter, "the one I want is the Gretsch". Harrison was starting to get a bit more money at this time and had saved around £75. "I saw an ad in the paper in Liverpool," he recalled later, "and there was a guy selling his guitar. I bought [a Gretsch Duo Jet from a sailor] who had bought it in America and brought it back. It was my first real American guitar – and I'll tell you, it was secondhand, but I polished that thing. I was so proud to own that."[26]

Harrison has described the Duo Jet as his "first good guitar", adding that it wasn't easy to acquire an American guitar in Liverpool back in the early 1960s, because of scarcity and cost. "I saved my money from the gigs I had started playing, and one night in the *Liverpool Echo* I saw the advert under For Sale. I rushed to the address that was given, with about £75 cash in my pocket, and returned home the very pleased owner of that

Sheridan also played a Gibson ES-175 archtop electric guitar (catalogue shot, right) while in Hamburg, which would have been The Beatles' first brush with a real American-made Gibson guitar.

Gretsch. I still have it till this day, after playing it through the Hamburg days and Cavern years, tours of Europe to America in '64 and many, many of The Beatles recordings."[27]

Gretsch had introduced the "solidbody" electric Duo Jet in 1953 to compete with Gibson's Les Paul model, in a quite similar body style. It was not in fact a true solidbody guitar, but rather semi-solid with hollow "pockets" in the body. Harrison's Gretsch model 6128 Duo Jet bears the serial number 21179, dating its manufacture probably to 1957.

A 1957 Gretsch Duo Jet is a rare guitar today, highly sought-after among guitar collectors. The playability and tone of most 1950s Duo Jets is outstanding. Its semi-solid mahogany body provides a deep, rich tone while the single-coil pickups help deliver a fine treble response, combining into a tone unique to these early Duo Jets. Another bonus is the guitar's very thin neck, which is comfortable and easy to play. So it's no surprise that this guitar started Harrison's love affair with Gretsch guitars – one that has lasted to this day.

A British-made Reslo microphone like the ones that The Beatles used at this time in and around Liverpool, especially at the Cavern.

Early days of PA systems

At the start of the 1960s, rock'n'roll bands with electric guitars were still a new idea. No one quite knew how they should sound – or how to make them sound the way they should. The general availability and quality of guitars was low, and the same was true of amplifiers, whether for instruments or voice.

PA (public address) systems, for vocal amplification, were primitive. The average PA system for a band used a single 12-inch loudspeaker cabinet, probably set on stage in line with the guitar amplifiers, and usually powered by a small, low-wattage amp built into the same box. Maybe two or three microphones were used, and only for vocals. A larger PA might have a couple of small speaker cabinets on either side of the stage. These set-ups were a long way from today's sophisticated high-tech sound systems where every instrument is miked three different ways, sent through automated 96-channel mixing boards, funnelled into massive, multi-thousand-watt power amps, and pumped out to huge walls of high-energy, blow-your-head-off speaker systems.

Watching a band perform back then through the sparse, primitive PA equipment would have been a completely different experience. Bands playing in the early 1960s through such relatively crude equipment must have given an instant impression of their capabilities, unhidden by grand effects or impressive sound.

Chris Huston, guitarist for The Undertakers, another Liverpool group of the time, reminds us to bear in mind that at the time none of the bands in Liverpool – or anywhere else in Britain – had any experience. Players were thrown into the situation and had to make the best of what they had. "But it certainly beat working," he laughs. "Here we were, probably working more hours than if you had a regular job – but it wasn't work. Everything was seat-of-the-pants stuff."

Brian Kelly – who as we've seen booked The Beatles for their run at the Litherland Town Hall, and also promoted events at the Aintree Institute – supplied PA systems for many venues in Liverpool through his Alpha Sound Services. Chris Huston reminisces about the kind of PA gear you might expect in those days: "There'd be Reslo ribbon microphones, and little amplifiers of 25 or 35 watts output. These were not sophisticated times, by any means. It was when music was fun. The very essence of music for us and for most of the groups in Liverpool was excitement. You needed it in a place that was depressed, where it rained every bloody day, where people were out of work. And the people who had jobs might work 60 hours a week on the docks. Here we were earning more every night than the average person earned in a week. Everyone knew everybody else and all the bands used to go and see each other. There was something happening. There was magic in the air."[28]

It seems that the Liverpudlian bands of the early 1960s managed to turn less into more at their live shows. With very little equipment, groups had to rely on talent and sheer energy to get themselves across. Perhaps this is what Lennon was getting at when, years later, he said, "Our best work was never recorded. We were performing in Liverpool, Hamburg and other dancehalls. What we generated was fantastic. When we played straight rock, there was nobody to touch us in Britain. As soon as we made it ... the edges were knocked off."[29]

Every Liverpudlian musician interviewed for this book has fond memories of the city's most famous music store, Frank Hessy's. We'll let Pete Best underline the importance of this store to the

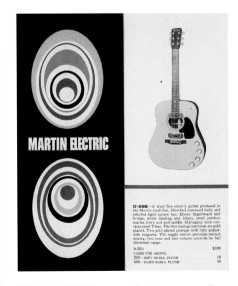

Martin's D-28E was a flat-top acoustic guitar with built-in electric pickup and controls – as used by Tony Sheridan.

The Beatles at the Cavern in the
summer of 1961. George has his new
Gretsch Duo Jet, with Bigsby vibrato,
and John his Rickenbacker 325 still
with its Kauffman vibrato – soon to be
changed to a Bigsby.

Mersey bands. "Everyone in Liverpool went to Hessy's," confirms Best. "It was *the* music store – the band's store. Rushworth's was the more musical store, if you wanted pianos, drum kits, and so on, and was up on London Row before it moved into the same vicinity as Hessy's.

"But it was Jim Gretty at Hessy's – Uncle Jim as we used to call him – who was a friend to everyone and every musician. Whether you went in there to buy strings or listen to him play or were with someone to look at guitars, or buy your sticks in there, it was normally Jim you ended up talking to. He was *the* man in Liverpool at that time. We all loved him."[30] It was at Hessy's that The Beatles bought most of their musical equipment and supplies while in Liverpool.

Lennon's Rickenbacker gets wobble and knobs

Photographs taken of The Beatles performing at the Cavern between mid-July and mid-August 1961 show Harrison with his new Gretsch Duo Jet and Lennon with his Rickenbacker 325, still with its factory-fitted Kauffman vibrato system and "oven" style knobs. Harrison's new Gretsch with its Bigsby vibrato must have intrigued Lennon, because he soon acquired a Bigsby for his own Rickenbacker. Lennon had quickly become dissatisfied with the Kauffman, which was a crude and unusual sideways-action system. The point of a vibrato was to slightly raise or lower the pitch of a string or strings when the arm was moved, giving a simple pitch-change effect or a more extreme "wobbling" sound.

Pete Best confirms that Lennon didn't think much of the poor Kauffman "twang arm", as he called it. "He liked the Bigsby simply because it was stronger and there was more leverage in it, he could twang the notes a little more, even though he didn't do it that much. He felt more comfortable with a Bigsby on it as opposed to the Kauffman which, to be quite honest, looked just like a spoon sticking out of the guitar."[31]

Bigsby

George's Gretsch Duo Jet. George bought this instrument in the summer of 1961 after seeing an ad in a Liverpool newspaper – and so became the second Beatle to own an American-made guitar. Geroge's Duo Jet, which he still owns today, was made in 1957. On the left is a Bigsby catalogue from the period.

Chris Huston of The Undertakers tells an interesting story about how Lennon acquired the Bigsby vibrato for his Rickenbacker. "I'd had a Gibson Les Paul Special," says Huston, "which came from the factory with a Bigsby unit behind the bridge. John had that little whammy bar on his Rickenbacker and we started talking about it one day. So he ordered a Bigsby unit from Hessy's – I don't think they were a stock item."

When Lennon's Bigsby came in to Hessy's he invited Huston to go with him to pick it up. "Jim Gretty was there, of course," recalls Huston. "He was a local legend. There were pictures of him all over the walls of the shop dressed in a cowboy suit – he was a player himself, did a sort of English version of country & western. So we just put John's Rickenbacker right on the counter, took the strings off, and put the new Bigsby on right there and then. A new aluminium bridge came with the separate Bigsby vibrato, so we just put that on as well."

Technically, the Rickenbacker's original bridge is better for individual string adjustment and intonation, but for some reason Lennon chose to install the more basic Bigsby "bow-tie" aluminium bridge that came with the vibrato system. "We just did it," says Huston. "It was something new, I suppose, and we just put it on."

When asked how Lennon liked the performance of the new Bigsby, Huston says, "It was like he'd graduated. The old one just didn't have the same excursion." Huston adds that The Undertakers' rhythm guitarist, Geoff Nugent, worked as an artificial-limb mechanic at Broad Green Hospital. "So he brought us the springs from artificial limbs which he'd grind down, and we'd put those in our Bigsbys instead of the Bigsby springs. Some of them were flesh coloured! So we had artificial-limb springs in our Bigsbys."[32]

Billy Kinsley, bassist for The Merseybeats, recalls hanging out in Hessy's one rainy afternoon with the group's guitarist, Tony Crane, when John Lennon walked into the shop. "He had the Bigsby on his Rickenbacker, but he kept losing the spring from it. In Liverpool at the time you couldn't get spare parts, like in America. So Jim Gretty would nick one from another Bigsby. Jim was a friend of John's, and he'd tell him to nick a spring off another guitar.

"Also that day I remember telling John that I'd ordered a Gibson bass from the States, a little EB-0, and he said that he and George really wanted Paul to get a different bass. They didn't like the violin bass, and they wanted him to get an EB-0. Obviously this was before The Beatles were famous, before the rest of the world saw that violin bass – and it became Paul's

John at the Cavern with his '58 Rickenbacker 325, complete with its new Bigsby vibrato and fresh set of control knobs.

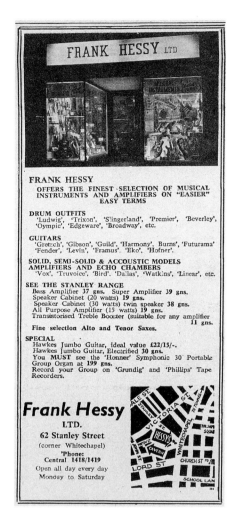

Frank Hessy's music store in the centre of Liverpool was the group's favourite place to buy instruments and supplies. It was here, with the help of the shop's manager Jim Gretty, that John changed the Kauffman vibrato on his Rickenbacker to a Bigsby.

trademark. But I often wonder what would have happened if he'd got one of those little Gibsons."[33]

The Bigsby model B-5 vibrato that Lennon had fitted to his Rickenbacker 325 at Hessy's was a British-made version, produced under license from the US Bigsby company by Selmer in the UK. The "British" B-5 is slightly smaller than the original US version and has a less strongly etched Bigsby brandname. The cost of the unit at the time was 12 guineas (£12.60, about $35 then; around £165 or $230 in today's money).

The addition of the Bigsby B-5 and "bow-tie" bridge to Lennon's Rickenbacker 325 was not the only change. He also decided, following many instances of the 325's knobs falling off, to remove the original art deco "oven" control knobs and replace them with more basic looking chrome knobs. Huston says the knobs came from a little hi-fi and radio store, Curry Electronics, near Rushworth's. "Maybe it was John's shot at customisation," he says.[34] As we've already seen, Lennon had an apparently continual problem with knobs falling off this guitar.

On August 19th The Beatles played a show at the Aintree Institute in Liverpool, and photographs taken at the performance show Lennon playing his newly modified Rickenbacker – with Bigsby vibrato and "bow-tie" bridge – through his Fender Deluxe amp. McCartney has his Hofner bass, playing through the Selmer Truvoice amp, and Harrison his new Gretsch Duo Jet plugged into the Gibson GA-40 Les Paul amp. Best is of course faithfully playing his Premier drum set.

One might wonder what Lennon did with the discarded Kauffman vibrato and Rickenbacker bridge. Another photograph taken this year, of Rory Storm & The Hurricanes, shows Johnny Guitar playing his Guyatone electric guitar with a non-standard Kauffman vibrato fitted. Johnny Guitar explains: "John gave me the vibrato arm and the bridge off his Rickenbacker. I put the vibrato on my guitar but it was no good, it didn't work properly, so I soon took it off again. But I've still got the bridge that was on John's first Rickenbacker."

The birth of *Mersey Beat* newspaper

By now the music scene in Liverpool was thriving, with hundreds of bands playing nightly at the different venues in and around the city. Bill Harry, a former schoolmate of Lennon's, was well aware of the scene, and decided to start a newspaper devoted to music in Liverpool, *Mersey Beat*. It was Harry who helped promote his old art-school friend's band by putting The Beatles on the front cover of the second issue of the paper, complete with the headline "Beatles Sign Recording Contract!" According to Harry, it may have been this issue of *Mersey Beat* that attracted a record shop manager named Brian Epstein to The Beatles.

"Nobody was really aware of what was going on in Liverpool until the advent of *Mersey Beat*," Harry says. "There was no publicity of any kind. The media completely ignored rock'n'roll. There were no papers or anything about the groups. But when *Mersey Beat* came out we wrote about all the groups, and how big the scene was.

"I took the first issue to the NEMS shop and asked to see the manager, who was Brian Epstein. He said he'd take a dozen, and by that same afternoon he'd sold them out. He was quite amazed that they sold out so quickly, so he kept ordering more and they kept selling out. So with issue number two he ordered 144 copies – which was amazing for one small store."

The entire front cover of the second issue, out in July 1961, covered the story about The Beatles recording in Hamburg. Epstein was intrigued, and invited Harry up to his office to have a chat. He was, says Harry, astonished that there was so much musical activity in Liverpool. Epstein appeared in *Mersey Beat*'s pages from issue three, as the paper's record reviewer, and soon began placing ads for his NEMS store.

"Then," continues Harry, "compère/DJ Bob Wooler wrote this big article about The Beatles and how sensational they were – and NEMS had an advert on the same page. Virtually every issue had The Beatles in. So Brian started asking about the groups, the scene, The Beatles and all the rest of it. Then he phoned me up and asked me if I could arrange for him to go down to the Cavern. So I fixed him up to go down there – and of course that was when he saw The Beatles."[35]

Epstein made his way to the Cavern club to see the group perform at a lunchtime session on November 9th. He wrote later that he had never seen anything like The Beatles on any stage. "They smoked as they played, and they ate and talked and pretended to hit each other," wrote Epstein. "They turned their backs on the audience and shouted at them and laughed at private jokes. But they gave a captivating and honest show, and they had very considerable magnetism... "I loved their ad libs and I was fascinated by this, to me, new music with its pounding bass beat and its vast, engulfing sound."[36] After the show Epstein met the group and tried to find out about their German single. It seems the reception he got was lukewarm at best.

Adrian Barber and the Coffin bass amplification

The "pounding" bass that Epstein described was due in part to a new addition to The Beatles' equipment line-up. In the early 1960s there was really no such thing as a proper bass amplifier. Most bass players would use the most powerful guitar amplifier that they could get their hands on. But these were not designed for bass guitar, and did not provide the deep, throbbing bass tones that bass guitarists wanted. As The Beatles evolved their sound and Best perfected his "atomic beat" the group were searching for a stronger and more solid bass sound.

The band considered by many to be the loudest and most aggressive in Liverpool was The Big Three. They had started out as Cass & The Cassanovas, a four-piece until leader and frontman Brian Casser left during the beginning of 1961. The remaining members stayed together to form The Big Three: Johnny Gustafson on bass, guitarist Adrian Barber, and Liverpool's loudest drummer, Johnny Hutchinson, on the skins.

Barber says that when they became a trio there was an instant problem: he and Gustafson weren't loud enough to project over Hutchinson's drumming. Even the relatively punchy Selmer Truvoice amp was not enough. Barber, however, had an interest in electronics from his days in the merchant navy. He'd met a local jazz guitarist, Denis Kealing, who said he could build him an amp along with a speaker cabinet with a 12-inch Goodmans driver. Barber agreed, and used that set-up with The Cassanovas.

When it came to The Big Three, Barber went out and bought a book about loudspeakers produced by G A Briggs, who owned the British Wharfedale speaker company, and inside he found construction details for various sizes of cabinets. "I decided on one, and Denis Kealing said he could get me a 15-inch speaker," recalls Barber. "I built a set-up for the bass guitar and for the vocal, in a cabinet about five feet tall by about 18 inches square. It was a 'ported' reflex cabinet made out of three-quarter-inch chipboard with inch-by-inch bracing inside. It was screwed and glued and was very well built – it didn't vibrate. It was filled with fibreglass padding on the inside to cut down the resonances.

"I happened to have a Quad hi-fi amp," Barber continues. "In those days hi-fi was mono, there wasn't stereo. So this amp was one-channel, with two KT66 valves [tubes], and a good output transformer that would pass a lot of bass frequencies. I used that and mounted it in a metal ammunitions case, so we could carry it around without killing it. Johnny Gustafson used it as his bass amp, and it was very successful.

"When we carried it we had to lower it on its side, because it was long and skinny. The first time we took it down to the Cavern, we struggled down the tiny stairs there. As we carried this black-painted thing across the room it looked just like a coffin – and that's how it got its name: the Coffin. Now, the Cavern was the underground basement of a warehouse, with three vaulted brick-built archways. Over the years water had seeped down and brought calcium deposits with it, which had settled in the ceiling bricks. So when Johnny plucked that first bass note it was like a shower of snow coming down. People went, 'Wow look at that ... and listen to that.' So we were really impressed, and I got ambitious at that point."

For his own guitar amp Barber added another 12-inch speaker to the design, plus some midrange horns and four tweeters, all from Goodmans, as well as a Leak amp to power it and a pre-amp that he built himself. "I got a lot of treble out of it," says Barber. "In those days treble was a big thing with guitars, the more treble the better. Then I built an 18-inch ported reflex bass cabinet for Johnny, and that's what we ended up with. Nobody had heard anything like this. People were freaking out."

Other bands began to notice the relative sophistication of The Big Three's amplification, especially the bass gear. "Liverpool wasn't a competitive scene, before it got commercial," explains

Two cool cats: Paul with his Hofner bass, and Pete with his marine-pearl Premier drum kit.

This picture captures the group in their classic leather-clad period, complete with their soon-to-be-famous Beatle guitars: Rickenbacker 325, Gretsch Duo Jet and Hofner violin bass.

Barber. "All the bands co-operated with one another and backed each other up. It was a cool scene, and I started to build these things for other people. Paul McCartney asked me to make him a Coffin. It had a single 15-inch speaker in a reflex-ported cabinet, with two chrome handles and wheels on the side."[37]

McCartney started to use a Barber Coffin speaker cabinet during the late part of 1961. He used his existing Selmer Truvoice to power the new cabinet by disconnecting the speaker on the Selmer and feeding the output of its power amp to the Coffin. This speaker/amp combination produced a much more powerful bass tone. McCartney himself recalls, "Adrian made me a great bass amp that he called the Coffin. And, man! Suddenly that was a total other world. That was bass as we know it now. It was like reggae bass: it was just too right there. It was great live."[38]

Pete Best too remembers the Coffin. "Neil Aspinall and I used to carry it. Every couple of shows there'd be a flight of stairs which you had to carry this thing up, and it was then we'd wonder why he couldn't have got something smaller. We'd have sweat streaming off us. But the beauty of it was, with all the laughing and joking aside, it did produce a great sound. The first time Paul plugged it in and used it, we just said my god, this is incredible. It added to The Beatles sound."[39]

The group were using their new equipment line-up by their November 24th Operation Big Beat performance at the Tower Ballroom, New Brighton, and on December 8th at the Cavern with singer Davy Jones. Lennon had his Rickenbacker 325 guitar equipped with Bigsby vibrato and "radio" knobs, played through his Fender Deluxe amplifier. Harrison played his Gretsch Duo Jet guitar through his Gibson G-40 Les Paul amp. Best was on his Premier drum set, and McCartney played his Hofner 500/1 bass through his Selmer Truvoice amp connected to the Barber Coffin speaker cabinet. Photographs of The Beatles' first London show, on December 9th, reveal that McCartney did not use the Coffin bass cabinet. This was probably due in part to the problems the group must have had in transporting the large cabinet south from Liverpool to London. For this gig, with the Coffin left behind, McCartney reverted to using the Selmer Truvoice with its self-contained single 12-inch speaker.

Many of the musicians in the bands that The Beatles performed with tell of how they would borrow one another's amps and guitars and often swap equipment for shows. Some groups copied Barber's Coffin set-up. Billy Kinsley of The Merseybeats, for example, remembers that they would regularly use The Beatles' gear, and vice versa. "This was before they got their Vox AC-30s," says Kinsley, "when John had the little Fender and George the little Gibson. Tony Crane in our band had a small Fender amp, and I had a bass amp which I'd made myself. The Beatles' equipment used to come back to our house quite a few times. I lived off the West Derby Road and Pete Best and Neil Aspinall lived in West Derby, so they had to go past our house going home from town.

"So let's say The Beatles were third on at the Cavern and we were fourth. Neil [Aspinall, Beatles roadie] would go home after their set, we'd use their equipment, and then our road manager would go home and take all their equipment back to our house on the way. So one day I measured Paul's cabinet, the Coffin, and made myself a copy of it."[40] Kinsley's Coffin copy is today on display at The Beatles Story museum in Liverpool.

Paris and the Beatle haircut

At the beginning of October Lennon and McCartney took a trip to Paris. Apparently, a relative of Lennon's had given him £100 for his birthday. "I'd never seen so much money in my life," Lennon recalled later. "Paul and I just cancelled all the engagements and left for Paris, and George was furious because he needed the work, the money..."

Lennon went on to explain how he was always torn between looking arty and looking like a rocker. But it was when the pair went to Paris and saw a different style of hair and dress that they picked up the so-called Beatle haircut.

"It was really trying to do a French haircut," said Lennon, "where they don't have it parted at the side, but they have it parted high, a bit forward. Paul and I were there trying to cut each other's hair in that style. Also, the kids by the Moulin Rouge were wearing flared trousers in '61 and the round-neck jackets. So we went to a shop and bought one and thought oh, we'll make suits out of this. And they became Beatle suits.

"We just tried everything, and because we got famous, they said we were leading the fashion. But when we came back from Hamburg with the hair combed forward, the people in Liverpool were laughing at us. They said, 'You're queer, fags on stage!' And we had a hard time with the haircut. But we knew we liked it."[41]

With the birthday money gone, Lennon and McCartney returned from France and The Beatles continued to perform almost daily in and around Liverpool.

Managing The Beatles

NEMS store manager Brian Epstein continued to frequent The Beatles' performances, and would sometimes meet briefly with the band after shows. Epstein said later, "There was something enormously attractive about them. I liked the way they worked and the obvious enthusiasm they put into their numbers ...

"It was the boys themselves, though, who really swung it. Each had something, which I could see would be highly commercial, if only someone could push it to the top. They were different characters but they were so obviously part of the whole. Quite frankly, I was excited about their prospects, provided some things could be changed."[42]

Slowly Epstein built a casual acquaintance with the group, and toyed with the idea of managing them. Harrison explains, "Eventually he started talking about [him] becoming our manager. Well, we hadn't really had anybody actually volunteer [to do so] in that sense. At the same time, he was very honest about it, like saying he didn't really know anything about managing a group like us. He sort of hinted that he was keen if we'd go along with him."[43]

Epstein invited The Beatles to a formal meeting at his office in Whitechapel to discuss the possibilities of managing the group. On December 6th, Epstein made his proposal. For a fee of 25 per cent of the band's total gross earnings he would take over the responsibility of booking the group, promising that they would see an increase in their pay.

Epstein also promised that he could expand their bookings to a wider radius, to towns outside Liverpool. But most importantly he promised to secure them a recording contract with a major record company. Epstein's pitch sat well with the group and they agreed to have him represent them as their manager.

Epstein had a great deal of work to do. Not only did he start booking them for higher fees, but he began to focus on their image and presentation. On December 17th he booked the group for their first professional photo session, with Liverpool photographer Albert Marrion. This shoot yielded the famous picture of them decked out in leather and holding their guitars, with Best at his Premier drum set (minus rack tom).

Epstein would use these pictures as The Beatles' first promotional photos. Years later one showed up as the cover photo for the *Savage Young Beatles* album, a US release containing some of the Polydor recordings.

The new manager put most of his efforts into seeking a recording contract. Using his position at NEMS, one of northern England's largest record retailers, he tried to gain the attention of the British record labels.

After some luck he managed to persuade Mike Smith, an A&R representative from Decca Records, to attend a Beatle performance at the Cavern on December 13th, although this failed to land an instant contract. But it did secure a recording audition at Decca's London studios, to be held on January 1st 1962.

It looked as if a big record deal was just a few hundred miles away.

Guitarist Adrian Barber designed and built speaker cabinets, nicknamed "Coffins", for his group The Big Three, as seen in the shots above. Barber also built a Coffin bass rig for Paul McCartney, who later acquired The Big Three's Quad amplifier (pictured in the top photo, bottom right).

" **They had such duff equipment. Ugly, unpainted, wooden amplifiers, extremely noisy with [humming] earth loops and goodness knows what.** "

NORMAN SMITH, EARLY BEATLES STUDIO ENGINEER, RECALLING THEIR EMI RECORDING AUDITION AT ABBEY ROAD

1962

THIS WOULD BE A YEAR OF GREAT CHANGES FOR THE BEATLES – INDEED THE FIRST DAY OF THE NEW YEAR STARTED WITH A BIG STEP FORWARD. ON JANUARY 1ST LENNON, MCCARTNEY, HARRISON AND BEST PACKED THEMSELVES AND THEIR GEAR INTO NEIL ASPINALL'S LITTLE VAN AND TRAVELLED TO DECCA'S STUDIOS IN NORTH-WEST LONDON FOR THEIR RECORDING AUDITION WITH THE COMPANY.

Mike Smith, the A&R representative for Decca who had set up the audition, met the group and Brian Epstein that morning for the 11am session. Smith's first reaction was that the group's equipment was not suitable for recording. His complaints about the inadequacies of their gear must have been a shock and an embarrassment for Epstein. This was the first time he'd been made aware of the value and importance of good equipment for a professional group – though not be the last.

We can assume that after countless shows and many long hours of use the group's amplifiers were not in optimum working condition. They were probably in dire need of a good overhaul, and most likely required the fitting of new sets of valves (tubes). In proper working condition, the Fender Deluxe and Gibson GA-40 amps would have been more than adequate in the studio. Even by today's standards a vintage Deluxe or GA-40 in good operational condition are considered prize finds, and would hold their own at any modern recording session.

In any case, the group's gear was battered and Smith deemed that they could not use their own amplifiers. Instead he said they had to use the studio's equipment for the recording session. The amplifiers that The Beatles used for these Decca sessions are unknown, but Best says he at least used his own drums.

The session was captured live on to a two-track tape recorder. Fifteen songs were recorded in all, including three Lennon & McCartney originals, 'Like Dreamers Do', 'Hello Little Girl' and 'Love Of The Loved'. After the hour-long session Smith hurried the group out and promised Epstein that he would be in touch to let him know the outcome of the audition. (Four tracks from the session were officially released decades later on *Anthology 1*.)

The group returned to Liverpool and continued performing at an intense pace. *Mersey Beat* published the results of its group popularity poll, placing The Beatles at number one. "Beatles Top Poll!" ran the paper's headline. It seemed that Epstein's plans were working out well. On January 5th Polydor officially released in the UK the 'My Bonnie' single that had been recorded in Hamburg the previous June, this time correctly crediting it to Tony Sheridan & The Beatles. It was not a proper Beatles single, but Epstein knew that their appearance on the respected Polydor label would be viewed with interest, and that he could use it to help elevate his group by boasting about them as "Polydor recording artists".

But the run of good luck didn't last. By the beginning of February, Epstein had the bad news that Decca had turned down The Beatles. Mike Smith had played the session tapes for Dick Rowe, head of pop A&R at Decca. Rowe rejected the tapes, saying famously that guitar groups were on their way out. Rowe was later dubbed "the man who turned down The Beatles" – but quickly redeemed himself by signing The Rolling Stones.

With resilience and without flinching from Decca's rejection, Epstein immediately began using the same Decca demo tape to try his luck with other major British record labels. After more disappointing rejections he was eventually introduced to George Martin, head of A&R (standing for Artiste & Repertoire) at Parlophone, a division of EMI. Epstein played the Decca demos for Martin, who expressed interest, even suggesting he might like to see The Beatles perform. But no formal arrangements were made. Epstein returned to Liverpool full of hope but unsure of Martin's true interest in The Beatles.

The Beatles blamed Epstein for the rejection at Decca, feeling they had lost their big chance. It was Epstein who had picked which songs they recorded at the demo session, and the group believed the selections failed to show their true abilities. This only made Epstein work harder to try to find a record deal. Meanwhile Epstein kept the group busy, adding ever more frequent dates outside Liverpool. On one such occasion, at the Kingsway Club in Southport on February 5th, Best was ill and could not play, so they turned to the drummer from Rory Storm & The Hurricanes. The Hurricanes did not have a show that day, and so Ringo Starr filled in for Best.

Starr recalled, "Back in Liverpool, whenever Pete Best would get sick I would take over. Sometimes it was at lunchtime. I remember once Neil [Aspinall] got me out of bed, and I had no kit.

I got up on stage with only cymbals and gradually Pete's kit started arriving, piece by piece."[1] It may have been on these occasions when Starr sat in with The Beatles that Lennon, McCartney and Harrison began to think about changes to the group's line-up.

Beatle suits

Epstein worked diligently to improve The Beatles' standards, pointing out the need for professionalism and always trying to raise the quality of their performance. The next change was to the group's appearance. Their dapper manager convinced the band that if they wore matching suits he would be able to book them in better venues and get them more money. At first they resisted, not wanting to look like the dreaded "established" bands such as The Shadows.

Lennon described later how they had all been in a "daydream" until Epstein had come along. "We had no idea what we were doing. Seeing our marching orders on paper made it all official. Brian was trying to clean our image up. He said we'd never get past the door of a good place. He'd tell us that jeans were not particularly smart, and could we possibly manage to wear proper trousers? But he didn't want us suddenly looking square. He let us have our own sense of individuality. We stopped chomping at cheese rolls and jam butties on stage. We paid a lot more attention to what we were doing, did our best to be on time. And we smartened up, in the sense that we wore suits instead of any sloppy old clothes."[2]

"We were pretty greasy," Lennon recalled. "Outside of Liverpool, when we went down south in our leather outfits, the dancehall promoters didn't really like us. They thought we looked like a gang of thugs. So [Epstein suggested suits]. A nice sharp, black suit, man ... we liked the leather and the jeans but we wanted a good suit, even to wear off-stage ... If you wear a suit, you'll get this much money ... all right ... I'll wear a suit. I'll wear a bloody balloon if someone's going to pay me. I'm not in love with the leather that much."[3]

Best says he wasn't so keen on the matching suits. His recollection is that he and Lennon were anti-suits, Harrison and McCartney for them. "We liked the image of the leathers, we liked the feel. We felt it was conducive to what we were playing on stage at the time. So it was yes, we'll do it – but we still like our leathers. And for a certain period of time there was a compromise, depending on the venue we were playing, whether we'd wear leathers or the suits."[4]

Perhaps when Lennon and McCartney had been to Paris the previous year and purchased collarless jackets they were thinking of having suits made later. Perhaps Epstein's idea for suits wasn't quite what they had in mind. Whatever the motivations, on March 7th The Beatles wore their new matching suits by Liverpool tailor Beno Dorn for the first time, on the stage of the Manchester Playhouse. This was an important date because Epstein had arranged for it to be their first radio broadcast, for a BBC programme called *Teenager's Turn – Here We Go*.

A new club had opened in Liverpool named The Odd Spot. On March 29th The Beatles performed there for the first time, smartly dressed in their new and now standard stage attire. Photographs of the performance show them dressed in the new matching suits, with Lennon on his natural-finish Rickenbacker 325 with added Bigsby vibrato and radio knobs, playing through his

At the Star Club in April 1962, with Roy Young on piano. The group used the club's own backline of Fender amps, but brought their guitars and Best's kit across to Hamburg.

tweed Fender Deluxe amp. Harrison is seen with his black Gretsch Duo Jet, going through his tweed-finished Gibson GA-40 amp. McCartney plays his left-handed Hofner 500/1 violin bass through the Selmer Truvoice amplifier connected to the Barber Coffin bass cabinet, and Best is behind his blue pearl Premier drum set.

The first 'Beatles' drum-head

All of the existing photographs of The Beatles with Pete Best on drums show him playing his Premier drum set with a plain white bass-drum head, and never with a Beatles logo. But during interviews for this book Best revealed that there was a Beatles drum-head during his time with the group. "I was trying to get the name on the drum kit, but I didn't have stencil sets or anything like that. So I painted the calfskin bass-drum head a bright orangey flame red. I think it was the most hideous colour you could think of, but it was something that was bright and eye-catching and it would stand out on stage.

"Then I over-painted the name Beatles on top of that in white paint, in capitals. There was no The, it was just Beatles. The others thought it was good. It added a little bit more to the act because not many people in Liverpool at that time had been blazing the front of their drum kits as we did. It was quite adventurous.

"But there's not many photographs of it. That's because when you break through one side of the bass drum you flip it over quickly and use the other side. And so my front skin ended up as the back skin. The head I'd painted ended up being the playing side, and I just played on that until I eventually broke through that too. In those days you didn't keep them for posterity. I never painted one again – it was a one-off experiment."[5]

Preparing to leave for yet another season of shows in Hamburg, the group made a special appearance on April 5th at the Cavern for The Beatles' fan club. For this special show they wore leather outfits for the first set, and for the second their new matching suits. Photographs of this performance show that in the second set Best took centre stage as lead vocalist, while McCartney played drums and Harrison used McCartney's left-handed Hofner bass right-handed. Lennon remained on his Rickenbacker.

Best says he didn't go out front that much, but on the odd occasion he'd sing a couple of songs, 'Matchbox' and 'Peppermint Twist'. It seemed that every drummer in Liverpool sang 'Matchbox'. "Then a couple of times Bob Wooler tried to move me forward with my drums to the front of the stage," says Best, "because he thought it would add another dimension to the band. But that was very shortlived because the minute I moved them to the front they were yanked off the stage. We used to try to do something different on the fan club nights, and on that particular night I decided I'd get up the front and sing 'Peppermint Twist' and dance the twist like Chubby Checker. It was a lot of fun and was just pure entertainment for the kids who were there."[6]

At this point Best was one of the most popular members of the group. He even had his own fan club, and *Mersey Beat* published reports of girls camping out in Best's garden. A little jealousy probably began to grow among the other three, along with some resentment at Best's refusal to conform to the new Beatle hairstyle.

Hamburg third trip – the Star Club

The Star Club was the newest venue in Hamburg to attract talent from Liverpool. During December 1961 Peter Eckhorn had come to Liverpool and met Epstein to discuss booking The Beatles for his Top Ten club. Epstein asked for more money than Eckhorn was willing to pay, so no deal was struck. In the following weeks Horst Fascher, a former bouncer at the Kaiserkeller, came to Liverpool to book bands for the new Star Club. Roy Young, house piano player at the club, accompanied him. Epstein not only booked The Beatles into the Star Club but also managed to negotiate bookings for some other artists in his growing stable, including The Big Three and Gerry & The Pacemakers.

For this trip Epstein decided that The Beatles should travel more comfortably, so manager and band flew to Hamburg, from Manchester airport. Upon arriving in Hamburg the group were met by Astrid Kirchherr who had the unenviable task of telling them that their friend Stu Sutcliffe had died of a brain haemorrhage.

BRIAN [EPSTEIN] WAS TRYING TO CLEAN OUR IMAGE UP ... WE STOPPED CHOMPING AT CHEESE ROLLS AND JAM BUTTIES ON STAGE. WE PAID A LOT MORE ATTENTION TO WHAT WE WERE DOING

John Lennon

The group's seven-week engagement at the Star Club started on Friday April 13th and, unlike some of the other dives, conditions were designed to cater for the bands that performed there. The club provided a complete backline of Fender amplifiers for visiting acts to use, and photographs taken of The Beatles performing show a complete line of cream Tolex-covered Fender amps and speaker cabinets. Some of these photos show piano player Roy Young, who sat in with the group during their stay.

Young was a rock'n'roll piano player in the style of Jerry Lee Lewis, with what he describes as "Little Richard vocal overtones". He'd appeared on British TV shows in the late 1950s and early 1960s – including the famous early rock programme *Oh Boy*, created by producer Jack Good, and the later BBC equivalent, *Drumbeat* – and he'd toured with Cliff Richard. Then he'd ended up in Hamburg for a few years, sometimes playing with Tony Sheridan in a band called The Beat Brothers and, at the Star Club, The Star Combo. Ringo Starr had played with Young in The Beat Brothers at the Top Ten club.

"When The Beatles played at the Star Club they asked me to sit in on piano," Young remembers. "They said they'd love to have me come up and play with them – and I ended up playing all the shows with them. I had the grand piano that the club provided for me: it had my name on the side in glitter. They also provided me with a Hammond organ, and that and the piano were on the stage permanently for me to use. The Beatles were playing with Pete Best at the time, and one night we were sitting around having a drink with John, George and Paul when they asked what I thought about Ringo. I think John and Paul knew they weren't going to pull it off with Pete. They knew I played with Ringo so they asked me what I felt about him, and John was a good friend of Ringo's. I told them he was obviously a great drummer."[7]

Another band booked into the Star Club at the time was The Big Three, which included guitarist Adrian Barber. He had not got on too well with the group's manager, Brian Epstein. Barber says that in Hamburg he'd left the group because he didn't like Epstein's plans. The Big Three were the second band Epstein had signed. They wore canary-yellow and pink suits, and Barber had long hair. Epstein had told them to get rid of the garish suits and to clean up their act.

"And then he wanted to put another guy in the band," recalls Barber, who thought this an odd idea given the name of the group. Arguments ensued, with the result that Barber left and gave his equipment to Epstein. He spent some 18 months in Hamburg working for Horst Fascher as stage manager at the Star Club. While there he built another of his Coffin bass cabinets for the visiting bands to use, feeling it would work better than the Fender Bassman cabinets already there. This new Coffin cabinet was powered by one of the club's cream-coloured Fender Bassman amps.

The Beatles brought their own guitars on this trip to Hamburg, but their amplifiers stayed behind in Liverpool. Lennon and Harrison each played through the club's cream Fender Bandmaster "piggy-back" amps while McCartney used a cream Fender Bassman head with the Coffin speaker cabinet. Best, however, brought his entire Premier drum set to the Star Club.

The new fifth Beatle?

Epstein had stayed in Hamburg for The Beatles' opening nights at the Star Club to ensure that all was going well. While there, he asked Roy Young to join The Beatles. Young says that one night as he was finishing playing with The Beatles and walking down through the club, Epstein came up to him. "He said, 'Oh, Roy,' with this very posh accent, 'may I have a quick word with you?' I said sure, what's up?"

Epstein told Young that the group wondered if he'd be interested in going to back England with them and getting a record contract. "Well," says Young, "I looked at my position. I had a three-year contract with a car written into it, everything that people would love to have, I had it all there. I was making great money, and I think up until then The Beatles weren't making much money. Not that money was the only reason, we all loved to play. But anyway, I said to Brian that I'd have to think about it."

Young then walked away across the bar, and began to think some more about the madness of giving up his good contract at the club. "So I turned around and went back to Brian and said to him that I'd made a decision right there. He said great! But I said I was declining his offer. He asked why, and I told him that I couldn't break my contract – even though I could. I don't know why, maybe it was just security."[8] To this day, Young still wonders how things might have been had he said yes to the offer. From Germany, Epstein left for London where he turned his sights once again on his main goal: to secure a recording contract for The Beatles.

Still with his foot in the door at EMI, Epstein met A&R man/producer George Martin for the second time on Wednesday May 9th at EMI's Abbey Road studios in north-west London. There Epstein and Martin formalised a deal and set a recording date at Abbey Road for June 6th. The excited Epstein left his meeting with Martin and immediately sent a telegram to Bill Harry at *Mersey Beat*. It read: "Have secured contract for Beatles to record for EMI on Parlophone label. 1st recording date set for June 6th."

Another telegram was sent to The Beatles in Hamburg: "Congratulations boys. EMI request recording session. Please rehearse new material." According to Epstein's later book, *A Cellar Full Of Noise*, the band replied to the telegram with postcards. "From McCartney: 'Please wire £10,000 advance royalties.' From Lennon: 'When are we going to be millionaires?' From Harrison: 'Please order four new guitars.'"[9]

As we've seen, Harrison had showed signs of his love of guitars before, but this comment surely indicates the depth of Harrison's guitar lust. While his bandmates were thinking of money, Harrison could only think about guitars.

The Beatles completed their 48-night stay at the Star Club and left Hamburg on June 2nd, returning to Liverpool where they held two days of private rehearsals at the Cavern. They then travelled to London for their big break.

Abbey Road, George Martin, and better amps

On Wednesday June 6th The Beatles, Neil Aspinall and Brian Epstein arrived at studio 2 at Abbey Road studios for a 7pm session. This first visit to EMI's recording base was initially intended as an artist audition. The group set up their equipment: Fender Deluxe amp, Gibson GA-40, Selmer Truvoice with Coffin speaker cabinet, and Best's Premier drum set. With their trusty guitars in hand they ran through a number of songs. Ron Richards, George Martin's assistant who was in charge of the session, then picked four of the songs to record. 'Love Me Do' had attracted Richards and Norman Smith, the balance engineer. Martin was then called in to listen to the track, and he stayed for the remainder of the session.

Smith later recalled the bad condition of the group's gear. "They had such duff equipment," he said. "Ugly, unpainted, wooden amplifiers, extremely noisy with [humming] earth-loops and goodness knows what. There was as much noise coming from the amps as there was from the instruments. Paul's bass amp was particularly bad and it was clear that the session wasn't going to get underway until something was done about it."[10]

Ken Townsend, a technical engineer on the staff at the studio, also remembers distortion from McCartney's speaker. "George Martin turned to Norman and I and said, 'You know, we've got to do something about this.' Fortunately that evening there wasn't a session in studio 1, which meant that studio's echo chamber wasn't in use. So Norman and I went in and carried out the echo chamber's great big Tannoy speaker, which weighed about half a ton. We carried that through – it was on the same floor – into studio 2 for the test. I then fixed up a Leak TL12 amplifier, soldering a jack socket onto its input stage. It wouldn't be considered very high wattage today, but they were quite powerful amplifiers at the time. I think it took about a quarter-of-an-hour to do. We plugged it in and there was no distortion any more on the bass guitar, so we used that system for the session."

That evening The Beatles recorded 'Love Me Do', 'Besame Mucho', 'PS I Love You' and 'Ask Me Why'. After the session George Martin explained some technical aspects of recording to The Beatles. Townsend says that at first this chat was done over the playback speakers in the studio. "He told them about the different techniques for recording compared to playing on stage, and that the microphones we used where much higher quality." Townsend mentions by way of example the Neumann/Telefunken U47 and U48 microphones used for vocals at Abbey Road. First sold in the late 1940s, these exceptional mikes were made by Neumann but at first branded Telefunken, the exclusive distributor of Neumann products until the late 1950s. "For their vocals we quite often used a U48," says Townsend, "with Paul sitting on one side and John on the other – just one mike to get the balance between the two."[11]

WHEN ARE WE GOING TO BE MILLIONAIRES?

John Lennon,

on hearing the band had secured a

recording session with EMI

PLEASE ORDER FOUR NEW GUITARS

George Harrison

Studio gear was not the only topic of conversation that evening. Norman Smith recalls another talk about their own equipment. "We gave them a long lecture about what would have to be done about it if they were to become recording artists."[12] This was now the second time that the group had been told by professional studio engineers about the inadequacies of their gear. The first time was at the Decca sessions, and now here was the same message at Abbey Road. At this point Epstein must have decided that something had to be done. He may have ignored Decca's warning, but now here he was hearing it all again. Perhaps after this latest lashing he might even have thought that a lack of good equipment may have been partially to blame for their failure at Decca – and that ignoring the need for decent gear could be their downfall at EMI as well. Epstein was not going to make the same mistake again. He took the advice from Martin and his EMI staff and set out on a new quest. New gear for The Beatles!

Epstein not only left with the idea that The Beatles needed new and better equipment. He also now faced a problem in the personnel department. After the session, Martin had expressed criticisms to Epstein about Best's drumming. Martin recalled recently: "I said to Brian, when we do the next session … I'm going to provide the drummer."[13] New equipment could be sorted out, but Martin's opinion of Best would not be so easy to resolve.

Time for new gear

Following the EMI session Epstein and the group took a fresh and more serious look at their equipment. The subject became a new focus for Epstein, and from this point on he would pay close attention to their musical equipment needs. There was another factor in addition to the complaints from Decca and EMI. On June 4th, prior to the recording date at EMI, Epstein had been contacted by Hessy's store about loans that had been unpaid by members of The Beatles.

According to the hire-purchase receipt for Harrison's Selmer Truvoice amp, Hessy's had tried to make collections in December 1961. The report reads, "Finance company rep called, [Harrison] not at home. Spoke to mother who informed him that goods were not in his possession. Was told as far as the finance company are concerned they still look to [Harrison] for settlement." The document also shows that Hessy's had discovered that McCartney now had the amplifier in question. Another entry for December 1961 reads simply: "Mr. Paul McCartney, 20 Forthlin Rd, LP 18. Has goods." The document backs up Harrison's amused recollections of buying guitars and amps on credit, as mentioned earlier. "We got them what they call 'on the knocker' – a pound down and the rest when they catch you!"[14]

Clearly, Epstein made a judgement: he knew he would have to deal with the music shops in the future, and so he paid off the group's outstanding loans. The hire-purchase receipt for the Truvoice amp, for example, shows that in June 1962 Epstein settled the account with Hessy's.

The Beatles made their second BBC radio appearance on June 11th. McCartney's brother Mike (later of The Scaffold) documented the BBC session, photographing the group in rehearsal as well as during their performance in front of a live audience. The pictures reveal McCartney still using the Selmer Truvoice amp and Coffin speaker cabinet with his Hofner bass, Lennon with Rickenbacker and Fender Deluxe amp, Best on his Premier kit, and Harrison playing the Gretsch Duo Jet through his Gibson GA-40 amp (which appears now to be painted black).

Beatles and Vox

Some time in July, Epstein made his way to the Jennings music shop in Charing Cross Road, central London. Jennings Musical Industries, or JMI, was owned by Tom Jennings. While the Jennings Organ Company had existed earlier in the 1950s, JMI was established in 1958, manufacturing and distributing Vox amplifiers, which were devised by JMI's chief design engineer, Dick Denney. The operation also started to produce Vox guitars during 1962. The Vox factory was at Dartford, Kent, just to the south-east of London.

Epstein met the Jennings shop manager, Reg Clarke. "Brian said he had a band that had been playing in Germany. They were now back in England and, he said, were going to grow very big," recalls Clarke. "But the equipment they were using was pretty clapped out. He said he'd like to do a

Vox amplifiers were made in England by Jennings Musical Industries. Pictured is the factory in Dartford, Kent, during the early 1960s.

deal with us to get some of the more up-to-date gear we were doing then. He meant our pretty recent [Vox] AC-30 amplifiers."

Clarke told Epstein that a deal was possible, but the group's manager said he wanted Vox to give The Beatles a set of amplifiers. "He told me his boys were going to be so big and do so much promotion for us that it would pay off a thousand times over," says Clarke. "So I had to phone Tom Jennings, the owner of Vox, telling him of this conversation. I remember Tom's exact words very well. He said, 'What does he think we are, a fucking philanthropic society?' But I took it upon myself to do that deal with Epstein … because Tom really didn't say no."

Epstein told Clarke that if the deal was done the way he wanted, Vox could use the group for any promotion at all, and it would never cost the company a penny. The group would never use anything but Vox, said Epstein, while he remained their manager. "They never did," confirms Clarke. "And every time I got photographs from Epstein, it never cost a thing. He kept his word."[15]

The first Vox amplifiers that The Beatles used were a pair of AC-30s, finished in Vox's tan, or beige, colour. Contrary to popular belief, The Beatles never used Vox AC-15 amplifiers. According to Clarke, the deal he made with Epstein was that Jennings would take Lennon and Harrison's old amps as a trade on the new AC-30s. Clarke can remember getting Lennon's tweed-coloured Fender amp as part of the trade. Had the group paid full retail for their AC-30s, each would have cost them £105 (about $300 then), around £1,340 ($1,870) in today's money. The official model name was AC-30/6 Twin Normal: "6" meaning six inputs, "Twin" meaning two speakers, and "Normal" meaning the guitar rather than bass version.

Why did Epstein choose Vox? The manager probably had a number of motives. He would be well aware that the most famous British group of the time, The Shadows, prominently used and promoted Vox amps. His boys were going to be big, too, so they should also be using the best. And as Vox was a British manufacturer, it would be easier to deal directly with the company. As it turned out, Vox was a perfect choice for The Beatles. The AC-30 was a great little amp, well made, with a loud, clean, punchy sound.

Dick Denney, chief design engineer at Vox and the man who created the AC-30, recalls those first Beatle amps and their "retrofitted" top-boost circuits. "I had designed a little add-on unit that could be fitted to the back. It was a simple treble-boost circuit with two knobs on a piece of bent aluminium. For those who wanted it, we would cut out a small square hole in the back of amp. The top-boost unit went in there – quite simple really. People used to swear that was the best AC-30, rather than having the boost built into the main circuit. And that's the type The Beatles had, with the add-on treble boost." Vox said the extra circuit would "give you ultimate top boost – over 30 decibel rise at 10 kilocycles". A contemporary news report confirms that this was the type of AC-30 the group received. "Both The Beatles and [Billy J Kramer's] Dakotas are using the same make of amplifier," it said, "but with a specially added treble booster supplied by the manufacturer."[16]

Denney had started the Vox line of amplifiers with a 15-watt unit in the late 1950s. But soon he reasoned that what musicians needed was a twin-speaker amp with six inputs. Denney recalls Tom Jennings's reaction to the idea. "He said to me, 'Well, you do what you like, Dick, but if it doesn't work, your head's on the chopping block'. As it turned out, the AC-30 became the jewel in Vox's crown, without any doubt. It's what put Vox on the map. I made the amp so that it sounded good to me. It was old technology – and I think old technology still prevails."

One of the design oddities of the AC-30 was the situation of its control panel at the back of the top of the cabinet. Denney explains that his fellow guitarists at the time often sat behind their amplifiers, providing a reverb-type effect into the hall from the front and a "dry" sound from the open back.

Another distinctive visual feature of the amp was its optional chrome stand. Denney says that at early trade fairs when Vox displayed their new amps he would get some beer crates, cover them, and put the AC-30 on top. Tom Jennings suggested that something more permanent and professional might be a good idea. "That's when we got this tubular engineer from Dartford to come down and have a look," says Denney. "That's how the first stand got designed – and I didn't have to put amplifiers on beer crates any more. Being a little hard of hearing, I liked to have the amp up higher

A recent reproduction of Paul McCartney's 'Coffin' bass rig.

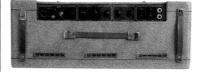

The Beatles acquired two tan-coloured Vox AC-30 amps like this during 1962.

on the stand, I used to like to hear that treble. If it was on the floor, once you get a load of bodies in a venue it sounds as if you have cotton wool in your ears."[17]

One of the first shows for which The Beatles used their new matching tan-coloured Vox AC-30 amps was on July 27th at the Tower Ballroom, New Brighton. This was a big event that Epstein's NEMS Enterprises promoted. The headliner was Joe Brown & His Bruvvers whose single 'A Picture Of You' had hit number two in May, and which Epstein regarded as one of his favourite records. The Beatles had even covered the song for their second BBC radio broadcast, on June 11th, with Harrison singing. A photograph taken by Mike McCartney shows The Beatles on stage at the Tower with their new Vox AC-30s, although the same picture reveals that Harrison's black-painted Gibson GA-40 amp was in position behind the new AC-30, presumably as a back-up.

The Beatles would soon become invaluable to Vox's promotional efforts, and the deal struck with Epstein would suit both parties well. But during 1962 the group barely registered in Vox advertising, reflecting their still lowly status. In a December ad in *Melody Maker*, for example, the Dartford-based company listed 20 endorsers of Vox gear, from the still top-of-the-pile Shadows right down to virtually unknown bands such as The Echos. But not a sign of The Beatles. Not yet.

George and the Gibson ES-335

Backstage at the Tower show, Harrison had his first brush with a Gibson ES-335 guitar. This thin, twin-cutaway, semi-hollow-body electric model had been launched by Gibson in 1958, its design effectively mixing the tonal advantages of a hollow-body guitar with the power and sustain of a solidbody electric guitar.

Joe Brown says his 335 was one of the first to arrive in England, and that he bought it at the Selmer shop in London's Charing Cross Road. He was pleased to have a Gibson with a Bigsby vibrato fitted, because he'd been impressed by the sound of the Bigsby on Eddie Cochran's Gretsch. "I'd done some work when I was only 18 years old backing Eddie Cochran and Gene Vincent when they came over to Britain. I learned this little trick from Eddie that presumably everybody was doing in America, but in England it was unknown. He would put a thinner second string on instead of the third string. Everyone does that now, but in those days it was unheard of. And with that thinner string, you could bend them much more easily. That was the sound everyone wanted. I used to get to do all the recording sessions because of that string."

Brown says that for the two dates he played with The Beatles in July, they would appear in the first half and he'd be on during the second. In a break, Harrison had a snap taken of him with Brown's Gibson ES-335. "Apparently I had gone out to go to the toilet," recalls Brown, "and George picked my guitar up. All the guys were saying put it down, he'll kill you! And he said no, I've got to have my picture taken with Joe's guitar. Which he did. I didn't even know about it."[18]

This incident once again reveals Harrison as the true guitar enthusiast in the group. If there was an unusual guitar around, Harrison wanted to see it. And, even better, have his picture taken with it. Brown and Harrison are now neighbours and good friends. It was Brown who in more recent years introduced Harrison to the ukulele and the George Formby society – which celebrates Britain's best-known ukulele player. Harrison is an avid uke enthusiast today and has a collection of the instruments.

A Quad for Paul

Now that Lennon and Harrison were set up with new gear, it was time to update McCartney's bass amplification. At the time Vox did not have a proper bass amplifier or any type of speaker cabinet that was equivalent to the Barber Coffin.

As we've seen, when Epstein and Barber parted, Epstein demanded Barber's Big Three equipment. According to Barber, one of the pieces of gear that Epstein acquired was a modified Quad amplifier that Barber had made for The Big Three's bass player, Johnny Gustafson. This same

Gibson ES-335T

The newest star in a long list of Gibson favorites, this revolutionary new double cutaway, thin electric Spanish guitar meets today's needs for individual performance, large or small ensembles, recording, television and radio. Engineered after consultation with leading players, the ES-335T presents a striking appearance and sensational response. New body construction, with solid fitting neck, pickups and adjustable bridge, provides the solidity essential for clear, sparkling, sustaining tone—while retaining a body size and shape that is easy and comfortable to hold. Provides easy access throughout the entire twenty-two fret range on all six strings.

The double cutaway, thin body, with arched top and back of curly maple has matching maple rims and pearloid binding • extra narrow, slim Honduras mahogany neck with Gibson Adjustable Truss Rod • attractive peghead with large pearl inlays • Rosewood fingerboard with pearl dot inlays • twin, humbucking pickups located for contrasting treble and bass response • individually adjustable polepieces • separate tone and volume controls which can be preset • toggle switch to activate either or both pickups • Tune-O-Matic bridge permits adjustment of string action and individual string length for perfect intonation • nickel plated metal parts • enclosed individual machine heads with deluxe buttons.

SPECIFICATIONS
16" wide, 19" long, 1¾" thick, 24¾" scale, 22 frets

ES-335TN—Natural Finish.............................$282.50
ES-335T—Sunburst Finish............................. 267.50
No. 519 Case—Faultless, plush lined.................. 46.50

George had to wait until 1965 to get his own Gibson ES-300 series electric, but in 1962 he tried out a 335 owned by British guitarist Joe Brown.

Quad amp ended up in McCartney's possession. A weekly accounting statement issued to McCartney by Epstein and dated July 27th shows calculations of booking fees, expenses, commissions… and an individual expense item detailing McCartney's payment for the amp. It reads simply, "To Adrian Barber for Amp – £5."

The Quad II valve (tube) amplifier was rated at 15 watts, though Barber says its output was closer to 40 or 50 watts and that he modified the associated model 22 pre-amp to pass more bass. The Quad II/22 combination was and still is considered a great mono amplifier, full of tone and punch. With Barber's modifications it became a great bass amplifier, and a perfect companion to the Coffin speaker cabinet.

Barber had mounted the Quad, as we've said, in an army-surplus ammunition box with a metal top and handles at the sides. He remembers acquiring this particular Quad amp in unusual circumstances. Promoter Allan Williams opened a new club in one of the rougher parts of Liverpool, on Soho Street, and Barber installed the sound system. "On the opening night, Allan threw out some teddy boys who were causing trouble," says Barber. "The next day the place burned down. He gave up on that club – but paid me with the sound system's Quad amp that survived the fire. It was the first Quad amp I got, and I worked on it to go with the Coffin cabinet. It became Johnny Gustafson's bass amp, and then Paul got it."[19]

McCartney would use the combination of Barber's modified Quad bass amplifier through the Coffin speaker cabinet as his bass rig for the next eight months.

From Pete to Ringo

Changes were not limited to the group's equipment. With no definite decision from George Martin and EMI on the fate of their single, The Beatles and Epstein took no chances with Martin's warning about the inadequacies of Best's drumming for recording. There was also the feeling that in some circles Best was more popular with the fans than the other Beatles – and he refused to go along with the band's newly adopted haircuts. Lennon, McCartney and Harrison were convinced that Best did not fit in to the band, and they decided to look for a new drummer.

They set their sights on a friend whom they had already played with on a couple of shows when Best was sick. They asked Richard Starkey – drummer of Rory Storm & The Hurricanes, stage-name Ringo Starr – to join them. The Hurricanes were playing a summer season at a Butlin's holiday camp when Starr was approached with the idea. He gave his group three days' notice and left to return to Liverpool and join The Beatles.

The task of telling Best the bad news was left to Epstein, and on August 16th he was dismissed from the group. The Beatles had an engagement that night and, unsurprisingly, Best refused to play. Starr had to fulfil his last three shows with The Hurricanes at Butlin's, so The Beatles – once again drummerless – had to enlist the help of Johnny Hutchinson, drummer from The Big Three, who filled in for two gigs. On August 18th at Hulme Hall, Port Sunlight, Birkenhead, Starr performed with The Beatles, officially joining the group. The band was now in place as the world would soon come to know them: John Lennon, Paul McCartney, George Harrison and Ringo Starr.

Starr had decided in his early teens that he wanted to be a drummer. "I had to wait until I was 18 to get my first drum kit, which was just a mish-mash that my father found me from a relation who had had enough of it," Starr remembers. "It probably cost me £12 or so. It was just old bits and pieces of stuff. And of course being 18 I wanted a new kit. So I bought one, made by Ajax. I've actually regretted getting rid of all those old drums ever since. It was in my soul, I just wanted to be a drummer. I didn't want to be a guitarist, I didn't want to play bass. I wanted to be a drummer, and that's how it is. My grandparents played mandolin and guitar and they gave me their instruments – and I just broke them. I had a harmonica; I dumped it. We had a piano; I walked on it. I just was not into any other instrument."[20]

He began his playing career as drummer for The Eddie Clayton Skiffle Group in 1957. Pictures of Starr with this outfit show him standing up to play a snare and floor tom. He then became drummer for The Raving Texans, who later evolved into Rory Storm & The Hurricanes. An early photograph of The Hurricanes performing in May 1960 at Liverpool's first rock'n'roll show, with Gene Vincent headlining, shows Starr playing his Ajax kit.

By July of that year Starr had purchased a basic four-piece Premier model 54 drum set which

> I DIDN'T WANT TO BE A GUITARIST, I DIDN'T WANT TO PLAY BASS. I WANTED TO BE A DRUMMER … IT WAS IN MY SOUL
>
> Ringo Starr

cost him a whopping £125 (about $350 then; around £1,600 or $2,200 in today's money). It came with a 20-inch-by-17-inch bass-drum, 12x8 rack tom, 16x20 floor tom and 14x4 Premier Royal Ace wood-shell snare-drum. The rack tom was mounted on the bass-drum using Premier's "disappearing" tom-tom holder. Starr's 54 kit came in a Duroplastic "mahogany" coloured finish, and was one of the least expensive Premier kits. It is listed in an early 1960s catalogue as being "for the busy modern group; for the recording drummer who wants the sharpest response and fidelity of tone". The 54 came with Premier's Zyn cymbals, and Starr used the standard Premier stands for the crash and ride cymbals and the hi-hat.

While with The Hurricanes, Starr decided to put the initials "R-S" on the front of the bass-drum, which also had the normal Premier logo toward the top of the head. Johnny Guitar of The Hurricanes says the initials could be interpreted two ways. "It could stand for Rory Storm, or for Ringo Starr. So he was killing two birds with one stone. Later on when we became more well-known he put his full name on the head."[21] Starr's Premier drum set with "Ringo Starr" on the front of the bass-drum is the one he used upon joining The Beatles.

On August 22nd the group had another lucky break. The Manchester-based Granada TV company had arranged to film them at the Cavern for a television show, *Know The North*. That morning, prior to this lunchtime session, the group held a private rehearsal at the club with their new drummer. Bill Connell and Les Chadwick, who worked for the Peter Kaye photo studio in Liverpool, photographed the rehearsal. Their candid shots of the group at work reveal a great deal of detail about The Beatles' guitars, amps and drums of the period.

Close-up shots show Lennon playing his Bigsby-equipped blond Rickenbacker and Harrison his Gretsch Duo Jet. Both guitarists are using their new tan-coloured Vox AC-30 amplifiers, with Lennon's on a "tray"-style Vox stand with a rim around the whole cabinet. Back shots of the AC-30s clearly show the two-knob top-boost circuits fitted to the back panel of the amps, as well as the distinctive "flat" leather handles used on the early AC-30s. This photo session also details McCartney's first Hofner bass and the Coffin speaker, and Starr's Premier drum set. That afternoon Lennon, McCartney, Harrison and Starr were filmed performing 'Some Other Guy', and this rare footage can be seen in *The Beatles Anthology* video box-set.

Second round at EMI

Soon after Starr's arrival in the group, they were summoned again by George Martin to EMI's Abbey Road studio for a further attempt to record a single. On September 4th they flew to London and started a session in studio 2 with engineer Ron Richards, rehearsing the potential songs 'Love Me Do', 'Please Please Me' and a Mitch Murray composition that Martin suggested, 'How Do You Do It'. Naturally the group would have preferred to have one of their own songs released as a single.

They recorded 'Love Me Do' and 'How Do You Do It' that evening. Photographer Dezo Hoffmann shot the rehearsal and recording session, and these pictures once again help to document the group's gear at the time. One interesting photo reveals McCartney playing his Hofner bass through the Barber-designed Quad bass amp. It seems that the Quad was accepted as a proper bass amp for an EMI recording session. Hoffmann's photo session also yielded a famous shot with the group's guitars and drums set up in a pile in the foreground with The Beatles themselves behind in the distance.

A feature that drew Martin to 'Love Me Do' as a possible single was Lennon's distinctive harmonica (or "harp") phrasing that sets the mood in the opening bars of the song. For years rumours have circulated that some time in the summer of 1962 Texan harmonica player Delbert McClinton may have shown Lennon how to play the part. McClinton was playing with Bruce Channel on a 1962 British tour, having appeared on Channel's March 1962 UK number two hit 'Hey! Baby'.

"We were playing with a group called The Barons," says McClinton. "I remember we toured in a British World War II ambulance with half of the floor gone and all the exhaust coming through. It was a nightmare. We only did one show with The Beatles, at the Tower Ballroom in New Brighton, but they came out to see us on at least two other shows. I think one was when we played at the Cavern.

Premier '58'

With the 14"×14" floor tom-tom, this outfit has set the smaller drum fashion. Easy to handle and quick to set up. Ideal for busy 'in-town' drummers. Shown here in Premier's exclusive Mahogany but the outfit may, of course, be had in any Premier finish.

	No.		No.
Bass Drum, 20"×17" (14" shell) with disappearing spurs	130	Sticks	545
Snare Drum, 14"×4"	19	Brushes	555
Tom-tom, 14"×14", with 3 legs	435	CYMBALS 1 pr. 14" Super-Zyn Hi-hats	354
Tom-tom, 12"×8"	442	18" Super-Zyn	358
Bass Drum Pedal	250		
Hi-hat	289	**OUTFIT**	
Snare Drum Stand	300	'58' with 20" Bass Drum	
Cymbal Stand with Tilter	304	'B58' with 22" Bass Drum	
Tom-tom Holder, disappearing	389	'C58' with 18" Bass Drum	
Bass Drum Post	469		
Cowbell and Clamp	771		

EXCLUSIVE PREMIER FINISHES (far more beautiful than it's possible to reproduce on paper). Extra thickness gives you the deep, lustrous beauty so exclusively Premier. And longer life too. All plating in Premier 'Diamond' Chromium. All B.D. hoops except B finished in high gloss black.

GLITTERS R Red   C Silver   A Aquamarine   DUROPLASTICS W White   B Black

"John Lennon was one of the many guys that would come to the dressing room. It got to be just about every night that somebody in one of the other bands would come around with a harp to ask me how to play. They'd ask how to play a part, but it's hard to show a guy how to play harp. To this day I still don't know how to show it, because you can't really see what you're doing," McClinton laughs. "One of those nights, I think in New Brighton, Lennon came around and we jammed, playing some harp. I hung out with John more than any of The Beatles because we had harmonicas going all the time. John took me to an after-hours joint one night that just freaked me out. This was 1962 and you didn't see anything at all like this in the States – and especially not in Fort Worth, Texas. I was shocked! I was thrilled! I felt that I had crossed the line into another world. It was such a magic time."[22]

Perhaps McClinton's harmonica style did influence Lennon's harp phrasings on 'Love Me Do' and later recordings. But it's much more likely that it was specifically McClinton's playing on Bruce Channel's 'Hey! Baby' single that was the primary influence on Lennon's work on 'Love Me Do'. Channel's record was a big hit, and The Beatles were trying to make a hit of their own, so lifting an

This kit was sold as Ringo Starr's Premier outfit, the one he was using at the time he joined The Beatles, and that he played until he got his better-known Ludwig in 1963.

idea probably made a lot of sense to Lennon. More importantly, however, the recordings made of 'Love Me Do' on the first EMI sessions, back on June 6th, already had Lennon's signature harp phrasing in place. This predates the group's gig with Channel and McClinton by two weeks.

New jumbos – Gibson's J-160E

Returning to Liverpool from the September 4th studio session, the group continued with daily live shows. Earlier in the year, just after Abbey Road staff had complained about the poor state of much of the group's gear, Lennon and Harrison had ordered a pair of new Gibson electric-acoustic J-160E guitars, and word now came through that these had arrived.

The J-160E had been launched by Gibson in 1954, and was an unusual hybrid. Looking like a regular flat-top acoustic, it was nonetheless fitted with an electric-guitar type pickup and controls. This meant that it could be used unplugged as a normal acoustic guitar, for example for songwriting on the road, or plugged-in to give an amplified approximation of an acoustic guitar, either on stage or in the studio.

The group's J-160Es were ordered from Rushworth's – one of the few shops in Liverpool where musicians could buy American-made instruments. The J-160E was not one of the Gibson models generally on sale then in the UK through distributor Selmer, so Lennon and Harrison had to order the guitars from a catalogue and wait for them to be sent specially to the store from the United States.

The reason the two guitarists chose this unusual model may be linked to Tony Sheridan. He recalls: "At the time everybody was using a cricket bat – a piece of wood with strings on it. Not too many people were into big jazz guitars, but I was. So I guess it rubbed off on the Liverpool crowd. I think that had something to do with The Beatles using those big hollow-body acoustic guitars." Sheridan believes that Lennon and Harrison intended to order the archtop Gibson ES-175 – the model he had used in Hamburg and that the two Beatle guitarists had tried – but that they somehow ended up with the flat-top J-160E. He says that they had enjoyed using his Gibson ES-175, and would refer to it as "the jumbo".

Perhaps Lennon and Harrison liked Sheridan's 175 so much that, when it came to shopping for new guitars, they really did mean to get that model for themselves. The two guitarists certainly did refer to their Gibson J-160Es later as "the jumbos". Maybe when Lennon and Harrison ordered the Gibson guitars at Rushworth's they asked for "the Gibson electric jumbo", with the intention of ordering a model like Sheridan's "jumbo". Early 1960s Gibson catalogues list the J-160E as the "Electric Jumbo Model" – hence the J and the E. The ES-175 is listed as an "Electric Spanish Model". Maybe this accounts for Lennon and Harrison ending up with their J-160Es.

But Sheridan also points to a more attractive second theory: that it may have been the influence of another guitar he used in Hamburg, his pickup-equipped Martin D-28E, an instrument much closer in style to the J-160E. Whatever inspired their purchase, Lennon and Harrison's J-160Es were certainly specially ordered through Rushworth's. The total credit price noted for Lennon's Gibson J-160E (and presumably Harrison's too) was a cool £161/1/- (£161.05, about $450 then; around £2,050 or $2,850 in today's money). Tracing the serial number 73161 listed on Lennon's original hire-purchase receipt to the log still in Gibson's archives shows that this J-160E (and, again, presumably the pair) was shipped by Gibson on June 27th. The receipt also reveals that Epstein paid for the guitar in full almost exactly a year later.

So when did the group start to use their new J-160E guitars? They may have been sent by sea from the US, which would account for them taking more than two months to arrive. Rushworth's boast that the guitars were "specially flown to England by jet from America"[23] was probably just part of the promotional hype. That receipt for Lennon's Gibson is dated September 10th, and certainly he and Harrison were never pictured with the J-160Es prior to that date. This seems to rule out the Gibsons from the first two recording sessions for 'Love Me Do', with Best on June 6th and with Starr on September 4th.

Dezo Hoffmann's photographs of that September 4th session do not feature the Gibsons, nor is there any evidence of these guitars being at the studio. Surely if Hoffmann and The Beatles took the time to set up the famous "pile of gear" shot in the studio the guitarists would have made sure that any lovely new instruments were prominent? The Beatles proudly displayed their J-160Es later in

Rushworth's, one of Liverpool's main music stores, was where John and George ordered their Gibson J-160E electric-acoustic guitars.

numerous photo sessions. So it is safe to assume that Lennon and Harrison did not use the Gibsons for the September 4th session – and indeed did not even have them in their possession.

To complicate matters further, the presentation of the guitars to the group at Rushworth's may not have happened on September 10th. In the photographs taken of the event, the guitars already have smudges on the finish, as if they had been well played. Both guitars have string tied around the headstock for a shoulder strap, which would not have been how they were shipped from Gibson. Perhaps the photo session was staged later, an afterthought by Epstein and Rushworth's with an eye to a promotional opportunity? Indeed Bill Harry, publisher of *Mersey Beat*, remembers[24] that the event was set up specifically for his paper, to help promote the group and the music store. The pictures did not appear in *Mersey Beat* until October.

On September 11th, the day after Rushworth's sold them their new guitars, The Beatles once again visited EMI's Abbey Road studio 2 in London to try again to record their first single. Dissatisfied with Starr's drumming, producer George Martin this time employed session drummer Andy White, with Starr left to play maracas and tambourine. White used Ajax drums for the session. The group once again recorded 'Love Me Do' and 'PS I Love You'. All three versions – June 6th, September 4th, September 11th – have since been released, and all bear a similar guitar sound. So maybe the same guitar was used for all three sessions – meaning either Lennon's Rickenbacker or Harrison's Duo Jet.

It is of course possible that the J-160Es were used for the recording on the 11th. When Lennon and Harrison first used their Gibson J-160Es in the studio they recorded them by plugging the guitars into their amplifiers – the guitars were not recorded acoustically, and the tone came from a miked-up amplifier. If one plays a J-160E, a Rickenbacker 325 and a Gretsch Duo Jet today through an AC-30, it's relatively easy to get the same sound quality from all three guitars – essentially a very clean and full tone.

Anyway, regardless of dates of delivery or how and why the guitars were acquired, all the indications are that the group and Brian Epstein were now taking a more serious and professional approach to their musical gear. In any case, George Martin had decided on 'Love Me Do' as the a-side and 'PS I Love You' as the flip-side for the band's debut single. The songs were mixed on the evening of September 11th and the first British Beatles single was released on the Parlophone label on October 5th 1962.

Painting the Rickenbacker 325

Improving on the group's equipment in any way was now seen as a distinct advantage, and the next major upgrade was a facelift to Lennon's Rickenbacker 325, which he decided to have painted black. Ex-Big Three guitarist Adrian Barber says that black was now the colour of choice for Beatles gear. "Brian Epstein was always trying to improve the way The Beatles looked on stage. It was Brian's idea to have matching suits, matching amps, so why not matching black guitars?"[25]

Billy Kinsley, bassist for The Merseybeats, says he played the freshly-painted black Rickenbacker before even Lennon did, because it was Kinsley's DJ friend, Chris Whorton, who brought the refinished guitar to the Cavern. "The Beatles were doing the lunchtime session, and Tony Crane and I got there about 11.30, way before the show commenced," says Kinsley. "Chris showed me the guitar and invited me to have a play. I just couldn't believe how good it looked resprayed black. But the guy who painted it didn't know that much about guitar electrics, and he'd put the pickup switch back to front. So when John played the guitar he threw it back at the guy, because he didn't understand why the switch wasn't selecting pickups properly. Everything was reversed, and John didn't realise it at the time. So he grabbed his Gibson jumbo and started playing that."[26]

It is popularly believed that Jim Burns of Burns Guitars painted Lennon's Rickenbacker black, but this is not true. In fact the job was done by a coach-painter in Birkenhead, effectively a suburb of Liverpool, just across the River Mersey. Chris Whorton was a small-time dance promoter there, and like most people in the local music business was familiar with The Beatles.

"I don't know how it came up in conversation," says Whorton, "but John wanted his guitar painted black, and I offered to get it sprayed for him. I worked for my father who had a meat haulage business in Birkenhead, with plenty of lorries. So we got Charles Bantam, who coach-painted my father's wagons, to spray the guitar. The Rickenbacker was natural-wood coloured, and had a gold

IT WAS BRIAN'S IDEA TO HAVE MATCHING SUITS, MATCHING AMPS, SO WHY NOT MATCHING BLACK GUITARS?

Adrian Barber,

guitarist with fellow Liverpool band

The Big Three

The Operation Big Beat show in September would have been among the first opportunities for the group to use their new Gibson J-160Es.

control panel which we left alone. When I took it back I'd put the control panel back the wrong way and he made a bit of a fuss about that. But John didn't pay me, it wasn't necessary to pay me, it was done as a favour. Bantam was a perfectionist. He used Tekaloid black coach paint, and did the job at his garage in Birkenhead. It took about three days because we had to let the paint dry."[27]

As well as having his Rickenbacker painted black, Lennon decided to change his volume control knobs to cream-coloured Hofner knobs with gold "dish" tops. Lennon's newly refurbished Rickenbacker is first evident in photographs taken by McCartney's brother Mike on October 12th at the Tower Ballroom in New Brighton, where the group performed as support with a number of other groups for headliner Little Richard.

For the Richard show the group used their two matching tan-coloured Vox AC-30s. Both amps were on Vox stands, Harrison's the standard type, Lennon's the "tray" style. Harrison played his Gretsch Duo Jet and Lennon the refinished black Rickenbacker with Hofner control knobs. McCartney used his Hofner 500/1 bass, plugged through the Quad amp and Coffin cabinet.

Starr played his Premier drum set with "Ringo Starr" and

George Harrison's Gibson J-160E. This is one of the two 160s that the group acquired in 1962 from Rushworth's store in Liverpool. George still owns this one today, although the serial number on the hire-purchase receipt (right) indicates that it was originally sold to John. The guitars became muddled later, and the one John used was stolen at the end of 1963.

Original Gibson shipping record indicating that John's J-160E, serial 73161, was shipped from the factory on June 27th 1962.

FLAT TOP JUMBO MODELS

Gibson guitars were distributed in the UK by Selmer in the 1960s; here's the J-160E in a Selmer catalogue. Gibson US still have the log book with the shipping record for George's J-160.

Premier logo on the bass-drum head. For this performance Starr also had a set of new Premier bongos, matching the brown colour of his kit and fixed to the bass-drum rim with a chrome-plated Premier bongo mount.

The Cavern PA system

The Beatles were putting in seemingly endless hours every week at their home-away-from-home, the Cavern, not only performing at the club but often using it as a rehearsal space.

"The Cavern had its own very basic PA system in those days," explains local promoter/DJ Chris Whorton, "with a Vortexion amplifier and Reslo ribbon microphones. But that was a Rolls Royce system compared to some of the PAs back then.

Epstein did some promotions at Queen's Hall in Widnes, a town just east of Liverpool, and he would hire a PA system from Alpha Sound Services, run by Brian Kelly. It had a simple 25-watt amp, with bass and treble controls for three microphone inputs, and two 12-inch speakers. But this 25-watt PA was still adequate to cut above the volume the groups were producing themselves with their amplifiers, in a fairly big place that held about 800 people. Quite astonishing these days!"[28]

With 'Love Me Do' peaking on the singles chart at number 17, Epstein was able to book The Beatles ever more frequently outside Liverpool, and the group's busy schedule was including an increasing number of radio shows and, now, television appearances.

But there was a brief pause in the new momentum. On November 1st they flew once again to Hamburg for a 14-night engagement at the Star Club, sharing the bill with Little Richard. For these shows the group took only their guitars and drums, again using the club's own Fender amplifiers.

John and George with their new matching Gibson J-160E guitars.

Entertaining a north London crowd: Paul with '61 Hofner; Ringo on his Premier kit; George with Gretsch Duo Jet; and John with recently repainted '58 Rickenbacker 325. (Picture from early 1963.)

Live at the Star Club in Hamburg, John with his Rickenbacker that has recently been repainted black. The guitar also shows signs of electrical problems: one control knob is missing, apparently inside the guitar, and more work seems to be planned as the pickguard is only held on with two screws.

Two receipts from the Star Club in Hamburg for performance fees. George signs for himself (top) but note that Ringo signs for the band (misspelled as "The Baetles").

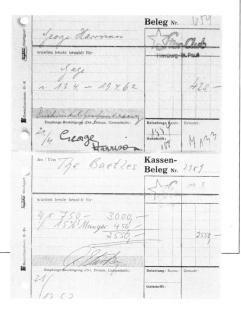

Returning to London on November 16th, they continued with live performances and promotional work for their single. With the chart success of 'Love Me Do', George Martin decided that it was time for them to record again. This meant another visit to Abbey Road, on November 26th, to record their second Parlophone single, 'Please Please Me' and 'Ask Me Why'. Another original song, 'Tip Of My Tongue', was also taped that day.

The group's career was moving forward ever faster as Epstein worked hard at pushing The Beatles. At the end of 1962 they won their second *Mersey Beat* popularity-poll award. On December 15th at the Majestic Ballroom in Birkenhead the group performed at a special award show where they received a celebratory plaque from master-of-ceremonies Bill Harry.

For this show they used their tan-coloured Vox amplifiers, McCartney played his Hofner bass, Harrison the Gretsch Duo Jet and Lennon his black Rickenbacker. Starr played a pearl-white Trixon set, most likely borrowed from one of the other bands performing on the bill, as The Beatles closed the show – at 4am – and probably didn't want to lug Starr's kit home at that time in the morning.

Just a few days after winning a popularity poll and with a new single on the horizon, the group had to fly once more to Hamburg to fulfil their final commitment there – a two-week engagement at the Star Club.

Fifteen clubs a day

This was the last time The Beatles would perform in Germany until their triumphant return in 1966. During these shows in Hamburg the group used their normal guitars – Rickenbacker 325, Gretsch Duo Jet and Hofner bass – through the Star Club's amplifiers, while Starr played his Premier drum set.

Photographs taken at the club again reveal Lennon having more problems with loose controls as a volume knob made a bid for freedom.

Some of these final shows at the Star Club were recorded by Adrian Barber, who had built a large PA (public address) system and installed recording gear at the club. Barber wanted to improve upon the generally poor PAs used in Hamburg clubs, and was given the opportunity by Manfred Weissleder, owner of the Star Club.

"With a partner he also ran 15 strip clubs," says Barber. "Remember in 'She Came In Through The Bathroom Window', the bit about 'she said she'd always been a dancer, she worked in 15 clubs a day'? Well, that was it. And with this many places, each with a PA, Weissleder had mountains of surplus gear."

Star Club on tape

So Barber was set to work to build a good PA for the Star Club, and he ended up creating a system that for the time was unusual in several ways. It had two 25-element speaker columns on each side of the stage, with a low-voltage line feeding each of the 10-inch speakers. Barber additionally used powerful Telefunken valve (tube) amplifiers rated at about 200 watts to drive the columns.

"I also had Binson Echorec echo units, which were Italian-made and used discs rather than the regular tape. It was most unusual to have separate systems for the lead vocal and the horns and the back-up vocals, and each with its own distinct echo unit. I even had side fills, or stage monitors, which was also unusual. The bands thought the system was wonderful. We'd have really good nights when every note was perfect and everything fell into place. And I thought wow, if only we could have recorded them."

So then Barber rigged up a recording system at the club. He says the idea was simply to record every gig in order to remember the good ones. Barber used a domestic-style Telefunken tape recorder that belonged to Weissleder, and the club owner also provided a small mixer.

"At first I had another little tape recorder that I used in order to record the ambience of the club room," says Barber, who would use the results to improve the system's sound.

"Once when I recorded the room ambience it happened to be The Beatles. As time went by I built better and better miking, and improved the general system."[29]

Fifteen years later, Ted "Kingsize" Taylor, who'd led Liverpool band The Dominoes in the 1960s, released Barber's recordings of The Beatles at the Star Club as the album *Beatles Live! At The Star Club, Germany, 1962*.

Meanwhile, with The Beatles willing to be guided by their enthusiastic and astute young manager, the prospects for 1963 looked good – although the group could surely not have guessed just how important the coming year would be.

> I'LL WEAR A BLOODY BALLOON IF SOMEONE'S GOING TO PAY ME. I'M NOT IN LOVE WITH THE LEATHER THAT MUCH...
>
> John Lennon

"**It's really a joke if you compare it to these days, because we used to have these little Vox AC-30 amps ... We were so naive in those days ... still just very modest in some respects.**"

GEORGE HARRISON, RECALLING THE DAYS BEFORE MEGA-WATT AMPLIFICATION, AND HOW THE BEATLES SHOULD HAVE ASKED FOR MORE

1963

THIS WAS THE YEAR THAT THE BEATLES CONQUERED BRITAIN. THE BAND'S CAREER WAS MOVING FORWARD AT AN EVER-INCREASING PACE AS BEATLEMANIA REVEALED ITSELF FOR THE FIRST TIME. BUT IT WAS ALSO THE YEAR THEY MADE SOME OF THE MOST DRASTIC AND EXTENSIVE CHANGES TO THEIR EQUIPMENT. HAVING LEARNED LESSONS DURING 1962 ABOUT THE IMPORTANCE OF GOOD "PROFESSIONAL" GEAR, BRIAN EPSTEIN AND THE GROUP TOOK ADVANTAGE OF THEIR POPULARITY AND NEW-FOUND INCOME TO ACQUIRE BETTER QUALITY DRUMS, GUITARS AND AMPS.

The year started with a brief five-date tour of Scotland – during one of Britain's most severe winter storms. Epstein worked feverishly, keeping the band constantly busy. He managed to use the chart success of 'Love Me Do' and the pending release of the group's second single 'Please Please Me' to land them their first proper British tour, as a support act to singer Helen Shapiro who'd enjoyed two top-ten hits during 1962. The tour was scheduled to start at the beginning of February 1963. But there was much work to be done before then.

Brian Epstein was forever trying to persuade the group to improve their stage appearance and performance. The way The Beatles looked on stage and the manner in which they presented themselves was almost an obsession for the manager. With this important British tour now scheduled, Epstein wanted his band – and their gear – to look good. So during the two weeks in which they were away in Hamburg at the end of 1962 arrangements had been made for Lennon and Harrison's Vox AC-30 amplifiers and McCartney's "coffin" bass cabinet to be sent to Barratt's music shop in Manchester for a facelift and overhaul. There the amplifiers were refurbished and re-covered with new black vinyl.

Billy Kinsley of The Merseybeats remembers the effect that the black Vox amps had in Liverpool. "You couldn't buy a black Vox back then," he reckons. "The Beatles had the original light brown ones. Some people think that they changed those for new black amps, but that's not right: they had them re-covered in black. Paul got his bass amp re-covered at the same time, because that was down to bare wood, though originally it had been painted black. When John and George had the Vox amps re-covered, he got his Coffin done too."[1]

Kinsley remembers that Harrison had been "pretty miffed" when Merseybeats guitarist Aaron Williams turned up at the Cavern a little later with a new black-finished Vox amp. The Beatles must have thought they had an exclusive. "George said, 'Who re-covered that for you?' And Aaron said, 'We bought it like that in London, at the Jennings shop.' So obviously, Vox must have heard about The Beatles and decided, hey, good idea, we'll issue AC-30s in black." Vox had in fact been offering black-finished amps since about 1961, at first in small numbers but gradually increasing.

On January 11th 'Please Please Me' backed with 'Ask Me Why' was released in Britain on Parlophone and started a steady climb up the charts. In the meantime, Epstein continued to book The Beatles into a heavy daily schedule to promote their new record with radio and television appearances, in addition to the group's already strenuous regime of live performances. It was becoming clear that Epstein was determined to get The Beatles to the top.

By the start of 1963 the band's arsenal of equipment had grown to include a healthy number of "professional" instruments. Lennon usually played his trusty '58 Rickenbacker 325 and Harrison his Gretsch Duo Jet, both using their newly re-covered black Vox AC-30 amplifiers. Lennon and Harrison used their Gibson J-160E acoustic-electric guitars as backups to their Rickenbacker and Gretsch instruments. Ever more frequently, the J-160Es were used live as well as on radio and television performances. McCartney played his '61 Hofner violin bass through his Quad amp and the newly re-covered "coffin" speaker cabinet. Starr meanwhile continued to play his mahogany-coloured Premier drum set with the Premier logo and "Ringo Starr" lettering painted on the front of the bass-drum head – although that would soon change.

With their first prestigious British tour scheduled to start on February 2nd, The Beatles decided once more to improve the appearance of their stage equipment. Starr's name had to be taken off the front of his drum-head. After all, the group were going to be seen by thousands of new potential fans during their first real tour. They didn't want people walking away after the performance wondering what the band was called … or thinking it might be The Ringo Starr Band. It was time to design a Beatles logo for the front of the bass drum.

Various drawings that McCartney made for a Beatles logo were published in his brother Mike's 1981 book, *The Macs*. These interesting documents show the preliminary sketches that would eventually become the group's "bug" logo. The ideas were taken to a local signwriter in Liverpool, Tex O'Hara, whose brother Brian was guitarist in another Epstein-managed band, The Fourmost.

Tex explains, "We played around with different ideas to find out which ones they liked. I did about five to ten drawings – which I've still got – and showed them to the group. They settled on one logo, which was put on a piece of linen and stretched across the front of the drum."[2] This second bass-drum head on Starr's Premier drum set was plain white, without the Premier brandname and with the new Beatle "bug" logo. This had a script-style "Beatles", the "B" of which was decorated with two bug-like antennae. It was simply drawn on a piece of cloth that was stretched across the drum head, and held down with the bass-drum's mounting hoops.

George sitting on a newly re-covered Vox AC-30, and holding a Gretsch Jet Fire Bird – similar to his Duo Jet – that he seems to have borrowed and used for only a short period in early 1963.

While this new logo was being created by O'Hara, Harrison had some work done to his Gretsch Duo Jet. Photos of the group rehearsing at the Cavern in January 1963 show him playing a Gretsch Jet Fire Bird. The model was similar to the Duo Jet, but had thumbnail-shape fingerboard inlays, a pair of Filter'Tron pickups, a black Gretsch pickguard, and the standard Gretsch trapeze-shape tailpiece. The guitar was almost certainly red in colour, although all the extant photographs of Harrison with it are black-and-white. When asked recently about this Gretsch, Harrison answered, "It was someone else's, I just tried it out at the Cavern."[3] The same rehearsal shots also show Starr's Premier drum set with a plain white front bass-drum head, as it was before the addition of the cloth with the Beatle "bug" logo.

Beatles' roadie Mal Evans

With an ever-more-busy schedule and an ever-growing mound of equipment to maintain, the group needed someone else to help roadie for them. Neil Aspinall's workload as road manager had become increasingly time-consuming.

In the middle of January 1963 Aspinall had fallen ill and was unable to drive The Beatles to London for a scheduled radio show. Fortunately, Aspinall had run into his friend Mal Evans at the Cavern. Aspinall asked Evans if he would run the boys to London and back. Evans agreed. On the return to London the windscreen (windshield) on the van shattered. Lennon later told Aspinall, "You should have seen Mal. He had this paper bag over his head with just a big slit for eyes. We were all in the back of the van [trying to keep warm]. It was freezing … Mal had to knock out the rest of the broken glass and just drive on. It was perishing. Mal looked like a bank robber."[4]

The group had a gig at lunchtime and an out-of-town show in the evening. Evans showed up at Aspinall's with the van in perfect condition, windscreen replaced. Aspinall: "We never knew how he'd managed to get it fixed again so quickly and, even if we didn't say so, it was something we remembered. Ten out of ten to Mal for not just bringing back the van and leaving it for someone else to get a new windscreen put in."[5]

Evans became the band's trusty roadie and confidant, looking after all of their musical equipment from 1963 and staying with The Beatles throughout the rest of their career. Everyone interviewed for this book described Big Mal as one of the nicest, kindest people you could ever meet, always looking after The Beatles and their equipment in fine detail. Evans alone could have been one of the greatest sources of information for this book, but tragically he was murdered in 1976.

The Helen Shapiro package tour started on Saturday February 2nd. During the tour Epstein managed to fill The Beatles' days off with sporadic shows at the Cavern and a full schedule of live radio and television appearances to help promote the new single. Amid all this work, producer George Martin and Epstein managed to book another recording session at EMI. On Monday February 11th The Beatles entered Abbey Road Studio 2 and recorded their first full-length LP, the 14-track *Please Please Me*. The whole album was recorded in one gruelling day. Judged by today's standards, when one day is unlikely to produce a decent drum sound, this seems a remarkable achievement. The session was recorded on to a two-track tape machine, almost entirely live and with few or no overdubs. The instruments and amplification that the group used for making *Please Please Me* were the same as for their live performances during the Shapiro tour.

By February 22nd the band's second single 'Please Please Me' neared the top of the British charts. Epstein's programme of never-ending promotion had paid off perfectly. On February 17th The Beatles had recorded a performance for the influential British television show *Thank Your Lucky Stars*, miming a performance of the hit 45. McCartney played his Hofner bass, Harrison and Lennon both used their Gibson J-160E acoustic-electric guitars, and Starr played his Premier drum set with the new "bug" Beatles logo displayed on the front drum head.

The Shapiro tour carried on, and the group continued to use their familiar equipment. But Lennon was again having problems with his Rickenbacker. The Hofner volume knobs that he had put on the guitar when it was painted black started to fall off: first one, then another. Lennon used the Rickenbacker with two knobs missing for a while before he once again replaced them all with a new set of Burns knobs. Burns was an Essex-based guitar manufacturer which by the early 1960s had established a line of guitars and basses in Britain. A myth has it that the company's founder, Jim Burns, had painted Lennon's Rickenbacker black. But as we've seen, this remains a myth. The only connections between Burns and Lennon's Rickenbacker are the volume knobs Lennon decided to put on the guitar when the old knobs fell off, and – as we shall discover – some work done later to the instrument's electrics.

As the Shapiro tour wound down, The Beatles had become the main attraction. With this growth in popularity the group decided it was time to take up permanent residence in London. It was important to be in the capital city, at the centre of the British music industry, with easy access to television and radio appearances, and more importantly to be near the Abbey Road recording studios. Martin and Epstein had devised a plan to release a new Beatles single every three months and at least two albums a year. At the close of the Shapiro tour Lennon and McCartney found time to write a new song, and on March 5th the group once again entered studio 2, to record their third single 'From Me To You'. Photographer Dezo Hoffmann again documented this recording session and his wonderful photographs not only show The Beatles at work in the studio but, more importantly for us, reveal some of the equipment used during the session. Lennon and Harrison play Gibson J-160E guitars through their Vox AC-30 amplifiers. Starr is on his Premier drum kit, with The Beatles "bug" logo, and McCartney plays his Hofner bass. But the most interesting equipment shown in these photographs is the bass amplification.

In order to get a sound that suited Abbey Road's exacting requirements, McCartney used two items borrowed from the studio's store: a large Tannoy speaker cabinet, and the Leak TL12 amplifier that Ken Townsend spoke about earlier. The bass rig was set up behind a sound baffle and miked for recording. During the session The Beatles also recorded 'Thank You Girl', to be the flip-side of their new single, and attempted two new Lennon & McCartney originals, 'The One After 909' and 'What Goes On', though these songs would not surface on record until years later.

Another British package tour

Just days after finishing one tour, and with just enough time to record their third single at EMI, the group started yet another British tour. This time the outing was shared with American artists Tommy Roe and Chris Montez. Roe's 'Sheila' had been

Liverpool signwriter Tex O'Hara's preliminary sketches for the Beatles "bug" logo, which ended up on Ringo's Premier drum set.

ABC TV's Teddington studios for Thank Your Lucky Stars on February 17th. Ringo has his Premier kit with its new Beatles "bug" logo, and Paul uses his '61 Hofner violin bass.

Mal Evans joined The Beatles in 1963 as their trusted roadie, and would look after the boys' gear for the rest of the group's career. He is pictured here in action at a concert in 1966.

a hit in summer 1962, while Montez had scored a few months later with 'Let's Dance'. The tour started on Saturday March 9th, and though The Beatles were not booked as headliners it took only a few shows before it became obvious which act was drawing the crowds.

Tommy Roe today looks back on this tour with fond memories. He hadn't heard of The Beatles until the tour. "They told me they had performed 'Sheila' in their show in Hamburg, at the Star Club," Roe recalls. "We toured together for a month, so we had plenty of time to talk. They were very interested in America, and had many questions. They really wanted to tour there. John let me borrow his Gibson guitar on the bus to write songs. I started my song 'Everybody' then, and that became a top-five hit for me. I could tell that The Beatles were special, and I tried to get my label ABC Paramount to sign them, but was turned down. When they came to the US in 1964 they invited me to perform with them in Washington DC, at the Coliseum. It was an exciting time, and I was very pleased by that invitation."[6]

During the Roe-Montez tour The Beatles' equipment remained unchanged. Once when Lennon had a cold and lost his voice the group were forced to perform as a three-piece, with Harrison and McCartney making changes in the set to cover Lennon's vocal parts. Halfway through the tour, on March 22nd, Parlophone released the group's first album, *Please Please Me*. It flew up the British charts. By the end of March 1963, with the Roe-Montez tour completed, The Beatles had managed to elevate themselves into Britain's newest hit makers.

New bass amp for Paul

After the Roe-Montez tour, the group decided to upgrade their bass amplification. McCartney had until now used the custom-made "coffin" bass amp, but that would soon change. Dick Denney and Tom Jennings were relishing the good fortune of having Britain's top new pop act endorsing their Vox amplifiers. By the spring of 1963 Jennings Musical Industries (JMI) were already taking advantage of this success by placing advertisements in the music trade papers showing The Beatles performing with their Vox AC-30 amplifiers. The ad copywriters could not contain their excitement: "Wonderful number – wonderful performance – wonderful audience! And, of course, wonderful sound – Vox sound! Top performers use Vox for its top star quality; brilliance, sensitivity, reliability. Vox sound is precision sound."

It was great advertising for Vox, but Tom Jennings realised that only two of The Beatles were presently using his amplifiers. Vox's first bass amplifier had been a 100-watt valve (tube) device, the AC-100, but recently the company's amp designer Dick Denney had developed the smaller T-60 solid-state bass amp. It came in two parts. The tall, vertical speaker cabinet was loaded with a 15-inch and a 12-inch speaker, employing a built-in "crossover" network for better efficiency from the two speakers. The T-60's amplifier section was a solid-state head housed in its own separate cabinet that fitted perfectly on top of the speaker cabinet.

McCartney was an early recipient of the new black-coloured Vox T-60 bass amplifier. It was supplied with a chrome-plated wheeled-stand that fitted around the bottom of the speaker cabinet. The T-60 was a step up from McCartney's "coffin" bass rig, but the solid state circuit of the amp was very new technology – and, as McCartney would soon find out, it was prone to instability. He received his new bass amp toward the end of March or the beginning of April.

Pictures taken by Dezo Hoffmann at a gig at Roxburgh Hall at Stowe School on April 4th show Lennon and Harrison respectively playing their Rickenbacker and Gretsch guitars, with their two Gibson J-160E guitars leaning behind their amps. McCartney plays his Hofner, with Starr on the Premier drum kit bearing The Beatles "bug" logo. The photographs show The Beatles equipped with a pair of Vox AC-30s on Vox amp stands – and the new Vox T-60 bass amp, without a stand.

Tom Jennings didn't take long to capitalise on The Beatles' now complete Vox amp line-up. An advertisement was quickly put together featuring a picture of the group posing with their amplification. It appeared in British music-trade magazines in late May and early June 1963, with the simple boast: "The Beatles Feature The Vox."

At EMI House in London The Beatles gave a short performance on April 5th for EMI record executives, to celebrate the release of their debut LP. During the ceremony the group were also presented with their first silver disc, for the sales of the 'Please Please Me' single. Once again, many photos were taken of this performance and they document The Beatles playing through their complete Vox backline. This equipment line-up would remain in place until the end of April 1963.

Buying gear in London

As their popularity grew The Beatles began to perform at larger venues for better fees. Their biggest concert to date took place on April 21st, the *New Musical Express*'s 1962-63 Annual Poll-Winners' All Star Concert at the Empire Pool in Wembley, north London, where the group performed in front of 10,000 fans.

As the band became more successful their appetite for better and newer equipment grew. They kept in mind lessons learned in the past, and from 1963 onward were continually striving, not only for improvements in their gear, but for new and different sounds. With London now the group's adopted home, the latest in musical equipment was on their doorstep. The finest music shops stocking the latest and best musical instruments in the world were all in London – the key British musical instrument manufacturers and distributors such as Selmer, Jennings and Arbiter all had shops located in and around central London's Charing Cross Road and Shaftesbury Avenue.

With such easy access to the latest fab gear, The Beatles couldn't resist frequenting these stores. Two in which they could often be found were Sound City and Drum City, both owned by Ivor Arbiter. These shops were already familiar to the band who, before they lived in London, had stopped by for supplies while passing through.

Gerry Evans was store manager at Drum City. "The first time I heard of The Beatles was when they turned up outside the shop in a van, probably in 1962 when they first came to London," says Evans. He was especially impressed by the fact that the vehicle had side windows and an on-board record player – both unusual and expensive extras for band vans of the time. The small truck

The group and their producer George Martin receiving their first silver disc for 'Please Please Me' at EMI House on April 5th 1963. Paul is standing in front of his very new Vox T-60 bass amp.

This first Vox ad using The Beatles was published in June 1963 as the group now had a full Vox line-up. Vox's first transistor (solid-state) bass amp was the T-60, and Paul was among the first to use one.

The surviving tom and snare from Ringo's first Ludwig 20-inch-bass drum set. They are still owned by Ringo today.

managed to contain four Beatles, road manager Neil Aspinall, and all their equipment, including PA and stage uniforms.

"They came into the shop to have a look around," Evans continues, "and we found out that they were from Liverpool and they were coming down to do some demos or something. The guys interested in drums – Neil Aspinall and Ringo Starr – came into Drum City, at 114 Shaftesbury Avenue, and the others who were interested in guitars went to Sound City. Later on roadie Mal Evans would come in a lot, but in the early days the musicians themselves used to come into the shop and choose their own equipment."[7]

Ringo's first Ludwig kit – and a new Beatles logo

The next Beatle to make a major change to his equipment was Starr. At first with The Beatles he had used the Premier drum set that had served him so faithfully through his years with Rory Storm & The Hurricanes, but it was time for an upgrade to a more suitably "professional" top-of-the-line kit.

Some time toward the end of April Starr and Epstein made their way to Drum City in search of new gear for the drummer. Gerry Evans recalls that Starr wanted a black kit. "Originally he was going to have a Trixon kit, but because we didn't have the right colour I showed him the oyster black pearl finish that Ludwig did, and he said, 'Oh, that's the one'." Evans says that Epstein then went to see the store's owner, Ivor Arbiter, and Epstein told Arbiter that his group were going to be big and he needed new equipment for them. "Arbiter said he could fix them up with everything," recalls Evans, "so they did a deal where they swapped old equipment for new. As far as Arbiter was concerned this was a promotional deal."

Ivor Arbiter was proud of his shop's position in the market at the time. "Drum City was quite original in England then in that it more or less copied the American idea of a store devoted to drums," says Arbiter. "We had recently started distributing Ludwig drums. Our main line was Trixon drums, but we were trying to get Ludwig going; the brand had been very famous before World War II, and we were getting some interest from the professional end of the market."[8]

Ludwig dates back to 1909 when the Ludwig & Ludwig company was founded in Chicago by German immigrants William and Theobald Ludwig. One of their early innovations was the first workable bass-drum pedal, and by the 1920s business was booming. But with the economic crash in 1929, the Ludwig brothers sold their operation and set up a new company of their own, WFL. By the mid-1950s they had bought back the Ludwig name, and soon took the percussive lead in the rising rock world – the loud, bright sound of their drums perfectly suited to the new music. By the early 1960s, Ludwig were making some of the most desirable drums in the world.

Ivor Arbiter's office was in Gerrard Street, just around the corner from Drum City. "One afternoon I had a phone call from the shop to say that someone called Brian Epstein was in there with a drummer. Epstein apparently wanted some drums for this guy, who was in a band that was doing very well in Germany. I think they wanted a bit of a deal. So the store sent them around to my office. Here was this drummer, Ringo, Schmingo, whatever his name was. I tried to help, because we wanted to promote Ludwig products at the time. You could give drums away all day long," Arbiter laughs.

"At first I tried to palm them off with a Trixon set. But I remember Ringo was looking at my desk, and on the desk I had a swatch of colours. We didn't talk about which brand at this point. Ringo said, 'I like this colour.' We didn't get too heavily into what the drums were or what they sounded like. They chose Ludwig because of the colour, and I made some sort of deal with Brian. I have a feeling that they paid a bit of money for the drums, maybe cost plus five per cent, something like that. We had the kit in stock."

The day that Starr and Epstein visited Drum City for the purchase of the new drum set turned out to be a landmark one – and not just because of the Ludwig drums in oyster black pearl finish, although they would play an important part in the way The Beatles sounded and looked. More significant was the birth of the new Beatles logo. Without much thought, and more or less on the

Ludwig Pearl Finishes

Ringo's Ludwig 20-inch-bass drum kit. This is Ludwig kit number two, and one of the two 20-inch-bass oyster black pearl kits that Ringo owned and used with The Beatles. He still owns it today. The Beatles drop-T logo drum-head has long since been removed.

spot, the now famous Beatles "drop-T" logo was designed (see full-page photo on page 109).

William Ludwig Jr, former president and owner of the Ludwig drum company, explains his version of the logo's origins. He had sent to Ivor Arbiter a swatch about six inches long and three inches wide of oyster black pearl, a new finish that Ludwig's pearl supplier was pushing. "Ringo spotted this on Ivor's desk and said, 'What's that? I want that. Put that on a Premier set.' And Ivor said, 'You can't have it on a Premier set. It's only on Ludwig.' So Ringo said, 'Well, then I'll use a Ludwig, because my friend uses a Ludwig. I'll have a Ludwig set in oyster black pearl.'"[9]

Ludwig thinks that Epstein worked out a price with Arbiter for the set. "Then Epstein said, 'Hold on, the group's not called Ludwig, it's called The Beatles. Where's "The Beatles" going to be? If the Ludwig name's on the head, I want The Beatles on there, and bigger.' Well, Ivor didn't want to lose the sale, and he said, 'OK, we'll put it on something like this.' And Ivor drew the Beatles logo, the way it is today. He alone took out a piece of stationery, drew a circle, and created the Beatles logo with the exaggerated capital B and the exaggerated capital T. That became the official Beatles logo known all around the world. And all that Ivor ever got out of it was that he sold them a drum set."

Ludwig says Starr was the most famous drummer that the company had ever encountered. "He was a likeable, good-looking fella. All Ringo wanted to do is play the drums ... and that's all. He kept good time and he didn't want to play solos. Drummers, as you know, are supposed to rock the rhythm and stay in the background."

Ivor Arbiter modestly agrees with Ludwig's story, and tells his version. "At that time I certainly

The drummer's view (below) of Ringo's second 20-inch-bass Ludwig kit.

hadn't heard of The Beatles. Every band was going to be big in those days. We were looking for endorsers, so I wanted to be as helpful as possible. The Ludwig logo was because of me. I wanted it on there for promotion, and I think Brian said, 'Let's get their name on the drums too.' I'm sure that they didn't give us the design and I'm sure that we designed the Beatle logo. There was a signwriter by the name of Eddie Stokes who used to do all our drum heads in Drum City. He used to come into the store, and amazingly enough he had a withered arm just half the size of the other one. He'd hold a stick to steady himself. I told him we needed to get this Beatle name on for Mr Epstein."

Gerry Evans, then manager of Drum City, confirms the story. "The Beatles logo that we know today with the drop-T was created in our store by Eddie Stokes, the signwriter who used to do the front of the bass-drum heads for us. He would come in during his lunchtime, because he worked locally. Ivor Arbiter drew the Beatles logo on a pad of paper, then had Eddie put what he had sketched on to the drum head.

"There were about three or four options, and they chose the one with the drop-T. Eddie did it in front of me, he painted it by hand on the first drum that we supplied. I think we charged £5 extra for the artwork. And when I see the drop-T logo today on everything, how I wish we could have registered it. The Drum City shop designed it from Ivor Arbiter's idea, and obviously if it hadn't been for Eddie the signwriter at Drum City then that logo would never have appeared."

Ludwig – "a drummer's dream"

As Starr's new drum kit was being prepared at Drum City, The Beatles and Brian Epstein took some time off for a 12-day holiday. McCartney, Harrison and Starr went away to Santa Cruz, Tenerife, while Lennon and Epstein flew to Spain. When they returned from their break, one of the first engagements on their schedule was in Birmingham for another appearance on the ABC television show *Thank Your Lucky Stars*.

It was at the Alpha Television Studios in Birmingham on Sunday May 12th that Starr took delivery of his first Ludwig drum set. Drum City's Gerry Evans explains that the kit was taken from the shop's stock to have the signwriting done, and then was delivered to Birmingham for the TV show. "I had to take the kit there, about 120 miles away from London, on a Sunday. I drove up in the morning, and that was the first time Ringo used the Ludwig set live. What most people don't know," adds Evans, "is that the drum kit we supplied was in a relatively small size." This first Ludwig kit of Starr's had a 20-inch diameter bass drum, with a 12-inch by 8-inch tom tom, a 14x14 floor tom tom, and a wooden snare drum. "This was a small kit compared to what most of the other bands were using," says Evans, who explains that the small size was needed so the relatively short Starr could sit "on top" of the kit and look big – and be seen.

Evans also supplied Starr with new Paiste cymbals, made in Switzerland. "He had those for quite a long time. I think the cymbals he already had were Premier Super Zyns, which were very cheap cymbals, and most likely he never used them again. We supplied cases as well, because the drum cases he had for his Premiers were too big for the smaller Ludwigs. So I supplied Premier vulcanised fibre cases in the smaller sizes.

"I also took his old Premier drum kit from him and brought it back to the store. We renovated it in our workshop, and then sold it. I ripped off the bit of material from the bass-drum head where he'd handwritten the Beatles name and threw it away. It was a terrible drum kit. It wasn't old: he'd only had it six months or a year. But it was a brown finish, one of the worst finishes that Premier ever did," says Evans. "It looked like furniture, and this kit was all the wrong styles for the time. It had very low-quality heads, and just sounded awful. I don't know why he got it in the first place, really. No wonder he wanted to change it. Anyway, we cleaned it up and sold it off the same week – and very, very cheaply. It would most likely be a collector's item if we still had it today." In fact Starr's Premier drum set did end up on the auction block, at Sotheby's in 1995, and was purchased by the Hard Rock Cafe.

Starr now had his new Ludwig drum set. Drum City celebrated the important sale by announcing in their regular *Melody Maker* ad, on May 18th, "Have just delivered new Ludwig Kit to the Fabulous Beatles." Some say the kit was a £275 Ludwig Super Classic set, but that came with a Supraphonic 400 chrome snare, unlike Starr's wooden drum. Others claim it was a £238 Ludwig Downbeat set –

Ivor Arbiter's Sound City and Drum City stores were quick to capitalise on The Beatles' fame as they were the main suppliers of gear to the group.

which may explain the 12-inch tom, 14-inch floor tom and 20-inch bass – but a Downbeat kit would have had a smaller snare than Starr's. The Beatle drummer's first kit was more likely just a mix of various Ludwig components that Drum City put together from stock.

More importantly, The Beatles had a new logo that would soon become known throughout the world. This same drop-T logo designed by Ivor Arbiter in 1963 is still in use today as The Beatles' official marque, and indeed was registered as a trademark by Apple Corps Ltd in the late 1990s. The first Beatles drop-T logo was painted on a 20-inch Ludwig Weather Master head, and marked the beginning of a series of similar Beatle-logo drum heads that Starr would use.

Ringo undoubtedly helped push Ludwig's profile, but the brand was already in demand among British drummers. In fact, *Mersey Beat* magazine dated November 15th-29th 1962 includes an intriguing picture of Pete Best behind an oyster pearl Ludwig drum set. It seems that The Beatles' first drummer was also first to use Ludwig. The *Mersey Beat* piece concerns Best's activities after his break from The Beatles in summer 1962, and it is clear from this report that the drummer had a Ludwig kit almost six months before Starr acquired his oyster black pearl Ludwig drum set.

Pete Best in 1962, after leaving The Beatles, with his new Ludwig kit.

Today, Best recalls that he really wanted a Ludwig, even though his Premier kit still had a great sound. "Ludwig at the time was a household name," says Best. "It was like a drummer's dream. So when I heard Ludwig kits were available in Britain I tracked them down. A music shop in Manchester called Barratt's had them, and I wanted one. I had done my penance on the Premier – which was a great kit and had a great sound, but now it was time to upgrade. Everyone else was upgrading their equipment, and drummers have pride as well. I knew if I could get my hands on a Ludwig, it would look great.

"I started the enquiries while I was in The Beatles," says Best. "The drums were beginning to come in to Barratt's – but I didn't know I was going to be out of the group. So when that happened things went on hold for a while, until I got my head back together again. Then it was a case of, 'OK… and I still need that Ludwig kit.' The colour was oyster blue pearl, and it had the Ludwig logo on the front of the bass drum. I still have it today. I sold my Premier kit way back in 1962."[10]

George and the Gretsch Country Gentleman

The Beatles continued with a packed itinerary as Brian Epstein booked the fab four on their third British package tour, this time with American headliner Roy Orbison. The singer had scored a number two in March '62 with 'Dream Baby' and another top-ten hit in February 1963 with 'In Dreams'. The tour kicked off on May 18th, but once again it wasn't long before it became clear that The Beatles were the real attraction.

The determined Epstein used The Beatles' ever-growing popularity to land the group their own BBC radio show, *Pop Go The Beatles*. On May 24th, during the busy Orbison tour, the band found time to record some early instalments of the new programme. The pre-recorded half-hour shows would feature The Beatles performing, plus other musical guests and a disc-jockey or comedian to break up the show. The first episode aired on Tuesday June 4th.

On the equipment front, Harrison was the next in line for an upgrade. Apparently Ivor Arbiter's central-London Sound City music store was the place to be in the summer of 1963. A magazine reported, "There were enough stars in Sound City one day last week to put on a full concert. Paul McCartney, George Harrison, John Lennon and [ex-Shadows bassist] Jet Harris were all looking at new guitars."[11]

One of these stars – George Harrison – certainly did find a new guitar. Of the three guitarists in The Beatles, it was Harrison who was obviously most interested in instruments. This, coupled with the fact that Epstein had already made a deal with Ivor Arbiter for Starr's kit, most likely made it easy for Harrison to acquire a new instrument from Arbiter's Sound City store. This time the guitar of choice was a Gretsch Chet Atkins Country Gentleman.

At the time, Arbiter was the exclusive distributor for Gretsch guitars in the UK, and Sound City was one of the prime places to find them. Arbiter explains, "Sound City was our little store in Rupert Street [later Shaftesbury Avenue] and The Beatles found their way in there somehow. The guy that ran the shop then was Bob Adams, who you would probably describe as a roadie type. He was actually a plumber. Bob had a lot of contact with The Beatles. He was a very low-key guy, and they liked that very much."[12] Adams himself says, "I remember outfitting George Harrison with a Gretsch, the

Country Gentleman. We had the full range of Gretsch guitars in stock, and we sold an awful lot of them."[13] Sound City ran a regular weekly ad in *Melody Maker* at the time, and a £264 Country Gentleman disappeared from the ad's stocklist in the first week of May 1963. That £264 was about $740 then, which works out to some £3,300 ($4,600) in today's money.

Harrison would later own a second Country Gentleman guitar, and was no doubt pleased to have a new guitar which had been designed by Gretsch in collaboration with Chet Atkins, the American country guitarist whom Harrison admired. Harrison's first Country Gent was most easily distinguished visually from the later model by its dual "screw-down" mutes that appear on the face of the guitar.

From around 1960 a number of Gretsch models began to feature these string-damping mutes (the company called them "mufflers"). Many players regularly place the edge of their picking hand near the bridge to "damp" or quieten strings. Gretsch decided to offer a mechanical device to do the job. Depending on the model and period, a single or double pad was positioned close to the bridge and under the strings. The pad(s) could be brought into contact with the strings by turning (on early models) one or two "screw-down" control-knob mutes situated either side of the tailpiece, or (a little later) two "flip-up" lever-action switches. But most players preferred the normal, manual method and ignored Gretsch's mechanical mutes.

Indeed the feature would be unworthy of further comment, except that the deployment of dual "screw-down" control-knob mutes or "flip-up" lever-action mutes provides about the only relatively easy visual clue to distinguishing between the two Gretsch Country Gentleman guitars that Harrison would acquire during 1963.

This Country Gent (main picture) is very similar to George's first, with dual "screw-down" mutes. These are controlled by the two knobs seen either side of the Bigsby vibrato. His second (like the smaller picture), which he acquired later in 1963, differs in that it has dual "flip-up" mutes. This time the controls each side of the Bigsby are smaller lever switches, activating the two independent mutes underneath the strings behind the rear pickup.

The Orbison tour continued and The Beatles' popularity grew. During the tour, on May 27th, the group released their third single, 'From Me To You' backed with 'Thank You Girl', which would become their first number-one. The tour ended on June 9th. A daily string of live performances followed throughout the rest of that month, and there were more visits to the BBC studios to tape instalments for *Pop Go The Beatles*, as well as another performance on a special summer edition of the TV show *Thank Your Lucky Stars* featuring all-Liverpudlian talent. For this June 23rd performance The Beatles mimed 'From Me To You' and 'I Saw Her Standing There' with McCartney using his Hofner bass, Lennon his black Rickenbacker, Harrison the new Gretsch Country Gentleman, and Starr playing his Ludwig drum set with the new Beatle drop-T logo. The film clip can be seen on *The Beatles Anthology* video box-set and perfectly documents the fab four with this classic instrumental line-up.

Back to the studio, then back on the road...

By mid 1963 it was beginning to seem as if the group's success was providing its own momentum. On Monday July 1st they were again summoned to studio 2 at EMI's recording base in Abbey Road for another recording session, where they recorded their fourth single, 'She Loves You', backed with 'I'll Get You'.

Photographs from the session show Starr playing his Ludwig drum set and Lennon with his Gibson J-160E plugged through his Vox AC-30 amp. McCartney played his Hofner, which by now had been slightly altered: the forward neck-position pickup must at some point have worked its way loose, most likely because the side set-screws fell out. A quick fix was rigged with some black adhesive tape holding the pickup in place. As McCartney described it a few years later, the bass had "seen so much work that it was held together with

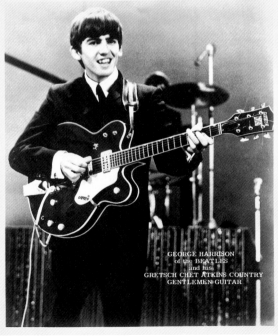

George with his first Country Gent, seen in a Gretsch promo shot.

GEORGE HARRISON
of the BEATLES
and his
GRETSCH CHET ATKINS COUNTRY
GENTLEMEN GUITAR

Paul's Hofner violin bass showing signs of wear and tear: note the tape holding the front pickup in place. Meanwhile, Vox continued to use The Beatles to publicise their amplifiers, especially the AC-30 (example right).

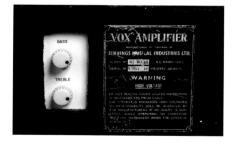

Some Vox AC-30 amps featured this treble-enhancing "top boost" circuit fitted to the rear.

sellotape".[14] McCartney's bass rig for this recording session was still the Vox T-60 amp head and speaker cabinet.

For this session Harrison used his Gretsch Country Gentleman played through his Vox AC-30 amp. Some photographs from the session show Harrison plugged into a small Gibson Maestro Fuzz-Tone unit that was sitting on his Vox AC-30 amp, though there's no evidence of him using the Fuzz-Tone on this recording. "Fuzz" was an electronic form of distortion, the Maestro the first unit to offer the effect, and Harrison's surprisingly early experimentation pre-dates any appearance of such a sound on a Beatle recording by years. It's interesting to imagine how 'She Loves You' or 'I'll Get You' would have sounded with the addition of a fuzz guitar.

Doug Ellis, who worked in Selmer's music store in Charing Cross Road in central London during the 1960s, recalls: "The Beatles were in the shop a few times, and I remember them buying a Gibson Fuzz-Tone on one occasion. I think it was a weekday morning when they pitched up to buy it, and so the shop wasn't swarming with screaming people."[15]

The fast pace continued as the group performed more live dates. For one such performance, on July 5th at the Plaza Ballroom, Old Hill, Birmingham, the opening act was a group called Denny & The Diplomats. The guitarist was a young Denny Laine who years later would team up with McCartney in Wings. "I remember it was in my home town, Birmingham," says Laine, "and I remember the stage was round. It was one of those gigs where we went off, then the stage revolved, and the main act came on. That was the first time I had ever met The Beatles, and I thought they were great."[16]

A new Vox line-up

During a six-night engagement at the Winter Gardens in Margate, Kent, from July 8th-13th, The Beatles made a change to their amplifier line-up. A visit was paid to the Vox headquarters, just 45 miles away in Dartford, also in Kent. It was time to upgrade their tired Vox amps. Now, however, it was no longer necessary for Epstein to negotiate a deal with Vox. As Vox man Dick Denney puts it, "We gave them whatever they wanted, no questions asked."[17]

Lennon and Harrison's original "re-covered" black AC-30s were taken back by Vox and replaced with a new pair of factory-stock black models. The new AC-30s had the same top-boost circuits, retrofitted on to the back of the amplifiers, as had those first AC-30s. The only visible difference between the older and the newer AC-30s was in the carrying handles on top of the amps. Instead of the older flat-style leather handles, the newer AC-30s featured checkerboard-pattern moulded handles with the Vox logo imprinted on them. These newer-style handles were slightly raised off the amp because of the fastening hardware, unlike the earlier-style handles that sat flush on the cabinets.

McCartney's Vox bass amp was also upgraded. Denney says the Beatle bassist's T-60 amp would regularly blow up and roadie Mal Evans was constantly having it fixed or exchanged. McCartney's new bass amp was an AC-30 bass head. Denney explains that he modified the company's existing AC-30 model so that it would suit bass guitar, producing a new head to power the bass cabinets. "So we began to offer the AC-30 head three ways: as a treble unit, as a treble boost, and for bass. They all looked identical from the front and from the top, but the circuits were different." Not many AC-30 bass heads were produced, and today they are rarely seen.

McCartney used his new AC-30 bass head to power the same T-60 bass cabinet that he had been using previously. At first he would simply place the AC-30 head on top of the T-60 cabinet, but the head was oversized for the cabinet and looked odd. So a stock AC-30 chrome amp stand was supplied by Vox to hold the head. This revised Vox line-up – two new AC-30s, plus the new AC-30 bass and old T-60 cabinet – would provide The Beatles' amplification until the end of 1963.

A reader of *Beat Instrumental* wrote to the magazine a couple of years later to ask the editor what had happened to the group's original amplifiers. He replied: "The Beatles' old amps have been completely overhauled and will be put into stock, which Jennings

PRECISION SOUND EQUIPMENT

retains for demonstration, hire and loan purposes. These amps could well be used for large beat contests and stage shows, or by visiting artists who use Vox in their home country but don't want the inconvenience of bringing their own gear with them."[18] As for McCartney's old "Coffin" bass amp, an article by Mal Evans and Neil Aspinall in *The Beatles Monthly Book* years later explained: "We still have it in storage and, with some modifications, it might be possible to use that equipment now."[19]

The second album

With a chart-topping LP and three singles behind them, and another 45 soon to be released, George Martin decided it was time for The Beatles to record a follow-up album. Keeping in step with Epstein and Martin's plan of four singles and two LPs per year, the group started work on their second album, eventually titled *With The Beatles*.

On July 18th, amid their still busy live schedule, the group popped into Abbey Road's studio 2 where they recorded 'You Really Got A Hold On Me', 'Money', '(There's A) Devil In Her Heart' and 'Till There Was You'. They bounced back out on the road for a number of shows, but were in the studio again on the 30th to continue work on the LP. This time they recorded some new original material, 'It Won't Be Long' and 'All My Loving', as well as covers of 'Please Mister Postman' and 'Roll Over Beethoven'.

By the summer of 1963 The Beatles were in great demand all over Britain, with continual offers for the group to do live shows as well as requests for radio and television performances. Looking back now at The Beatles' schedule for 1963 it appears that Epstein turned down none of these offers. His

The group with their new Vox amplifier line-up (left to right): Paul's T-60 bass cabinet; George's AC-30; AC-30 bass head; John's AC-30. The new AC-30s have raised-style handles. The picture was taken at the prestigious Royal Command Performance at the Prince of Wales Theatre, London, in November 1963.

objective was always to push the band on to greater heights. What is remarkable is that with such a frenzied schedule the band still managed to find the time to write and record such great records.

Birth of *The Beatles Monthly Book* fan magazine

By the summer of 1963 Brian Epstein had managed to capitalise further on The Beatles' success. Sean O'Mahony, the publisher of *Beat Instrumental* magazine, aware of the group's huge popularity, approached Epstein with the idea of publishing a magazine catering exclusively for Beatle fans. O'Mahony had started *Beat Instrumental* in May – it was dedicated to the British music boom in general, with a focus on musical instruments and equipment. With this background, it would be relatively easy for O'Mahony to publish a Beatle-fan magazine.

The Beatles Monthly Book began publication in August 1963, edited by O'Mahony under the pseudonym Johnny Dean. It was a great success, not least in that it provided rare insights for Beatle fans because O'Mahony was given unique access to the group's recording sessions as well as some of their more private moments. O'Mahony and his staff became part of The Beatles' inner circle.

The photographs taken for the magazine have proved to be one of the best sources of information for this book. Many of the pictures showed The Beatles with their instruments, providing an insider's view of the equipment used for particular recordings and live performances. These pictures were an enormous help in piecing together the complex puzzle of the group's use of specific musical equipment, and they provide a fascinating historical record.

Sean O'Mahony, publisher of The Beatles Monthly Book and Beat Instrumental, backstage with the group.

George's Rickenbacker 425. George bought this guitar, his first Rickenbacker, while visiting his sister in the US in 1963. It originally had a single pickup but has since been modified. It is presently on display at the Rock & Roll Hall Of Fame in Cleveland, Ohio. Rickenbacker's September 1962 internal document (below left) includes this guitar, serial BH439.

WE GAVE THEM WHATEVER THEY WANTED, NO QUESTIONS ASKED

Dick Denney,

Vox designer, recalling the company's promotional deal with The Beatles

A Maton Mastersound MS-500 on display at the National Centre for Popular Music in Sheffield, England, and said to be the one used briefly by George in the summer of 1963. The Australian-made guitar is featured in the manufacturer's catalogue.

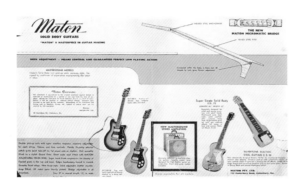

George and an Australian Maton

During August Harrison started to use an Australian-made Maton solidbody guitar. Billy Kinsley of The Merseybeats recalls that when Harrison's Gretsch Country Gentleman was being repaired he borrowed the unusual Maton. "It was an MS-500 Mastersound model. It can be seen in quite a few photographs, but he only borrowed it because he was getting the Gretsch fixed. He got it at Barratt's music shop in Manchester." Maton is one of the few high-profile Australian guitar-makers, and was set up in Canterbury, Victoria, by Bill May in 1944. Electric guitars were added to the line five years later, and the Mastersound MS-500 was a solidbody model launched in the late 1950s.

There has been a story in circulation that Harrison later gave the Maton guitar to Tony Hicks. But Hicks, who played a similar Maton briefly in the early 1960s with his group The Hollies, says he was never given a Maton guitar by Harrison.[20] Harrison's Maton is also said to have ended up in the hands of a Sheffield musician, Roy Barber, who in the 1960s was guitarist with Dave Berry & The Cruisers. Barber claimed that he received the guitar from one of The Hollies in exchange for his Fender Stratocaster, and kept the Maton from that time on. Recently Barber's widow Val loaned the Maton guitar to the National Centre For Popular Music in Sheffield, where it is currently on display. What exactly happened to Harrison's Maton after his brief possession of the guitar remains less than clear.

Photographs taken of The Beatles at the Grafton Rooms, Liverpool on August 2nd and at the Queen's Theatre, Blackpool on

Filming Ready Steady Go in October, George uses his new Rickenbacker 425 for the first time. And it was the last time Paul played his first violin bass in its original state.

CAN WE HAVE A COMPRESSOR ON THIS GUITAR? WE MIGHT TRY TO GET A SORT OF ORGAN SOUND.

George Harrison,

pushing engineer Norman Smith

to try new effects in 1963

the 4th show Harrison playing the Maton guitar. Lennon meanwhile was playing his black Rickenbacker 325, and both guitarists were using their new Vox AC-30 amps with stands. McCartney played his Hofner bass with the "taped" forward pickup, and used his Vox AC-30 bass head on top of the T-60 bass cabinet. Starr was beating away on his new Ludwig drum set – so much so that the "g" of the Ludwig logo had come off.

In the first week of August 1963 The Beatles gave their last performance at the Cavern. Merseybeats guitarist Tony Crane remembers the night well because his group was one of several others on the same bill. "The Beatles had already had big hit records, and they played one more time at the Cavern. So it was a big night, and people had queued for hours. We went on just before them and absolutely stormed the place, everyone went mad.

"I don't know whether The Beatles thought they shouldn't be playing there, or something, but they were very quiet in the dressing room when we were chatting, very subdued. And when they went on, within about five minutes all the electrics went off. The place was so full, the walls were pouring with sweat, with water … everything was wet. All their amps went, the lights went off, it was pitch black. Whatever could go wrong went wrong on that night. It was ominous really. When we'd been on, everything was perfect. It was weird that they should come back for just one more show, and then everything went wrong."[21]

The Beatles non-stop success continued as the new single 'She Loves You' was released in Britain on August 23rd. It became the first Beatles 45 to sell a million copies. The BBC filmed the group for a 30-minute documentary, *The Mersey Sound*, showing how Beatlemania and Liverpool groups had come to prominence. Clips from this documentary can be seen on the *Beatles Anthology* video box-set, superbly capturing the group with their equipment line-up in the summer of 1963.

Early studio effects

Continuing with their relentless schedule of live gigs, television appearances and radio shows, The Beatles found time to get into Abbey Road studio 2 again to continue work for their second LP, *With The Beatles*. On September 11th and 12th they recorded 'All I've Got To Do', 'Not A Second Time', 'Don't Bother Me', 'Little Child' and 'I Wanna Be Your Man'. Lennon and McCartney had written the latter song just days before and given it to The Rolling Stones, who also recorded it, as the a-side of their second single. Gibson's Maestro Fuzz-Tone distortion box, first experimented with by the group on the 'She Loves You' sessions a few months earlier, was tried again, this time by Lennon on early takes of 'Don't Bother Me', but again it did not make the final issued version.

A journalist present at the session reported that the first take was not too successful. "When they had rearranged the opening bars, John produced a fuzz box … John was knocked out with the result, but George Martin wasn't too happy. 'You'll have to do something, John,' said Martin. 'It's already distorting from the amplifier. Do you think it sounds OK? Are you sure about it?'" The vote went against the fuzz box. Harrison, the report continued, asked engineer Norman Smith, "'Can we have a compressor on this guitar? We might try to get a sort of organ sound.'"[22]

With their chart success, The Beatles were enjoying greater freedom in the studio. No longer were there strict time limitations. The session that included 'Don't Bother Me', for example, had gone on until after 10pm – very late by the conservative standards of Abbey Road in those days. And at this relatively early stage the group had already started to add different instruments to their recordings, beyond the usual guitars and drums line-up, and to play with recording effects. Although these decorations were not yet elaborate or extreme, instruments such as bongos, claves, piano and Hammond organ as well as harmonica, tambourine and other percussion were all used to enhance the recordings, and the group would continue to develop these ideas in the studio.

The issued version of 'Don't Bother Me' ended up with amplifier tremolo – a rhythmic fluctuation of volume – on the rhythm guitar. Though relatively polite, this was the group's first evident use in the studio of an electronic effect on the guitar sound, and thus marked the start of a search for unusual sounds and the group's role as studio experimenters in coming years. Fortunately, producer George Martin was responsive to such developments, and increasingly it seemed as if The Beatles were willing to try anything. This open-mindedness proved to be one of the major reasons for the artistic success of the group's records, and ensures that these discs remain as milestones in the history of recorded pop music.

Holidays ... and a Rickenbacker for George

At the pace The Beatles were moving, it was time for a much-deserved break, and a brief two-week holiday was planned to begin on September 16th. Starr and McCartney travelled to Greece, Lennon and his wife Cynthia went to Paris, while Harrison and his brother Peter went to the United States to visit their sister Louise who had relocated to Benton, Illinois, in the 1950s.

During Harrison's visit to the US his sister introduced him to a friend, local musician Gabe McCarty. McCarty says Harrison purchased his first Rickenbacker guitar during this trip, long before most Americans had even heard of The Beatles. "I played some guitar with George a few times at his sister's house during that visit," McCarty recalls. "I had a band called The Four Vests, and George played two gigs with us. We played one in Eldorado at the VFW [Veterans of Foreign Wars club] where he came and sat in with us. He brought his sister and his brother-in-law along. Then the following week we had a birthday party in Benton at the Boccie Ball Club, and he played there with us.

"George wanted to buy a Rickenbacker guitar, so I took him up to Mount Vernon, to Red Fenton's Music Store. That was the only place around here that had a Rickenbacker franchise, and he bought a guitar that they had in stock. I think there were two or three, and he was wanting a black one. Fenton didn't have anything but red sunburst ones in stock. That was a popular colour then. I think the reason George wanted it black was that John Lennon had a black Rickenbacker, and they would match. So Fenton told George that if he left the guitar there for a week he would have it refinished black for him.

"George went ahead and bought it. He played the guitar in the store there, we had a little jam session for about 45 minutes, Fenton on piano, me on bass, and George playing the guitar. Then he left the Rickenbacker with the store to have it refinished. About seven or eight days later I took George back there and he picked it up. This was a couple of days before he left. George was crazy about the guitar. I guess he had wanted one for a long time and had never had a chance to get something."[23]

This first Rickenbacker of Harrison's was a single-pickup model 425 solidbody with serial number BH 439, dating its manufacture to August 1962. Rickenbacker usually gave vibrato-less guitars a model number ending in "0", but for some reason 425 was the official number for this non-vibrato guitar until 1965. In 1963 a 425 retailed for $179.50 (about £65 then), which would be about $1,030 (£730) in today's money. Harrison would use it for only a relatively brief period, and years later gave the instrument to George Peckham, a guitarist in Liverpool band The Fourmost who became a record-cutting engineer at Apple. Through the years the guitar was modified. A second pickup was added, plus associated extra controls. The inside cavity of the guitar was routed to accommodate the additional pickup, a new faceplate was made for the guitar, and the original Kluson tuners were changed to Grover Sta-Tite models.

The modified Rickenbacker was sold at auction in September 1999 at Christie's, and the purchaser contacted Harrison, enquiring about the guitar and its alterations. Harrison confirmed that it was indeed the guitar he had given to Peckham – but he did not remember making the modifications to it, which remain a mystery. The Rickenbacker 425 is currently on loan for display at the Rock and Roll Hall of Fame in Cleveland, Ohio.

Jim Burns and John's Rickenbacker

He may not have painted John's Rickenbacker 325, but Jim Burns did do some work for Lennon ... on the guitar's electrics. In September 1963 reporter Chris Roberts became involved in an important journey for Lennon's guitar. Roberts worked for the top British musicians' newspaper *Melody Maker* from 1962 to 1964, and often interviewed The Beatles during that time. Roberts was also a guitar player, and knew the technical side of instruments. He became quite close to the band, even appearing fleetingly on their BBC *Saturday Club* version of 'Kansas City' after McCartney hauled him into the studio to swell the choir.

Roberts recalls: "The Beatles and I were in the back of a black London taxi swapping guitar stories, just chatting like guitar players. Then John said to me, 'Can you do something about my Rickenbacker? Do you know anyone who can fix the electrics?' The guitar just didn't work, and that's as much as he knew. So we made a loose arrangement that the next time I was in the NEMS office in Monmouth Street – which I used to visit at least once a week – I'd pick up the guitar. So I took it

Paul's 1963 Hofner 500/1 violin bass. This became Paul's main instrument and the one with which he is most associated – so much so that it was later nicknamed "the Beatle Bass". Along with John's original Rickenbacker 325, this bass is considered the most important Beatle guitar. The pickguard was removed during the 1966 US tour, and the set-list taped to the side of the body (close-up below) also dates from that last Beatles tour.

The Maestro Fuzz-Tone was an early fuzz-box that the group experimented with in the studio, although it was never used on the final released recordings.

away ... without a case! No big deal: I took it back to the *Melody Maker* office in Fleet Street and leaned it against the wall by my desk.

"I was acquainted with guitar-maker Jim Burns and thought he would be ideal for the job. I wanted someone who could sit down with a guitar and know what they were doing. When I rang Jim I asked if he'd help out an acquaintance of mine, John Lennon, with a guitar repair. He said, *Lemon*? I said no, Lennon, in The Beatles. He said, '*Beatles*?' ... as if I was speaking a foreign language. I never found out if he was having me on or was actually ignorant of the name. He had a pretty droll sense of humour.

"I explained what Lennon thought was wrong, that one of the pickups was not functioning and was making the rest of the pickups not work. One pickup had been giving trouble, and now it had taken the rest with it. There was no electric sound at all. I went to Burns's factory at Buckhurst Hill in Essex, and Jim opened the electrics to look at the wiring. He was intrigued by the way another manufacturer worked. He said they could fix it, so I left it with him. I'm sure that was the first time Jim had dealt with a Beatle instrument. About two weeks later it was delivered back to me, and I made the handover back at the NEMS office. No ceremony: here's the guitar. John gave it a go. So what do you think? 'Oh, not bad. Thanks a lot.' I remember seeing Lennon with the guitar again on a TV performance soon afterward."[24]

Burns did his work to Lennon's Rickenbacker while the group were on holiday during the last two weeks of September 1963. A day after they returned they were back to work. This time it was a live performance for the key British pop TV show, *Ready Steady Go!*. On the afternoon of October 4th the group attended a camera rehearsal in Studio Nine at Television House in London, and later that evening they performed 'Twist And Shout', 'I'll Get You' and 'She Loves You' for the live broadcast. Photographs taken of the rehearsal show Starr on his Ludwig kit and Lennon with his newly-repaired '58 Rickenbacker 325, while Harrison is pictured for the first time playing his new Rickenbacker 425 guitar with The Beatles.

New Hofner bass for Paul

The photographs taken of the October 4th *Ready Steady Go!* rehearsals also reveal McCartney holding a new Hofner violin bass. Most previous accounts have Selmer (Hofner's distributor in the UK) handing over this new second bass to McCartney at the group's Royal Command Performance on November 4th. But clearly McCartney received the instrument earlier. He explained to a reporter: "I ordered another Hofner bass ... because it was the only left-handed bass available and I thought I'd better have a spare."[25] At those *Ready Steady Go!* rehearsals McCartney at first played the new '63 Hofner 500/1 violin bass, holding it very high and without a strap. Later at the same rehearsals he switched back to his original '61 Hofner, but for the actual broadcast later that day he again chose to play his new bass.

McCartney's '63 Hofner 500/1 violin bass is similar in many ways to his first. The most noticeable

visual difference is in the placement of the pickups and the style of the Hofner logo. His second bass has two Hofner "staple"-style pickups mounted apart, one near the neck and the other near the bridge. This is in contrast to his first Hofner where both pickups are mounted close together and near the neck. The second bass has the more common horizontal Hofner script logo, as opposed to the vertical block-type logo of McCartney's first bass.

This second Hofner 500/1 violin bass would become McCartney's main instrument, and the Beatle bass with which most people would identify him. He used it on almost all the rest of The Beatles' live performances and television appearances, and many recordings, until the group's break-up. In recent years McCartney pulled out this '63 Hofner bass and started to use it again for recordings and performances.

Almost gone in Scotland

With their new instruments on board, The Beatles started a mini-tour of Scotland. But at the first show on October 5th, in Glasgow, Harrison's new Rickenbacker 425 guitar was stolen. The guitar was taken from the group's van outside the Concert Hall. Fortunately, police were watching, and the instrument was recovered.

Scotland's *Press & Journal* newspaper reported the incident, its headline reading "They Stole A Beatle's Guitar". The news item continues: "Two 18-year-old youths who stole a £150 guitar belonging to The Beatles while the pop group were in Glasgow appeared at Glasgow Sheriff Court yesterday. The youths, James Armstrong and Thomas McNama, had at a previous court appearance admitted breaking into a van on October 5th and stealing the guitar. What they did not know was that the van belonged to The Beatles and that the guitar was the property of George Harrison, one of the group. When the case came up originally the sheriff adjourned it so that he could study background reports. Yesterday McNama was committed for Borstal training and Armstrong was put

George pictured playing his new Country Gent with dual "flip-up" mutes, and Ringo's kit has lost some letters from the Ludwig logo, which is down to "Lu". The occasion is a charity show at the Grosvenor Hotel in London in December 1963.

on probation for three years and ordered to find £25 security for his good behaviour. It was his first offence. Armstrong said as he left the court that he was not a Beatle fan and in fact was not 'with it'."[26]

This had been a close call for Harrison's new Rickenbacker. But it would not be the last Beatle guitar to be stolen, as we'll see. Harrison used his new Rickenbacker 425 for a few live performances and for a BBC radio programme, *The Ken Dodd Show*, but then went back to favour his Gretsch Country Gentleman.

The Beatles' October 13th television appearance on *Val Parnell's Sunday Night At The London Palladium* was seen by 15 million viewers in Britain. After hordes of screaming fans greeted the group's performance, the press coined the term Beatlemania to describe the wild, chaotic, exciting scenes. For the Palladium performance McCartney used his new '63 Hofner bass, Harrison played his Gretsch Country Gentleman, Lennon had his Rickenbacker 325, and Starr was on the Ludwig drum set. This was the equipment line-up that The Beatles used for the following handful of live shows. Lennon also took his J-160E along, and Harrison his Rickenbacker 425.

Amid more gigs the group found time to return to the studio, and on October 17th recorded their fifth single, 'I Want To Hold Your Hand' backed with 'This Boy'. The recordings were made on a new Studer J-37 four-track machine which had just been installed at Abbey Road studios. Willi Studer had founded his company in Switzerland in 1948, soon making Dynavox, Revox and Studer brand tape recorders. The four-track offered new possibilities, allowing four independent tracks to be recorded side by side, giving the group yet more flexibility for studio experimentation. No photographs exist from these sessions, but it's likely that the instruments used were the same as their contemporary concert line-up. Another appearance on ABC Television's *Thank Your Lucky Stars* was taped on October 20th, and broadcast on the 26th. Harrison once again used his Rickenbacker 425, Lennon his Rickenbacker 325, McCartney his new '63 Hofner bass, and Starr his Ludwig set.

Another Country Gent for George

On October 23rd the band flew to Sweden for a week-long tour. During the Swedish shows Harrison used his Country Gentleman, but played his Rickenbacker 425 almost as much. Some of the pictures taken of the group in Sweden show them posing with Harrison's Rickenbacker, while other shots reveal Lennon playing the 425 backstage. Live photos taken at the October 29th concert show Harrison with the guitar, while for the performance on the Sveriges Television show *Drop In* filmed the following day Harrison uses his Country Gentleman. (This clip can be seen on *The Beatles Anthology* video box-set.)

Returning to the UK, the group appeared at a show that would be seen later as a landmark: the Royal Command Performance at the Prince Of Wales Theatre in London. The event was recorded with Queen Elizabeth in attendance on November 4th and broadcast on television throughout Britain on Sunday the 10th. Photographic evidence of the performance reveals an interesting detail on Harrison's Country Gent guitar. There is a hole where the top "screw-down" string-mute's control-knob would normally sit. Because the mute knob sat so high off the body of the guitar, perhaps

About to make an appearance on the British TV programme Thank Your Lucky Stars, the group talk over a few final points with the show's director. George has his second Gretsch Country Gentleman, with dual "flip-up" mutes, and Paul his second Hofner violin bass. (The picture was taken in December 1963.)

Harrison removed it for comfort? According to Bob Adams of the Sound City store, the Gent was in need of repair at this time. If Harrison did remove the knob, it's possible that the mute mechanism became loose inside the guitar and rattled around or, in the worst case, interfered with the guitar's wiring. So Adams supplied Harrison with a replacement Country Gent.

Adams says he had to go to the Prince Of Wales Theatre to deliver the second Country Gent. "I took a Gretsch to George myself," he recalls. "It wasn't far from our store, just down from Piccadilly Circus." This second Gretsch Country Gentleman guitar was virtually identical to the first, but had dual "flip-up" lever-action switches either side of the bridge to control the guitar's string-mutes, with red felt pads under the switches, rather than the "screw-down" control-knob mutes of the earlier Gent.

Adams's recent recollection is confirmed by a report from the time. "One of [Harrison's] worn-out guitars, a Gretsch Country Gent in a falling-to-pieces case, fills a corner in Sound City, in London," wrote a *Beat Instrumental* journalist. "No good for George ... but it could raise thousands of pounds if put up for charity."[27] Adams explains that the Gent in for repair was then stolen from Sound City. "They broke the side window and took the Gretsch out of the shop."[28] The guitar was later found and returned.

A tour for the autumn

By the beginning of November the group had started their fourth package tour – but this time they were the headliners. Billed as The Beatles Autumn Tour, the month-and-a-half round of English theatres (plus a gig each in Dublin and Belfast) featured an almost daily ritual of live shows. A mix of radio and television interviews and performances were fitted into the schedule wherever possible.

The equipment used on the Autumn Tour saw little change. Starr played his Ludwig drum set, Lennon his Rickenbacker 325 as his main guitar and Gibson J-160E when required, through his '63 Vox AC-30 amp. McCartney used his new '63 Hofner bass, with his original '61 as a spare, played through the AC-30 bass head and T-60 bass cabinet, while Harrison used his '63 AC-30, playing his Gretsch Country Gentleman with dual "flip-up" mutes as his main guitar and another Country Gent as a spare. Pictures taken at the November 26th show at the Regal Cinema, Cambridge and at the Grosvenor House Hotel's Ballroom in Park Lane, London, on December 2nd confirm the guitars Harrison used on the tour. He's seen playing the dual-"flip-up" Gretsch, with a spare Country Gent leaning on the back of his AC-30.

The Gent with dual "flip-up" mutes was the one that Harrison came to favour, the guitar that he was most photographed with and most identified with, and the instrument he would take to the United States and use on many of the Beatle world tours, television appearances and films. The deep dark-brown "mahogany" finish of this prime Country Gent has often been mistaken as black. When this particular guitar was originally manufactured by Gretsch a healthy amount of brown stain finish must have been used, giving the guitar its extremely dark finish. So today, among guitar collectors, an early Gretsch Country Gentleman with a very dark brown finish can command a higher price than a similar guitar with a lighter brown finish – entirely due to the fact that Harrison's favoured Country Gentleman happened to feature this especially intense colour.

During the group's Autumn Tour they made an appearance on the Granada television programme *Scene*, taping a performance of 'I Want To Hold Your Hand' and 'This Boy' on November 25th. The television studio's stage was set up with large headlines from a fictitious *Daily Echo* newspaper and a drum riser made to look like a camera lens. For the miming of 'This Boy' Harrison and Lennon both used their Gibson J-160E guitars – one of the last occasions that Lennon would be filmed with his, because the instrument was stolen soon afterward. On November 22nd the group's second LP *With The Beatles* was released in the UK, with advance orders of 300,000 copies. A week later the single 'I Want To Hold Your Hand' came out, with over one million advance orders. The Beatles had conquered Britain.

Ringo and the Lu

The group finished their Autumn Tour on December 13th, with a grand finale concert at Wimbledon Palais in London the following day. By this time Beatlemania was rife in Britain. For the special Wimbledon concert a steel fence was erected as a barrier between the band and their fans. It was the first time such extreme measures were taken to protect The Beatles, but it would not be the last. Similar sights would become common at many future concerts.

The last television appearance that The Beatles made in 1963 was on ABC's *Thank Your Lucky Stars*, for an all-Merseyside edition, taped on December 15th and broadcast on the 21st. Gerry Evans of Drum City watched this appearance on TV and was horrified when he saw Starr's drum set. "I could see Ringo's Ludwig kit that we'd supplied no longer said 'Ludwig' on it," reveals Evans. "All it said was 'Lu...'. That first Beatle drum head we provided had a stick-on Ludwig logo that must have started to peel off as Ringo used the set. Obviously it was in our best interest to have the Ludwig logo visible on the drums, for promotion. So I rang up Mal Evans the next day and arranged to have Eddie Stokes paint the Ludwig logo on the drum head, so that it would not come off. I later found out that John Lennon was making jokes about it on stage. He'd introduce the drummer: 'And on the

A late-November Granada TV show in Manchester – one of the last appearances where John still has his first Gibson J-160E guitar. The guitar was stolen soon afterwards.

Lu, Ringo!' As you know, 'loo' is British slang for toilet. We were trying to sell Ludwig drums, not Lu drums." Starr's bass-drum head was taken back to Drum City where Eddie Stokes hand-painted the Ludwig logo on to the existing 20-inch head, above the Beatle drop-T logo. This new hand-painted Ludwig logo turned out to be slightly larger than the original stick-on version, aiding Drum City's promotional efforts for Ludwig.

Christmas show and Gibson lost

For the close of 1963 Brian Epstein had planned his first year-end seasonal extravaganza. The Beatles' Christmas Show was held at the Astoria Theatre in Finsbury Park, north London, and featured comedy, pantomime and, of course, music. Other members of the cast included Tommy Quickly, The Fourmost, Billy J Kramer With The Dakotas, and Cilla Black. The 16-night run of two shows every night was sold out well in advance of its start on Christmas eve, December 24th.

It was at the Christmas shows in London that Lennon noticed his Gibson J-160E had been stolen. An account of the Gibson's abduction printed a couple of years later in *The Beatles Monthly Book* described how Lennon and Harrison took pride in their Gibson "Jumbos" and how they'd saved up their money for the hire-purchase deposits with much determination. "By the time of the Finsbury Park show the total collection of Beatle guitars had grown, but John and Paul were using their Gibson jumbos in the dressing room and they were there as stand-by replacements if strings snapped during a performance. Recalls John: 'George and I often took a jumbo home with us, so nobody noticed until the end of the season that one was missing. A week or two afterwards I asked Mal where he'd put my jumbo. It was only then that we realised the guitar had been pinched, at Finsbury Park. No, I never got it back."[29]

At some point between September 1962 when they acquired their Gibsons and December 1963, Lennon and Harrison had in fact swapped their guitars. Perhaps it was because of playability or sound preference. Or maybe, because the instruments were identical, the guitars were unknowingly switched, and neither Lennon nor Harrison noticed... or cared. So Lennon's Gibson guitar stolen in 1963 was actually the one that had been registered to Harrison under the hire-purchase deal made at Rushworth's music shop. And the J-160E guitar that Harrison currently still owns, serial number 73161, is the guitar that was logged to Lennon on the original hire-purchase document.

The sold-out Christmas shows were met with near hysteria. Screaming fans made so much noise that it was almost impossible to hear the group's performance. The Beatles themselves were also finding it harder to hear what they were playing. Gerry Evans of Drum City remembers how this became clear to him. "They used to go away on tour without any spare drum parts, because they would just go and pick them up locally whenever they needed them. It wasn't organised like it is today. On one of the Finsbury Park Astoria shows Ringo broke his bass-drum pedal, a Speed King model. For a drummer, this would be like losing half your sound. So they rang us up to see what could be done, but we said we couldn't get out there until Monday. And so Ringo says, 'Oh well, it doesn't matter, because they can't hear it anyway, it's all just screaming.' He said he'd make do – and he actually went on without a bass-drum pedal."

Vox supply more volume

It was during the extended series of Christmas shows that The Beatles took the opportunity to make some major upgrades to their equipment. The Vox AC-30 amplifiers that had served the group so faithfully were just not loud enough to overpower the racket made by their boisterous fans. A serious decibel boost was a must. The simple solution would be louder amplifiers, so they turned to Vox.

Head Vox engineer Dick Denney remembers the group continually asking for louder gear. "They couldn't hear themselves on stage," he shrugs. "That's why I came up with the AC-50 guitar amplifier. I made up the first ones using an AC-30 cabinet with two 12-inch speakers plus a 'horn' speaker for more top end. The horn didn't fit, so I cut a hole for it in the back of the cabinet. I didn't have the time to make up a new cabinet, because we had to get them their new amps. There was always a rush. The new amplifier was in 'piggy-back' style, in other words with separate amplifier and cabinet, and I used two EL-34 valves [tubes] to get the power. But I still think the AC-30 with the EL-84 valves was a better design. It sounded more musical to me."

In the 1990s, Harrison looked back on the question of volume and The Beatles. "It's really a joke if you compare it to these days, because we used to have these little Vox AC-30 amps, and then … Vox decided to make these bigger amplifiers for us. We were so naive in those days: [we could have had anything we wanted made for us] but we were just very modest still in some respects. … And the PA system [had] probably just two microphones on the stage … Any sound that comes across from any guitars or drums is purely coming from those two vocal mikes. Nothing else is miked. Nowadays you'd have the whole drum kit with five or six mikes on it and [its] own mixing system being pumped back out through the PA system. So it's a miracle, really, that anything came across – but when you're competing with 55,000 people it was ludicrous. You can see in the film of [the Shea Stadium concert in 1965] that there's a bit of us just playing to ourselves because we were not quite sure if anybody can even see us, let alone hear us."[30]

The new Vox amplifiers had been ordered during The Beatles Autumn Tour and were delivered to them at the beginning of the Christmas Shows at Finsbury Park. Lennon and Harrison both received a pair of custom-made single-channel Vox AC-50 amplifier heads. From this point on The Beatles were almost always the first to be offered every prototype that Vox built. According to Denney, in most cases new Vox designs and products were specifically and intentionally made with The Beatles in mind.

A poster for the group's sold-out Christmas season of shows at the Finsbury Park Astoria in north London.

While Lennon and Harrison received their new AC-50s, McCartney acquired a new Vox bass amp. With all the problems he'd experienced using the solid-state T-60 head, the switch to the modified AC-30 bass head had generally proved to be a good one – but it was not providing enough power for the Beatle bassman's current requirements. Denney remembers the Vox solution. "The AC-30 head was not loud enough, so I said to [Vox boss] Tom Jennings that we needed something more like the size of a T-60. So I managed to achieve that by simply dropping the valves (tubes) into the bottom of a sub-chassis which reduced the valve height and, of course, made it much slimmer."

McCartney's new single-channel AC-100 bass head delivered a total of 100 watts output power. And with the new head came a new cabinet, almost identical to the T-60 cabinet but with a pair of 15-inch speakers where the T-60 had a 12-inch and a 15-inch speaker. From afar it would have been virtually impossible to tell the two cabinets apart.

Denney says, "Often we didn't have time to re-design things, we just used what we had. That's why it's so hard to identify the various types we made. Later we came up with little tags that looked like flags or banners which we put on the front of the amps so that you could tell the model. The only problem was," he laughs, "they used to fall off." This more powerful AC-100 bass rig – the head and 2x15 cabinet – would remain as McCartney's amplification set-up for the next two years.

All of the new Vox amps for the Finsbury Park Christmas Show season were supplied without the specialised stands that became available later. For these shows all three Vox speaker cabinets were placed in a row in front of Starr's drum riser. The AC-50 cabinets were placed at each end, with the AC-100 bass cabinet set on its side horizontally between them, while the heads were placed on the stairs of the drum riser, behind the speaker cabinets. Vox would put the new rigs on general sale in 1964, the AC-50 for £184 (about $515 then; around £2,200 or $3,120 in today's money) and the AC-100 bass for £205/16/- (£205.80, about $575 then; some £2,500 or $3,500 today).

With The Beatles hard at work performing, Epstein spent the end of 1963 with his sights on the United States. He was carefully scheming for the group to perform on the popular and prestigious *Ed Sullivan Show* on CBS TV. To coincide with a planned US trip, a deal was finally struck with EMI's American affiliate, Capitol Records, to release The Beatles' new single.

On December 26th 'I Want To Hold Your Hand', backed with 'I Saw Her Standing There', was released by Capitol in the US. The invasion plan was almost ready.

"**You are about to be 'invaded' by a series of British performing groups who feature Vox equipment...**"

ADVERTISEMENT PLACED IN US MUSIC PRESS BY TOM JENNINGS, BOSS OF UK COMPANY VOX, EARLY 1964

1964

AS 1963 ENDED, THE BEATLES WERE THE BIGGEST BRITISH MUSICAL SENSATION EVER TO ENGULF THEIR HOME COUNTRY. BUT 1964 WOULD PROVE TO BE THE YEAR WHEN THE GROUP BEGAN TO CONQUER THE WORLD. BEFORE THE START OF 1964, PLANS HAD ALREADY BEEN SET IN MOTION BY MANAGER BRIAN EPSTEIN TO PUSH THE BEATLES OUT AND SPREAD BEATLEMANIA WELL BEYOND BRITISH SHORES.

Epstein made deals in several countries to release records and to present the group in live performance. It was probably hard to imagine for the musicians themselves, but their 1964 schedule would prove even more hectic and busy than that of 1963.

As the year got underway the group were finishing their sell-out series of Christmas performances at the Astoria cinema in Finsbury Park, north London. As we've seen, they had a new Vox backline in place – but now another significant change was made. During the round of Christmas shows in London, Harrison acquired a new Gretsch guitar – this time a Chet Atkins Tennessean.

It was different to his Country Gentleman model in several ways. Most noticeable visually was the body's single cutaway, where the Gent had twin cutaways. From the player's point of view, the Tennessean had single-coil pickups rather than the Gent's humbuckers, providing a more cutting sound. Harrison's new Gretsch was without string mutes, and was in a deep maroon-burgundy wood-grain colour. The guitar was most likely manufactured in 1963, possibly 1962, but it's impossible to tell for sure as no documentation exists and the guitar is no longer in Harrison's possession. Such a Tennessean would have sold new for $350 (about £125 then; around $1,980 or £1,400 in today's money). Harrison used this Gretsch Tennessean on numerous recordings and for live appearances throughout 1964 and then more prominently in 1965.

On January 12th, the day after the string of Christmas shows ended, the group once again appeared live on national British television, this time on the popular show *Val Parnell's Sunday Night At The London Palladium*. For the performance Harrison used the new Gretsch Tennessean while Lennon played his trusty Rickenbacker 325 and McCartney his second Hofner violin bass, the '63 model 500/1. Starr played his Ludwig kit with its newly painted "Ludwig" logo. The exposure on this influential TV programme further solidified the group's grip on Britain. The world beckoned, but for now the next stop was Paris.

Epstein's carefully orchestrated season of 18 days of shows at the Olympia Theatre in Paris began quietly enough but soon turned into a mass frenzy. The run started on January 16th and continued through February 4th. One of the opening acts was French singer Sylvie Vartan – and a member of her backing group was a young British guitarist named Mick Jones, who later found fame in Spooky Tooth and Foreigner. Today, Jones recalls his joy at being on the same bill as The Beatles for the Paris shows. "I was just in seventh heaven. I was still pretty young, around 18, and it was an incredible experience. The first time I saw them they had their Nikon cameras, photographing everything. I couldn't believe I was playing on the same stage with them."

Jones says he would go on with Vartan for their performance, then the curtain would come down and roadie Mal Evans would dash on stage, hastily moving gear. "John would be coming on with his guitar and amp – they were all carrying their own stuff, even though they were already big at this point. When they went on, I watched from the wings. I'd never heard anything like it before."

One night, Jones recalls, the curtain came down and snagged his beloved Gibson SG – a guitar his father was still paying for on hire-purchase. "So I said out loud, 'Oh, fuck!' John came up behind me and said 'Hey, what did you say? Didn't know you were English. We thought you was a frog.'" Lennon asked Jones to come and have a drink with the lads after the show. "Well, I almost fainted," says Jones. "So, I went up and they kind of took me under their wing for the next two or three weeks. I was virtually living with them in the hotel in Paris. We used to go out to clubs, and then they'd sit around and play guitars, just playing music and fooling about. George was definitely more of the guitar aficionado."[1]

It turned out that Jones wasn't the only one having equipment problems at the Olympia shows. On the opening night the group's new Vox amplifiers broke down. A report at the time revealed: "When The Beatles were appearing [in Paris] their amplifiers failed three times, but it wasn't Mal Evans's fault. Mal recalls: 'I've never seen anything like the electrical wiring they had at the back of that theatre. It amazed me that we didn't all go up in smoke in the first five minutes.'"[2]

A further item clarified the position: "Their amps did not break down in Paris. Lots of reports

from Paris stated that The Beatles' amplifiers broke down during their first evening performance at the Olympia. This upset Jennings Musical Instruments who made them especially for The Beatles. Everything turned out right, though. It wasn't the amps at all … the French electricity supply just couldn't take the load of The Beatles' equipment plus lighting and supplying power for French radio engineers to record the show."[3]

The Beatles' fire-power at this point was considerable, certainly by the standards of the day. Lennon and Harrison had their two custom-made Vox AC-50 "small box" amplifiers with matching AC-50 cabinets set on top of a pair of Vox AC-30 stands. One photograph from Paris shows a prototype AC-30 cabinet with a built-in Goodmans Midax horn extending from the back of the cabinet, with the amplifier head placed on the stage floor. McCartney used his new Vox AC-100 bass set-up, through which he played his '63 Hofner 500/1 bass. Harrison played both his second Gretsch Country Gentleman guitar (with dual "flip-up" mutes) and the new Gretsch Tennessean. Lennon relied on his Rickenbacker 325, with Harrison's Gibson J-160E on standby (serving as a replacement for Lennon's own J-160E which, as we've seen, had been stolen in December 1963). Starr, of course, had his trusty Ludwig drum set, with the freshly-painted Ludwig logo clear and bright on the 20-inch bass-drum head.

During the stay in Paris, George Martin and The Beatles managed to squeeze in some sessions at EMI's French recording studio. This was the only time that The Beatles as a group recorded outside of England. There at the Pathe Marconi studios they recorded German-language vocals on to their hit songs 'I Want To Hold Your Hand' and 'She Loves You' for a special release in West Germany. Also recorded at these sessions were the basic tracks for a new Lennon & McCartney song, 'Can't Buy Me Love'.

This 1963 Gretsch Tennessean is similar to the one George acquired during the group's 1963/64 Christmas shows. Like George's, this Tennessean is finished in a deep maroon colour, and has "fake" painted-on f-holes.

WE'VE BEEN PROMISED THE USE OF EVERYTHING WE NEED OVER THERE.

George Harrison, as America gets geared up for the Beatles arrival

Conquering America

While they were in Paris, *Meet The Beatles!*, the group's first album on their new US record label, Capitol, was released on January 20th. It helped boost the already explosive sales of their first single on Capitol, 'I Want To Hold Your Hand', which had come out on December 26th. Indeed the biggest and most exciting news to reach them in Paris was that the single had reached the number one position on the US charts. This was perfect timing for Epstein. The group had apparently said to him that they would not dare go to America unless they had a hit. With the news of the number-one single, everything was in place for The Beatles to play in the United States. Next stop: New York City.

They arrived at New York's John F Kennedy international airport on February 7th and were met by thousands of screaming American fans. Beatlemania had struck in the US. After a brief but chaotic press conference at the airport, the group set up camp at the Plaza hotel in Manhattan. There were countless interviews with press and radio. It seemed that everybody in the media wanted a piece of The Beatles, and Epstein did his best to please everyone. It was all part of his plan.

On Saturday February 8th at 1.30pm the group began camera rehearsals for their big TV appearance on *The Ed Sullivan Show*. Harrison was ill and did not attend, so road manager Neil Aspinall acted as a stand-in, Gretsch guitar and all. Lennon played his '58 Rickenbacker 325 and McCartney his '63 Hofner bass, while Aspinall simply stood holding Harrison's Gretsch Country Gent.

If the static Aspinall wasn't odd enough, photographs taken during the *Ed Sullivan* rehearsals reveal that Starr was playing a white-pearl coloured Ludwig drum set rather than his regular kit, with no Beatles logo on the front of the drum head. Danny Burgauer, former head of the drum department at Manny's music store in Manhattan, explains that they had been asked to supply the group with a Ludwig set for the show. Burgauer recalls: "Ringo didn't like the colour of the original one we supplied, so we had to send over another kit with the colour he normally used. Later they came to the store and we changed the hardware, and Ringo got some cymbals."[4]

In an interview with Harrison by British reporter June Harris on February 6th – the day before they left for America – Harris asked, "Will you have any baggage problems?" Harrison replied, "Not as far as our equipment is concerned … Ringo's not taking his drum kit. We've been

George frequently used his Tennessean throughout 1964 and 1965. The picture below shows him with the guitar recording 'Baby's In Black' at Abbey Road studio 2 on August 11th 1964.

Right: Ringo playing his second Ludwig 20-inch-bass kit at the group's first live US concert, in Washington DC on February 11th 1964. Ringo had a series of seven distinctly different Beatles "drop-T" drum-head logos between 1963 and 1969. The drum head here is number two, featuring the heaviest and most prominent lettering.

Roy Morris of UK instrument distributor Rose-Morris alerts Rickenbacker's Francis Hall to The Beatles in this November 1963 letter (above). The tip would prove to be of great importance to the California guitar maker.

Rickenbacker met with Brian Epstein and The Beatles early in 1964 (hotel message, above).

promised the use of everything we need over there."[5] Starr did indeed leave most of his drum set at home and, as we've just seen, acquired a new one while in New York. He did, however, bring from London his own Ludwig snare drum, his cymbals, and a new freshly-painted Beatles drop-T logo drum-head. (We'll call this "number two" logo head – and each subsequent new logo head will be numbered accordingly.) Photos from the appearance confirm what Starr brought with him: his new Ludwig 20-inch kit reveals fresh heads on the tom toms but a well-worn snare-drum head, and the cymbals too are clearly not new.

The group had no choice but to take their new Vox amplification to the States. Dick Denney of Vox says that the group had been given the first AC-50s the company made, and these were not yet available in the US. A news item in an American music trade magazine provided more detail. "The Beatles ... brought with them not only the famous haircuts but £1,000-worth of British-made equipment. The four Liverpool boys, creators of the famous Mersey Sound, insist on taking their Vox amplifiers with them on every tour. The extra-powerful amps they are using now were specially created for The Beatles by Jennings Musical Industries Ltd of Dartford, Kent, England. The extra power was really necessary to make 'I Want to Hold Your Hand' heard above the screaming of the teenage fans, a spokesman said. At the moment The Beatles are using two AC-50 amps driving a Vox Super-Twin loudspeaker, and a 100-watt amp driving a [bass cabinet]."[6]

No to Rickenbacker amps... yes to their 12-strings

Prior to the group's arrival in the US, Capitol Records had orchestrated a large press campaign and media blitz to prime America for their coming. One shrewd businessman who saw an opportunity in the Beatle invasion was Francis Hall, then owner and president of the Rickenbacker guitar company.

Hall believes it was Harold Buckner, one of the company's sales representatives, who'd reported to him about a popular British band that would be coming to the States. Roy Morris of the Rose-Morris musical instrument distribution company in London was also among the first to alert Hall to The Beatles. A letter still in the Rickenbacker archive, dated November 15th 1963 and from Morris to Hall, includes a newspaper clipping of a picture of The Beatles. Morris, who was angling for UK distribution of Rickenbacker, writes: "Here's a better illustration – this shows both the Rickenbackers used by the group I mentioned to you. We'll need samples of both these models, please." The clipping shows Lennon and his '58 325 and Harrison with his 425.

Another letter from Morris to Hall several weeks later – dated December 23rd 1963 – gives more detail. Morris urges, "We think that it would be an excellent idea if you, as the manufacturer of Rickenbacker guitars, were to contact The Beatles' manager and offer them a certain amount of American publicity on their forthcoming visit to the States. If you address your letter to: Mr Bryan [sic] Epstein, Nems Enterprises, 24 Moorfield, Liverpool 2, England, you will reach their manager, who is, I believe, a very charming fellow."

So Hall tracked down Epstein well in advance of The Beatles landing in the US and was able to set up a meeting with them in New York City. In a letter from Hall to Epstein dated January 7th, he says: "Enclosed with this letter, please find a copy of Rickenbacker's amplifier brochure. We would like to recommend Rickenbacker's model B-16 for the amplification of your bass guitar. For the electric guitars, we recommend two Rickenbacker model B-22D stacked-deck amplifiers. The three amplifiers will give you ample amplification for any size auditorium. Our company will loan, without charge, these amplifiers to you not only for the *Ed Sullivan Show*, but also for all of your other appearances and record sessions while you are in the United States. The amplifiers will be available to you at the Hotel Plaza on February 7th. Rickenbacker has just developed a new echo accessory unit using a patented static electricity principle. We will have one for the boys to try out." Luckily for Jennings, however, Epstein's gentleman's agreement held and the group would stay loyal to Vox amplification.

Francis Hall was clearly aware of the importance of the scheduled meeting with The Beatles, and wrote to his salesman Harold Buckner: "I have a definite date to talk to The Beatles in New York; however, *please* do not mention this to a soul as I do not want our competition to know I will be in New York while they are there."

After the *Ed Sullivan* rehearsals on the 8th, the group and Epstein headed for The Savoy Hilton to meet Hall. The time of the meeting had been pre-arranged by Epstein, who left a message at the

desk: "Will be here to see you with the boys between 4:00 and 4:30pm today – Brian Epstein."

Hall had taken a suite at the Savoy and set up a display of guitars to show to The Beatles. He'd asked New York-based Belgian harmonica player and guitarist Toots Thielemans to be at the meeting to demonstrate the equipment. Thielemans remembers well the events of that day. "Hall wanted me to show them the guitars – but they didn't need anyone to play the guitars, of course. So I went to say hello to them, and when John Lennon saw me he said, 'Oh, you're the guy.' He said that he'd bought his original guitar after seeing a photograph of me using my Rickenbacker with the George Shearing Quintet on a live album made in 1955 or so. That must have impressed him, because he then said to me in a thick Liverpool accent, 'If it's good enough for George Shearing, it's bloody good enough for me.'"[7]

Hall brought along the company's new electric 12-string model. "We'd just developed that," he says. "We had it on display for The Beatles along with another six-string guitar. We may have brought a left-handed bass along, too, but I don't recall. George was sick so he didn't come over. John Lennon played the 12-string and he said, 'You know, I'd like for George to see this instrument. Would you mind going over with us and letting him play it?'

"So we all walked across the park together, and there was George in bed listening to the radio. I unpacked the 12-string and he fingered it for a while. Pretty soon the phone rang, and it was a radio station. They said they'd heard he wasn't feeling well and asked him what he was doing. He said, 'I'm fingering

NOW, A NEW DIMENSION IN SOUND!

TWELVE STRINGS

Rickenbacker

George's 1963 Rickenbacker 360-12 12-string guitar. Described in the press at the time as "the beat boys' secret weapon", the electric 12-string guitar's chiming sound became an important part of many Beatle records, which influenced countless other bands and helped shape the sound of the 1960s. George still owns the guitar today.

TOM SPRINGFIELD HAD A BIG 12-STRING GUITAR ... I SAT IN THE DRESSING ROOM ALL AFTERNOON PLAYING IT. WHAT A SOUND...!

George Harrison, on his first encounter with a 12-string, in 1963

a Rickenbacker 12-string guitar.' They asked if he liked it, and he said it was great. So the station asked if they bought it for him, would he play it? And he said, 'Sure I would.' So that's how he got that guitar."[8]

However, Hall's son John points out that it was Rickenbacker who gave Harrison this first 12-string, and that a radio station in fact paid for a second Rickenbacker 12-string that the guitarist acquired in 1965.[9] The origin of the 1964 radio-station story may lie with Harrison's sister Louise who, still resident in the US, had come to New York to see her brother. She recalls that on the evening of Saturday 8th, with Harrison still in bed with flu, there were a number of people outside his room from a radio station, possibly WMCA. They told her that they'd been inundated with mail after a Beatles contest, and invited her to the station to see it.

"The next thing I knew I was on the air talking to the DJ," recalls Louise Harrison. "They were saying: keep her going, keep her going – forget all the commercials, forget the station breaks, forget everything – everybody is listening to this station!" Then came the inevitable question: could she get her brother on the phone? "I said that probably I ought to check and see how he is anyway. So I called the hotel and he was there playing with his 12-string Rickenbacker. They asked how it was, and I think he sang a little and did a few notes on the guitar over the air. Then for the whole weekend these people would play that every hour on the hour. Brian got very annoyed with me because I'd messed up the exclusive deal he'd made with that DJ called Murray The K. So I'd kind of put both my feet and my arms and my legs in it all at the one go."[10]

George Harrison has said he immediately took to the Rickenbacker 12-string guitar. "Straight away I liked that you knew exactly which string was which. [On some] 12-strings you spend hours trying to tune it, and you're turning the wrong [tuner, because] there's so many of them."[11] But Harrison's apparently instant love for the 12-string may have had earlier origins. He'd first tried out an acoustic 12-string guitar back in the early part of 1963. In an interview in a British music paper at the time he explained: "When we were at the Albert Hall ... Tom Springfield [of The Springfields] had a big 12-string guitar which he'd had made for him – in Liverpool, strangely enough. I asked if I could have a go, and borrowed it, and sat in the dressing room all the afternoon playing it. What a sound on it!"[12]

Anyone who owns a Rickenbacker 12-string knows how time-consuming it can be to change the strings. Pictured here, George makes his way through a Rick string-change while his second Country Gent waits nearby.

1964

IF IT'S GOOD ENOUGH FOR GEORGE SHEARING, IT'S BLOODY GOOD ENOUGH FOR ME.

John Lennon,

on meeting the guitarist who inspired

him to buy his first Rickenbacker

The Rickenbacker model 360-12 guitar that Harrison acquired was one of the first electric 12-strings Rickenbacker had made. Its headstock boasted one of the guitar's cleverest features: to accommodate 12 tuners, Rickenbacker had devised a way to combine classical-guitar style "slotted" fittings alongside traditional electric-guitar type mountings, alternating the position of each tuning peg. This unique design meant the headstock was not unduly elongated, even if it did give this part of the instrument an unorthodox look.

Twelve-string guitars have the six strings of a standard guitar doubled to make six close-together pairs of strings, the extra set of strings an octave above the originals (except for the first two, which are doubled in unison). The result is a big, ringing sound, almost as if two guitars are being played at once. Harrison's 12-string was the first that Rickenbacker made with non-traditional stringing, reversing the regular arrangement so that the player would hit the lower-pitched string of the pair before the octave string. Rickenbacker still employs this method today. Harrison's 360-12 came equipped with both mono and stereo ("Rick-O-Sound") outputs mounted on a chrome plate located on the side of the guitar. This plate also bears the guitar's serial number, CM107, which dates its manufacture to December 1963. Harrison still owns the instrument today.

In some ways his Rickenbacker 360-12 guitar could be considered a prototype. It was not yet a proven product in the Rickenbacker guitar line – and in fact only a handful of small US makers had already tried to market an electric 12-string guitar. Had it not been for Hall's insight and faith in the guitar the Rickenbacker boss may not have even brought the 360-12 to show to the group. Like Lennon's original 325, the 360-12 could easily have become a forgotten and unpopular model. But as Hall would soon discover, that was not to be the case. These two Rickenbacker models went from almost certain obscurity to virtually instant fame, and all because of The Beatles. The 325 and the 360-12 became two of the most in-demand models in the company's line, and Rickenbacker was to be one of the hottest guitar brands of the 1960s, selling thousands of instruments beyond any dreams they might have had in February 1964. When the 360-12 went into general production during 1964 it retailed for $550 (about £200 then; around $3,120 or £2,200 in today's money).

The Rickenbacker 12-string would soon become an important part of The Beatles' sound, influencing a generation of bands who would seek out similar Rickenbackers to emulate the sound heard on Beatle records. Most music historians agree that the unique, chiming, bell-like tone of the Rickenbacker 12-string became not only a Beatles signature but a sound virtually synonymous with 1960s pop music.

Along with the Rickenbacker 12-string guitar, Francis Hall also brought over a Rickenbacker amplifier to the Plaza hotel where the group were staying. Photographs of Harrison trying out the 12-string while still in bed reveal a silver-coloured Rickenbacker "piggy-back"-style amplifier – a rare model that never went into general production. Though Harrison clearly tried the 12-string through the amp, The Beatles never officially used any Rickenbacker amplifiers.

More Rickenbackers

The other Rickenbacker six-string guitar that Hall recalls taking to New York was a model 365, also manufactured in December 1963. The guitar was evidently passed over by The Beatles, but would turn up again at a later date. Another musician whom Hall had arranged to be at the Savoy demonstration was a guitar teacher, Tony Saks. It was Saks who purchased the 365 six-string. Later he wrote to Epstein's personal assistant Derek Taylor in London to arrange to have the guitar autographed the next time the group were in the US.

A meeting was eventually arranged during their later 1964 American tour, on September 13th at a Holiday Inn in Baltimore, Maryland. Saks took his Rickenbacker 365 to the hotel, with gold foil signature tape applied to the guitar where he wanted the autographs. "The Beatles (all four of them) were kind enough to autograph the guitar," ran a magazine report at the time. "It was done by writing on gold leaf, removing the sheets after the impression, and then lacquering over the handwriting. Possibly this guitar, the only one of its kind that Tony knows of, will some day have historical or monetary value. Up to now it has been a conversation piece, and an added attraction at Tony's guitar studios."[13] Saks's intuition did indeed prove sound; his Rickenbacker 365, autographed by all four Beatles, recently sold at auction in Tokyo for a considerable sum.

The Rickenbacker 4001 bass that Hall brought to the Savoy hotel in February 1964 was specially built left-handed for McCartney. The intention was to present it to him at that meeting. The bass has serial number DA23, which indicates it was manufactured in January 1964. A letter from Hall to Epstein dated May 23rd 1964 reads: "We have a left-handed electric solidbody Rickenbacker bass similar to the one Paul tried while he was in New York City. If he would rather use a Rickenbacker bass than the one he has been using, our company would be willing to send one to him free of charge, or he may prefer to try this instrument again while he is in the United States." Recently, McCartney confirmed that he saw the Rickenbacker bass in New York for the first time in 1964.[14] For some reason, though, McCartney refused to take the bass from Rickenbacker, only to accept it later (in the summer of 1965).

While it is widely believed that Lennon too received a new guitar at the Rickenbacker meeting in New York, documents from the company's archives show that Lennon's new model 325 guitar, intended to replace his original, was not present then. In fact it was shipped from the Rickenbacker factory in California on February 13th to Lennon at the Deauville hotel at Miami Beach, Florida, as the group prepared for a further *Ed Sullivan* appearance. The new-style Rickenbacker 325 must have been intended for the New York gathering, but presumably was not ready in time.

The final arrangements made between Rickenbacker and The Beatles on February 8th consisted of a request by Lennon for a custom-made 12-string 325 model that would match his 325 six-string. Epstein also asked for an additional 360-12 12-string guitar to be made and sent to England for another of his artists, Gerry Marsden of Gerry & The Pacemakers.

Enthralling the States – the first *Ed Sullivan* TV show

The next day, February 9th, saw the main event of the US visit – and it turned out to be a milestone in the history of television and music. The Beatles were to perform on *The Ed Sullivan Show*. That Sunday morning more rehearsals took place at CBS's Studio 50 in Manhattan. Harrison was now feeling better and participated. Starr rehearsed on his new oyster black pearl-coloured Ludwig drum set – although for the moment it was without "The Beatles" on the front drum-head.

In the afternoon they taped a live performance – 'Twist And Shout', 'Please Please Me' and 'I Want To Hold Your Hand' – for later broadcast on the February 23rd *Ed Sullivan Show*. For this, the same stage set was used as in rehearsals, but Starr's kit had The Beatles drop-T logo in place. This was number-two Beatles-logo head, similar to the first but with larger, thicker, bolder lettering and a larger Ludwig logo. It was painted on to a 20-inch Remo Weather King drum-head, identified by the Weather King "crown" badge at the top.

At 8pm Eastern Standard Time, The Beatles made their live debut on American national television before an estimated 73 million people. This single television appearance mesmerised an entire generation. How many future musicians' dreams began that day? How many kids were inspired to form bands and be like The Beatles? Virtually every famous American rock musician of the following 25 years would say: "When I saw The Beatles on *Ed Sullivan* it changed my life."

For the most important single performance in the group's career – they played 'All My Loving', 'Till There Was You', 'She Loves You', 'I Saw Her Standing There' and 'I Want To Hold Your Hand' – Harrison used his dark-brown Gretsch Country Gentleman guitar (the second one, with dual "flip up" mutes), Lennon played his '58 black-painted Rickenbacker 325 guitar, and McCartney his '63 sunburst Hofner 500/1 bass. Starr played his oyster black pearl-coloured drum set, its Ludwig logo almost as bold and visible as the group's own.

This instrumental line-up would become America's first impression of The Beatles, an image permanently etched on the minds of US Sixties youth. The instruments that they used that night on TV instantly became known as "Beatle instruments" and provided a shopping list for every aspiring group, thousands of which sprang up in the days and weeks following the *Ed Sullivan* broadcast. Gretsch, Hofner, Rickenbacker and Ludwig could not have asked for a better advertising campaign, nor could they have imagined what the future held. Every music store throughout the US was soon clamouring for these Beatle instruments. The demand was far greater than the supply. It was every manufacturer's dream.

William Ludwig Jr, then president of the Ludwig drum company, felt the impact created by Starr's choice. "That was the first time I ever saw my name on TV," he laughs. "There I was sitting watching *The Ed Sullivan Show* and I see my name on the front of the drum-head. Yeah! It was also

This January 1964 Rickenbacker document lists Paul's left-handed bass (serial DA23) as a special "verbal" order, and calls it a "4000 + 1 pickup". (Rickenbacker's parent company was called Radio & Television Equipment Co at the time.)

The Beatles' most influential performance was on The Ed Sullivan Show in February 1964 (right). The appearance on CBS television was watched by more than 70 million people, instantly launching Beatlemania in the United States and creating an unforgettable image in the minds of thousands of musicians-to-be.

Pictured below is the number-two Beatles drop-T logo drum-head – the one used for The Ed Sullivan Show – as it appears today.

the first time I'd seen The Beatles and the first time I was aware of Ringo using Ludwig drums. Our company was besieged with calls the next day with people looking to order that Ludwig drum set. Well, we got after the suppliers and put on a second shift, a night shift till 1am. All day, every night, six days a week, including Saturday, we got geared up to make 100 sets a day – and we still had nine months' backlog. We had 85,000 on back order. And they were all ordering it with the Ludwig logo on the front head.

"We were riding on the coat tails of a good thing. But I thought to myself, this is ironic. I spent my earliest years with the company chasing drummers day and night. I'd be in the deep nightlife, smoking and drinking like fury as I waited for a drummer to take a break. While I'm begging them to take a free set to get my drums out-front, Bud Slingerland is down at the other end of the bar, doing the same thing. I'd go on the road, calling up the dealers, and I'd hit the joints and try to get Gene Krupa away from Slingerland. It was a battle. Then, Ringo just fell into my lap – and I didn't even know him. It was amazing, this wonderful thing from heaven that fell into our laps without trying. It'll never happen again."[15]

A news item in a music trade magazine headed "Beatle George Harrison Rocks Nation on Gretsch" provided another indication of the way the group's instrumental choices immediately affected the lucky manufacturers. "The recent appearance of The Beatles, England's famous rock-and-roll group, on American television screens, revealed the fact that one of them, George Harrison, who plays lead guitar in the combo, uses a Gretsch instrument. In fact, the name Gretsch was clearly visible when close-ups were flashed on the screen during *The Ed Sullivan Show* on three separate Sunday evenings.

"Says a spokesman for the Fred Gretsch Manufacturing Company: 'Have you any idea what this has done for the Gretsch image? It has made Gretsch one of the most desired guitars in America. This is what we in the business consider to be "beautiful timing". Product associations such as this are rare, but when they do occur they can do more for the product than millions of dollars of paid advertising. The Beatles inadvertent "selling" of the Gretsch guitar should mean millions of dollars in sales for music merchants handling this line,' he continued, adding: 'Just think what effect you can make on your customers when you show them a Gretsch guitar and mention, incidentally, this is the kind of guitar that one of The Beatles plays.'"[16]

Vox fared least well from the broadcast itself. Though the group did use their Vox gear for the Sullivan show, the amps did not appear on screen. They were concealed to the right and left sides of the stage, facing inward, as photographs taken during dress rehearsals reveal. But despite missing out visually, Vox too would soon enjoy massive popularity thanks to their Beatles association.

First American concert

After the TV success, the group travelled by train to Washington DC for their first US concert, on February 11th at the Washington Coliseum, where they played in the round. It seems laughable now, but at several points during the set Starr was forced between songs to spin his drum set on the pedestal to different sides of the audience in order to give everyone an equal view of The Beatles.

This first American Beatles concert also provided the nation's introduction to Vox amplifiers. To their fans the group themselves were a phenomenon – but they had brought with them these new never-before-seen Vox amplifiers, made in Britain. At the time, Gibson and Fender guitars and amps were the standards among most professional American musicians, and the "big two" brands dominated the market. But here were The Beatles presenting an excitingly different range of equipment. With Beatlemania came completely new choices for musical gear. Because of The Beatles, America's hopeful teen musicians would want Rickenbacker, Gretsch and Hofner guitars, Ludwig drums, and Vox amps. These instruments and amplifiers would become as strong a part of Beatle identity as the group's mop-top hairstyles.

A good number of American Beatle fans were fascinated by the very Britishness of The Beatles' music and image. So naturally many of them assumed that Rickenbacker, Gretsch and Ludwig were made in Europe, just like Vox and Hofner. John Hall, now head of Rickenbacker, says: "We used to get all kinds of letters that were addressed, believe it or not, to 'Rickenbacker, Liverpool, England'.

The Beatles live at the Washington Coliseum, with Beatlemania in full swing and the stage strewn with jelly babies. It was the American audience's introduction to Vox amps: John and George have an AC-50 each, and Paul uses an AC-100 bass rig – a mere 200 watts of power to fill a vast arena full of screaming fans!

And they got to us! I still wonder who figured that out. Yes, many people thought we were British … but I think even more thought we were German."[17]

The equipment used during the Washington performance was the same as that used for their earlier Paris shows. There were two Vox AC-50 "small box" amps with matching AC-50 speaker cabinets on AC-30 amp stands, a Vox AC-100 bass head with 2x15 AC-100 bass speaker cabinet, the second 20-inch-bass Ludwig drum set with number-two Beatles logo, the Gretsch Country Gentleman guitar, the '63 Hofner 500/1 bass, and Lennon's original '58 Rickenbacker 325. Harrison also had his Gretsch Tennessean on hand as a spare.

The following day the group travelled by train back to New York City for two shows at the prestigious Carnegie Hall. Tickets were oversold for the theatre and some of the audience ended up sitting on stage behind the group. Fans would never get this close to The Beatles again. The equipment used at Carnegie Hall was the same as in Washington, although photographs from this performance reveal that McCartney's original '61 Hofner bass was present as a spare. After the two Carnegie Hall shows, they flew to Miami Beach, Florida, where they stayed at the Deauville Hotel. It was from this location that they would make their second live appearance on *The Ed Sullivan Show*.

John's second Rickenbacker 325

On Friday February 14th and Saturday 15th the group spent time relaxing, enjoying the fine weather in Miami and rehearsing for their upcoming TV show. Photographs taken during the first day of the rehearsals in a meeting hall at the Deauville Hotel reveal Harrison using his new Rickenbacker 12-string guitar. McCartney has his '63 Hofner bass and Starr the Ludwig set. Lennon plays the original '58 Rick 325, but it was at the Deauville that he took delivery of his new Rickenbacker guitar. According to the original receipt in the Rickenbacker archive, the new black model 325 guitar was sent directly to the hotel from the guitar-maker's factory in California. The following day's rehearsals on the set of *The Ed Sullivan Show* marked the first time that Lennon played his new Rickenbacker 325 guitar with the group.

The short-scale guitar was similar to Lennon's first 325, but with a thinner body, a five-control layout with extra "balance" knob mounted on a white two-layer pickguard, and a new-design Rickenbacker Ac'cent vibrato unit. The headstock on the '64 Rick 325 was slightly smaller than the earlier guitar, with a white Rickenbacker nameplate. The black finish was officially called jetglo by Rickenbacker. Contrary to popular belief, this second Rickenbacker 325 of Lennon's was not manufactured in 1963 but in February 1964, as indicated by its serial number DB122. If Lennon had bought the 325 in a store it would have cost him $399.50 (about £145 then; around $2,265 or £1,600 in today's money).

Francis Hall had obviously planned for this second 325 to be made and given to Lennon as a better replacement for his road-weary '58 325. Fortunately for Rickenbacker, the new guitar had been manufactured and delivered just in time for another important TV appearance. It was first used publicly on The Beatles' second *Ed Sullivan Show*, broadcast live from Miami. This marked one of Hall's finest marketing achievements.

So it was that on Sunday February 16th the group made their second live appearance on American TV. Across the nation an estimated 70 million viewers tuned in to the show. The Beatles performed 'She Loves You', 'This Boy', 'All My Loving', 'I Saw Her Standing There', 'From Me To You' and their hit, 'I Want To Hold Your Hand'. Guitars used were the '63 Hofner 500/1 bass, the second Gretsch Country Gentleman and the new '64 Rickenbacker 325. Starr performed on his already famous oyster black pearl Ludwig drum set. The Vox amplifiers were again set off to the sides of the stage. Many a music retailer and manufacturer had Sullivan and the boys from Liverpool to thank for a very good season as crowds of teenagers rushed to buy Gretsch and Rickenbacker guitars, Hofner "Beatle" basses and Ludwig drum sets. Gretsch, Ludwig and Rickenbacker greatly expanded operations. It was the dawn of a golden age for garage bands.

Fred Gretsch, current owner of Fred Gretsch Enterprises, was a teenager at the time, working for his uncle who ran the Gretsch operation. "There's no question that George Harrison's use of the Gretsch Country Gentleman and Tennessean affected sales. Everybody was aware of that. I used to drive the delivery truck and when we'd go over to 48th Street in New York to deliver to Manny's store, it was The Beatles that everybody was talking about. The Country Gentleman was our number-one selling guitar. On 48th Street we were delivering them six at a time, and they still wanted more. We had thousands of back orders. The demand far exceeded what we could supply."[18]

Virtually overnight Gretsch, Rickenbacker and Ludwig tried to increase production to meet the demand, while in Germany Hofner worked to set up US distribution. Calls and telegrams started to pour in to Jennings Musical Industries back in England requesting the Vox "Beatles" amplifiers. Tom Jennings too was keen to establish an American agent.

Whatever happened to John's first Rickenbacker?

As soon as he got his new '64 Rickenbacker 325, Lennon retired his original '58 model and never used it on-stage again. Instead he played the new Rickenbacker as his main electric guitar almost exclusively through to the end of 1965 – when it too would be retired. This second Rick 325 would appear with Lennon in Beatle films, for live performances and on Beatle records, becoming a memorable part of his classic Beatlemania image.

The '58 Rickenbacker 325 was left unplayed and unmodified until the 1970s when Lennon decided to have it refurbished and put back to its original natural finish. The job fell to New York guitar repairer Ron DeMarino, who had recently supplied an old amp and a guitar to Lennon. When he received the 325 from Lennon it still had its 1962 black refinish. "It had been painted black with a brushed-on finish," says DeMarino. "It was not a professional job, and had a lot of brush-marks. I found out by working on his instruments that John messed around with his guitars a lot. He didn't know much about guitars. For instance, he wanted one with 'humberdinker' pickups in it. Obviously he was referring to humbucker pickups, but he didn't know. He would say, 'I'm a rhythmer, I don't know nothing about these things, I'm a rhythmer.'"

DeMarino says the 325 was in a pretty poor state, and looked like it had not been played for a long time. Some strings were missing and those that remained were a mix of roundwound and flatwound types. The repairer also reports that the guitar's wiring was "messed up". He asked Lennon what he wanted done, and was told to "do it brown". So DeMarino refinished the guitar to a honey-coloured natural wood.

"It had the original gold pickguard," he says, "which appeared to have a line crack in it, so I made a new pickguard. I did a gold one, but then we were referring to pictures of him playing the second Rickenbacker with the white pickguard. I think that's why we made a decision to use a white pickguard. He was adamant about the colour, which I did, and as it turned out John was very, very

THERE'S NO QUESTION THAT GEORGE HARRISON'S USE OF THE GRETSCH COUNTRY GENTLEMAN AND TENNESSEAN AFFECTED SALES ... THE DEMAND FAR EXCEEDED WHAT WE COULD SUPPLY.

Fred Gretsch

Rickenbacker's shipping document for John's '64 model 325 guitar, sent direct to Miami where the group were shooting another Ed Sullivan TV show. Rickenbacker were clearly in a hurry: the serial number is wrongly noted as BD122, instead of DB122.

satisfied with it. I asked him if I could keep the old pickguard and he agreed. I also have the original open-back Grover tuners from that guitar."[19] This is how Lennon's '58 Rickenbacker 325 has come to exist today with a natural finish, a white pickguard, and a newer set of Grover Sta-Tite tuners. All the other parts are original. Yoko Ono now owns both of Lennon's Rickenbacker 325 six-string guitars.

Meanwhile in 1964, The Beatles returned to England on Saturday February 22nd and were treated to a heroes' welcome by large crowds at London airport. The Jennings company devised their own form of welcome, with a Vox promotional campaign: "Vox! went The Beatles USA," proclaimed the ads. "Congratulations, Beatles, on your overwhelming success in the United States ... and thanks for phoning your appreciation of the new Vox amps featured in your fine performances. The Beatles, like Britain's other top radio, TV and recording stars, feature Vox Sound Equipment." This was a dramatic turnaround from just over a year earlier when The Beatles had failed to appear at all in a Vox ad featuring 20 of Jennings's most important amplifier-using artists.

After being home for just a couple of days, the group found themselves at Abbey Road studio 2 on Tuesday February 25th, Harrison's 21st birthday. The Beatles started the session by recording 'You Can't Do That' for a b-side to their forthcoming single, 'Can't Buy Me Love'. Harrison's new Rickenbacker 12-string guitar was used for the first time on this track, and Lennon introduced his new 325 to Abbey Road by way of a spirited lead break. McCartney later overdubbed a cowbell and Starr added a conga drum.

On the same day they recorded 'I Should Have Known Better', with Lennon on harmonica and Harrison once again gracing the song with his new Rickenbacker 12-string. 'And I Love Her', another new Beatles original, was also cut for the first time, this preliminary take recorded with a 12-string lead. It was apparent that The Beatles were trying to use the glorious new sound of the Rickenbacker 12-string wherever it would fit.

The group used virtually the same equipment at this session as they'd employed on *The Ed*

John's 1964 Rickenbacker 325. Made specifically for John by Rickenbacker to replace his original road-weary 1958 325, this one became his favourite stage and studio guitar through 1964 and 1965. The instrument – with a Beatles 1965 set-list (below) still attached – is owned by Yoko Ono. The detail (right) reveals the poor repair made to the neck crack that the guitar received during the Christmas '64 UK shows.

A 1970s snapshot taken in the workshop of Ron DeMarino showing John's battered 1958 Rickenbacker 325 just before it was returned from black to its original natural finish.

Sullivan Show in Miami: two Vox AC-50 guitar amps and an AC-100 bass amp, Lennon's new Rickenbacker 325, McCartney's '63 Hofner bass, the Gibson J-160E, and Starr's Ludwig kit. Harrison of course used his new Rickenbacker 12-string, and Starr had some extra Ludwig drums on hand thanks to the second kit he'd acquired in the US. He now had a pair of matching Ludwig black oyster pearl kits, each with a smaller-size 20-inch bass drum.

Ringo tries Turkish, George goes classical

Gerry Evans, manager of London's Drum City store at the time, says that when Starr returned from the first American trip the drummer brought with him a 20-inch Zildjian cymbal he'd acquired at Manny's store in New York. Earlier, Drum City had supplied Starr with Swiss-made Paiste cymbals, but now he'd evidently got a taste for Turkish Zildjians.

"Mal Evans used to choose cymbals for Ringo," explains Gerry Evans (no relation). "Ringo never ever chose a cymbal back then. It wasn't because he was superior, it was just that he had no interest. He didn't know what was good or bad or indifferent. All he did was play them. So Mal used to come to our store and make the selections. Over the years the Paistes got replaced by Zildjians. They were more open sounding and somehow louder, where the Paistes had more of a dry, European sound."[20]

The second day's sessions at Abbey Road brought a new feel for the track 'And I Love Her', and a new guitar as well. A more laidback version of the song was recorded, with Starr on bongos and claves instead of the kit. Harrison meanwhile switched from the Rickenbacker 12-string to a José Ramírez classical acoustic guitar, while Lennon used Harrison's Gibson J-160E and McCartney played the '63 Hofner bass.

Harrison had a fond admiration for classical guitar. In an interview published later in 1964 he admitted that one of his big ambitions was to play classical guitar really well. "You really have to learn some intricate finger work," he explained. "Segovia is a person that I admire very much. He gets more feeling out of his guitar than anyone else I've ever heard. He's fantastic. Chet Atkins is another guitarist that I wish I could imitate at times, but once again he's too intricate for me … My trouble is I don't practise enough. It's not that I don't want to, it's just that I can never find the time."[21]

Whether through practice or not, Harrison's successful use of the nylon-strung classical on 'And I Love Her' gave the song an entirely new guitar tone for The Beatles, his melodic lead an impressive highlight. The Spanish-made classical guitar he used was a José Ramírez Guitarra de Estudio. The

The Beatles seen here during rehearsals in Miami for another Ed Sullivan appearance in February 1964. Rickenbacker had just delivered John's new 325 guitar, in time for him to use for this performance.

Ramírez dynasty of guitar-makers had begun with José Ramírez I in Madrid, Spain, in the 1880s; by the time Harrison's guitar was made, José Ramírez III headed the family business. In fact the model name of his guitar indicates a mid-price instrument designed by Ramírez but not built at their own workshops. The guitar had an extended fingerboard for the three treble strings, providing them with an extra fret over the soundhole.

Harrison's Ramírez had most likely been acquired at Ivor Mairants's guitar shop in Rathbone Place, central London. Mairants was one of the only British importers of classical guitars from Spain at the time. It was Mairants, a leading British danceband guitarist and session player, who had helped Boosey & Hawkes devise their Zenith line of guitars back in the 1950s – one of which had been bought then by a young Paul McCartney.

A Hard Day's Night

The Beatles continued their recording sessions at Abbey Road for the next few days. The majority of songs recorded – 'Tell Me Why', 'If I Fell', 'I'm Happy Just To Dance With You', 'I Should Have Known Better' and the re-make of 'And I Love Her' – were aimed for their new project, a major full-length movie, not yet titled. 'Long Tall Sally', not intended for the film, was recorded as the title song for the group's next EP (an "extended-play" 7-inch disc, usually with two songs each side). 'I Call Your Name', originally recorded for the film, also ended up on the E.P.

Harrison's Rickenbacker 12-string was used on the majority of the tracks recorded during all of these sessions. Its unique chiming tone played a big part in keeping The Beatles sonically ahead of the pack. The British musicians' newspaper *Melody Maker* soon dubbed the Rickenbacker 12 as "the beat boys' secret weapon". In the same paper, Harrison was asked about the Rickenbacker. "How do I like it? Marvellous. It's gear. It sounds a bit like an electric piano, I always think, but you get a nice fat sound out of it."[22]

On Monday March 2nd the group started filming for their movie, which would of course become *A Hard Day's Night*. The film's director, Richard Lester, went for a free, spontaneous style, aiming to capture the group's rambunctious spirit and wry humour. The loose plot featured a comical romp through the supposed life of The Beatles. The black-and-white film has since been called revolutionary, with the style becoming widely imitated. It effectively prepared the way for the later rock video and MTV booms.

Throughout the film the group are featured performing various songs, with the equipment they used in these sequences the same as for the recent recordings at Abbey Road: '63 Hofner bass, '64 Rickenbacker 325 and new Rick 12-string, played through the Vox AC-50s and AC-100 amps. Starr used his newer Ludwig oyster black pearl kit, with an added Rogers Swiv-O-Matic tom tom holder instead of the stock Ludwig tom mount. There was also a new front drum-head with a further slightly different Beatles logo. This number-three drum-head logo was painted on a 20-inch Ludwig head with the identifying Weather Master emblem at the bottom. One of the major differences compared to earlier Beatles heads comes in the unique lettering of the Ludwig logo, its script-style L extending well below the D.

Gerry Evans was manager of the Drum City store in London who were responsible for producing the heads. He recalls that a number of other heads were made beyond those for Starr's kit. "There would be promotions where they wanted a drum-head for the launch of a film. They'd put a drum-head in the foyer of a cinema, for example. And then a record shop would want one too, and then Madame Tussaud's waxworks in London wanted one for their Beatles kit. From our point of view it was promotion for Ludwig. I think we used to do it for free. So over the years Eddie Stokes painted many extra heads. I don't know how many exactly, but it must have been at least six for special things. All the heads for Ringo's kits were Ludwig Weather Masters, but often we'd put the logo on a Remo head. We figured as it was only a front head it could be a cheaper one."[23]

The filming took up all of March and a good part of April. It was not until April 16th that the group recorded the main song after Starr came up with the film's definitive title, *A Hard Day's Night*. The Rickenbacker 12-string once again played a big part in the sound of the song, notably the famous opening chord and the central lead break.

A highlight of the film came with the various mock rehearsals where the group performed on the sound stage of a supposed television studio set, and an in-depth view of The Beatles' equipment

occurs during their performance of 'If I Fell'. The scene opens with Starr setting up his Ludwig drum kit as Lennon breaks into the song using Harrison's Gibson J-160E. McCartney is playing his '63 Hofner bass while Harrison uses the Rickenbacker 12-string. During the song's performance, various stage-hands set up the group's Vox AC-50 amps.

Later, a moodier stage set provides a backdrop for the performance of 'And I Love Her' which features Lennon using the J-160E, McCartney on Hofner bass, Starr playing bongos and Harrison with his Ramírez classical guitar. During the solo the camera zooms in so close that the alert guitar fan can almost read the label inside the Ramírez's soundhole!

Harrison is featured singing 'I'm Happy Just To Dance With You' in the next clip, playing his Gibson J-160E. McCartney uses the Hofner and Starr is on the Ludwig set, while Lennon has his new '64 Rickenbacker 325. Throughout the film Richard Lester's camera direction highlights the group's instruments – whether intentionally or otherwise. Many of the film's camera angles and shots offer close-ups and detailed views of gear that would soon be considered by fans virtually as extensions of The Beatles' own personalities.

The film's finale features the memorable "live TV broadcast" scenes. Filmed at the Scala Theatre

George plays his Ramirez classical guitar during a break in the filming of A Hard Day's Night.

in London, these performances freeze in time the essential aura, excitement and innocence that was Beatlemania. Here preserved on film is the classic image of the four Beatles with their individual instruments – Harrison and Rickenbacker 12-string, Lennon and Rickenbacker 325, McCartney and Hofner violin bass, Starr and Ludwig drums. It was an image that changed popular music forever.

With the film's release in August, thousands of potential young musicians could watch The Beatles' every move and study the group's instruments. Many of them would later carve their own niche in rock'n'roll history. Hundreds of now-famous rock legends cite *A Hard Day's Night* as their inspiration to go out and play their own music. Harrison's use of that Rickenbacker 360-12 is a striking example of the profound influence The Beatles had on other musicians. Countless young rockers adopted the 12-string sound as their own, most notably Roger McGuinn of The Byrds – or Jim McGuinn as he was called at the time.

"I was influenced from the very first film clips that Brian Epstein released, the ones in England with the girls screaming," says McGuinn today. "When we saw that, I was convinced that they were something really hot. I was still into folk music at the time, I guess late '63, early '64, and was a Beatles fan. In fact I started doing folk songs with the Beatle beat in Greenwich Village before I came to LA and formed The Byrds. I played a 12-string acoustic then because we came out of folk music. I probably got my first one about '57."

McGuinn says that as The Byrds got together they made a couple of trips to see *A Hard Day's Night*, taking note of the instruments on display. They saw Lennon with a little Rickenbacker 325. "And George had this other guitar that looked like a six-string from the front," says McGuinn. "But when he turned sideways you could see six more pegs sticking out the back. I said ah, that's an electric 12, that's really cool. So I went out and bought one off-the-shelf from a music store in Hollywood – this was early '65. It was brand new and they only had one in stock. It didn't have the 'squared off' body edges like George's, it had rounded edges. I traded in my Gibson acoustic 12 that Bobby Darin had bought me, plus a Vega five-string long-neck Pete Seeger model banjo – which I regret losing now.

"I really got into electric 12-string and started learning how to play it. I used some banjo techniques instead of just flat-picking. George had been mostly flat-picking. I used a combination of flat-pick and finger-picks, kind of a rolling sound that came from my five-string banjo playing – that's where I got that technique. I don't have my original Rickenbacker 12-string any more. Unfortunately it was stolen in 1966 at a Byrds concert at Fordham University."[24]

As McGuinn explains, The Byrds' sound was directly shaped by The Beatles' use of the Rickenbacker 360-12. The Byrds, in turn, influenced countless other bands who would use the Rick 12 at the centre of their own sound. Directly and indirectly, Harrison's use of his Rickenbacker 12-string guitar changed the musical landscape of the 1960s. One of the most striking studio outings for a Rick 12, après Beatles, was Pete Townshend's "chord machine" rhythm parts on The Who's 'I Can't Explain', recorded in January 1965.

The third Hofner bass: a gold-plated caper

It appears that during the spring of 1964 McCartney was presented with his third Hofner violin bass. This particular instrument has become shrouded with much speculation and generated many stories. Did McCartney ever actually own or use the bass? Despite the uncertainty, at the heart of this episode are some basic facts worth relating.

McCartney had been using Hofner 500/1 violin basses exclusively throughout the group's rise to fame. With The Beatles' popularity now at its height, Selmer, the British distributor of Hofner, sought to capitalise on this excellent marketing opportunity. They had approached Epstein with a business proposal and received permission to use a "swing-ticket", a small card that could be attached to Hofner instruments in retail stores. It was printed with McCartney's one-liner, "Wishing you every success with this guitar," plus his signature and a picture of the bassist offering an encouraging thumbs-up to the prospective purchaser.

In return, Epstein would receive £5 for every Hofner guitar sold, and McCartney would be presented with a custom-made Hofner bass. Selmer commissioned Hofner to make this custom left-handed Hofner 500/1 bass with gold-plated hardware and a very figured, or patterned, maple back. The one-off bass was without a serial number.

A label of the type seen inside George's Ramirez classical guitar.

RAMIREZ

INSTRUMENTOS
PARA RONDALLA

CONCEPCION JERONIMA Nº 5

MADRID

Tº 227 - 99 - 35

Christian Benker, today managing director of Hofner in Germany, confirms that Hofner made this unique bass for Selmer specifically to be presented to McCartney.[25] Alby Paynter, Selmer's import manager from 1954 to 1967, said that the gold-plated-hardware bass was formally presented to McCartney some time in March or April of 1964.[26] Paynter has said that photos were taken of the presentation to McCartney, one of which was enlarged and placed in the window of Selmer's London shop.[27] Unfortunately, these photographs have never surfaced.

The odd thing about this presentation is that McCartney did not leave with his new Hofner bass. Allegedly, the bass remained with Selmer so that they could exhibit it at the upcoming summer 1964 British music trade show. A musicians' magazine covering the show reported: "Vox demonstrated the 100-watt amplifier specially made for The Beatles in the States. Paul McCartney's specially ordered gold-plated violin bass was on the Selmer stand."[28] There are two further contemporary reports that refer to the bass. In August, a piece about The Beatles' instrumental taste reads: "...but don't expect Paul to change – he's sticking to his famous violin bass. And Selmer recently presented him with another copy of his instrument from the makers in Germany – with gold-plated metal parts!"[29]

The last and most compelling evidence in associating the gold-plated-hardware Hofner bass to McCartney comes in an article published in July 1967 where popular British bass players of the day discuss their personal equipment and instruments. In McCartney's section, he says: "I have had a Hofner violin bass ever since I first started. I've got three or four models but the ancient one is still my favourite. It's seen so much work that some of it is held together with Sellotape. Its pickups are the ones that came on the guitar and I haven't souped any of my basses up. The only difference in any of them can be seen on the one that Selmers had made for me, that has gold pickups."[30]

All that glitters...

Controversy over this gold-hardware bass persists to this day. In 1994, Justin Harrison of Music Ground, a music shop in Doncaster, South Yorkshire, England, which specialises in vintage instruments from the 1960s, was approached by another store, in Biggleswade, Bedfordshire. The store wanted a pickguard for a left-handed Hofner bass. Harrison became interested, because old left-handed Hofner basses are rare and valuable. He asked how much they wanted for the instrument, and was later told £800. Music Ground bought the bass. "We stripped it down and noticed the gold-plated hardware on it," says Harrison.

He rang British guitar expert Paul Day who researched references to the presentation bass story. "Then we took it to Hofner in Germany. They verified it was the one, because it did not have a serial number on it, and had a very, very 'flamed' back on it. Then we contacted Alby Paynter who worked for Selmer, and he too verified the bass is the one."[31]

Realising what they seemed to have stumbled upon, Music Ground proprietor Richard Harrison, knowing the bass's potential value beyond its regular market price of around £4,500, decided to offer the Hofner gold-plated-hardware bass for auction at Sotheby's in September 1994. However, at the time Harrison did not have all the documentation now available on the bass, and it failed to sell at the auction. Music Ground finally turned up more documentation, and again tried to offer the bass for auction, this time through Bonhams. The bass was put up for sale in March 1997 as part of a Bonhams Tokyo event, "The Beatles Auction of the Century". It was during the preparation for this event that the public controversy began.

In a Bonhams catalogue published prior to the Tokyo auction, an exaggerated history was printed, claiming that "McCartney owned and played it from 1964 through to the end of the 1960s".[32] There is in fact no evidence that McCartney ever used the bass in a live performance, in the studio, in a film, or in a television appearance. Indeed, upon hearing of the auction, McCartney himself made it clear in a public statement that he had never owned or used the bass.

McCartney's assertion is corroborated in a remarkable way by one John Bunning. Reading in the *Daily Mail* newspaper that the gold-plated-hardware Hofner was to be offered by Sotheby's in 1994, Bunning remembered a similar bass that he owned when he was in a band in the 1960s. Interviewed today, Bunning, a left-hander, recalls making his first bass himself when a teenager. Gradually he realised he needed a proper instrument, but discovered it was hard to find a left-handed one. He remembered Paul McCartney playing a Hofner violin bass left-handed, and decided to look for one of those. Bunning's local music store, in Luton, Bedfordshire, modified a right-handed Hofner bass,

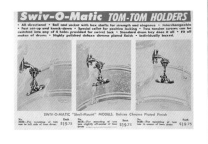

Ringo had a new Rogers Swiv-O-Matic drum-mount system fitted to his Ludwig kits to allow more flexibility when positioning the tom tom. The catalogue illustrates the various types available, and the close-up shows the Swiv-O-Matic on Ringo's second 20-inch-bass drum kit.

The fab four about to be preserved on film in A Hard Day's Night. Paul has his 1963 Hofner violin bass, George is playing the "secret weapon" Rickenbacker 360-12 12-string, and John uses George's Gibson J-160E guitar. Ringo has his second 20-inch-bass Ludwig kit that has a newly painted logo on the bass drum head (number three in the sequence) with its distinctive "L" of Ludwig that extends under the "d". This particular kit was not used much after the filming, as Ringo acquired a new set with a 22-inch bass drum soon afterwards.

SPECIAL PREVIEW • ADMIT ONE

Wed. Aug. 12th at 2:00 p.m.
THE BEATLES
in their First Feature-Length Motion Picture
"A HARD DAY'S NIGHT"
Produced by Walter Shenson/Released Thru United Artists

ALL SEATS $1.00
This Ticket Is Good Only For This Performance
at the
EMBASSY
THEATRE

№ 1378

DO NOT DETACH, Present Entire Ticket To Doorman

THIS TICKET IS GOOD ONLY AT

EMBASSY
THEATRE

All Seats
$1.00

The almost-Beatle Hofner bass. UK Hofner agent Selmer had this guitar made with special gold-plated hardware, with the intention of presenting it to Paul ... who never actually received the bass.

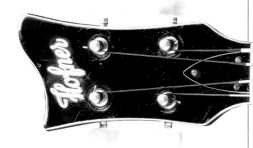

Brian Epstein made a deal with Selmer for a promotional "swing tag" (right) designed to be placed on new Hofner instruments in music stores. An illustration of Paul was accompanied with the line: "Wishing you every success with this guitar."

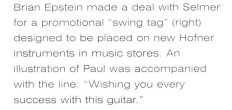

but the results did not please the bassist and he did not buy the instrument.

"About a week later the shop rang back to say they could get a left-handed Hofner bass but it would take two months to come," says Bunning, recalling events around April 1965. "So a couple of months down the road they called to say it was ready – and that it was slightly more than the standard one which cost about £45. Mine, they said, would be about £65 because it was left-handed, plus it had gold-plated fittings."

An excited Bunning collected his bass. He says the manager took him to one side and said the bass was special, that it had been "made for Paul McCartney, but it's a spare", and that this explained the lack of a serial number. Bunning examined the bass and wondered where the gold plating was. "It was gold plated," he says, "but it was very, very weak gold. Like an antique gold. It had special tuners with small gold covers on them. I took one of the covers off, and on the inside the plating was a strong, rich, gold, but on the outside it was this weak gold. Anyway, I thought no more of it. I took the guitar home, gave it a good inspection, and noticed on the rear there was a manufacturing imperfection in two places. The shop repaired this – and the repair can be seen on that guitar to this day."

Bunning played the bass until about 1971, when he traded it with a friend. Now, having read some of the subsequent reports tracing the bass's history, he suspects that the friend went almost immediately to Jim Marshall's music shop in Bletchley, Buckinghamshire, to sell the bass. Bunning believes the bass he once owned and the McCartney presentation bass are the same instrument, and in 1994 took some action. "I wrote a letter to Paul McCartney, because no one would listen to me," he says. "I came home from work one day and on the answerphone was a message from Geoff Baker, Paul McCartney's PA. He said that Paul had read my letter and that he knew I was telling the truth."[33]

Supporting Bunning's story is an article published in September 1965 in the *Leighton Buzzard Observer* newspaper. Under the headline "Left-Hand Guitarist Has Gold in His Grasp" the story reads: "It's quite a handicap being a left-handed guitarist, as most guitars built for the left-hander cost about 25 per cent more, but sometimes being left-handed has its advantages. John Bunning, bass guitarist of The Clifftops, of Leighton, thinks so, for his new guitar is left-handed and was one that was originally made for Paul McCartney. To cap it all, the guitar is gold-plated!"[34] A photograph of The Clifftops with John Bunning holding the Hofner bass accompanied the article.

Back again to 1997, and now a BBC consumer-rights television show, *Watchdog*, pounced on the story. In a programme that tried to show how auction houses at times go too far in trying to sell supposed collectables, John Bunning was featured. The show portrayed the bass as a fake, obviously causing problems for the upcoming Bonhams sale of the instrument, and further challenging Bonhams' claim that McCartney used the bass throughout his career with The Beatles. The story was

picked up by other elements of the British media. The bass did sell at the auction, although amid some confusion the final sale of the bass did not go through. At the time of writing the bass is still owned by Richard Harrison of Music Ground.

A review of all the available evidence relating to the gold-plated-hardware Hofner "presentation" bass points to a promotional-association-only with McCartney. Our conclusion is that here was a custom Hofner 500/1 bass made with gold-plated hardware, and the intention was to present it to McCartney. Selmer did make a deal with Brian Epstein and did use the McCartney hang-tags for Hofner instruments sold in the UK at the time. If Alby Paynter's story about the presentation of the bass is true, then clearly that is how McCartney became aware of the instrument, which would account for his later reference to it in the magazine article.

We further conclude that Selmer kept the bass after the presentation to exhibit at the upcoming trade show. Selmer's intention was to give the bass back to McCartney after the show. With McCartney currently denying owning or using the bass, we must assume the bass never made it back to him. After the trade show the bass may have been sent to the NEMS office, or to Abbey Road studios, from where it may have been stolen. Or it may just have been put back into Selmer's stock. No one will ever know for sure. But for some reason it did not end up in McCartney's hands. Surely if McCartney had received the bass he would have used it in live performances, television appearances, in the studio or in the filming of their upcoming colour

John Bunning (second right, below) holding the almost-Beatle Hofner bass, with his group The Clifftops in 1965.

1964

feature? But there is no evidence of McCartney ever using the gold-plated-hardware bass.

Somehow, the bass ended up in a music shop in Luton where John Bunning, also a left-hander, purchased it during 1965. The bass later arrived at Jim Marshall's music shop in nearby Bletchley and was purchased by Stephen Boyce, who used the bass for a decade. After his death in 1981, Boyce's widow Anne sold the bass to the Biggleswade store for £200. This is where Music Ground found it and purchased it for £800.

Our overall view is that the bass was made for McCartney, but he never owned it or used it. So it is not a true Beatles guitar – although there is strong evidence that it almost was.

Missing 12-strings, and a hacked-off Backer

Now we're back in 1964. With the title song recorded and the filming almost at an end, *A Hard Day's Night* was finally completed toward the end of April. The release of the film was scheduled for July. In the UK, The Beatles were at their peak. They were awarded the *New Musical Express* Annual Poll Winners award for 1963-64, topping the All-Star Concert bill at the Empire Pool, Wembley, on April 26th where they received their gong from actor Roger Moore, then star of the British television show *The Saint*, and a future James Bond. For this show the group used the same equipment as they had during the finale of *A Hard Day's Night*.

Their next endeavour was to film *Around The Beatles*, a television special taped before a live audience. The group mimed to a pre-recorded music track made for the show at IBC studios in London. Second engineer for the session was Glyn Johns, who would later work with them on the *Get Back/Let It Be* sessions.

During the show they performed a medley of hits: 'Love Me Do', 'Please Please Me', 'From Me To You', 'She Loves You' and 'I Want To Hold Your Hand'. The other highlight was their version of The Isley Brothers' classic, 'Shout', which can be seen now on *The Beatles Anthology* video box-set. A full-length version of this performance has also been available through the years, and the clips show very clearly the instruments that the group were using at the time, as well as full views around Starr's Ludwig drum set. After filming their television special, the group took the greater part of the month of May off for a much-needed holiday.

At the end of April and throughout May there was much correspondence to try to locate the two guitars that had been ordered at the February meeting with Rickenbacker in New York. The guitars – Lennon's custom 325 12-string and a 360-12 for Gerry Marsden – had been sent by Rickenbacker to the NEMS offices in London. Receipts and shipping records from Rickenbacker's archives show that the guitars had been shipped from their factory in Santa Ana, California, on March 17th. The REA Freight Company then held the shipment until April 8th when it was loaded on to a boat in New York headed for England.

John Hall, owner of Rickenbacker today, says Lennon's 325 12-string was originally intended to have a vibrato. "Of course, with it being a 12-string, one push of the vibrato and it was hopelessly out of tune. So very quickly it was converted to our regular 'trapeze' non-vibrato tailpiece."[35]

In Rickenbacker's model scheme, Lennon's 12-string should properly be called a 320-12 – the closing 0 indicates no vibrato – but it is generally known as a 325-12, and evidently was originally intended to be. The Rickenbacker 325 12-string's serial number, DB155, indicates it was manufactured in February 1964 – and is only 33 numbers away from Lennon's second Rick 325 six-string. The short-scale 325 12-string is identical in every way to that second 325, except for the trapeze tailpiece and, of course, the 12-string headstock.

The other guitar shipped, the 360-12, reveals a manufacturing date of March 1964. This guitar was an exact duplicate of Harrison's. Gerry Marsden says that Epstein ordered it for him as a surprise, to go alongside his acoustic 12-string. "I loved it," he recalls. "I was going on tour and I thought, well, I don't want to damage my Rickenbacker, so I made a travelling box. But when I was measuring up, I forgot that the wood adds an extra half-inch at each end of the guitar...

"So I made it, it was wonderful, I went to put in the guitar... and it wouldn't fit. I wasn't going to make another box – it had taken me a week. So I cut the top off the Rickenbacker. Not the tuning pegs, just the top where it said Rickenbacker. So now it was called a Backer. I got rid of it later in New Zealand as a gift to somebody."[36]

NEMS ENTERPRISES LTD

SUTHERLAND HOUSE, 5/6 ARGYLL STREET, LONDON, W.1
TELEPHONE REGent 3261

BE/MTD   23rd March, 1964.

F. C. Hall, Esq.,
Radio & Television Equipment Co.,
2118 South Main Street,
Santa Ana,
CALIFORNIA,
U.S.A.

Dear Mr. Hall,

Many thanks for your letter of the 12th instant, to which by way of reply I would advise you that we have now received the sets of strings for which the boys are most grateful.

We expect to return to the States for a nation-wide tour on or about August 18th, the details of which have not yet been completed. The tour is at present being set by:-

                    Norman Weiss, Esq.,
                    General Artistes Corporation,
                    640, Fifth Avenue,
                    NEW YORK, 19,
                    N.Y.

We will look forward to receiving John's guitar in due course. In the meantime many thanks for all your help and consideration.

                    Yours sincerely,
                    for NEMS ENTERPRISES LTD.

                    Brian Epstein
                    Brian Epstein

March 1964, and Brian Epstein asks Rickenbacker's Francis Hall about the custom 325 12-string guitar specially ordered for John that has so far failed to arrive in England.

Another Ludwig for Ringo – and a piano that sounds like a guitar

After their holidays, the group re-assembled on May 31st for a live performance at the Prince of Wales Theatre, London. It was at this show that Starr received his third Ludwig drum set. A brief item in a music paper marked the event. "What better for the world's most publicised drummer, Ringo Starr, than to come back home to a shiny new drum kit? Ringo took delivery of the kit at the Prince of Wales Theatre, London, on Sunday, shortly before Brian Epstein's Pops Alive show. But not before a six-year-old son of Ivor Arbiter, managing director of Drum City, who supplied the £350 Ludwig kit, could bash out a beat from the white skins."[37]

Ivor Arbiter today looks back on the time with amused disbelief. "Bill Ludwig couldn't believe his luck," he laughs. "Ludwig started to look after The Beatles, sending Ludwig sets over. They just got huge overnight. We were selling 40 or 50 Ludwig kits a month, just in Britain, and the brand took off all over the world. The British drum companies like Premier probably thought The Beatles should be using British drums, but I think Epstein and Ringo were loyal to Ludwig because we had helped them a bit when they were not all that well known."[38]

Starr's third Ludwig oyster black pearl kit was a larger-sized set, with a 22-inch by 14-inch bass drum, 13x9 rack tom, 16x16 floor tom and a 14x5 Jazz Festival snare drum. The kit came with standard Ludwig hardware except for the tom mount, once again customised by Drum City to a Rogers Swiv-O-Matic tom mounting system.

It can be difficult to distinguish in photographs between Starr's 20 and 22-inch bass drums, but a relatively easy way is to count the number of bass-drum lugs (the metal brackets visible around its diameter). A 22-inch Ludwig bass drum has ten lugs; a 20-inch bass has eight. Generally, Starr only used the larger-sized Ludwig sets from this point. In a music store, the kit would have cost about £350 ($980 then). That would be about £4,200 ($5,900) in today's money.

Along with this third, larger Ludwig kit came another new Beatles head. This was number-four drum-head logo, painted on to a 22-inch Remo Weather King head. It had a more traditional, unexaggerated Ludwig logo, while the lettering of "The Beatles" was again slightly different compared to the previous types.

Performing on the same bill of the May 31st concert was the group's old friend from Hamburg, Roy Young, now a member of Cliff Bennett & The Rebel Rousers. Young recalls using a Hohner Pianet at the time, an electric piano about which the group were very curious. "Paul, John and George were asking, 'Hey, man, what kind of piano is that? Wow, what a great sound.' The Pianet had almost a percussive sound," says Young, "like a guitar or something, which they really liked. They had just really cracked, and they were making phenomenal money, so they said, 'We're gonna get two of those!' It was like what was wrong with getting just one? But they wanted two! They could just go out and buy anything they wanted. And they did."[39]

The next day the group reconvened at Abbey Road where they continued to record songs for their next EP. With 'Long Tall Sally' and 'I Call Your Name' complete, they taped 'Matchbox' and 'Slow Down'. Also on June 1st they put down 'I'll Cry Instead' and 'I'll Be Back' for the non-soundtrack side of the *Hard Days Night* LP. The following day work continued on 'Any Time At All', 'When I Get Home' and 'Things We Said Today'.

According to correspondence between NEMS and Rickenbacker, Lennon's Rickenbacker 325 12-string must have arrived in London during the group's holidays. It's possible that Lennon used his new guitar during these early-June EP sessions, though there is no evidence of this.

Beatle strings and things

Some Beatles guitar enthusiasts have speculated about what kind of guitar strings the group used. The general consensus among Liverpudlian musicians and others interviewed for this book is that none of the bands from that time – including The Beatles – cared much about what strings they used, just so long as they were new. "It wasn't like today where you have people that only use a certain brand," Gerry Marsden says, typically. "There was no such thing as gauges. We really didn't care."[40]

Commonly used brands then in Liverpool, according to our poll, included Cathedral, Fender, Gibson (Sonomatic), Maxima, Monopole, Picato, Pyramid and Selmer, and generally roundwound rather than flatwound. Although good strings were available from manufacturers in Britain and

> I'M NOT TECHNICAL ... SOME GUY IN A GUITAR SHOP I WENT INTO SAID, 'WHAT KIND OF BASS STRINGS DO YOU USE, PAUL?' I SAID, 'LONG SHINY ONES'
>
> Paul McCartney

Germany, for some reason it was generally believed among British musicians that American-made Gibson and Fender strings were better.

Guitarist Colin Manley of The Remo Four was described in the 1960s by Harrison as "so far advanced [he makes] most other British guitarists, including myself, sound old-fashioned".[41] Manley's recollection is that Monopole was among the most popular string brands. "They were flatwounds," he says, "but as soon as we heard The Shadows' 'Apache' we knew we could only get that sound with roundwound strings, so I tended to use Gibson Sonomatics. You had to change those often to get that sustaining, ringing sound that comes from roundwounds. And of course when you're playing in the Cavern and places like that, all the sweat would clog up the strings and make them sound duller. So when I was broke, I used to boil the strings in water to clean them, and then put them back on again to get that sound."[42]

Epstein made an arrangement with Selmer, around the same time as the McCartney/Hofner swing-tag deal, to offer sets of Beatles-brand guitar strings. The Hofner Beatle strings were noted as "Empire Made" and "Made under licence from Selcol Ltd". The strings were distributed by Selmer and offered in "wire-wound" (roundwound) or "tape-wound" (flatwound) sets, with an extra 1st and 2nd string supplied in each set. The strings came in a green pack with a picture of the group and the slogan "made to The Beatles' own specification". The bass set came with the same artwork but in red. It's not known if The Beatles actually used these strings. Chances are that roadie Mal Evans was given numerous sets when they were first issued in 1964.

McCartney himself has admitted not knowing what strings he used. "I'm one of the least technical people you're likely to meet," he said recently. "Some guy in a guitar shop in America that I went into a few years ago said, 'What kind of bass strings do you use, Paul?' I said, 'Long shiny ones.' I don't know! Now I've got a tech, and he knows what I like. I'm not technical. I don't know about

John's custom-made Rickenbacker 325 12-string. This is the guitar that John ordered from Rickenbacker in February 1964. He used it briefly in the summer of 1964 as a back-up for his six-string 325. The guitar is owned today by Yoko Ono.

amps, I don't know about names, serial numbers ... People say to me: I've got a fantastic L-35. And I say oh, yeah? It could be a motorbike for all I know. I'm just not like that, you know? For us it was just like Vox, it was Hofner, it was Club 40 ... I never really got into the analytical end of it."[43] It seems likely that The Beatles were not fussy about what kind of guitar strings they used. Most reports indicate that Lennon and McCartney didn't tend much to their guitars and would usually only change strings when they broke. In most cases they probably used whatever was available.

Dealing with Starr's drums, heads, cymbals and sticks was also the responsibility of Mal Evans. A steady supply of sticks was always required for Starr, so a deal was made with Arbiter's Drum City store. Manager Gerry Evans says that Ivor Arbiter, always aware of a commercial opportunity, suggested a Ringo Starr stick.

"We told Ringo we would supply as many drumsticks as he would require for himself," says Evans. "We just bought a British drumstick and called it the Ringo Starr, similar to the one that he used. I think we sold hundreds of thousands of them. It just had the name Ringo Starr in block capitals, not a signature. In each pack of sticks was a little piece of paper with a photograph of Ringo and his printed signature."[44] Arbiter advertised the special Ringo Starr drumstick as being made of "American white hickory".

The Beatles on Dutch TV in June 1964, and the first time that John uses his new Rickenbacker 325 12-string, with Vox Python strap.

The Vox Python strap

Dick Denney and Tom Jennings were forever working on new ideas for the Vox line. Because of the magnitude and popularity of The Beatles, any product tie-in would be virtually guaranteed financial success, so in the spring of '64 Denney designed a new and very different looking guitar strap. He named it the Python.

Denney thinks that Lennon had asked for a strap made of snakeskin, complete with scales. "So Tom and I came up with armoured metal pieces that would look like a python's skin," he says. "I made up the first prototype from brass, but it wasn't long enough. So we elongated the strap and decided to have it in black and chrome.

John was the first to have one. I took the original chrome and black leather strap to The Beatles,

WHEN THE BEATLES WENT TO AMERICA FOR THE FIRST TIME, THEY FOUND THAT THEIR 50-WATT AMPS COULDN'T PIERCE THE SCREAMS OF THE AUDIENCE.

Tom Jennings, of Vox

on the reason they started making

100-watt amps

Vox made the metal-clad Python Strap in 1964 (example left), designed to resemble snakeskin. John used one on his Rickenbacker 325 throughout 1965.

but we also made one in gold with brown leather. Later we made a horse-brass strap for them, and George used it. John used the Python strap, but I think they turned out a bit too heavy."[45]

As soon as Lennon started to use the Vox Python strap, fans became interested. One reader wrote to a musicians' magazine: "Could you please give me some information about John Lennon's guitar strap and tell where I can obtain one?" The editor replied: "John's strap is a Vox Python strap which is made up of springy steel and leather. It costs 6 guineas [£6.30, about $18 then; around £75 or $105 in today's money] and can be obtained from any of the larger musical dealers."[46]

Instant Beatle

During a morning photo session on June 3rd, Ringo Starr was taken ill and soon hospitalised for tonsillitis. With a big tour scheduled to start the very next day, Epstein moved quickly and recruited drummer Jimmy Nicol. He was asked to fill in for Starr during the upcoming tour of Scandinavia, Hong Kong and Australia.

Nicol was a session drummer, and was also in a group signed to Pye Records called The Shubdubs. That same afternoon Lennon, McCartney and Harrison had a brief rehearsal with Nicol at Abbey Road. During the rehearsals, Nicol was pictured using Starr's Ludwig 20-inch-bass set with the number-three Beatles logo – in other words the same kit that had been used for filming *A Hard Day's Night*. The studio photos also show Harrison with his Ramírez classical guitar, McCartney playing his Hofner bass, and Lennon using his Rickenbacker 325 with the new Vox Python strap. The Beatles rehearsed their short set-list with Nicol, and the next day were off to Copenhagen to perform live. Nicol became an instant Beatle almost before he knew what was happening.

Nicol not only performed live with the group but was also seen on national television in The Netherlands on the show *Vara-TV*. They mimed to a tape, but had their microphones switched on and sang live with the existing vocal track. The clip can be seen on *The Beatles Anthology* video box-set. During the performance of their last number, 'Can't Buy Me Love', the Dutch fans took over the stage set as Neil Aspinall whisked the group off to safety while the song continued over the playback – with no one left performing but stand-in drummer Nicol.

For this chaotic performance Harrison used his second Gretsch Country Gentleman, McCartney his '63 Hofner bass, and Nicol played on Starr's third Ludwig set with the larger 22-inch bass drum and number-four Beatles logo. It was during this television show that Lennon first performed using his new Rickenbacker 325 12-string guitar, suspended on the new Vox Python strap. The Rickenbacker 325 12-string stayed with Lennon as a spare to his main '64 325 six-string for all live performances until the end of 1964. There is much speculation about Lennon's use of the 325-12 during studio sessions, but no evidence has surfaced to indicate that the guitar was used on any Beatles recording.

Nicol continued with The Beatles to Hong Kong where they performed two shows on June 9th. The equipment line-up for the tour was Harrison on Gretsch Country Gentleman and Rickenbacker 360-12, Lennon on his '64 Rickenbacker 325 with 325-12 as backup, McCartney on his '63 Hofner 500/1 bass, and the Ludwig drum kit with 22-inch bass which Nicol and, later, Starr used.

One of the major changes in the group's equipment for this tour was made to their Vox amplifiers. Jennings now fitted the group's AC-50 guitar amplifiers and AC-100 bass amplifier with new swivel-style Vox stands. These gripped the speaker cabinet on each side, allowing the cabinet to be tilted backwards. The stand was joined at the top, forming a platform for the amplifier head. Vox's Dick Denney says this new type of stand proved to be very expensive to make, but the company considered the cost worthwhile.[47] The swivel stands were sold as optional extras, retailing for ten guineas each (£10.50, about $30 then; around £125 or $180 in today's money).

From Hong Kong the group flew directly to Sydney, Australia, where Nicol would perform his last shows. Starr rejoined them in Melbourne on Monday June 15th and stayed with the group for the rest of the Australian and New Zealand tour. The Beatles returned to England from their triumphant concerts to attend the world premiere of their first full-length motion picture, *A Hard Day's Night*, at the London Pavilion on July 6th. They then headed up to their hometown, Liverpool, for the film's northern premiere at the Odeon Cinema four days later.

McCartney had arranged for extensive work to be done to his original '61 Hofner bass while he was away on tour. The guitar was refinished with a polyurethane sunburst finish, similar in appearance to Fender's well known three-colour sunburst. His old Hofner was also fitted with a new mounting system for the two forward pickups, one of which had come loose and had been temporarily taped in place. Replacing the regular individual pickup surrounds, a new large black rectangular plate was made to hold the two Hofner pickups in place. The bass's pickguard was cut to accommodate the new mounting plate, and a new set of volume knobs replaced the originals.

"Sound City has some very distinctive guitars on its walls at the moment," ran a contemporary news report, "including one of Paul McCartney's very first violin basses. Another is Harrison's first Gretsch and the third is Lennon's second Rickenbacker, but they are not for sale. 'The boys wouldn't part with any of them,' says [store manager Bob Adams], 'they're just in for overhauls.'"[48]

Today, Adams recalls the work done to McCartney's bass. "We worked on it at our shop in Shaftesbury Avenue and I had to send it out to have it re-sprayed. I had one of my staff do it. We needed to make a new mounting system for the pickups because they were falling out."[49]

McCartney first used his newly refinished and refitted '61 Hofner bass on July 11th for a television performance on the British ABC programme *Thank Your Lucky Stars*. During this same day's shooting, McCartney talked to a journalist about the work done to his bass. "Sound City did a great job re-varnishing and re-wiring it," he said, "so that most people think it's a brand new model."[50]

During July the group continued with more live performances in the UK, as well as radio broadcasts and television appearances to promote their new film, LP and single. *A Hard Day's Night* was an immediate success, with the title-track single going straight to the top of the charts.

Yet more new Vox gear

At the end of July the group embarked on a brief two-day visit to Stockholm, Sweden. During the four shows they played, on the 28th and 29th, Harrison and Lennon used a pair of new Vox AC-50 amplifiers while McCartney continued with his Vox AC-100 bass rig. The two new-style AC-50 speaker cabinets were visually distinctive: unlike the prototype AC-50 speaker cabinets the group had used earlier, which were completely covered at the front with Vox's diamond-pattern grille cloth, the newer production-version AC-50 cabinets had grille cloth only on the lower half of the front, giving a look similar to an AC-30. These newer-style Vox AC-50s were only used by Lennon and Harrison during this short period in July 1964.

With the return to Britain came more live performances. The Beatles played the Gaumont Cinema in Bournemouth on August 2nd, with "new London group" The Kinks on the same bill. This was the last show at which Lennon and Harrison would use Vox AC-50 amplifiers. By now Beatlemania was out of control. It became almost impossible for the group to hear themselves live on stage over their screaming fans. Tom Jennings of Vox said at the time, "When The Beatles went to America for the first time they … found that their 50-watt amps just couldn't pierce the screams of the audience, so they asked us to produce something even more powerful. The results are their present 100-watt monsters."[51]

Once again Vox's Dick Denney went to the drawing board to design a new, louder guitar amp. His creation was the Vox AC-100, and according to Denney the prototypes were made specifically for The Beatles. "There was always a rush," he explains. "They always had some tour to go on and needed their new amps. I remember hand-soldering the first AC-100 guitar heads for The Beatles and finishing them the night before I delivered them in Scarborough."[52] A total of three original AC-100 prototypes were made: one each for Lennon and Harrison, plus one for a spare. The group were keen to try out the amps before taking them on their forthcoming US tour.

The Vox AC-100 was designed with seven valves (tubes) delivering 100 watts of power. The simple, single-channel head had two inputs, with single volume, bass and treble controls located on the top rear of the head. The speaker cabinet was enormous for its day, loaded with four 12-inch Vox-Celestion 25-watt speakers and two Goodmans Midax high-frequency horns, with a crossover

Paul had his first Hofner violin bass repainted and repaired. Pictured here at a TV studio in July 1964, the bass has a new mounting system, installed to hold the two pickups in place, along with a new three-colour sunburst finish and a pair of new knobs to replace the old ones.

Part of Epstein's deal with Selmer was to produce a line of guitar strings, supposedly "made to the Beatles' own specifications".

network to improve its efficiency. The amp came with a specially designed chrome-plated Vox swivel/roller stand. Never before had the music industry seen such a massive amplifier. And who better to receive the biggest amp? The biggest band.

It was on Sunday August 9th at the Futurist Theatre in Scarborough that the group received their new AC-100 amps. Denney remembers taking the amps to that gig himself, along with his wife and a Jennings engineer. Members of a support act local to Vox's Dartford factory, The Candy Choir, transported the speaker cabinets separately. "When we had everything set up at Scarborough, I noticed the stage had a slight forward slope to it," says Denney. "Just one number into their set, the amplifiers started rolling forward. I had to kneel behind the cabinets and hold on to their stands so they wouldn't move!

After Scarborough, The Beatles left for the States."[53] Denney also remembers bringing McCartney a spare AC-100 bass head to be used as back-up during the US tour. The AC-100 Super De Luxe "with Beatles type speaker cabinet" would retail in 1964 for £252 (about $700 then; around £3,050 or $4,270 in today's money).

So the group's new amp line-up now consisted of two Vox AC-100 guitar amps plus AC-100 bass amp – all equipped with swivel stands. These new Vox amps were christened in the studio the very next day. With the excitement of *A Hard Day's Night* still fresh, the group embarked on a new recording session at Abbey Road as they started work on yet another LP, eventually to be titled *Beatles For Sale*.

On August 11th The Beatles recorded 'Baby's In Black', and the session was well documented by *The Beatles Monthly Book* photographers. Into the new Vox AC-100 amplifiers Harrison plugged his Gretsch Tennessean and Lennon his '64 Rickenbacker 325, while McCartney played his '63 Hofner through the AC-100 bass head and cabinet.

At these sessions, or shortly before, the Ac'cent vibrato arm on Lennon's Rick 325 was changed from its original shape into a more exaggerated almost 45-degree bend. This is the way the vibrato arm exists on the guitar today. It's not known why it was altered. Perhaps Lennon felt it would help keep the arm out of the way? Lennon is also pictured using Harrison's Gibson J-160E on the 11th, as he had not yet replaced his own, stolen the year before.

It was during the 'Baby's In Black' session that the group first experimented with volume swells on the guitar. Harrison told an interviewer in the 1980s how much he'd admired Remo Four guitarist Colin Manley's ability to play two-part Chet Atkins-style pieces. Manley also had a volume pedal and had tried to show Harrison how to play a note with the pedal up, and then gradually bring in the note by depressing the pedal, creating a gradual "swelling" effect. "But I could never co-ordinate it," said Harrison. "So what we'd do is, I played the part, and John would kneel down in front of me and turn my guitar's volume control."[54] This is the method they used at the 'Baby's In Black' session; photographs show Lennon manually changing the volume knob on Harrison's Tennessean guitar while Harrison played. The result can be heard on the released take on *Beatles For Sale*, at the beginning and end of the song, and in the brief solo. The group would also use the effect later on 'I Need You' and 'Yes It Is'. They were evidently as keen as ever to venture beyond normally accepted studio guitar sounds.

The sessions continued on the 14th with the group recording a new original, 'I'm A Loser', and a cover of Dr Feelgood & The Interns' track 'Mr Moonlight'. Also recorded that day was 'Leave My Kitten Alone', a track that remained unreleased until *Anthology 1* in 1996. During these sessions Harrison used his second Gretsch Country Gentleman in addition to the Tennessean.

Before leaving for their much anticipated tour of the United States, the group performed at Blackpool Opera House on August 16th. The Who, then called The High Numbers, were the support act. Bassist John Entwistle remembers using McCartney's lead (cord) at the gig. "Mine didn't work, so I borrowed one off Paul," he says. "Their roadie Mal Evans gave it to me – and I never gave it back, so I guess he didn't have one for the show.

"Paul asked me if I liked my Rickenbacker bass, and I said no. At that time the neck was starting to warp, so it was pretty unplayable. I was stupid enough to buy one – I had the second one into Britain, through Jim Marshall's shop. Later, when

Live in Australia 1964 (below), the group are using "swivel" stands for their Vox amps, and the new 22-inch-bass Ludwig kit is seen in action.

Ringo's Ludwig 22-inch-bass drum kit. This is Ludwig kit number three, the first of two 22-inch oyster black pearl kits he played with The Beatles, and which he still owns today. The drop-T logo head is long gone. This was his most important Ludwig kit, which he used from 1964-1968, live and in the studio. Note the extra Rogers Swiv-O-Matic drum mount, added at a later date.

we left the show, the police thought that The Beatles were escaping in our van. This huge crowd of kids rushed after us, so our roadie drove off and Roger [Daltrey] was running behind. I think *Hard Day's Night* had just come out. The Beatles were enormous!"[55]

Vox in America

The Beatles' huge success had created an overwhelming demand for Vox amplifiers in the United States. Around the start of 1964 Vox boss Tom Jennings had placed ads in the music trade magazines seeking a US distributor. One such ad, headed "A Message To The American Music Trade", described Vox as British manufacturers of musical merchandise, and in particular "Vox electronic aids to music". The ad boasted how Vox had exported to 60 countries throughout the world during the past five years, but emphasised that this did not include the United States. "You are about to be 'invaded' by a series of British performing groups who feature Vox equipment," it continued, "the forerunners of whom were The Beatles, a group that has made a very strong impact upon the teenage population of America.

"We are open to negotiate with music firms in the US for distribution of our products throughout the American continent. Those interested and who have the capacity for such distribution should write to me personally. British promotion could mean many hundreds of thousands of dollars being spent this year on Vox musical merchandise. This is an opportunity you cannot afford to miss."[56] It was signed by Tom Jennings.

By early 1964, the Thomas Organ company of California had seen the great potential in Vox equipment and quickly approached Jennings, offering a proposal to acquire Vox distribution in America. Jennings had already distributed Thomas organs in Britain, so he blindly struck a deal with Thomas. Jennings would export Vox guitars and amps to Thomas Organ, and in return Thomas would provide Jennings with their organs. The difference would be made up financially.

Jennings himself was well aware that The Beatles were the main reason for the Stateside success of Vox. "Their tours of the States created a terrific demand for our equipment," he told a magazine, "and led to our contract with the Thomas Organ company to supply them with five million dollars' worth each year."[57]

Unfortunately, Jennings was not ready or able to meet the manufacturing demands of the US market. The Beatles had singlehandedly created a bigger market for Vox amps than Jennings could ever have imagined. Unable to fulfil the demand, he was forced to make business decisions that he would soon regret. To gain the capital needed to expand his Vox manufacturing facility in England, Jennings sold the controlling interest of his company to the Royston Group of London.

At first all went well, with large numbers of British-made Vox amplifiers and guitars being exported to the US. By the time The Beatles had landed for their summer 1964 US tour, a dealer network had been set up throughout the United States and Vox amplifiers were available – but only in small quantities, because demand far exceeded supply. For a short time in mid-to-late 1964 a steady supply of imported British-made Vox amps became more readily available for the US market. But all that would change quickly. The Thomas Organ company had other ideas for Vox.

Beatles first American tour

After their last show in Blackpool, The Beatles headed for what would turn out to be their most extensive and lengthy tour of the United States and Canada. Even though it was actually their second trip to the States, the concerts were billed as the group's first US tour. By the summer of '64 the American market was primed. *A Hard Day's Night* was in theatres throughout the country. The group's singles and LPs topped the US charts. Beatlemania was running loose in the States. The Beatles could do no wrong.

The summer of 1964 was in some ways a turning point in pop music. The Beatles' earlier appearances on *The Ed Sullivan Show* had whetted everyone's appetite. But that was not enough. It seemed as if every teenager in America wanted to see and hear them first hand, up close and live, to find out what it was that created the Beatle magic. Tickets for Beatle concerts sold out almost instantly, only adding to the pandemonium.

Epstein's constant work to refine The Beatles' image and stage presence was at its peak. The group's look and sound during this '64 US tour would become the standard at which almost every American teen garage band would aim. The Beatles alone changed the landscape of the music industry and inspired thousands of bands to be formed. Any group with enough cash copied the whole Beatle package: Rickenbacker, Hofner and Gretsch guitars, Ludwig drums, Vox amps, matching suits, Beatle boots and, of course, mop-top haircuts. Many outfits successfully aped The Beatles' look and sound. Others would take the basic ideas and evolve their own, creating some of the best one-hit-wonder bands of the 1960s. Successful American groups such as The Knickerbockers, The Outsiders, The Beau Brummels, The Standells and countless others could trace their roots directly or indirectly to The Beatles.

The equipment used during the '64 US tour was the same as the group had used in Blackpool. Starr played his third Ludwig drum set with the 22-inch bass drum, on the Remo head of which was painted the number-four Beatles drop-T logo. McCartney used his '63 Hofner violin bass, with his refinished '61 Hofner along as a spare, which he played through the Vox AC-100 bass rig. Harrison had his second Gretsch Country Gentleman, alternating with his Rickenbacker 360-12, and played through the Vox AC-100 guitar amp. Lennon used his '64 Rickenbacker 325 guitar with Vox Python

I COULD SEE THE BEATLES WERE GOING TO BE A REAL FORCE IN THE BUSINESS, AND I WANTED TO GET HOLD OF THEM.

Don Randall, co-owner of Fender

on the company's plans to get the band to use their gear – which proved harder than they'd hoped

Ringo has a tea break at Abbey Road studio during the recording of 'Baby's In Black' in August 1964. He's using his new Ludwig 22-inch-bass drum set, fitted with Beatles drop-T logo head number four.

strap as his main guitar, with the new Rickenbacker 325-12 along as a spare, and also played through a Vox AC-100 guitar amp. Reportedly, a complete extra set of Vox AC-100 guitar and bass amps were brought on this tour as spares.

It had only been a few months earlier that Americans had had their first glimpse of Vox amplifiers, but now The Beatles returned with matching mammoth-size Vox AC-100s, later renamed Super Beatle amps in the US.

The idea for a guitar amplifier "stack" has its roots in The Beatles and their Vox gear. The size and volume of the Vox AC-100s were designed from sheer necessity, to project the group's sound over their screaming fans. The idea of a wall of guitar amplifiers for a live performance was unheard of in America at the time. When The Beatles came there in summer '64, no US manufacturer made amplifiers that even came close to the physical size of a Vox AC-100.

Unknowingly, The Beatles and Vox started another fashion in the music industry: the idea that bigger amps are better. While we now know this is not necessarily true, the trend started nonetheless.

The AC-100 was Vox's biggest and most powerful amp so far, and the first examples were made especially for The Beatles.

Dick Denney (left) of Vox shakes hands with Mal Evans at the Futurist Theatre, Scarborough, on August 9th 1964, the day he delivered a set of new AC-100 amps for The Beatles.

From that point, the race was on. Every manufacturer wanted to create a bigger and better amplifier.

The 26-date US tour started at the Cow Palace in San Francisco on August 19th. Support acts were The Bill Black Combo (led by former Elvis bass player), The Righteous Brothers, and Jackie DeShannon. As with most Beatle tours, an almost daily schedule of shows ensued, with few days off. The group criss-crossed the country in a chartered plane.

Highlights included the famous Hollywood Bowl concert on August 23rd, which was recorded by Capitol Records and planned as a live LP release for the US market only. But after the performance the recordings were shelved as unsuitable for release. They would not re-surface until the 1977 *Beatles At The Hollywood Bowl* album.

Fender wants The Beatles

Every guitar manufacturer in the world wanted their instruments in The Beatles' hands. One of the leaders in the music industry at the time was Fender. Considered by many as the best, the brand enjoyed a huge market share. Many professional and non-professional musicians would choose Fender instruments and amplifiers.

But by mid-1964 a problem had arisen for Fender. The world's biggest band, The Beatles, did not use any Fender products. With Beatlemania in full flow, kids wanted the instruments their heroes played – and they weren't Fenders.

Leo Fender's business partner and co-owner of the operation was Don Randall. "I could see The Beatles were going to be a real force in the business," says Randall, "and I wanted to get a hold of them. And we were doing a lot of business in Britain at the time."

The Vox company, Jennings, had been the first UK distributor of Fender gear, starting in 1960 and joined by Selmer in 1962. "Jennings did an incredible job for Fender," says Randall, "maybe for two or three years. Then all of a sudden I see The Beatles using his Vox amplifiers, so I asked Tom Jennings what was going on. You know, I said, we didn't give you this line for you to copy it!" So Randall pulled distribution from Jennings and Selmer around the summer of 1965 and moved Fender's British agency to the apparently tireless Ivor Arbiter.

Randall says it was not company policy to pay musicians to endorse Fender. "The only time I ever tried to do that was when I mistakenly sent our Jim Williams to New York to talk to Brian Epstein, to see if we could interest them in playing our equipment. I felt I'd broken my cardinal rule, but it was imperative to do it. It was our intent to line them up with all the Fender equipment they wanted – but nothing ever came of it. And it was a huge amount, I can tell you that much. Not by today's standards, of course, but it was a lot of money for us at the time.

"Jim never even got to meet with Epstein. I think he got to some secondary director who said that the boys had been successful with what they were playing and they were going to continue to use it. They didn't see any reason to change. I couldn't argue with that."[58]

The Fender meeting was scheduled to take place while the group were in New York on August 28th and 29th for their shows at the Forest Hills Tennis Stadium. Unconfirmed reports indicate that Williams was so nervous he decided to have a few cocktails to calm himself and that this may have affected his reception. Whatever the reason, the emissary from Fender probably never made it anywhere near the group themselves, maybe only getting to Neil Aspinall or Mal Evans.

It's interesting to imagine how it might have been had he reached the musicians. Another close call with a Stratocaster for Harrison? Still, Don Randall and Fender would have better success with The Beatles in the years to come.

Ringo's gold-plated snare

The US tour continued with a stop-off in Chicago on September 5th for a performance at the International Amphitheater. Chicago was also the home of the Ludwig drum company. William Ludwig Jr, then owner and president of the operation, decided that they ought to honour the group in some way. He remembered that his father had made a gold-plated snare drum for Western film star Tom Mix. "We dug it out of our archives and there it was," recalls Ludwig, "engraved and everything. So I said let's make the same thing for Ringo, only we'll use 14-karat gold. All the parts were sent out, the shell and everything, to a jeweller."

Ludwig learned that the group were reluctant to come to the factory, because the fans would soon find out and mob the event. The drum company boss had noticed vehicles already parked outside the factory as news began to spread.

"I went from car to car and explained that I would be taking the drum to the Amphitheater and giving it to Ringo there at a press conference" he remembers. "I had

The group's 1964 US tour would be their most extensive, and this shot from Las Vegas on August 20th details the gear line-up. Paul plays his '63 Hofner bass through the AC-100 bass rig, and has his refinished '61 Hofner as back-up. George uses his '64 Rick 12-string through an AC-100, with a Gretsch Country Gent nearby. John plays the Rick 325, with his 12-string version by his amp, through another AC-100. (Other amps on-stage are for the various support acts.) Meanwhile, Ringo plays his 22-inch-bass Ludwig kit (set number three).

The first concert on the 1964 US tour, at Cow Palace, San Francisco, on August 19th. The invasion commences, with Gretsch, Hofner, Rickenbacker, Ludwig and Vox.

A shipping log from Gibson's archive notes that John's second J-160E, serial 64309, was shipped from the factory on January 17th 1964.

tickets for the press conference, but they didn't believe me. They stayed all night and day. Some of them had learned about it from our employees who were buzzing about the gold drum."

Ludwig and his daughter took the gold-plated snare drum to the Amphitheater press conference and presented it to Starr. "We didn't know what the heck happened to it," he admits now. "The last I saw of it in '64 was when a Chicago cop was walking out of the press conference with the drum under his arm. I thought well, that's the end of that.

"I never got a chance to talk to them. It was always a shoving match with The Beatles. I just gave a little speech and that was the extent of it. There was a line of people waiting to get in to be photographed with The Beatles after us, as there was before. We stood in line like a cattle drive. I never saw them play in person – you couldn't get in to the concert.

"But Ringo still has the drum. I checked with him years later when he came through Chicago. During a soundcheck, I said, 'Hey, Ringo, you still got that drum?' He said, 'Yes I do. It plays marvellous. It's at my estate in Essex.'"[59]

Ludwig's moment at the press conference, which was held in the upper ballroom of the Stock Yard Inn with 150 members of the press, radio and television media in attendance, was documented in a contemporary news item. "The drum was presented to Ringo in recognition for his worldwide popularity, Mr Ludwig said. In making the presentation Mr Ludwig stated, 'I have never known of a drummer more widely acclaimed and publicized than you, Ringo Starr. Your millions of fans throughout the world have honored you and the other members of the famous Beatles group by their overwhelming acceptance of your many recordings, movies and concert appearances. On behalf of the management and employees of the Ludwig drum company I would like to express our appreciation to you for choosing our instruments and for the major role you are playing in the music world today.' …

After the presentation The Beatles held a 20-minute press conference and then appeared before a capacity audience of 13,500 screaming fans in the Chicago Amphitheater."[60]

Right: Ringo is presented with a gold-plated snare drum (see photo top right) by William F Ludwig Jr on September 5th in the company's home town, Chicago.

Above: the drum in its special case – it is engraved "Ringo Starr, The Beatles", and is still owned by Ringo today.

John's second Gibson J-160E

During the tour another guitar was added to the group's ever-growing arsenal when Lennon acquired a replacement for his original '62 Gibson J-160E acoustic-electric guitar that had been stolen the previous December. His second J-160E was an almost identical match to his first. Both had a sunburst finish. One of the only visual differences was that this later guitar had two sets of white rings in the soundhole rosette where his first had only a single set. Also, the second J-160E had an orange Gibson label inside the soundhole, while his first guitar did not. Otherwise the second J-160E was identical in specifications and in all other ways to Lennon's first. The serial number 64309 was stamped on the back of the headstock of this second J-160E indicating the guitar's manufacturing date as early 1964.

Lennon's '64 Gibson J-160E appears in photographs taken of him playing backstage at the September 8th show in Montreal, Canada. This guitar would become Lennon's main acoustic which he would use throughout the remaining years of the group. And as we shall see, as Lennon's life evolved, so this Gibson J-160E would also go through changes.

Following the two shows at the Forum in Montreal, the tour moved on to Florida for a performance at the Gator Bowl in Jacksonville. The September 11th concert was somewhat hindered by Hurricane Dora, which had hit the city the day before, but went ahead as scheduled. To help promote the performance, local promoters staged a battle-of-the-bands contest for local groups. It was sponsored by Music Mart, the Vox dealer in Orlando. The winners would be given The Beatles' Vox amplifiers.

One of the members of the winning band was Charlie Lytle, who later became a sales representative for Korg USA (still American distributors of Vox at the time of writing). Lytle's band, The Rockin' Roadrunners, were Beatle copyists. He recalls that they had to go up to Jacksonville to get their prize, the Beatles' amps. "After their show at the Gator Bowl we took our van right in and drove up to the stage. They'd played on a little stage toward an [American football] end zone. Some road guys helped us. It seemed like they had a bunch of Vox amps with them on stage, including spares. I later found out from Dick Denney of Vox that they needed the spares because the amps were unreliable. We got the bass amp and an AC-100 guitar amp."[61]

Lytle says his group continued to use the prize amps, although after a while the combination of general wear and tear and the Florida weather did for the speaker cabinets. He remembers the bass cabinet had a 15-inch and a 12-inch speaker inside, the guitar cab four 12s. Fortunately, the two amplifier heads fared better, and Lytle still has these. A detailed examination of them was recently made at Korg's US headquarters in New York. When taken apart, they showed signs of being non-production prototype AC-100 heads.

Meanwhile, next stop on the tour was the Boston Garden in Massachusetts on September 12th. This was one of the only shows on the tour where Lennon was pictured using his Rickenbacker 325 12-string in live performance. Perhaps he broke a string on his 325 six-string, or maybe it went out of tune? The 12-string was usually only present as a spare during this tour.

The tour lasted a little over a month, with a total of 32 shows in 24 cities, netting The Beatles and Epstein a small fortune. The last show was on September 20th, a special charity concert for the United Cerebral Palsy & Retarded Infants Services, staged at the Paramount Theater in New York City. The Beatles performed for free: all proceeds from the $100 tickets went to the charity.

Back to the UK

Returning to Britain on September 21st, the group could confidently claim to have conquered the United States. In doing so they had paved the way for many other British bands to follow: The Rolling Stones, The Animals, The Yardbirds, The Who, The Kinks and more. The Beatles had also inspired a generation of young American bands to form, not only influencing them musically but also having a profound effect upon the kind of equipment they wanted to use.

With barely a few days off to rest, the group was hurled back into the studio to continue work on their new LP – the record they had started working on before leaving for the tour. On September 29th they began three new songs, 'Every Little Thing', 'I Don't Want To Spoil The Party' and 'What You're Doing'. The sessions spilled into the next day as Starr put down a timpani accent track for 'Every Little Thing' while McCartney simultaneously added single notes on the piano. Overdubs and

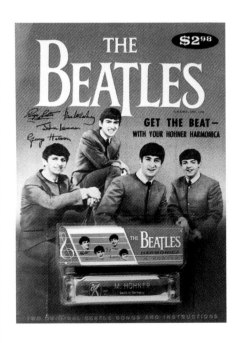

Instrument manufacturers tried to capitalise on The Beatles' popularity in any way possible. Hohner issued this tie-in harmonica packaged with a Beatles songbook.

vocals were worked on, and a recording of 'No Reply' was also completed. The following day's session in studio 2 was documented photographically, producing pictures that would later appear on the back cover of the *Beatles VI* album, first released by Capitol in the US on June 14th 1965. Some of the photos taken on the 30th show Lennon with his original '58 Rickenbacker 325, among the last pictures known of him using this guitar.

The same pictures show Lennon for the first time playing with a new harmonica holder. This type of "harness" was favoured by artists such as Bob Dylan and Donovan, but it took Lennon's use of one to provoke some comment in musicians' magazines. "When The Beatles recorded 'I'm A Loser'," ran one report, "John Lennon sang and played his guitar on one take and then added a harmonica track later. Problem: how to do all three at once when they perform the number on stage. Answer: John fitted [an] ingenious contraption round his neck to hold his harmonica. He could then alternately sing and play harmonica while at the same time playing rhythm guitar through the number."[62] A later item noted: "John Lennon is using [a harness] made for him in Liverpool, which incorporates springs ... The other harness is manufactured by a British firm called Menlove."[63] This seems a typical piece of Lennon foolery: "Menlove" was the name of the road where he'd grown up in Liverpool with Aunt Mimi, and had presumably been offered as a spur-of-the-moment answer to a gullible journalist.

Whoever really made it, the new harmonica harness was put to good use a few days later for the filming of a Beatle performance for the top-rated American television show *Shindig*. A special all-British show was filmed in London to be aired in the US on the ABC network. The Beatles performed 'Kansas City'/'Hey-Hey-Hey-Hey!' and 'Boys', with McCartney playing his '63 Hofner bass, Harrison his Gretsch Tennessean, Lennon his '64 Rickenbacker 325, and Starr his 22-inch-bass Ludwig kit with the same number-four Beatles-logo drum-head used on the summer American tour. For the performance of 'I'm A Loser' Lennon switched to Harrison's Gibson J-160E and, for the first time live, played harmonica using his new harness.

German-based harmonica manufacturer Hohner struck a "merchandising arrangement" with Epstein to capitalise on Lennon's popular use of the instrument, as reported in an American trade publication at the time. "A harmonica set starring The Beatles is being marketed. The Beatles package contains an especially designed ten-hole 20-reed harmonica, similar to the Marine Band model; two of The Beatles' song hits, 'Please Please Me' and 'Little Child'; a basic harmonica instruction chart; and photographs of The Beatles and their signatures. The retail price is $2.98 ... Says a Hohner spokesman: 'The contract with Hohner, The Beatles' first in the US musical instrument field, is a logical development of their featuring the harmonica in a number of their recordings. Sparked by John Lennon, the oldest of the group, who has long played the harmonica, The Beatles are credited with accelerating the new popularity upsurge of the harmonica which has been making music news in Britain and now on this side of the Atlantic. The Beatles will spotlight the harmonica in future records and it is anticipated that the harmonica will be featured in their forthcoming motion pictures.' ... It is anticipated that The Beatles' identification will make their harmonica package a best-seller, as the mop-headed entertainers have done with other products using their name. Hohner expects to keep the merchandise in adequate supply."[64]

Further studio work continued at Abbey Road on October 6th and 8th to record future classics 'Eight Days A Week' and 'She's A Woman'. Epstein wouldn't think of letting his boys rest, and put them on another month-long 25-city tour of Britain. The package included nine support acts including Sounds Incorporated, Mary Wells, and The Remo Four, and opened in Bradford, Yorkshire, on October 9th.

During the tour the group were expected to use the very few days off from the intensive schedule to make their way back to London and finish off the recordings for the new LP. So it was that on October 18th, during a marathon session, a series of songs were recorded, often in just a few takes each – including cover versions of 'Kansas City'/'Hey-Hey-Hey-Hey!', with George Martin on piano, 'Mr Moonlight', with Hammond organ played through a Leslie speaker cabinet by McCartney, 'Rock And Roll Music', 'Everybody's Trying To Be My Baby' and 'Words Of Love'.

John (opposite) during filming in England on October 2nd 1964 for the US Shindig TV show. He's wearing his new harmonica harness that allows him to play harmonica and George's J-160E at the same time.

The Rockin' Roadrunners, winners of the Florida Battle Of The Band competition, pose with their prize: one of the The Beatles' Vox AC-100s.

The Beatles feed back

Two new Beatle originals were also recorded on the 18th: 'I'll Follow The Sun' and 'I Feel Fine'. One reporter present at the session described 'I Feel Fine' as having a distinctly country-and-western flavour. "It begins with a very odd sound," he wrote, "which, Paul McCartney says, started off as a mistake when he produced the opening note and feedback noises were heard from his amplifier. The Beatles love oddness and decided to leave it in."[65]

Geoff Emerick, second engineer on the session, remembers that it was Lennon's J-160E guitar plugged into an amplifier that started to feed back when McCartney played a low A on his Hofner bass.[66] Feedback is a noise produced when the sound from the amp/speaker feeds back into the pickups of the guitar. The group decided to try to fit this "found sound" on to the start of their new recording. At the time, McCartney described the 'I Feel Fine' feedback intro as "the biggest gimmick thing we've ever used".[67] Later, Lennon said it had been "the first time feedback was used on record"[68], before more noted exponents such as The Who and Jimi Hendrix. George Martin has said that Lennon had been "mucking around" with feedback, and confirms that its appearance on the front of 'I Feel Fine' was intentional. "He found it quite difficult to get the right amount of feedback," Martin recalled, also noting this was the first time feedback was used on record. "He liked things like that. He loved weird kinds of effects – and it was his idea. It was great."[69]

'I Feel Fine' was recorded with Lennon playing his Gibson J-160E, Harrison his Gretsch Tennessean, McCartney his '63 Hofner violin bass and Starr his Ludwig kit. On October 26th, during another day off from the British tour, the group again found time to attend a mixing session in studio 2, to record 'Honey Don't', and to re-record 'What You're Doing', in the process completing their fourth British album. *Beatles For Sale* would be released on December 4th.

Paul acquired his Epiphone Texan toward the end of 1964. This photo taken on the set of the TV show Blackpool Night Out in August 1965 shows him demonstrating his versatility.

Rickenbacker 12-String or Vox Mando-Guitar?

For years many guitar enthusiasts have believed that songs on the *Beatles For Sale* album such as 'Words Of Love' were recorded using a Vox Mando-Guitar. This instrument was effectively a mini electric 12-string, with short-scale 20-fret neck and an odd body shape. But it would have been impossible for the group to have used it on that album, because the instrument was not yet available. Vox did not display the instrument publicly until the summer 1965 UK instrument trade show. It was probably around that time that Dick Denney of Vox showed it to The Beatles, although he recalls that even then they "didn't think much of it", and stresses that it was Brian Jones of The Rolling Stones who really took to the Mando-Guitar.[70]

It's easy to hear why some listeners might believe that a Mando-Guitar was being played on 'Words Of Love', given the intense, chiming guitar sound heard on the record. But it's likely this was produced with a pair of regular electric 12-string guitars played in unison. The various songs for the LP were recorded with heavy use of the Rickenbacker 12-string sound. Harrison, of course, had his

**IT WAS JOHN'S IDEA
... AND IT WAS GREAT!**

George Martin, on the feedback start

of 'I Feel Fine'

This Epiphone Texan is like the one used by Paul for writing, in the studio, and on live performances of 'Yesterday'. Paul's Texan was also right-handed and turned upside down, but of course his would have been strung left-handed.

360-12. And if Lennon did ever use his Rickenbacker 325 12-string guitar in the studio, it would have been during the sessions for *Beatles For Sale*. To Lennon, this guitar was still relatively new, so experimenting with it in the studio would have been a natural move.

Recently, some previously unseen photographs revealed Lennon in the studio using his Rick 325 12-string, apparently on September 30th (the same day that he was last pictured using his '58 Rickenbacker 325). One of these photos even shows McCartney playing Lennon's '64 325 six-string upside-down, indicating that all three of Lennon's Rickenbacker 325 models were present in the studio. It appears that after these sessions and the '64 British tour Lennon retired his Rick 325 12-string and the '58 325.

Lennon's Rick 12-string did get some use during The Beatles' 64 British tour – but not by Lennon. Colin Manley, lead guitarist for one of the tour's support groups, The Remo Four, was a friend of McCartney and Harrison from schooldays. "For that British tour we were backing a guy by the name of Tommy Quickly," he recalls. "We used to play for 15 or 20 minutes before The Beatles came on, so we used their amplifiers. I also used that Rickenbacker 12-string which had been made for John. We'd play a song called 'The Wild Side Of Life' which had a riff for piano and guitar, and the only way I could get the sound on it was with a 12-string. So John let me use his. It was only a tiny thing, same size as his black one. It had a strange sound, not like George's big Ricky 12. It sounded like a little harpsichord. It had a very small neck, and I remember it was very easy to make a mistake on it."[71]

Gretsch George Harrison 12-String

Colin Manley recalls another 12-string guitar custom-made for a Beatle. This time the maker was Gretsch, who delivered a guitar for Harrison during the group's British tour this year. Manley reminisces about how he and Harrison would talk guitars at school: the pair discovered Chet Atkins together at a Duane Eddy concert, where Eddy played 'Trambone' and announced it as by Atkins. Keen to discover more about this new name, the two got hold of an Atkins LP with 'Trambone' on it, and revelled in its multiple picked parts. "Well," says Manley in astonishment, "that was it! It was like: how does he do that? So we found out about Chet and just took it from there. We liked some different guitar players but we both loved Chet. George came around to my house a couple of times and we'd listen to Chet and try to work out how he did it."

Both Atkins and Eddy played Gretsches, and this too made an impression on the young Liverpudlians. As we've seen, Harrison indulged his passion for Gretsches from The Beatles' early days. "He had that lovely Country Gent," says Manley. "And then Gretsch made him a 12-string – but he didn't like it. It was on one of the dates of that British tour that it was delivered, possibly in London. But that guitar was a dog to play. The neck was too wide and the action was bad. It wasn't like his Rickenbacker, which was almost as easy to play as a six-string. As far as I know George gave the Gretsch 12-string to John St John, the lead guitarist in Sounds Incorporated, who were also on that tour, backing Mary Wells."[72]

Gretsch's guitar-playing representative Jimmie Webster had visited England in 1964 on a promotional tour for the company, and had hopes of arranging a meeting with Harrison. It seems the meeting never happened – but perhaps there would have been talk of Gretsch producing a George Harrison signature guitar. A magazine report in September mentioned: "... at long last one manufacturer is planning to make a special guitar which will be named after [George Harrison]."[73] A later reply to a readers' letter in another magazine offered a further clue: "Gretsch do not have an electric 12-string on the market although they have made one experimental model which is now being given the once-over by George Harrison. Arbiter, who handle Gretsch in [the UK], say that even if the 12-string does come on to the market it is unlikely it will cost more than 250 guineas."[74]

Manley's account suggests that Harrison accepted the Gretsch 12-string but was not impressed, and quickly shelved the guitar. There is no evidence that he ever used it with The Beatles. What is certain is that John St John of Sounds Incorporated ended up with the guitar. Sounds Incorporated members had first met The Beatles when both groups worked in Hamburg in the early days.

"We had sax players, so we'd back Gene Vincent and Little Richard – that was with Billy Preston on organ, aged 16. Brian Epstein always wanted to handle us," says St John. "He always liked the band, and asked us to play on Beatles tours, in Australia and the States. We had to go on before The Beatles – and that was one of the hardest gigs ever for a band. Some of our horn section ended up playing on *Sgt Pepper*."

On a later tour alongside The Yardbirds, guitarist Jimmy Page had accidentally damaged a Guild 12-string of St John's. St John happened to be discussing this in a tea break with The Beatles when both bands were recording at Abbey Road. "George said, 'Do you want to try the Rickenbacker?' And I said no, my Guild wasn't that sort of guitar. So George said he'd got another 12-string, a Gretsch. Mal Evans went and got it down from their big pile of guitars. George said it was too big for him – it had a very wide fretboard – and he said, 'Well, why don't you have it? I don't need it, you know. I can't play it, it's not right for me.' So that's how I got it. It was great for what we were doing."[75]

A keen observer wrote to a magazine's letters page toward the beginning of 1967: "I remember reading that George took delivery of a Gretsch electric 12-string. A little later I saw John St John of Sounds Incorporated using one and I thought that perhaps [Gretsch 12-strings] were on distribution over here, but I haven't seen any since. Are these guitars in fact a set Gretsch line, and are they on

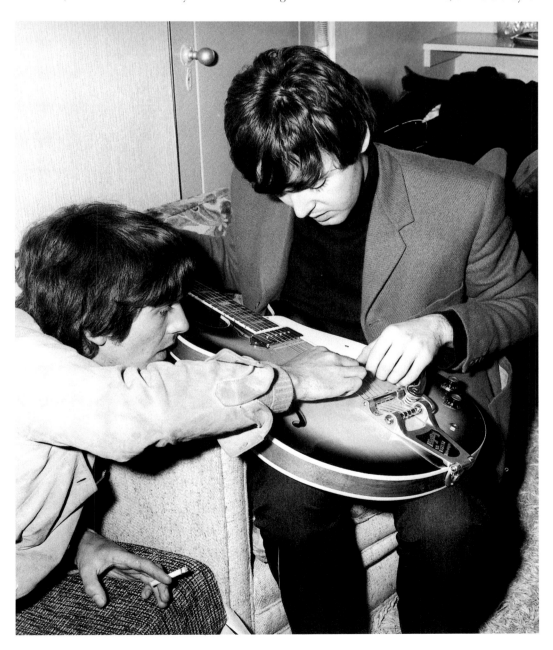

IF I HAD TO PICK ONE ELECTRIC GUITAR, IT WOULD BE THIS.

Paul McCartney, referring to his

all-time favourite electric, the

Epiphone Casino

At the same time as acquiring his Texan acoustic, Paul also got an Epiphone Casino electric guitar. Pictured right, backstage at the group's 1964/65 Christmas shows, George and Paul try to figure out a way of adapting the new right-handed guitar for left-handed playing.

An original log from Gibson's archive recording the shipping of Paul's Casino, serial 84075, on November 1st 1962.

Paul's Epiphone Casino ES-230TD. The guitar is set up for left-handed playing, has had the original pickguard removed, and features a British-licensed Bigsby vibrato. The Gibson-style headstock here differs from the later Epiphone shape. Paul still owns the guitar.

This one-of-a-kind Gretsch George Harrison Model electric 12-string (headstock close-up right) was given to the Beatle by Gretsch in 1964. George later gave it away to a member of Sounds Incorporated.

sale over here or in the States?" The magazine replied that the guitar was not generally available. "George had his custom-built and it was the same model which you saw being used by John St John, who borrows it from George on odd occasions."[76]

The very unusual Gretsch George Harrison 12-String has an old-style model 6120 single-cutaway body finished in black, with white bound f-holes. The label inside reads "Special", a name Gretsch often applied to custom guitars, and bears serial number 45708. The engraved chrome plate on the headstock reads "George Harrison Model". This type of 12-string never appeared as a regular Gretsch production item. The only other example known is an identical 12-string used by Mike Nesmith with The Monkees in the first season of episodes of their television show (not the regular double-cutaway Gretsch 12 he used later). The only difference was that Nesmith's was without the chrome nameplate on the headstock and had a Bigsby vibrato.

With all the new guitars The Beatles were receiving, one wonders what happened to the old ones. In most cases, if they weren't stolen, the extra guitars would be kept at individual homes or in storage at Abbey Road. But on occasion the group did give instruments away, such as the Gretsch 12-string. A further example was another Harrison guitar, his Futurama. *Beat Instrumental* magazine held a contest this year to win it. "This is the actual instrument he used during the Cavern days right up to The Beatles' last visit to Hamburg in 1962," ran the blurb. "It can also be heard on the historic Polydor recording of 'Ain't She Sweet' etc."[77]

Beat Instrumental's publisher at the time, Sean O'Mahony, recalls Harrison donating the Futurama for the competition. "I asked if they had any old equipment we could give as a prize, and George said, 'Yes, you can have this old guitar, I don't want it'. This was in the days when nobody thought they were worth anything." The winner of the guitar was one AJ Thompson of Saltdean, Sussex. O'Mahony remembers the prizegiving. "I asked the winner if he played guitar. He didn't. So I said, 'Would you rather have the money?' and he said yes, so I gave him some money. He didn't want the guitar, he wanted the money – which I was very pleased about. I still have the guitar today. There are some Hamburg stickers on the case."

Beat Instrumental also ran numerous competitions to win old Beatles strings and drumsticks. "I've still got loads of strings used on *Sgt Pepper*," says O'Mahony. "Mal Evans used to bring them in and say, 'Do you want these?' and I used to stuff them in a drawer. I hardly knew what to do with them."[78]

Meanwhile, the group's British tour ended on November 10th, in Bristol. The remainder of the month was taken up with television and radio appearances to promote the latest releases, including a special filming on the 14th of the ABC Television show *Thank Your Lucky Stars*, and later their final appearance on *Ready Steady Go!* which aired on November 27th.

New guitars for Christmas

The group's next great adventure planned by Epstein was Another Beatles' Christmas Show, this time held at London's Hammersmith Odeon. The bill featured Sounds Incorporated, The Yardbirds, Freddie & The Dreamers, The Mike Cotton Sound and other acts. Freddie Garrity of The Dreamers recalls the sense of fun that surrounded the production. "I opened the show swinging on a rope wearing a tutu, just like a fairy. I mean, it was a Christmas show,"[79] he laughs.

Rehearsals started on December 21st. Reports at this time indicated that McCartney bought two new Epiphone guitars, which he said he planned to use for "composing". Photographs taken during the rehearsals for the Christmas performances show him playing a new Epiphone Casino, the guitar still strung right-handed. Another picture shows McCartney and Harrison examining the right-handed Casino, evidently discussing how they would alter the regular right-handed guitar so that the left-handed McCartney could use it.

The Epiphone Casino ES-230TD that McCartney purchased has an early-style Gibson-design headstock rather than Epiphone's later "hourglass"-shape headstock. The Epiphone brand dates back to the 1920s, the New York company quickly becoming well-known for fine archtop and flat-top guitars. But the company's luck did not continue, and Gibson agreed to purchase the faltering operation in 1957. The hollow-body double-cutaway Casino model, launched in 1961, was based on Gibson's ES-330.

McCartney's sunburst Casino has serial number 84075, and according to Gibson's records was shipped by the company on November 1st 1962. McCartney did alter it for playing left-handed, turning the guitar upside down, re-stringing it and modifying the bridge for correct intonation. A strap button was added to the top horn of the guitar's body, too, so that he could play the Casino using a guitar strap.

McCartney has said he was influenced to buy the Casino by his friend, blues musician John Mayall. "He used to play me a lot of records late at night," said McCartney. "He was a kind of DJ type guy. You'd go back to his place and he'd sit you down, give you a drink, and say, 'Just check this out.' He'd go over to his deck, and for hours he'd blast you with BB King, Eric Clapton ... he was sort of showing me where all of Eric's stuff was from. He gave me a little evening's education in that. I was turned on after that, and I went and bought an Epiphone."[80]

Mayall recalls the late-night record sessions. "I showed him my hollow-body guitar that I'd bought when I was in the army, in Japan in 1955. When people get together and listen to records they talk about all kinds of things related to the music, so obviously we must have touched upon the instruments and it struck home. He got a hollow-body after to get that tone."[81]

Remember that McCartney had started in the group as a guitarist and then switched to bass guitar. He would use his Casino extensively in the studio with The Beatles and throughout his solo career, and still owns the guitar today. Indeed he has referred to it as his favourite electric. "If I had to choose one electric guitar," he said, "it would be this."[82]

At 164 guineas (£172.20, about $480 then; around £2,080 or $2,910 in today's money) the Casino wasn't the most expensive Epiphone in 1964 – and you might have expected a Beatle to have opted for the best. But McCartney recently explained that he wanted one with a Bigsby fitted – and the Casino was the only Epiphone of its type offered by UK importer Rosetti with the vibrato arm.[83]

The other Epiphone McCartney bought was an acoustic flat-top Texan FT-79. Again, the guitar is similar to a Gibson model, the J-45. It was another right-handed model that was then converted to a left-hander. McCartney used it for much of his acoustic work, most notably for the recording of 'Yesterday'. A Texan retailed for 84 guineas (£88.20, about $250 then; around £1,070 or $1,500 in today's money).

The group's Christmas shows ran from December 24th to January 16th. As with the previous year's Christmas events, there were musical guests, comedy, pantomime and, of course, a performance by The Beatles, this time of 11 songs. Also on the bill was one of London's hippest new groups, The Yardbirds. Eric Clapton was lead guitarist, and it was during these shows that Harrison and Clapton became friends. The band's rhythm guitarist, Chris Dreja, remembers above almost anything else the sheer noise created by the screaming crowd and the number of objects they threw on to the Hammersmith Odeon's stage.

"They had two guys on either side of the stage who used to sweep up after every performance," says Dreja. "I remember Lennon going on stage and picking up this gift-wrapped thing that had been thrown on. Inside was a lump of coal. So it was pretty dangerous stuff."

He remembers one day during the shows when McCartney came into The Yardbirds' dressing room to ask

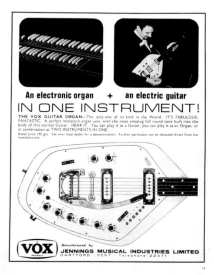

An electronic organ + an electric guitar
IN ONE INSTRUMENT!

VOX
Manufactured by JENNINGS MUSICAL INDUSTRIES LIMITED

An ad (right) for Vox's unusual and shortlived guitar organ.

what they thought of a new song he was working on. "He sat down with the guitar, and at that point hadn't got the lyrics, just the melody. He said it was called 'Scrambled Eggs'. And of course it was 'Yesterday'. There we were witnessing the start of one of the most famous songs of all time, and Paul was just playing it for us on an acoustic."

The Hammersmith Odeon was a big cinema, says Dreja, with a large car park at the rear. For half the show The Beatles were dressed in furry "yeti" costumes, based on the alien yeti character in the BBC TV programme *Doctor Who*. "This was obviously the time they'd decided to buy their first Rolls Royces," explains Dreja. "So they had the car company bring some Rolls Royces down to the Odeon. I remember Lennon and McCartney at the backstage door saying, 'All right boys, bring the next one around.' And these amazing Rolls Royces would be driven around this car park for them to choose from – while they were standing there in their yeti costumes. It was wild."[84]

When is a guitar not a guitar?

With the music scene booming, manufacturers were experimenting with new methods of creating unusual sounds. During 1964 Vox, Watkins (WEM) and Burns London were all in a race to turn out the first guitar-organ hybrid. This was an instrument that looked and played like an electric guitar, but produced organ-type sounds. Burns completed the earliest prototype, and Lennon was among the first to try it. For some reason, however, Burns shelved their idea.

Vox was first to market with a guitar organ. At first it had been designed simply to attract people to the company's trade-show exhibit, but when salesmen took orders for the instrument at the show, Vox had little choice but to actually produce guitar organs. The Vox was made with the company's standard five-sided Phantom body shape, but part of a Vox organ was built into the body to create the sounds. There were special contacts wired into the first 14 "sectioned" frets. The instrument was designed to be able to produce organ or guitar sounds, individually or simultaneously.

Dick Denney of Vox says he presented a guitar organ to The Beatles. "I took the first one up to John Lennon and Paul McCartney, to the Hammersmith Odeon in London during their Christmas show. When they first saw it they were in awe, but they couldn't suss it out. It was too much trouble to run. But I think they liked it, because John kept it. I remember him coming up to me and pulling my beard and saying, 'Dick, you're an old nanny goat, but we love you.'"[85] The negative opinion of the guitar organ was shared by most other musicians who tried it, and the unreliable instrument soon disappeared from the market.

After Beatle roadie Mal Evans's death in 1976, his wife wrote to Harrison enquiring about some guitars she had, including Lennon's Vox guitar organ. Harrison replied: "The white Vox guitar was presented to John by the makers, at Abbey Road studio some time during the mid-1960s, and I seem to recall that it was a prototype guitar with built-in organ facility incorporated into the fingerboard. This was a short time before the advent of synthesisers and therefore I am not too sure if this model ever went into serious production …

"It is difficult to give you an estimate of their value because alone the guitars are not too expensive by today's standards. However, if you do decide to sell them, I would remind you that because they once were John's they will be much more valuable than you may suspect. I paid £1,000 to Sotheby's last year to retrieve a one-page letter I'd written in the early 1960s. In the same sale an acoustic guitar of mine was auctioned for £3,000 – and that was a guitar I only owned for ten minutes! So you could most likely get £5,000 to £10,000 for them. If you decide not to sell them now they will only appreciate in value as [does] all Beatle memorabilia."[86]

The Vox guitar organ eventually sold at auction for £10,000. It's not known if Lennon ever made use of his on any Beatle recordings – but there is no evidence at all to suggest that he did.

Rickenbacker Beatlebacker in the UK

By autumn 1964 electric 12-string guitars were in great demand in the UK as a result of Harrison's popularisation of the instrument. British distributor Rose-Morris commissioned Rickenbacker to make six exclusive models from the California maker's existing line, renamed and slightly modified for the British market.

Some of the "British" line of Rickenbackers came with traditional f-holes instead of the more

I REMEMBER LENNON GOING ON STAGE AND PICKING UP THIS GIFT-WRAPPED THING THAT HAD BEEN THROWN ON. INSIDE WAS A LUMP OF COAL. SO IT WAS PRETTY DANGEROUS STUFF.

Chris Dreja, of The Yardbirds,

who supported the Beatles at their

1964 Christmas show

common Rickenbacker "slash"-shape soundholes, and all were available only in Rickenbacker's fireglo (red sunburst) finish. "It's here at last," trumpeted a Rose-Morris press release. "And now anyone can go and buy a 12-string Rickenbacker identical to the one George Harrison uses ... You can rest assured that you will have exactly the same guitar as The Beatles."

In fact, the 12-string model sold by the UK distributor was the equivalent of a Rickenbacker 330-12 model, and not the more deluxe 360-12 used by Harrison. Rose-Morris used their own four-figure model numbers for the guitars, with the 330-12 known as a model 1993 and the 325 equivalent a model 1996. These numbers were purely for Rose-Morris's purposes, and did not appear on the guitars themselves. The 12-string 1993 sold for 212 guineas (£222.50, about $620 then; around £2,700 or $3,775 in today's money), and the 325-like 1996 for £166/19/- (£166.95, about $465 then; around £2,020 or $2,830 in today's money).

To launch the new "British" line of Rickenbackers, Rose-Morris started an advertising campaign in the instrument press, at first indirectly and then directly using The Beatles to help promote the Rickenbacker line. Thus Rose-Morris's promotions started out with slogans such as "Yeah! Yeah! Yeah! It's Rickenbacker" and tag-lines like "Listen to Beatles John and George ... That's the great Rickenbacker Sound"[87]

During one of the Christmas performances Lennon damaged his '64 Rickenbacker 325. "John Lennon has broken the Rickenbacker guitar that was specially made for him," ran a news item, "and Rose-Morris have provided him with a production model, the 1996, from stock which is very similar to his original, while the broken one is being repaired. He is apparently very pleased with his replacement and may well use it as his main guitar when he has the repaired one returned to him. He dropped it off stage during the current show at the Hammersmith Odeon and at the time thought little of it. When he took it on stage for the next performance, however, he noticed a slight

An original Rickenbacker model 1996, made in 1964 especially for sale in the UK. During the Christmas shows of 1964/65 John briefly played a similar model, which today is owned by Ringo.

AN ACOUSTIC GUITAR OF MINE WAS AUCTIONED FOR £3,000 – AND THAT WAS A GUITAR I ONLY OWNED FOR TEN MINUTES!

George Harrison,

on the value-added aspect of

ex-Beatle gear

crack in the neck just below the machine heads and found that it began to go out of tune as he played it. So he was left with only one guitar – the Rickenbacker model he bought in Germany four years ago, because the one he uses is not a standard model."[88]

A recent examination of Lennon's '64 Rickenbacker 325 reveals a very serious-looking headstock crack still visible. The splintered, jagged crack starts at one side of the nut and goes around the neck to the rear. The repair was poorly executed, and was not correctly touched up with new black finish.

Lennon's misfortune became Rose-Morris's great fortune. The Beatles had so far only dealt with Rickenbacker in the US, but now the British distributor was able to act directly – and cash in. By giving Lennon a new fireglo-finish 1996 model – the "British" equivalent of the 325 – Rose-Morris felt justified in using The Beatles and Lennon in their own advertising campaign. New ads appeared, the best known bearing the slogan: "Rickenbacker the Beatle backer." It featured a picture of Lennon and the 1996 guitar, adding: "This is the famous Rickenbacker guitar model 1996 as used by Beatle John Lennon. For a long time now John and his Rickenbacker have been inseparable, so why don't you try one at your local music shop?"

The "British" Rickenbacker 1996 model was identical to Lennon's '64 Rick 325 except for two differences. One was the f-hole in the body, the other its red "fireglo" colour. Lennon only used the 1996 briefly during the Christmas shows, after which it was retired to his house. It was spotted again in photographs taken for a story about Lennon's home music room published in 1967. Lennon later gave the guitar to Starr, who still owns it to this day.

The Beatles finished 1964 with the continuing Christmas shows, their stage equipment remaining almost unchanged. Starr played on his 22-inch-bass Ludwig drum set. The amplifiers stayed the same: two Vox guitar AC-100s and the AC-100 bass amp with 2x15 speaker cabinet. McCartney played the '63 Hofner violin bass as his main instrument and the reconditioned '61 Hofner as a spare. Harrison used his Rickenbacker 12-string, Gretsch Tennessean and Gretsch Country Gent guitars. Lennon played his new Rickenbacker 1996, with the Gibson J-160E electric-acoustic for use when required, while during the performance of 'I'm A Loser' he played harmonica using the harness.

But it was in the studio that the group's expertise would really become evident in the year to come.

Rose-Morris, UK agents for Rickenbacker, took advantage of John's brief use of the 1996 model by advertising it as "the Beatle backer".

RICKENBACKER
the Beatle backer

This is the famous Rickenbacker guitar model 1996 as used by 'Beatle' JOHN LENNON. For a long time now John and his Rickenbacker have been inseparable, so why don't you try one at your local music shop! You too may find that this is the guitar you just cannot put down.
Remember—if this particular model doesn't suit you, there are five other Rickenbackers including a fabulous 4-string bass and of course the famous 12-string.
Model 1996—illustrated
complete in luxury case **159 GNS.**

Rose-Morris SPONSORED INSTRUMENTS   See your dealer

" **The more I listened to it, the more I decided I didn't like the guitar sound I had. It was crap.** "

1965

BRIAN EPSTEIN'S MANAGEMENT HAD BEEN OVERWHELMINGLY SUCCESSFUL FOR THE BEATLES IN 1964, AND NATURALLY HE HOPED FOR MORE OF THE SAME THIS YEAR. ANOTHER RIGOROUS SCHEDULE WAS PLANNED: RECORDING SESSIONS, A NEW FILM, MORE RECORDING, AND EXTENSIVE INTERNATIONAL TOURING, INCLUDING ANOTHER SUMMER TOUR OF THE US AND A BRIEF TOUR OF THE UK.

One difference for 1965 was that with the group's increased popularity came the opportunity to be more selective about appearances. They tried to schedule more time off, playing fewer radio and television shows. The year started with the completion of the Christmas performances at the Hammersmith Odeon, with the final night on January 16th. Keeping in step with their schedule of two LPs and four singles a year, the group started a week-long series of recording sessions at Abbey Road studio 2 on February 15th. A multitude of new tracks were recorded for use in their forthcoming film, as well as for the next album release, both of which would eventually be named *Help!*. One side of the LP would feature songs from the film, the other the non-soundtrack cuts.

Some of the week's sessions were documented by reporters from Sean O'Mahony's Beat Publications for a feature in an upcoming issue of *The Beatles Monthly Book*. Photos taken show The Beatles with their familiar instruments: McCartney and his '63 Hofner bass; Harrison and his Gretsch Tennessean, with his Rickenbacker 12-string also to hand. Lennon's repaired '64 Rickenbacker 325 made its way back into the guitar line-up, while Starr used the same 22-inch-bass Ludwig kit seen during the '64 US tour. More importantly, the photos show the studio littered with new Beatle instruments.

Sonic blue Fender Strats for John and George

Lennon was playing a Fender Stratocaster during these sessions. The Fender company had been established by Leo Fender in California back in the late 1940s, at first making amps and electric lap-steel guitars. In 1950 Fender introduced the first commercially-available solidbody electric guitar, soon known as the Telecaster, and after adding the Precision Bass (1951) and the Stratocaster (1954) to the line, as well as great amps like the Deluxe and the Twin Reverb, the company was well on the way to world-beating success.

The Stratocaster – widely abbreviated, simply, to "Strat" – had fired Western swing and Buddy Holly, Dick Dale's surf tones and The Shadows' twangy pop, but now it was set for a new journey. Lennon was used to a three-pickup guitar, but this was something else altogether.

His Strat was in Fender's pale blue custom-color finish, officially known as sonic blue. Harrison later recalled that both he and Lennon acquired Strats at the time. "It was funny," he said, "because all these American bands kept coming over to England, saying, 'How did you get that guitar sound?' And the more I listened to it, the more I decided I didn't like the guitar sound I had. It was crap. A Gretsch guitar and a Vox amp, and I didn't like it. But those were early days, and we were lucky to have anything when we started out. But anyway, I decided I'd get a Strat, and John decided he'd get one too. So we sent out our roadie, Mal Evans, said go and get us two Strats. And he came back with two of them, pale blue ones. Straight away we used them on the album we were making at the time, which was *Rubber Soul* – I played it a lot on that album, [most noticeably] the solo on 'Nowhere Man' which John and I both played in unison."[1]

Although Harrison's recollection places the acquisition of the Fenders later, the photographs featured in *The Beatles Monthly Book* show Lennon at the February 1965 sessions with his new Fender Stratocaster. It's not certain if either Strat ended up on any of these *Help!* recordings, but when one listens to some of the results – such as the single A notes hit on the beat in the verses of 'Ticket To Ride' – the tone of a Fender Stratocaster seems evident.

It's ironic that only a few months earlier Fender would, as we've seen, have paid The Beatles to use a Fender Stratocaster – and here only four months later Harrison and Lennon decide to send out Evans to buy a pair of Strats. Like their two matching Gibson J-160Es, the sonic blue Fender Stratocasters were virtually identical. They had rosewood fingerboards, white pickguards and standard Strat hardware. A recent examination of Harrison's Strat reveals that the guitar had at some point in its life been sold by a music dealer in Kent. A worn label on the back of the headstock reads: "Grimwoods; The music people; Maidstone and Whitstable."

The original label for the American-release of the 'Ticket To Ride' single boasted, rather prematurely, that the track was from the forthcoming film Eight Arms To Hold You – which was the working title of what later became Help!

The serial number on Harrison's Strat is 83840 and the neck is dated December 1961. A new custom-color Strat in 1965 would have cost £180/12/- (£180.60, about $500 then; around £2,080 or $2,900 in today's money).

First task on the group's recording agenda was to cut a new single, 'Ticket To Ride'. McCartney overdubbed the memorable lead-guitar break on the recording using his new Epiphone Casino, now strung left-handed. This was the first time that lead guitar had been played on a Beatles session by anyone other than Harrison or Lennon. This change to the group dynamic did not, of course, go unnoticed. In a music-paper report on the February 15th session Lennon, pointing to a running tape machine nearby, commented, "Hey, listen. Hear that play by Paul? He's been doing quite a bit of lead guitar work this week. Gear. I reckon he's moving in."[2]

Harrison said later he thought that 'Ticket To Ride' was the last Beatles song on which he used his '63 Rickenbacker 12-string. "There's a strange thing about that guitar," he said. "I don't think the electronics in it are very good. I don't know if they improved it – they probably have by now – [but] it had a whole bunch of controls on it … four knobs and a little tiny knob. [That tiny knob] never seemed to do anything. All it ever seemed was that there was one sound I could get where it was bright, which was the sound I used, and another tone where it all went muffled, which I never used. [The bright sound was] the sound you hear on 'Ticket To Ride'."[3]

Harrison also remembered that his 12-string was quite easy to play, as long as it was in tune – although 12-string guitars are notoriously difficult to get (and keep) in tune. "Having not played it for years, I just played it again recently and was surprised that the neck is so narrow," he said later. "You have to be very careful when you're clamping the strings down there because the first and sixth strings can slip off the side of the neck if you're pressing at an angle. But it's pretty good from what I remember. I used to play it in concerts for years and it never gave me any trouble. I'm pleased to say I've still got that guitar – and it's a great classic guitar now, I think. I've got it hanging on the wall at home … That sound you just associate with those early 1960s Beatle records. The Rickenbacker 12-string sound is a sound on its own."[4]

John at Abbey Road studios in February 1965 with his new sonic blue Fender Stratocaster. Together with George's matching instrument, these were the first Fender guitars owned by the group.

While 'Ticket To Ride' was indeed the last Beatle recording on which Harrison used his '63 Rickenbacker 360-12, it wasn't the last time he would use a Rick 12-string on record. Only months later he would receive a new-style Rickenbacker 360-12 which he went on to use for further sessions and concerts.

'Another Girl' and Harrison's 'I Need You' were also recorded on February 15th, for use in the group's upcoming film. Harrison again experimented with guitar volume swells on 'I Need You', this time using a traditional volume pedal for the effect rather than relying on Lennon to manipulate his volume control. The sessions spilled into the next day as McCartney overdubbed a lead-guitar part on 'Another Girl', again playing his Epiphone Casino. A new song, 'Yes It Is', was also cut, as the flip-side for their new single. Harrison again used the volume pedal to create the song's distinctive volume-swell guitar sound.

IT NEVER GAVE ME ANY TROUBLE ... AND IT'S A GREAT CLASSIC GUITAR NOW ... THAT SOUND YOU JUST ASSOCIATE WITH THOSE EARLY 1960s BEATLE RECORDS.

George Harrison,

still proud owner of his

'63 Rickenbacker 12-string,

last used on 'Ticket To Ride'

This early-1960s sonic blue Fender Stratocaster is similar to the pair that John and George acquired in 1965.

The Framus Hootenanny

Other new instruments appeared for these *Help!* sessions, including a German-made Framus Hootenanny 5/024 acoustic 12-string, with full-size flat-top natural-finish body. Framus had been set up in Germany in 1946 by Fred Wilfer, and by 1965 the instruments were being distributed in Britain by the London-based Dallas company. The 5/024 sold for £42/10/6 (£42.52, about $120 then; around £490 or $690 in today's money).

Another new German-made instrument, the Hohner Pianet, made its way into the group's instrument collection. It seems that Roy Young's use of a Pianet on the same bill as the group last year had left an impression. McCartney and Lennon, at least, played the new Pianet during these February recording sessions. Hohner was an old German-based musical instrument manufacturer, founded by Matthias Hohner in the 1850s. Perhaps best known to the group for its harmonicas, Hohner also made keyboard instruments. Their first electric piano was the Cembalet of 1958, followed by the Pianet four years later, both designed by Ernst Zacharias. The Pianet has an unusual "acoustic" mechanism. Each key was linked to a short metal rod with a leather-and-foam adhesive pad on the end; the pad rested on an accordion-style reed, from which it pulled free when the key was pressed, vibrating the reed, the sound of which was then amplified. As a result the Pianet had a very distinctive and percussive piano-like sound that was subsequently used on many Beatle recordings. The model the group used was a Pianet C, with its classic wooden case, "coffee table" legs and a folding lid that doubled as a music stand when opened. At the time it retailed for £114/9/- (£114.45, about $320 then; around £1,400 or $1,950 in today's money).

As with many new instrumental arrivals, the group tried to fit the Pianet's sound into virtually any new song. Recording continued on February 17th with work on a new Harrison tune, 'You Like Me Too Much', which clearly features Pianet. The group's classic 'The Night Before' was also cut on this day, with Lennon playing the Pianet while McCartney and George Martin took to Abbey Road's Steinway grand piano.

Further recording and mixing continued the next day and included 'Tell Me What You See', again featuring Pianet, this time played by McCartney. He also overdubbed the Latin-percussion sound of a guiro on to this track. Another song recorded on the 18th was Lennon's acoustic Dylan-like ballad 'You've Got To Hide Your Love Away' which featured the sound of the new Framus Hootenanny 12-string, as well as Harrison playing his Gibson J-160E – and Starr playing the drums with brushes. 'If You've Got Trouble' was also committed to tape, with Starr on lead vocal, although the track would not be released until *Anthology 2*.

The week-long sessions continued on Friday February 19th with the new Lennon original 'You're Going To Lose That Girl'. Overdubs included McCartney on the Steinway and Starr on bongos. Another new track recorded and shelved during these sessions was a ballad, 'That Means A Lot', later given to singer PJ Proby. Once again The Beatles' version of the song would not be released legitimately until *Anthology 2*.

With the bulk of their new album recorded, the group headed off for a few weeks in The Bahamas to start filming their new as-yet-untitled movie. The working title was *Eight Arms To Hold You* – another Ringoism – but of course this became *Help!*. Various location scenes were shot around the islands, and one of the freshly-cut tracks was immediately put to use as the group were filmed on the waterfront miming to 'Another Girl'. This light-hearted sequence shows all four Beatles switching instruments throughout the song: Lennon's Rickenbacker 325 with Vox Python strap, Harrison's Gibson J-160E, McCartney's Hofner '63 bass, and Starr's third Ludwig kit with the larger 22-inch bass that he'd used on the '64 US tour, with the same Beatles drop-T logo.

After the warm, sunny climate of The Bahamas, the group switched to the snow-capped mountains of the Austrian Alps. For almost a week, filming continued here with madcap antics on the ski slopes. No Beatle instruments were used during these sequences, but a grand piano was dragged out into the snow to film the 'Ticket To Ride' segment. This is not recommended.

Returning to England on March 22nd, the group continued work on the new film at Twickenham Film Studios. Amid an ever-hectic schedule, Epstein booked them for a further personal appearance on the *Thank Your Lucky Stars* television programme. They mimed to 'Eight Days A Week', 'Yes It Is' and 'Ticket To Ride'. Lennon used his Rickenbacker 325 with Vox Python strap, McCartney his Hofner bass and Harrison his Gretsch Tennessean, while Starr had his 22-inch-bass Ludwig kit. This would be the group's final appearance on the show.

Other TV appearances and recording sessions were slipped between film work. On April 10th they appeared on the BBC TV chart show *Top Of The Pops* performing 'Ticket To Ride' and 'Yes It Is'. The following day the group once again played at the Empire Pool, Wembley, for the *New Musical Express* 1964-65 Annual Poll-Winners' All-Star Concert where they performed 'I Feel Fine', 'She's A Woman', 'Baby's In Black', 'Ticket To Ride' and 'Long Tall Sally'. Harrison played his Gretsch Tennessean with his Country Gentleman as a spare, while Lennon used his Rickenbacker 325 with his '64 Gibson J-160E as back-up. Both guitarists went through their Vox AC-100 amplifiers. McCartney played his '63 Hofner bass through his AC-100 bass rig, and Starr used his 22-inch-bass Ludwig kit.

Finishing the *Help!* sessions

With the title of the new film established, Lennon and McCartney now had to compose a title song. They did so quickly and brilliantly. On April 13th the group found time in their shooting schedule to hop into Abbey Road and work on 'Help!'. It was completed the same day. A recent bootleg which unveiled the building of the track in the studio revealed that Lennon played the Framus Hootenanny 12-string for the song's acoustic rhythm part.

Filming for the movie progressed, but back at Abbey Road producer George Martin completed final mixes of the songs needed for the film. The group were shot in further performance sequences, including one of the highlights, the superb opening scene with the group playing 'Help!'. The black-and-white scene shows Harrison using his Gretsch Tennessean, McCartney his '63 Hofner bass, Starr on his 22-inch-bass Ludwig kit with the number-four drop-T logo drum-head, and Lennon playing Harrison's Gibson J-160E.

More memorable clips include the mock recording-studio scene – actually made at Twickenham film studios – for 'You're Going To Lose That Girl'. Again Lennon uses Harrison's Gibson J-160E and McCartney his Hofner bass, while Harrison opts for his second Gretsch Country Gentleman. The sequence presents a "studio" set-up with the group recording, and Harrison, McCartney and Lennon singing through a pair of Neumann U-47 microphones. Starr is seen using his smaller Ludwig drum set with the 20-inch bass drum – the same kit used during the filming of *A Hard Day's Night*, with number-three Beatles-logo drum-head (the one with the exaggerated script-style L in Ludwig).

Another highlight from the film is 'You've Got To Hide Your Love Away', where Lennon uses the Framus Hootenanny acoustic 12-string while Harrison plays his Gibson J-160E and McCartney his Hofner bass. Starr hangs out in Lennon's sleeping pit and accompanies the tune on a tambourine.

Some of the most visually effective scenes of the film were shot on location on Salisbury Plain. The surrealistic setting has the group ostensibly making a recording outdoors, protected by a division of British troops, and all against the backdrop of Stonehenge. The sequence for 'I Need You' has Harrison playing his Gibson J-160E, Lennon on Rickenbacker 325, McCartney using his Hofner bass, and Starr playing his Ludwig 22-inch-bass kit with number-four drop-T logo drum-head. 'The Night Before' was also filmed on this set, but with Lennon playing the Hohner Pianet and Harrison his Gretsch Tennessean.

Filming for *Help!* was concluded on May 12th, with post-production work commencing and the group called in to do various voice-overs for the film's audio track. The Beatles still needed to finish their forthcoming LP and yet another single release, so on June 14th they again journeyed to Abbey Road to record three more songs: 'I've Just Seen A Face', 'I'm Down' and 'Yesterday'. McCartney used his Epiphone Texan acoustic guitar to record the basic track for 'Yesterday' while simultaneously singing the lead vocal.

A few days later, producer George Martin arranged a string quartet of two violins, cello and viola for the song's string accompaniment. 'Yesterday' marks the first time that the group discarded their traditional instrumentation, instead employing an arrangement unexpected of a modern pop-group recording of the time.

The same day's sessions yielded a cover – of Buck Owens's 'Act Naturally' – with Starr on lead vocal, while another new Lennon-McCartney song, 'Wait', was also taped but, appropriately for a song with such a title, was shelved. It would be unearthed again in November during the *Rubber Soul* album sessions.

McCartney recently described the stringent recording schedules at Abbey Road. "It was so

WE JUST HAD TO DO IT. SING THE ROCKER, THAT'S DONE, SING THE BALLAD. AND YOU SEEMED TO HAVE PLENTY OF TIME FOR IT ... WHATEVER TIME THEY GIVE YOU IS ENOUGH.

Paul McCartney,

on the Beatles astonishing work-rate

The scene where the band record 'You're Gonna Lose That Girl' from the movie Help! – actually shot in a mock studio set at Twickenham film studios. John is playing the Gibson J-160E, Paul his Hofner bass, George the Gretsch Country Gent, and Ringo his second 20-inch-bass Ludwig kit, with a good view of the Rogers Swiv-O-Matic drum mount on the bass drum. It looks like there's a Vox AC-100 amp lurking in the shadows too.

organised, and there was not really [anything] laid-back about it. There were three main sessions of the day, 10.30 to 1.30, 2.30 to 5.30, 7.30 to 10.30, and that was how everyone worked. They used to give you time for lunch, which was mainly a cheese roll and half a beer, or tea – and that might be a quick meal.

"We hardly ever worked in the evening, actually – it was only later we got into those evening sessions. We mainly worked the two day sessions, so it was the pub in the evening, to talk about our exploits. Now, people drive themselves mad recording, going crazy, up all night, still up there doing funny things at six in the morning."

He recalls recording songs as diverse as 'I'm Down' and 'Yesterday' at the same day's session, and being asked now how they managed that. "We just had to do it. Sing the rocker, that's done, sing the ballad. And you seemed to have plenty of time for it ... whatever time they give you is enough."

For a 10.30am session, he remembers, they would arrive at Abbey Road at 10 o'clock. "You'd let yourselves in, test your amps, get yourselves in tune – which didn't take long really, as long as you knew you weren't going to fart around. It takes about half an hour to do that. And then George Martin would be there: 'Right, chaps, what are you going to do?' You'd sit around for about 20 minutes, and me and John normally would just show everyone what the song was ...

"We never rehearsed. Very, very loose. But we'd been playing so much together as a club act that we just sort of knew it. It would bore us to rehearse too much, we kind of knew the songs. So we'd get quite a lot done at those sessions."[5]

The Continental

To complete their new single 'Help!' a flip-side was needed. 'I'm Down' was recorded with McCartney tearing through one of his best rocking vocal performances to date. The song featured another new instrument, a Vox Continental Portable organ, which Lennon played. Later he would use it for live performances of the song, too.

Production of the British-made solid-state Continental began in 1962, although in years to come Vox would manufacture their organs in Italy. The Continental Portable model that The Beatles used had a four-octave keyboard. Wood-weighted black and white keys, reversed from the conventional arrangement so that the main notes were black, along with a detachable chrome Z-shape frame stand and bright orange top helped to give the Continental its classic 1960s futuristic look. The Continental Portable retailed for £262/10/- (£262.50, about $735 then; around £3,030 or $4,250 in today's money).

The unique full-toned voice of the Continental organ, with built-in vibrato, was popular not only with The Beatles but became a key sound with other British groups such as The Dave Clark Five, Manfred Mann, The Zombies and, most notably, The Animals and their hit 'The House Of The Rising Sun' with Alan Price on Continental. The Continental can also be heard on a number of American hit records by groups including Paul Revere & The Raiders, The Blues Magoos, and especially on the Question Mark & The Mysterians hit '96 Tears'. Yet again The Beatles had popularised a distinctive new voice in pop music. As with the Rickenbacker 12-string guitar, the sound of the Vox Continental organ became virtually synonymous with the 1960s.

As always, Epstein kept the group working at a keen pace. A brief 14-day tour of mainland Europe was next, with stops in France, Italy and Spain, commencing in Paris on June 20th. After two shows there the group travelled to Lyon for two more performances on June 22nd, and from there to Milan, Italy, where they performed another two shows. Further concerts occurred the following day in Genoa, Italy, and then four shows in Rome on June 27th and 28th. From Italy they flew back to France for a performance in Nice, after which they went to Madrid, Spain, for a single show in a bullring on July 2nd and then one more concert, in Barcelona, on July 3rd.

Equipment was unchanged: Harrison favoured his Gretsch Tennessean, alternating with his Rickenbacker 12-string and keeping his Gretsch Country Gent close by as a spare. Lennon used his Rickenbacker 325, with J-160E as back-up, and played harmonica with his harp harness on 'I'm A Loser'. Both guitarists used their Vox AC-100 amp rigs. McCartney played his '63 Hofner bass with his refinished '61 along as a spare, going through his Vox AC-100 bass rig. Starr played on his trusty Ludwig 22-inch-bass kit, as for the '64 US tour, and with the same number-four drop-T Beatles logo drum-head.

While in Spain, Lennon acquired a new guitar. A report from the time said it was Lennon who did most shopping during the European tour. "He bought loads of hats and a Spanish guitar," ran the item. "He didn't intend to buy any new instruments but the maker brought the guitar he had just finished to The Beatles' hotel in Madrid and John decided that he would add it to his collection."[6] Lennon was first pictured using his new standard-size Spanish-made classical guitar in the studio during the autumn 1965 *Rubber Soul* sessions. Through the years he would use it on a few Beatle recordings, as we shall see.

George loses a Gretsch

Back in England, the group attended the July 29th royal premiere of *Help!* held at the London Pavilion cinema on Piccadilly Circus. Next on the agenda was to prepare for another American tour. So the day after the premiere, the group held a private rehearsal on the stage of the Epstein-run Saville Theatre in London. Here the group ran through songs for two important upcoming television programmes as well as their imminent US tour.

The first of the TV shows, on the following Sunday, was *Blackpool Night Out* for British ABC. After the Saville Theatre rehearsals the group travelled up to the Lancashire town, just north of Liverpool, but during the journey an incident occurred that depleted the group's instrument collection. The colourful story is told by Beatles' chauffeur Alf Bicknell.

"Prior to leaving," recalls Alf, "roadie Mal Evans had gone on ahead and left me with two guitars, a Rickenbacker and a Country Gentleman. I had to strap these on to the back of the car, because it

This example of the German-made Hohner Pianet electric piano is the kind that The Beatles used extensively in the studio during the recording of the Help! soundtrack, on songs such as 'The Night Before'.

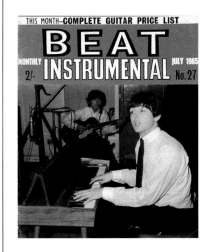

Paul playing the group's Hohner Pianet at Abbey Road studio 2 in February 1965 during the Help! sessions. In the background George plays his Tennessean, with the Rick 12 nearby.

The Framus Hootenanny 12-string, played here by George, was used on many sessions throughout 1965, including 'You've Got To Hide Your Love Away' and 'Help!'.

was very rare for me ever to carry anything like this. We'd left London and probably travelled about 30 or 40 miles, and it was getting a little dark. We passed a big heavy truck, and a few hundred yards down the road Ringo says to me, 'Alf, I think some guy following us is flashing his lights at you.' I pulled over and stopped, got out, and went back to the guy. He said, 'You've just lost a banjo.' So I walked to the back of the car. The straps had broken and one of the guitars was gone."

Bicknell saw that the Rickenbacker case was still in place. By this time road manager Neil Aspinall had got out of the car to have a look. Bicknell wondered aloud what they were going to do. "I asked Neil if he was going to tell them what had happened. He said no, so we stood there arguing for several minutes, not knowing what to say. So then I walked around and opened the passenger door. I leaned in and said, 'John, we just lost a banjo,' trying to make light of it. So he leaned forward and with a whimsical smile on his face said, 'Alf, if you can find the guitar, you can have a bonus.' I said, 'Thanks, John. What's that?' And he says, 'You could have your job back.'"

There then followed some complicated and, for Bicknell, agonising moments as he re-traced their steps and searched for the missing Gretsch. "We found it," he remembers, "which was quite a surprise to everybody. We found a piece here and a piece there and pieces all over. The guitar and its case were smashed to bits. I'm convinced it was the big truck we passed that ran over it. We never even bothered to pick it up, but just left it there lying in the street, because by now we were pushed for time. Nobody blamed me after that – nothing more was said about it. It just turned out to be one big joke."[7] The guitar lost was Harrison's first Gretsch Country Gentleman, with the dual "screw-down" mutes, which by this time was carried only as a spare. The guitarist's favoured Country Gentleman, his second, with dual "flip-up" mutes, managed to survive with Harrison throughout the remainder of 1965.

The Beatles themselves arrived safely in Blackpool and spent the afternoon of Sunday August 1st on-stage at the city's ABC Theatre rehearsing for the evening's live performance. They played six songs: 'I'm Down', 'Act Naturally', 'I Feel Fine', 'Ticket To Ride', 'Yesterday' and 'Help!', the last four of which can be heard on *Anthology 2*. The group had their familiar backline for the show, as used during the recent European tour. Lennon and Harrison played through their Vox AC-100 guitar amps and McCartney through his Vox AC-100 bass rig. Harrison used his Gretsch Tennessean, alternating with his Rickenbacker 12-string, and with his second Gretsch Country Gentleman as a spare. Lennon played his Rickenbacker 325, while McCartney used his trusty '63 Hofner bass. Starr played the 22-inch-bass Ludwig kit with number-four drop-T logo. But there were also a few additions to the live equipment. For the first time 'Yesterday' was performed live, for which McCartney played his Epiphone Texan, accompanied by a string quartet. For 'I'm Down' Lennon sat and played the Vox Continental Portable organ, which was plugged into a Vox AC-30 amp-and-speaker combo.

Another new Ludwig for Ringo, and a Mellotron for John

After their television appearance in Blackpool The Beatles had barely two weeks off before departing for their second American tour. Prior to leaving, Starr received yet another Ludwig drum set – his fourth, and the second standard-size set with a 22-inch bass drum. Starr now had two such Ludwig kits, larger than his earlier sets, and they were virtually identical, including the added Rogers Swiv-O-Matic tom mount. The only noticeable difference between Starr's third and fourth 22-inch-bass Ludwig sets is in the distinct swirling patterns in the drums' oyster black pearl covering. Like fingerprints, no two of these coverings are exactly the same.

Along with the drum set came a new Beatles drop-T logo drum-head, number five. The logo was painted on a Ludwig Weather Master head, and the clearest difference between it and the earlier heads is that the Ludwig logo is larger, heavier and appears somewhat crooked on the left side in relation to "The Beatles". Starr used this fourth Ludwig set with 22-inch-bass and number-five drop-T logo for the group's 1965 American tour. (Starr's two 22-inch-bass Ludwig kits would show up together in photographs taken at Abbey Road in 1966 during the recording of 'Paperback Writer'.)

Always searching for new sounds from different instruments, Lennon became one of the first artists in Britain to acquire a unique new keyboard, the Mellotron. It was like 70 tape-recorders in a box. Pressing a key activated one of the pre-recorded tapes inside, loaded with sounds as diverse as pitched strings and brass to rhythm effects and entire musical passages (although any held note would stop after ten seconds). In effect it was a forerunner of today's sampling keyboards.

The Mellotron was the younger brother to a US invention, the Chamberlin keyboard devised in the late 1940s by Harry Chamberlin. A Chamberlin representative, Bill Fransen, visited Britain in the early 1960s, ostensibly in search of tape-head manufacturers, but more likely on the look-out for a marketing opportunity. Fransen stumbled upon electro-mechanical engineers Bradmatic in Birmingham, run by the Bradley brothers, Les, Frank and Norman.

Soon Fransen and the Bradleys collaborated – minus Harry Chamberlin – to form the British sales and distribution company Mellotronics, with the Bradleys set to manufacture a copy of the Chamberlin, the Mellotron Mark I, beginning in 1963. Changes were soon made to this prototype, and the Mark II appeared in 1964. It was this production version that Lennon saw.

Its retail price then was a phenomenal £1,000 (about $2,800 then; around £11,500 or $16,200 in today's money). The sometimes out-of-tune and eerie but always atmospheric sounds of the Mellotron later became widely used by many bands, including The Moody Blues and King Crimson.

I MUST HAVE ONE OF THESE.

John Lennon,

reportedly after five minutes

on a Mellotron

The inside of an early Vox Continental organ with orange top removed, showing how at this period the instrument had wooden keys. Later examples had plastic keys and modified electronics, giving a different feel and sound.

Paul with an early-style wooden-key Vox Continental Portable organ which the group used live and in the studio.

Despite Lennon's early enthusiasm, The Beatles would not use a Mellotron until the end of 1966 when they added some of its distinctive sounds to the recording of 'Strawberry Fields Forever'.

Lennon's acquisition of his Mellotron was noted in a contemporary news item. "On the day before they left for their current American tour, The Beatles did some very secret recording at the IBC studio in [London's] Portland Place. John Lennon was persuaded to try a Mellotron during a break and after just five minutes said, 'I must have one of these.' It was delivered on August 16th."[8]

This report not only provides the precise date for the arrival of Lennon's Mellotron, but also refers to a recording session that has never before been documented. Unfortunately no further information about this "secret" recording session at IBC was given. There seems no particular reason why the group would be recording there at this time. Perhaps there was no "secret" other than a visit to IBC to see an early demo of the fabulous new Mellotron?

Back in the USA

The group travelled to New York to start their American summer tour, arriving on August 13th. First on their busy schedule was the filming of a live performance for *The Ed Sullivan Show*, for broadcast in September. The Beatles ran through the same numbers that they had performed weeks earlier in Blackpool. They attended rehearsals at CBS TV's Studio 50 on the afternoon of August 14th, with McCartney playing his '63 Hofner bass, Harrison his Gretsch Tennessean, Lennon the Rickenbacker 325, and Starr his new fourth Ludwig drum set.

McCartney again played his Epiphone Texan acoustic guitar during the performance of 'Yesterday'. During the afternoon camera rehearsals, McCartney was accompanied by three tuxedo'd violinists standing in a row in front of him. But for the actual taped performance later that evening, he played alone to a pre-recorded accompaniment of the three violins.

Also present during this *Ed Sullivan* appearance was Lennon's Vox Continental Portable organ. It had a non-standard "Vox Continental" logo in black letters on white added to the right of the front of the case, presumably at the request of Vox who must have thought that two name-tags would help publicise their keyboard to the big TV audience. Lennon used the Continental on 'I'm Down', playing the organ break in the song with his elbow.

This US television appearance marked the first time that The Beatles used their Vox amplifiers in front of Ed Sullivan's 70-million-plus viewing audience. The group's backline of Vox AC-100 amps, plus an AC-30 combo for the organ, acted as the best advertising campaign that Vox and their US agent Thomas Organ could have wished for. What a way to break into the American market and kick the Vox line into high gear – and all for free! Thomas would capitalise on the group's use of the Vox AC-100 amp, renaming it for the US market as the Vox Super Beatle – an amp that every Beatles-inspired US teenage band and musician would want.

The following day, August 15th, marked the first date of the group's ten-city 1965 American tour, with a concert that would prove to be the biggest and one of the most memorable of their career. Over 55,000 screaming Beatle fans packed into New York's Shea Stadium to witness the group's live performance. John St John, guitarist with one of the tour's opening acts, Sounds Incorporated, remembers what he describes as a "wild" concert. "You just couldn't imagine how loud the crowds were. I could barely hear myself on stage. When The Beatles went on, it was even more deafening. You've never heard anything like it!"[9]

Harrison said later that by this stage in their career, they had enough confidence to play more or less anywhere. But Shea Stadium was different. "It was such a screaming crowd, and it was such a long way to get to the stage, and we all were very nervous," he recalled. "We'd still get nervous doing concerts, even in small theatres. I'd always get a little bit of the butterflies. But at Shea Stadium, although in the film we look very casual when we're lying around waiting to go on, we were very nervous, with that mixture of excitement and anticipation with the biggest crowd that had ever gathered in history. But once we got out there and got on stage and started doing it, it became apparent we were doing it for our own amusement – because nobody could hear a thing."[10]

In conjunction with Ed Sullivan, Epstein had arranged to have the concert filmed as a television special to air in Britain and the US. The film was simply titled *The Beatles At Shea Stadium*. This important document not only presents Beatlemania at its height but provides a detailed view of the instruments and equipment used during the group's second US tour.

Brian Epstein chats with John during rehearsals for the group's appearance on Ed Sullivan in August 1965. John's '64 Rick 325, complete with Vox Python strap and set-list, lies on top of the Vox Continental organ. In the background, Ringo's second 22-inch-bass Ludwig kit has a new Beatles drop-T logo, head number five in the sequence.

This organ was recently sold at auction as John Lennon's first Vox Continental, as used during the Beatles 1965 American tour.

The line-up was the same as in Blackpool. The amplifiers were two Vox AC-100 guitar amps and one AC-100 bass amp. Lennon played his '64 Rickenbacker 325, with his '64 Gibson J-160E as a spare. Harrison played his Gretsch Tennessean, alternating with his Rickenbacker 12-string, and had his second Gretsch Country Gentleman as a spare. McCartney used his '63 Hofner violin bass with his original '61 Hofner nearby as back-up. Starr played his new Ludwig 22-inch-bass kit with number-five drop-T logo drum-head. Also on-stage for each date of the tour was the Vox Continental Portable organ, played through a Vox AC-30 combo amp mounted on a Vox side-swivel stand. Lennon used it on the closing number, 'I'm Down'.

For the grand finale at Shea Stadium, Lennon savagely attacked the organ during the lead break of 'I'm Down' in a way that would have made Jerry Lee Lewis proud. But Lennon's frenzied performance resulted in the Continental's malfunction for the next show, on August 17th in Toronto, Canada. The following day, while in Atlanta, Georgia, the group made arrangements to have the organ replaced. The local Atlanta dealer, The Vox Shoppe, swapped out a Vox Continental organ from the store's stock for Lennon's faulty keyboard. Apparently, Epstein even managed to arrange to have an Atlanta policeman carry out the exchange. Lennon's "Shea Stadium" Vox Continental remained in the possession of the shop's owner until recently when it was sold at auction.

George's second Rickenbacker 12, and a Rick bass for Paul

The tour pressed on through Houston and Chicago. During the stop in Minneapolis, Minnesota, on August 21st another new guitar joined the group's ever-growing instrument array. At a press conference held prior to the evening performance, radio station WDGY in association with B-Sharp Music, a local music store, presented Harrison with a new-style Rickenbacker 360-12 electric 12-string guitar.

The press conference was covered by an instrument trade magazine. "George Harrison, who spoke for the group when I asked them if they had any plans to become musical instrument manufacturers, replied in the negative," wrote the reporter, "while Lennon and McCartney shook their heads 'no' in tacit agreement. 'All we do is play them,' Lennon chirped in when Harrison was finished … [but] McCartney and Lennon felt that they were responsible for increased sales of guitars and drums in this country.

"Randy Resnick and Ron Butwin, representing B-Sharp Music, a Minneapolis store … presented Harrison with a 12-string Rickenbacker guitar at a press conference. Butwin said the guitar was custom-made especially for his store. 'When The Remo Four (another English group) were in town a few weeks back,' said Butwin, 'we showed them this guitar when they visited our store, and they flipped over it. The group knew The Beatles, and one of the fellows said that George Harrison would love to have a guitar like this. I decided that Randy and I should present it to him when he came to town, with our thanks to The Beatles for causing the guitar business to boom.' Harrison was all smiles as he accepted the guitar from the young men,"[11] the magazine piece concluded.

This second Rickenbacker 360-12 was in Rickenbacker's new recently-introduced style and thus differed from Harrison's first: it had rounded edges to the body's top and checkerboard-pattern binding on the back. Other differences on the '65 Rick 12 included the more common "R"-motif tailpiece and a white-bound slash-shape soundhole. Like his first 12-string, Harrison's new guitar was finished in Rickenbacker's fireglo (red sunburst) finish. He did not use this second Rick 12-string during the 1965 American tour, but instead waited to christen it in the studio when the group returned to Britain.

The North American tour continued with a show in Portland, Oregon, on August 22nd. From there the group flew to Los Angeles, California, on August 23rd and rented a house in the exclusive Benedict Canyon neighbourhood out toward the Santa Monica Mountains. It was during the group's week-long stay there that they managed to arrange a meeting with their one-time hero Elvis Presley.

While relaxing at their Benedict Canyon retreat The Beatles entertained several guests and fellow musicians. During one of these days off, Rickenbacker's Francis Hall and his son John managed to arrange a meeting with the group. It was then that McCartney was presented with the left-handed Rickenbacker 4001S bass he'd first seen in New York in 1964.

"I believe it was Burt Lancaster's home that they had rented," says John Hall. "We only brought the left-handed bass. Neil Aspinall had asked to have it. Paul had a little tiny Vox amplifier, just an itty-bitty thing there in the house. He plugged in the bass and was playing away. He really liked it – he didn't want to put it down. He was definitely enthusiastic about it."[12] McCartney recalls receiving his new bass. "I just remember [Rickenbacker] giving me it, and they invited us down to the factory, which I never made, I never got down there. It was a little bit out of LA, I think. But I liked the instrument a lot."[13]

This particular Rickenbacker 4001S bass was one of the first left-handed basses the company had ever made. Their earlier single-pickup 4000 model, launched in 1957, was the first through-neck solidbody electric bass – that is with a neck section extending the entire length of the instrument, with added "wings" to complete the body and headstock. The similar two-pickup 4001 and export 4001S had been added to the line in 1961 and 1964. McCartney's 4001S was finished in Rickenbacker's popular fireglo (red sunburst) finish, and had serial number DA23, indicating a manufacturing date of January 1964.

From 1964 the 4001S was sold in the UK through Rose-Morris as the company's model 1999

Manufacturers were always quick to demonstrate the instrumental activities of the world's favourite group – this Vox ad from 1965 shows the Beatles at Shea Stadium.

and retailed for 175 guineas (£183.75, about $515 then; around £2,120 or $2,970 in today's money). McCartney used this bass a great deal throughout the remaining years with The Beatles as well as later during his solo career. Along the way, McCartney would have several alterations made to the instrument, which he still owns personally at time of writing.

During their rest in Hollywood, the group had time to hang out with LA's latest smash group The Byrds. According to ex-Epstein assistant Derek Taylor, by now working for an LA radio station, The Beatles even managed a studio visit. On his liner notes to The Byrds' *Turn! Turn! Turn!* album, Taylor wrote: "Two of the Fab Four came to the recording sessions at Columbia's Hollywood studios when they could have been sprawling beside their Bel Air pool gazing at Joan Baez. Some choice. Anyway, down from the hills rode George and Paul because they'd liked The Byrds' 'Mr Tambourine Man', and they know that a record like that doesn't happen by accident. ('Ho,' John had said, 'The Byrds have something,' and the others had nodded.) So there they were, at Columbia – bachelor Beatle twosome, denims and fringes and so much experience, heads bent to pick up the sound-subtleties of the Los Angeles Byrds, whom The Beatles publicly named as their fab gear fave rave American group."[14]

Byrds guitarist Roger McGuinn recalls spending time with The Beatles. "We talked a lot about old records, like Gene Vincent, Carl Perkins and of course Elvis. I remember being at their house the day they went to meet Elvis and they wouldn't let me tag along," McGuinn laughs. "I wanted to go with them, but they wouldn't let me." So The Beatles had influenced The Byrds ... and then in turn The Byrds gained The Beatles' respect and in some ways influenced them. It wasn't long before Harrison started to wear "granny" glasses (like McGuinn's), to make good use of his new-style Rickenbacker 12-string (exactly like McGuinn's, except for colour), and to write 'If I Needed Someone', a song that chimes with Byrds-like echoes.

To finish up their tour, The Beatles played two consecutive nights at the Hollywood Bowl in Los Angeles on Sunday August 29th and Monday 30th. Once more, Capitol Records recorded these performances, but as with the 1964 recordings made at the venue the tapes were shelved and remained unreleased until 1977 and *The Beatles At The Hollywood Bowl* LP.

The final date of the group's 1965 American tour was in San Francisco at the Cow Palace, on August 31st. The following day they travelled home to Britain, a million dollars richer, and began a much-needed six-week break in the action. The success of the American tour was immediately reported in the British press – and Vox started a new ad campaign using photos from the group's already famous Shea Stadium concert.

During their time off Harrison experimented with his Gibson J-160E, moving its P-90 pickup from its original location close to the neck to a new position near the bridge. Holes were drilled into the face of the guitar to accommodate the six polepieces of the pickup. Harrison seems to have been trying to get a different or better sound from the instrument, but the pickup would not stay in its new position for long.

Back in the studio – George and the sitar

The group's time off had given them a chance to formulate fresh ideas and write new songs for the next LP and single, which were due out before the end of the year, in time for Christmas sales. On October 12th they re-grouped at Abbey Road, and work immediately commenced on what would become *Rubber Soul*. That day's session started with the taping of a new piece, 'Run For Your Life', followed by early takes of 'Norwegian Wood (This Bird Has Flown)', another new Beatle song destined for classic status.

The recording of the primarily acoustic 'Norwegian Wood' marks the introduction of yet another new Beatle instrument, the sitar. Harrison explained his introduction to the exotic stringed instrument during the filming of *Help!*. "We were waiting to shoot the scene in the restaurant when the guy gets thrown in the soup, and there were a few Indian musicians playing in the background. I remember picking up the sitar and trying to hold it and thinking, 'This is a funny sound.' It was an incidental thing, but somewhere down the line I began to hear Ravi Shankar's name. The third time I heard it, I thought, 'This is an odd coincidence.' And then I talked with David Crosby of The Byrds and he mentioned the name."[15]

In another interview, Harrison continued the story. "I went out and bought a [Ravi Shankar]

I JUST PICKED UP THE SITAR AND KIND OF FOUND THE NOTES.

George Harrison, who discovered an affinity with Indian music during the filming of *Help!*, and first used the sitar in the studio on Lennon's 'Norwegian Wood'

1965

I PLAYED IT ON PIANO AT EXACTLY HALF NORMAL SPEED, AND DOWN AN OCTAVE ... WHEN YOU BRING THE TAPE BACK TO NORMAL SPEED, IT SOUNDS PRETTY BRILLIANT.

George Martin, multi-talented Beatles producer and collaborator, who wasn't averse to cheating now and then – as in the 'harpsichord' solo for 'In My Life'

On-stage in Sheffield, England, on December 8th 1965, George plays his second Rickenbacker 360-12 guitar. It has a capo fitted at the seventh fret for George to play 'If I Needed Someone'.

record and that was it ... it felt very familiar to me to listen to that music. And so it was around that time that I bought a ... cheap sitar in the shop called India Craft in London. And it was lying around, I hadn't really figured out what to do with it. When we were working on 'Norwegian Wood' it just needed something. It was quite spontaneous, from what I remember. I just picked up the sitar and kind of found the notes and I just kind of played it. We miked it up and put it on and it just seemed to hit the spot."[16]

Harrison's interest in Indian music brought new sounds to The Beatles, but also provided an entirely fresh musical outlook for the 1960s. As with the Rickenbacker 12-string, Harrison's use of a new instrument prompted widespread imitation among other pop musicians, especially when the electric sitar was developed a few years later. The Beatles themselves would turn to the sitar for an individual sound texture on some of their future recordings.

The *Rubber Soul* sessions marked the group's first serious efforts to go beyond the normal pop album as they explored a consciously wide range of musical styles. Studio experimentation was developed too.

Discussing the track 'In My Life', producer George Martin explained how the group were becoming bored with conventional ideas. Even the hallowed guitar solo was under threat. "It was quite common practice for us to do a track and leave a hole in the middle for the solo," said Martin. "Sometimes George would pick up his guitar and fool around and do a solo, and we would often try to get other sounds. On 'In My Life' we left the hole as usual, and The Beatles went out and had their cup of tea or something.

"While they were away, I thought it would be rather nice to have a harpsichord-like solo ... I did it with what I call a 'wound up' piano, which was at double speed – partly because you get a harpsichord sound by shortening the attack of everything, but also because I couldn't play it at real speed anyway. So I played it on piano at exactly half normal speed, and down an octave. Of course, when you bring the tape back to normal speed again, it sounds pretty brilliant. It's a means of tricking everybody into thinking you can do something really well."[17]

A 1965 Rickenbacker 360-12 like the one that George acquired during the group's '65 US tour. It was his second 360-12, with Rickenbacker's new "rounded" body style. George used his in the studio and live from the end of 1965 and into '66. The photo on the far right shows George being presented with his new Rick 12 by B-Sharp Music at a press conference in Minneapolis.

The plentiful instruments and equipment at the *Rubber Soul* sessions accentuated this continuing search by the group for new sounds. Photographs reveal Abbey Road's studio 2 littered with instruments. At least 12 guitars were present during the sessions: Lennon's Rickenbacker 325 and the new classical guitar he'd acquired while on tour in Spain; both Gibson J-160Es; McCartney's '63 Hofner bass; the Framus Hootenanny 12-string acoustic; and both sonic blue Fender Strats. McCartney had his Epiphone Casino electric and Texan acoustic, as well as his new left-handed Rickenbacker 4001S bass, while Harrison also had to hand his new Rickenbacker 360-12. Starr used his 22-inch-bass Ludwig set.

A guitar soon gone from the sessions was Harrison's second Gretsch Country Gentleman (the one with dual "flip-up" mutes). Brian O'Hara, lead guitarist and singer of Liverpool band The Fourmost, says Harrison gave him the guitar. "We were friends with The Beatles before they really made it," O'Hara explains today, "and Brian Epstein also managed our group, so we did a lot of shows together.

"We were doing a season in London at The Palladium for nine months, and at night when we finished we'd sometimes go down to Abbey Road and pop in if the lads were recording. We'd just go in and watch them or listen to them until late into the night. On one of those occasions I got a Gretsch Country Gent from George Harrison, which he didn't use – everyone was giving them dozens of guitars by now. I mentioned that the Gent seemed nice, and he said, 'Well, you can have it,' and just like that he handed it over in the studio. God knows what happened to that guitar later. I haven't got a clue. I think I traded it in on another one somewhere along the way."[18]

Here then is news of another tantalising out-there-somewhere Beatles guitar, of untold value both historically and monetarily … but with no means of identifying itself.

Fender Bassman and Hammond organ

During the *Rubber Soul* sessions the Vox AC-100s were used for amplification, although some photographs reveal a pair of Vox AC-30s also set up for recording. The same photos show that a new amplifier had made its way into the group's line-up: a Fender Bassman. It was set up behind a studio "baffle" and was used to record McCartney's bass.

Fender's piggyback-style Bassman – that is, with separate amplifier head and speaker cabinet – was covered in the company's cream-coloured Tolex material, with wheat-coloured grille cloth and cream knobs. The amp head produced 50 watts of power and sat on a matching cabinet containing two 12-inch speakers. This Bassman was most likely a so-called "transitional" model made in late 1963 or early 1964. It's not known which amps the group used for particular songs, but it seems that they had by now figured out that using smaller amps in the studio should provide better and more controllable sound.

Among the keyboard instruments at Abbey Road studios was a Hammond RT-3 organ (below), used with a Leslie rotating-speaker cabinet. The Beatles used the RT-3 and Leslie on a number of recordings.

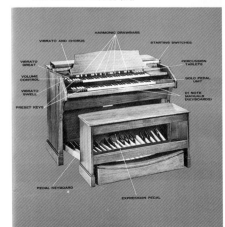

THE CONCERT MODEL (RT-3)

Keyboards too filled the studio during the recording of *Rubber Soul*, including two acoustic pianos – a Steinway grand and a Challen upright. Steinway is one of the best-known and most respected piano makers, founded in New York by German immigrants Henry Steinway and his brothers in 1853. Henry and Theodor Steinway together devised the design of the modern grand piano in 1860. Since then many top concert halls and studios have chosen Steinway instruments – including Abbey Road. Challen was a British maker founded in 1830 by William Challen in London; a century later they began supplying the BBC with pianos, and Abbey Road would probably have been influenced by this prestigious connection.

There was also a Hammond RT-3 organ with Leslie rotating speaker-cabinet at Abbey Road, and a harmonium, all widely used during these sessions. The Hammond RT-3 organ was a top-of-the-line console, similar to the manufacturer's classic B-3. The main difference was that the RT-3 had a 32-note concave pedalboard and a different, larger cabinet. The model was approved by the stringent American Guild of Organists, which set standards for length, height and tension of the pedals and keys of organs. The Hammond RT-3 met all of the AGO's requirements for professional organists, and this is the most likely reason why an RT-3 rather than a B-3 was installed at Abbey Road. An RT-3 was an expensive investment: retail price was around $3,400 (£1225 then) which would translate to a whopping $19,000 or £13,500 in today's money.

Laurens Hammond invented his revolutionary organ in the early 1930s in Chicago. The basis of the instrument's sound was a series of small metallic discs, or "tone wheels". A magnetic pickup was situated near each disc, and the individual cuts or indentations in each disc determined the pitch and type of sound produced. Hammond and his partner John Hanert designed the wheels to produce fundamental pitches and developed a system of controls, or "drawbars", to blend in various harmonics. The result was the wonderfully rich and full Hammond organ sound that became popular not only with churches and classical organists, but more importantly with jazz greats like Jimmy Smith as well as pop and R&B crossover artists such as Georgie Fame.

The amplified speaker cabinet used with Abbey Road's Hammond RT-3 was a Leslie 145 loaded with a model 147 power amp. Donald Leslie invented his speaker cabinet in the early 1940s in California. Inside was a rotating horn, drum or baffle, depending on the model, through which the amplified sound was directed. The speed of the rotation could be controlled by the player: fast for a swirling tremolo-type effect or slow for a churning chorale sound. Abbey Road's Leslie 145 had a pair of rotating horns as well as a rotary drum which directed the sound from a downward-facing 15-inch speaker. This particular combination of RT-3 organ and 145 cabinet was used on most of the occasions when a Hammond organ was called for during Beatle sessions. It's thus likely that this set-up was used back in August 1964 for the group's first Hammond-assisted recording, 'Mr Moonlight', a song soaked in McCartney's atmospheric keyboarding.

A fourth keyboard, a harmonium, was introduced as a new sound to The Beatles and heavily used on the *Rubber Soul*-period recordings – for example on 'We Can Work It Out'. A harmonium is a type of reed organ, using air compressed by bellows and then driven out through the reeds. Along with these four studio-owned keyboards, the group also had their own Vox Continental organ and Hohner Pianet electric piano to hand.

Slap on a capo

By the time Harrison had come to record *Rubber Soul* he'd moved the pickup on his J-160E guitar again. Now it was mounted at the side of the soundhole away from the neck – the opposite side to its original position. Lennon followed suit, moving the pickup on his '64 J-160E to the other side of the soundhole. They must have both liked the more trebly sound that this alteration made because this is how both guitars remained for the next few years.

The October 1965 sessions also produced the group's next single, a double-a-sided disc, 'Day Tripper' and 'We Can Work It Out'. They were recorded with standard Beatle instrumentation, although a highlight on the latter song was the harmonium, played by Lennon. The sessions were yielding some of the group's greatest work, as they started to move away from their familiar tools and experiment with fresh tone colours and new instrumental voices.

McCartney used his new left-handed Rickenbacker 4001S bass almost exclusively on the *Rubber Soul* sessions. He has described the Rickenbacker as being "a slightly different style" to his familiar

Hofner bass. "It stayed in tune better, that was the great thing, because that had been a major problem with the Hofner. I liked everything about that, but it was embarrassing if you weren't quite in tune for something ... Normally you were sort of buried in the mixes; it wasn't until [this period] that the bass and drums came up in the mix."[19]

The Rickenbacker's unusual maple body seemed to aid its punchier, clearer tone, with more 'presence' to each note when compared to the sound of the Hofner.

As we've already seen, Fender Stratocasters were prominent on the solo of 'Nowhere Man', where Lennon and Harrison each played their new blue Strats, in unison. Harrison unleashed his new Rickenbacker 360-12 too, for his composition 'If I Needed Someone'. He chose to record the song using a capo, a small moveable device which can be fitted over the fingerboard behind any fret, shortening the string length and thus raising the strings' pitches.

For 'Someone' Harrison fixed a capo at the seventh fret of the 12-string, lifting his guitar part into a suitable key. Until this point the group had rarely used capos, but for these sessions they used them for many songs, including 'Norwegian Wood' which was played with one at the second fret. Photographs taken while they worked on 'Michelle' show capos on McCartney's Epiphone Texan, on Harrison's J-160E and on Lennon's Spanish classical guitar.

McCartney is even pictured during these sessions using a capo on his new Rickenbacker bass. Capos are rarely used by bass players. Recently asked to explain what he was doing, McCartney himself seems baffled. "I'd try anything once," he laughs. "So ... I'll try a capo.

"I often do that when I'm writing a song – stick a capo on just so it's a different instrument than the one I normally play. Everything goes up a little bit and goes more tingly, and you get a song that reflects that. So it may well have been that we'd written a song on guitars in a certain key, so I only knew it in that key. Or maybe it was to get a higher sound? I often used to tune the strings down a tone, too, so the E would become a D. You'd have to be careful how hard you hit them, but it was kind of interesting. I would just mess around with any experimental effect."[20]

The Vox Tone Bender

'Think For Yourself' was another Harrison original recorded for *Rubber Soul*, this one featuring the new sound of a fuzz bass. "Fuzz" is generally used to describe electronic distortion, normally available by using a box plugged between guitar and amp. Ken Townsend, ex-Abbey Road technician, explains that the studio's owner, EMI, built their own distortion boxes, which at times The Beatles would use.[21] However, it's possible that the fuzz-box used on the bass for this song was a prototype Vox Tone Bender unit.

Dick Denney of Vox says that he delivered the first Vox Tone Bender prototypes to the group in the early part of 1965. As we've already seen, Harrison and Lennon had fiddled around with a Maestro Fuzz Tone unit as early as 1963. Denney recalls that Vox's Tone Bender began life around 1962 when the company was sent a Maestro to try out.

Vox owner Tom Jennings declared the sample American unit useless: surely, he said, their job was to get rid of distortion? Jennings was of the old school, and did not understand the desire among the new pop musicians to find unusual sounds, including electronically "incorrect" ones.

Denney then made up a trial Vox fuzz-box based on the Maestro, but did nothing further. "However, there was a rogue working for us," he says, "and he grabbed hold of the circuit diagram and started making up fuzz-boxes and selling them for himself. We later introduced it ourselves as the Vox Tone Bender."[22] In 1967 Vox would offer their Tone Bender for 10 guineas (£10.50, about $25 then; around £115 or $160 in today's money).

A break in recording on November 1st and 2nd allowed the group to tape mimed performances of 'Day Tripper' and 'We Can Work It Out' for a Granada Television special, *The Music Of Lennon & McCartney*. For these performances McCartney used his '63 Hofner bass, Lennon his '64 Rickenbacker 325, and Harrison his Gretsch Tennessean. Starr went back to using his third Ludwig kit, the first of his two 22-inch-bass sets, which would continue as his main kit until the end of 1968.

For the Granada appearance, the Ludwig set received yet another new Beatle drop-T logo drum-head. Number six was painted on a Ludwig Weather Master head and was similar to its predecessors, but with slight differences in the lettering of "The Beatles". This drum-head stayed on Starr's kit until the middle of 1967.

The Tone Bender fuzz-box as it appeared when Vox marketed the effects unit starting in 1966. The Beatles had earlier used a prototype version given to them by Vox chief designer Dick Denney.

I'D TRY ANYTHING ONCE ... I WOULD JUST MESS AROUND WITH ANY EXPERIMENTAL EFFECT.

Paul McCartney

Ringo's fourth oyster black pearl Ludwig kit, the second of the two with 22-inch bass drums (but minus the drop-T drum head). He used this kit during the 1965 US tour, and still owns it today.

As the sessions for *Rubber Soul* continued into November, the group received some new Vox amplifiers. "Vox have just delivered a new set of amps to The Beatles," ran a news item. "The old ones were still functioning perfectly but their cases had received so many knocks on their travels that they had begun to look shabby."[23] The new Vox amps were a further pair of Vox AC-100 guitar rigs plus another Vox AC-100 bass rig.

The deadline for completion of the new LP loomed and so the final recordings for *Rubber Soul* were concluded on November 11th with a marathon session. 'Wait' was pulled from the left-over tapes from *Help!*, with Harrison adding guitar overdubs again featuring volume-pedal work. McCartney's 'You Won't See Me' and Lennon's 'Girl' were also recorded. Final production and mixing of the album was completed on November 15th.

A Gibson ES-345 for George

The group by now considered it laborious to have to promote their new recordings. Nonetheless, requests poured into Epstein's office for Beatle television appearances, so instead of scurrying around from studio to studio trying to fulfil the impossible demand, they decided to produce their own promotional film clips.

"The idea [was] we'd send them to America, because we thought, well, we can't go everywhere," explained Harrison later. "We'll send these things out to do the promo ... So I suppose in a way we invented MTV."[24] By making their own clips, the group could simultaneously promote new records on television stations around the world. As Harrison says, this idea would eventually prompt a widespread reassessment of methods for music publicity and promotion.

On Tuesday November 23rd at Twickenham film studios the group filmed their promos for 'We Can Work It Out', 'Day Tripper', 'Help!', 'Ticket To Ride' and 'I Feel Fine'. Three members used their familiar instruments: McCartney the Hofner bass, Lennon his Rickenbacker 325, and Starr the 22-inch-bass Ludwig kit with new number-six logo drum-head. But a new guitar was evident. Harrison had a sunburst Gibson ES-345.

Gibson's ES-345TD double-cutaway hollowbody guitar was in effect an upscale version of Joe Brown's 335 that Harrison had tried out back in 1962. The 345 had a six-position Varitone rotary

switch for choosing different tonal settings, and all the metal fittings were gold-plated. A sunburst 345 then cost £236/5/- (£236.25, about $660 then), which would be about £2,730 ($3,820) in today's money. Harrison used his new Gibson only for the filming of these promo clips, and later again this year during the last UK Beatles tour.

Although a British tour had originally been planned by Epstein for autumn 1965 and then cancelled by the group, he had finally persuaded them to venture out on a very brief British round of gigs, visiting just nine cities and with each date consisting of two shows. The support acts for the tour where The Koobas from Liverpool and the latest addition to Epstein's stable, The Moody Blues – featuring a young Denny Laine who, as we've mentioned, would later play with McCartney in Wings.

Prior to this British tour The Beatles met at the London flat of Mal Evans and Neil Aspinall for a brief rehearsal, at which all four group members were presented with Russian-made acoustic guitars. "The Beatles agreed to be photographed with them so that the shots of themselves playing the instruments could be sent to the Russian factory where they were made,"[25] said a news item. The resulting photographs of the group with these student-size flat-top acoustic guitars reveal instruments apparently of primitive quality. It's most improbable that the guitars were ever seriously used by the group, and the photo-session was almost certainly the last time they saw them.

The British tour started on December 3rd in Glasgow at the Odeon Cinema and continued through Newcastle, Liverpool and Manchester. On the 8th in Sheffield, Yorkshire, Lennon and Harrison were photographed using their two new Vox AC-100 guitar amps while McCartney used his new Vox AC-100 bass amp, playing his '63 Hofner bass and with his original '61 Hofner as a spare. Harrison played his new Gibson ES-345 as his main guitar, switching to the '65 Rickenbacker 360-12 for 'If I Needed Someone'. Lennon played his '64 Rickenbacker 325, with the '64 Gibson J-160E along as a spare.

A photograph taken of the group's guitars before the show in Sheffield reveals all these guitars as well as various guitar cases, drum cases and a Vox organ. But most interesting is an unexplained guitar among the expected Beatle instruments. The black-and-white photo shows a dark-coloured Fender Stratocaster with matching coloured headstock and rosewood fingerboard. Could this have been a spare six-string for Harrison? Such a Stratocaster has never before been itemised among The Beatles' instrumental line-up.

Starr used his familiar 22-inch-bass Ludwig kit for the tour with number-six Beatle drum-head. A report on the tour described a "new instrument" invented by Mal Evans. The group's roadie had fitted an additional "ching ring" inside a tambourine, removed its skin, and installed a rod across the diameter. Then he fitted the modified tambourine to a cymbal stand. The idea, said the news item, was "so Starr could get the right sound for 'Day Tripper' during their December tour".[26]

The group's repertoire for this final British tour included a live performance of 'Yesterday'. According to reports and photographic evidence from the Sheffield show, McCartney accompanied himself for this song on the Vox Continental organ. Try to imagine that combination.

The organ was played through the group's cream Fender Bassman amplifier, and Lennon too used the Continental on 'I'm Down', the group's set-closer. The December 1965 British tour ended on Sunday December 12th at the Capitol Cinema in Cardiff, marking one of the last occasions when The Beatles would perform live in the UK.

With their evident enjoyment in recording the wonderfully diverse *Rubber Soul*, the group were clearly becoming more absorbed with the creative potential of studio work and growing less enthusiastic for live performances.

The year to come would see a dramatic decision that would put an end to this division – and produce some spectacular results.

Sheffield, England, during The Beatles' final British tour, and George plays his Gibson ES-345, a guitar which he used only for a short time at the end of 1965.

"I was getting frustrated listening to American records like the Motown stuff because the bass was a lot stronger than we were putting on our records."

GEOFF EMERICK, BEATLES STUDIO ENGINEER FROM 1966, WITH SOME NEW IDEAS FOR THE SOUND OF THINGS TO COME.

1966

BY THE START OF 1966 THE BEATLES HAD BECOME THE WORLD'S MOST POPULAR BAND. THEY HAD ALSO BECOME FOUR VERY WEALTHY YOUNG MEN WHO HAD LITTLE OR NO PERSONAL TIME TO ENJOY THEIR SPOILS. THEIR MANAGER, BRIAN EPSTEIN, HAD HOPED FOR A REPEAT OF THE SUCCESSFUL 1964 AND '65 SCHEDULES. UNFORTUNATELY FOR EPSTEIN, THE GROUP HAD STARTED TO TAKE CONTROL.

No longer were The Beatles willing to sacrifice themselves to an apparently never-ending sequence of live tours and TV appearances. Epstein had hoped to begin the year with another film. By the middle of 1965 plans had been set for a third Beatle movie, a Western to be titled A Talent For Loving. Time had been scheduled for the film's production, starting at the beginning of 1966. But it never happened. The Beatles rejected the script along with the notion of playing cowboys. Epstein's idea of making them into Elvis-style movie stars was foiled.

So it was that Lennon, McCartney, Harrison and Starr found themselves with three full months off. Almost no group activity was planned. There loomed the virtually unknown luxury of personal freedom. They were called upon only once during this period, on January 5th. They went to CTS Studios, a post-production film studio in west London, because the audio tape of the recorded 1965 Shea Stadium concert needed some work before the planned TV film of the show could be released. The group were required to recreate their live sound at CTS while watching the concert performance footage on a large screen.

A contemporary report described the session and some of the equipment being delivered to the studio. "When The Beatles' management filmed and recorded their performance at the Shea Stadium, Manhattan, in August 1965, the 57,000 fans killed pretty well all their sound. So the film company decided that all their songs would have to be dubbed on. Recently, The Beatles found time to go into a Bayswater studio to record them but had to borrow a complete set of equipment from Sound City as they had taken their gear to their own separate homes instead of leaving it all with the road manager, Mal Evans."[1]

The idea of having a fully equipped studio in each of their homes had become appealing to the group. By the beginning of this year, Starr and McCartney had just purchased new houses, joining Lennon and Harrison as property owners. Each Beatle now had several Brenell reel-to-reel tape recorders which they used to work out new ideas for songs.

As far back as late 1964 Harrison's studio had been mentioned in a magazine item. "George decided that he wanted to put all his guitars, amplifiers and other musical gear into one big room at his new house," wrote the visiting journalist. "He's had one wall knocked down and the result is a sort of small recording studio. He also likes to have the ends of his guitar strings sticking all over the place. Says they're useful to stick ciggies onto, especially when there's no convenient ashtray near."[2]

Also in late 1964, Lennon's set-up had been reported. "John is having his new house completely redecorated, and one of the rooms is being equipped as a small recording studio. In future, he wants to make demos of new songs in the comfort of his own home."[3] It had also been noted that Lennon had ordered an electric piano for the new home studio – presumably one of the Hohner Pianets the group had acquired. "Knowing the genius he has for extracting the most sounds out of ordinary equipment, everyone in the recording world is waiting to see what Lennon does with his piano."[4] As we've learned, the results were plainly heard on *Rubber Soul*.

Just over a year later, in early 1966, visiting reporters had even more to see and scribble about. "Anyone who has visited John's home will no doubt be impressed by his music room," wrote one. "It is situated at the top of the house and its decor is a multi-coloured effort by John. Amplifiers, guitars, organ, piano and jukeboxes: you name it, he's got it. Everything is littered all over the place. He just can't keep it tidy like George does."[5]

During their three-month hiatus, the group began to write and demo new material for an upcoming record. It was reported at the time that they planned to reconvene in the spring of 1966 to record in Memphis, Tennessee. "There is a very strong possibility that The Beatles' new single will be recorded in America. After working on arrangements during late March and early April in EMI's St John's Wood studios they plan to fly to Memphis to actually record several numbers on April 11th. They have wanted to do a recording session in America for a long time now."[6] Another item added: "They've heard so much about the American techniques and sound engineers so they want to see for themselves whether it makes any difference. George Martin will be accompanying them."[7]

Fender catalogue shot from the period showing the 'black-face' piggy-back style Showman amp and cab, which The Beatles used in the studio on the Revolver sessions.

Unfortunately the group never made the recording trip to Memphis. A Beatles single made at Sun studios would have been an interesting experiment. Instead, they wound up back at Abbey Road for another string of sessions, starting on April 6th. The sessions would eventually become part of the *Revolver* LP.

The idea to record in the US grew from the group's continuing desire to improve and refine their sound on tape. So even though the trip to the States was off, the April sessions at Abbey Road found them pushing ever forward in the studio, striving to set fresh standards for new kinds of recording and production. The key word for these sessions would be experimentation.

One element in the new direction came with a change in recording personnel. At the start of the *Revolver* sessions the group's long-time head engineer, Norman Smith, was replaced by Geoff Emerick, a young EMI engineer eager and willing to experiment. Emerick had worked on various Beatles sessions as second engineer as far back as 'A Hard Day's Night' in 1964, but now he joined George Martin's production team as chief engineer to help translate The Beatles' ever-expanding musical ideas.

Geoff Emerick and The Beatles

During the *Revolver* sessions the group explored and invented new studio recording techniques – often by the relatively simple expedience of their efforts to achieve different sounds. As they requested better or more unusual sounds on their recordings, engineer Geoff Emerick tried to oblige, sometimes by using non-traditional methods.

Emerick's open-minded approach and willingness to ignore standard recording practices and techniques when necessary was exactly what the group were looking for. His input to the *Revolver* sessions was immediate, as he employed new working methods that helped change the sound of The Beatles' recordings. Ironically, some of Emerick's innovative approaches to recording, such as close-miking and bass-drum damping, are now considered standard practice.

Discussing his work today, Emerick says his approach to studio recording and experimentation then was simple but logical. "Recording is like painting a picture," he says. "The different sounds are like the different colours that you have to blend correctly to paint a picture." Emerick explains that

A 1965 Gibson SG Standard similar to the one used by George in the studio and briefly on-stage during 1966. At the time this distinctively styled instrument was the flagship model in the Gibson solidbody electric line. Gibson's 1964 catalogue (left) offered the SG model in three different styles: the three-pickup Custom and two-pickup Standard and Special.

A 1962 Gretsch 6120 like the one John used very briefly in the studio in 1966 (below). The model was another in Gretsch's Chet Atkins signature series that included the Country Gentleman and the Tennessean.

John pictured in April 1966 at the 'Paperback Writer' session at Abbey Road, playing the Gretsch 6120. In the foreground is a Vox 7120 amplifier, with its tubes (valves) clearly visible.

he achieved The Beatles' studio drum sound by using a basic two-microphone technique. Starr, of course, produced his own sound. "He knew when it was too 'live' sounding," recalls Emerick, "and then he used to put a cigarette packet on top of the snare, to dampen the sound. That would always work."

The sound of Starr's kit would end up on one track of the tape while the group recorded on to four-track machines (which they had done since October 1963 and would continue to do until the onset of eight-track at Abbey Road in summer 1968). "A lot of this was because of the limitations of the mixing desk," Emerick explains, recalling his frustration at wanting to get more material on to tape. "There were only eight inputs and four outs on our mixers at Abbey Road then. Going in, you also had access to one of the channels with a four-way pre-mixer, but that didn't have its own EQ." Emerick reports that he would use AKG D19C mikes for the overhead on the drum kit, and an AKG D20 on the bass drum, virtually throughout his time recording the group. For some instruments – possibly close-miking drums – he would return to classic "ribbon" microphones, usually Telefunken 4038s.

Emerick developed one of his pioneering drum recording techniques on the *Revolver* sessions. "There was this woollen sweater with four necks that they had received from a fan – they wore it for one of their Christmas shows. It was around the studio, so I stuffed it into the bass drum to deaden the sound. I moved the bass-drum microphone very close to the drum itself, which wasn't really considered the thing to

THAT'S YOUR BABY, AND IT WILL GO ON FOREVER.

Vox boss Tom Jennings,

to AC-30 designer Dick Denney

Abbey Road studios in April 1966, and Paul digs into his Rickenbacker 4001S bass while John and George sing a backing vocal. By this time The Beatles had started to use headphones in the studio for monitoring, which would soon become common practice.

do at that time. We then ran the kit sound through a Fairchild 660 valve compressor."[8] Compressors were widely used on individual instruments on Beatle recordings, generally resulting in a more punchy, louder sound.

The first track recorded for *Revolver* was 'Tomorrow Never Knows' and it effectively set the pace for these sessions as well as many future Beatle recordings. The song was the most drastically different composition the group had recorded to date. Its hypnotic pulse derives from a core of Starr on his Ludwig 22-inch-bass kit and McCartney playing his Rickenbacker 4001S bass. The sound of a single drone note on a Hammond organ played through a Leslie speaker cabinet, layered with fuzz and backwards-recorded guitar, added to the mystical sound.

The most remarkable additions to the song were the numerous tape loops that the group apparently created themselves, expanding still further the song's mind-bending atmosphere. Emerick recalls that The Beatles recorded odd sounds using their Brenell tape machines at home, and then the tapes were looped to create repeating sounds and added to the basic track. 'Tomorrow Never Knows' stands out as one of the first recordings to use the technique now known as sampling and looping, widely employed in today's studios thanks to more user-friendly electronic systems.

New Vox and Fender amps

With the new recording sessions came much new equipment. Photographer Robert Freeman captured some fine images that help document the equipment used during the creation of *Revolver*. Pictures taken in studio 3 show McCartney playing his Rickenbacker 4001S bass through the cream-coloured Fender Bassman amplifier. Joining the Bassman at Abbey Road were a new pair of Fender Showman amplifiers – so new that some photos show empty Fender shipping boxes in the background. The "blackface" (black control-panel) Fender Showman was in piggy-back style – separate head and cabinet – and produced 85 watts of power. The head was essentially the chassis of a Fender Twin Reverb, without the reverb. The separate Showman speaker cabinet came with a single 15-inch JBL speaker. In 1966 the Showman with 1x15 cabinet was second from top of Fender's line of 15 amplifiers, and retailed for $660 (about £235 then; around $3,580 or £2,540 in today's money).

Freeman's photos also reveal a series of new Vox model 7120 guitar and 4120 bass amplifiers present in the studio. These 120-watt amps were designed using a solid-state pre-amp coupled with a valve (tube) output section. According to Vox man Dick Denney, The Beatles received the first Vox 4120 and 7120 amps made. He says the company were keen to innovate and constantly produced prototype designs. "The only amp that my boss Tom Jennings would never allow us to change was the AC-30. He told me, 'That's your baby, and it will go on forever.' And how right he was."

Denney had visited Vox's US distributor, Thomas Organ, in California. "They poured loads of money into Vox," he says. "They were making the Super Beatle, the Royal Guardsman amps and others. I was sent there to help work on the various models. I tried out the prototype for the Super Beatle, and I voiced it up almost like an AC-30. They had their own concept on it all, and they had a very good transistor [solid-state] vibrato unit. I had to work up the fuzz for them that was built into that amp. I brought back the circuit from America, and we took the pre-amp circuit and put it on a powerful valve [tube] output section. That became the 7120 guitar and 4120 bass amps."

The 7120 had a 4x12 speaker cabinet and the 4120 a 2x15. Denney says that these shortlived rigs are the rarest Vox amps – not many were made, and they never went into proper production. "They had all the effects, like the American amps, but with a valve [tube] output. We gave the first ones to The Beatles and the Rolling Stones."[9]

New guitars: Casinos and an SG

The *Revolver* sessions also saw the appearance of a number of new Beatle instruments. Some would only be used briefly in the studio, while others became mainstays in the group's instrumental line-up. McCartney frequently used his Epiphone Casino on the sessions, and Lennon and Harrison too decided to join the Casino club. In the spring they each acquired a sunburst Epiphone Casino.

The most obvious difference between these two virtually identical guitars was that Harrison's Casino had a Bigsby vibrato fitted (though different to that on McCartney's), where Lennon's had the regular Epiphone "trapeze" tailpiece. Lennon's was unusual in that it had a small black rubber

ring mounted around its pickup selector switch. Both Casinos had the more commonly seen Epiphone-style headstock, unlike McCartney's which had the earlier Gibson-style headstock. Both Lennon and Harrison's guitars were fitted with gold-coloured volume and tone knobs, where McCartney's had black knobs.

Lennon used his new Epiphone Casino as well as his '64 Gibson J-160E throughout the *Revolver* sessions. Harrison meanwhile played his sonic blue Fender Stratocaster, his Gibson J-160E ... and yet another new Beatle guitar, a Gibson SG Standard. The SG line had in effect been introduced by Gibson during 1961 as new-design Les Paul models, although the "Les Paul" name was dropped from them in 1963 when they properly became SGs. The new body shape was modern and highly sculpted, with sharp double-cutaway horns.

The SG Standard kept the powerful and effective humbucking pickups of the original single-cutaway Les Paul models that were being brought to the fore in Britain in 1966 by players such as Eric Clapton and Jeff Beck. Harrison knew Clapton and must have noticed the effect that the guitarist and his Les Paul were having. Harrison would also have been familiar with the appeal of Gibson's humbuckers from his earlier ES-345 guitar, but maybe wanted something without that guitar's unwieldy Varitone selector, and probably liked the look of the smaller, hipper, solidbody SG. His new Gibson had been made around 1964, was finished in translucent cherry red, and had a Maestro Vibrola tailpiece unit. The SG remained one of Harrison's favoured guitars from this time through into 1968.

As the *Revolver* recordings progressed, the group's sound experiments took them in several more new directions. McCartney's 'Got To Get You Into My Life' was inspired by Motown arrangements. After the basic tracks were recorded the sound of a full brass section was added to the song, with members of Georgie Fame's Blue Flames enlisted to provide tenor saxophone and trumpet for the track. Harrison's 'Love You To' had a strong Indian flavour. Initially titled 'Granny Smith', the song featured the help of London-based Indian session player Anil Bhagwat, who would be credited on the *Revolver* sleeve for his work on tabla, a pair of small hand-drums. The track began with Harrison singing and playing his Gibson J-160E acoustic, and then layers of overdubs were added with Harrison playing sitar, tambura (an Indian lute-style instrument used to create drones) and even fuzz guitar, probably using a Vox Tone Bender. (This was the same fuzz-box that was perhaps used during the *Rubber Soul* sessions to create the distorted bass on 'Think For Yourself'.)

Gretsch 6120 and Burns Nu-Sonic Bass

Keeping in step with their scheduled LP and 45 releases, the group set out to record a new single, 'Paperback Writer'. The April 13th session was photographically documented for *The Beatles Monthly Book* providing detailed information on the instruments used. New to their guitar line-up was a Gretsch Chet Atkins 6120 that Lennon used. The early-1960s orange-finished double-cutaway 6120 hollowbody guitar had gold-plated hardware apart from its aluminium-coloured Bigsby. The other new guitar at the 'Paperback Writer' session was a Burns Nu-Sonic Bass. Strangely, it was Harrison who was pictured playing it, while McCartney used his Casino and Lennon the Gretsch 6120. The solidbody short-scale Nu-Sonic Bass was only available in a translucent cherry red finish. Lennon and Harrison were only ever photographed using the Gretsch 6120 and Burns Nu-Sonic bass during the 'Paperback Writer' session, and the instruments were never seen again.

Perhaps the Burns was used as part of the experimentation going on during Beatle sessions at this time to try to achieve a better bass sound? Engineer Geoff Emerick has said the group had been listening to records by artists such as Wilson Pickett and wondering why their own recordings did not have as much low-end. McCartney said later, "By then bass was coming to the fore in mixes ... you listen to early Beatles mixes and the bass and bass drum aren't there. We were starting to take over ourselves and bass was coming to the fore in many ways. So I had to do something ... I was listening to a lot of Motown, Marvin Gaye and Stax stuff, [who] were putting some nice little basslines in."[10]

Chief engineer Geoff Emerick relates another bass recording experiment made during the work on 'Paperback Writer'. "I was getting frustrated listening to American records like the Motown stuff because the bass content was a lot stronger than we were putting on our records. We were governed by certain rules and regulations at Abbey Road, so I could never get the sound I really wanted on the bass. In desperation one day I figured that we could use a loudspeaker as a microphone – it works

On the right of this picture from a Burns catalogue is the Nu-Sonic Bass, the kind George Harrison experimented with in the studio during the 'Paperback Writer' sessions.

the same way in reverse, so it's effectively the same thing. That way the speaker could take the weight of the air vibrations from a bass. So we used that on a couple of tracks. It sounded all right."[11]

The photographs from the 'Paperback Writer' session also reveal both of Starr's 22-inch-bass Ludwig drum sets present in the studio. The kit that he used to record with has Mal Evans's tambourine "invention" set up on the bass-drum's cymbal holder.

Other photos show two Vox organs – a single-manual and a new dual-manual Continental. The newer Continental had two keyboards, the lower manual with an extended bass section, and drew a wider tonal range from two sets of drawbars. The instrument was similar in appearance to the single-manual Continental, with the distinctive Z-shaped chrome stand, reversed black-and-white keys, and orange-red top, but of course with two rows of keys. The group would briefly use the dual-manual Vox during their 1966 tour. The two-manual Continental cost £273 (about $765 then) which translates to about £3,030 ($4,250) in today's money.

The Beatles pictured filming promotional clips for 'Rain' and 'Paperback Writer' in studio 1 at Abbey Road. John plays his Epiphone Casino, Paul uses his '63 Hofner violin bass, and George is on his new Gibson SG Standard. Behind George is a Vox 7120 amplifier. Ringo plays his first 22-inch-bass Ludwig kit, fitted with a new Beatles drum-head logo (number six in the sequence).

According to studio documentation, another new sound tried out for 'Paperback Writer' came from a "jangle box" put through a Leslie rotating speaker. Geoff Emerick explains that the jangle box was also known as a "tack piano". "It was a piano that had felts with little copper tips on them, to give more of a clacky, ragtime sound."[12] Ex-Abbey Road technical engineer Ken Townsend says that in order to get the sound they would also detune the piano. "A popular pianist called Russ Conway recorded some big hits at the studio using the sound of the jangle box."[13] The best of Conway's jangling hits was 'Side Saddle' in 1959.

'Rain' was destined for the flip side of the group's next single, and was recorded on April 14th. To aid the song's remarkable sound, tapes were run backwards, slowed down and speeded up. As work on the *Revolver* album continued, 'Doctor Robert' was recorded with a more traditional instrumental line-up of lead and rhythm guitars, bass guitar and drums. Overdubs of harmonium played by Lennon, piano by McCartney and maracas by Harrison were added later. 'And Your Bird Can Sing' and Harrison's 'Taxman' were also recorded with more familiar Beatle instrumentation, but whenever possible studio trickery was being used to create unusual sounds.

The *Revolver* sessions saw a variety of new recording techniques created for and first used by The Beatles. One of Emerick's ideas for a new vocal sound was to run a microphone through a Leslie rotating-speaker cabinet. He devised a way to do this where the Leslie was miked-up and fed back to tape. The result was the vocal effect heard on 'Tomorrow Never Knows'. "It wasn't long before they were requesting everything to be run through a Leslie speaker cabinet,"[14] comments Emerick.

ADT: Ken's flanger... and using headphones in the studio

Another studio effect first invented and widely used during the *Revolver* sessions was ADT. It was Townsend who came up with Artificial Double Tracking after an especially long night watching McCartney endlessly double-tracking a vocal part. Double-tracking means recording a new second take of the same part to thicken the sound. For vocals in particular this can be a tricky process, because the "match" of the two takes needs to be just right.

"As I was driving home from that session," Townsend recalls, "I began to think that there must be an easier way of double-tracking if you simply want to reinforce your own voice." He thought about the work that Abbey Road engineer George Barnes was doing to apply "frequency control" to tape recorders, primarily to vary the speed at which the machines could run in order to facilitate various special effects, as on 'Rain'. "Without that invention," says Townsend, "I couldn't have done ADT." By meddling with the speed-controlled tape recorders, Townsend devised a method to electronically add an "automatic" time-delayed version of an existing recording on to itself, usually done at mixing stage.

"ADT allowed you to set a time-delay difference between the second voice and the first," he explains. "Also, by wobbling it around you could get a phasing effect, like we did later in 'Lucy In The Sky With Diamonds'. It was three devices in one, really. By just sitting there and fiddling the oscillator, it could be an automatic double-tracking device, a flanging device, or a phasing device."

In the early stages of development of his new effect, Townsend demonstrated it to another Abbey road engineer, Stuart Allen. "He said we'd better give it a name, so we came up with artificial double tracking. Everything had initials then. There was STEED, which was single tape echo and echo delay, and FITE, which was fader isolated tape echo. So ADT became the official name.

"George Martin worked with [comedian] Peter Sellers a lot. George was explaining to The Beatles what it was that I had invented, and the word 'flanging' had come out in one of Sellers's things. So they immediately called the ADT effect a flanger. Later it became known as Ken's flanger. Double-tracking to The Beatles was a flanger."[15] (More technically, flanging is a more extreme form of phasing, which itself is a swirling effect produced by time-delaying one of a pair of identical taped pieces. Think of 'Itchycoo Park' by The Small Faces.)

During the *Revolver* sessions the group also pioneered the use of headphones while "tracking" or overdubbing, in other words adding vocal or instrumental parts to recordings previously taped. At Abbey Road, as in other studios, the common practice when overdubbing a vocal, for example, was simply to play back the existing track through loudspeakers in the studio while the performer sang along to it into a microphone. Some of the backing would inevitably "bleed through" into the vocal microphone ... and, irritatingly, on to the vocal track on the tape.

> IT WASN'T LONG BEFORE THEY WERE REQUESTING EVERYTHING TO BE RUN THROUGH A LESLIE SPEAKER CABINET.
>
> Geoff Emerick,
>
> Beatles sound engineer

Headphones had never been used while tracking. Ken Townsend recalls Abbey Road's wall-mounted Altec Lansing speakers which had been used for some time for playback, and that in their earlier sessions The Beatles used two large Vox PA-type column speakers powered by a Leak TL-25 amplifier for the purpose. "These were made up at EMI by a Dr Dutton. When we did start to use headphones, they were models made by SG Brown."[16]

Engineer Geoff Emerick insists that The Beatles were the first artists at Abbey Road to overdub using headphones to listen to backing tracks, so that nothing would "bleed through". Says Emerick: "At that time it was totally alien to any other producer or pop band to wear headphones for working. It started during the time of *Revolver*."[17]

Pulling strings

On April 28th work started on 'Eleanor Rigby', and a new kind of musical arrangement for The Beatles. To accompany McCartney's lead vocal a double string-quartet featuring four violins, two violas and two cellos was used. George Martin scored the arrangement for the eight studio musicians hired for the session. 'Eleanor Rigby' was a very significant piece of work, not least in that it marked the first Beatles recording that featured no traditional Beatle instruments. No guitars, no bass, no drums, no keyboards. Just strings and the vocals.

Experimentation with yet another new instrument graced the next cut recorded. Initial takes of 'I'm Only Sleeping' featured the sound of a vibraphone, an instrument similar to a marimba but having metal bars and rotating disks in the resonators to produce a vibrato effect. The final mix of the song did not include the vibraphone, but years later *Anthology 2* offered a snatch of the original working version complete with the dulcet instrument.

On May 1st The Beatles made what would turn out to be their final live public appearance in Britain. The occasion was the *New Musical Express* Annual Poll-Winners' All-Star Concert at Wembley's Empire Pool, where the group performed five songs. The instrumental line-up for the show had Lennon playing his new Epiphone Casino, McCartney his '63 Hofner bass and Harrison his new Gibson SG. They played through their new Vox 7120 and 4120 amplifiers. Also set up on stage was a Vox Continental organ which was plugged into the cream-coloured Fender Bassman amp. Starr used his trusty 22-inch-bass Ludwig kit. Although the other acts on the Wembley bill were filmed for an ABC television programme, The Beatles' performance was unfortunately not included.

Then it was back to the studio. To finish work on their forthcoming LP, the group recorded 'For No One' – and yet another new instrument, a clavichord, was introduced as the dominant sound, providing *Revolver* with a further sonic novelty. The clavichord has roots back to medieval times, being a forerunner of the piano. Small brass wedges striking horizontal strings produce the instrument's soft, percussive sound. The clavichord for this session was rented from George Martin's own AIR studios (which he'd set up in 1965). Later a decision was made to add the sound of a French horn as the solo passage on the track, played by Philharmonia horn-man Alan Civil.

With a new 45 and LP scheduled for release, promotion was usually the next step. As they had done for *Rubber Soul*, the group set forth to produce their own promotional film clips, filming them at Abbey Road studio 1 on May 19th. Both colour and black-and-white clips for 'Rain' and 'Paperback Writer' were filmed for distribution to British and American television programmes.

The classic promo films show the group miming, with Lennon using his Epiphone Casino, McCartney his '63 Hofner bass and Harrison his Gibson SG, with one of their new Vox 7120 amplifiers thrown on to the set for good measure. Starr used the first of his two 22-inch-bass Ludwig kits with number-six Beatles-logo drum-head. This kit/head combination would remain as Starr's main set-up into 1968. More filming for 'Rain' and 'Paperback Writer' continued the following day in the gardens of Chiswick House in west London, with Lennon, McCartney and Harrison using the same guitars and Starr without drums.

Of the final songs to be recorded for the *Revolver* LP, 'Yellow Submarine' would become an unexpected highlight, given the often throwaway status of the songs written for Starr to sing. It was originally conceived as a simple children's song, but ended up as a single and later the title track of an animated film loosely based on the song. Initially recorded with the simple arrangement of Lennon on Gibson J-160E, McCartney playing his Rickenbacker 4001S bass, Starr on drums and Harrison playing tambourine, the song was quickly festooned with the experimental sounds and techniques that had become such a hallmark of the *Revolver* recordings. The day after the basic track was cut, 'Yellow Submarine' had a number of tape sound-effects added, with more noises provided by the group and their guests at an unruly recording session held on June 1st. According to Geoff Emerick it was "anything goes" as Brian Jones of The Rolling Stones, Marianne Faithfull and other friends contributed to the chorus. The use of non-musical sound effects in the song marked another fresh area for change. Later the group would take this to almost unlistenable limits when they used sound effects to create 'Revolution No. 9' – which would have no basic instrumental track at all.

A new Harrison song was recorded next. 'I Want To Tell You' featured a basic rhythm track of guitars, drums and piano, plus a later bass overdub. Under pressure to complete the album, the group continued to work on more new original tunes. 'Good Day Sunshine' with its basic instrumentation of guitars, bass and drums was highlighted by George Martin's honky-tonk-style piano. 'Here There And Everywhere' featured a soft arrangement of electric and acoustic guitars, bass and Starr's great brush work on the drums. But it is McCartney's lead vocal and the simple yet effective harmonies that really make the recording stand out. In the midst of so much sonic experimentation, the group knew that pure singing still had the power to shine through.

As the record deadline quickly closed in, The Beatles made an appearance on the important TV show *Top Of The Pops*. On June 16th they entered the BBC's London studios to mime to both sides of their new single, 'Rain' and 'Paperback Writer'. It would be one of the last occasions on which they made a personal appearance as a group on a British television show, and the first that Lennon and Harrison performed together with their almost matching Epiphone Casino guitars. McCartney left his Rickenbacker bass in the studio and took along his trusty '63 Hofner. Perhaps the group thought that the similar sunburst finishes on all three instruments would provide an attractive match – just like their newly tailored matching suits. Starr, as always, used his signature black oyster pearl Ludwig drum kit.

The Beatles were scheduled to start a tour in Germany on June 24th, but with only days to spare they recorded a last-minute final song for the upcoming LP, Lennon's classic 'She Said She Said'. The standard Beatle mix of two electric guitars, bass and drums drove the song along to provide one of the best and most rocking tracks on the album, with only a Hammond organ providing anything unusual in its soundscape.

The *Revolver* sessions had underlined a new determination by the group to think and play experimentally in the studio, resulting in a mass of new musical sounds – as well as new guitars. Beyond the scope of any previous Beatle recordings, the tracks on *Revolver* offered a mesmerising array of musical instrumentation. By all accounts, the studio had become littered with all kinds of instruments ready to be played at will. While we know about most of the gear present, determining exactly which guitars were used on particular songs is sometimes difficult. No detailed documentation on the subject exists. Ears are not wholly reliable. Some useful clues are tucked away in photographs taken during the sessions. But, of course, the debates will continue.

Back on tour – plus the original thriller in Manilla

As the final mixes for *Revolver* neared completion, the group started their 1966 world tour. They headed for West Germany where they would perform six shows in three days in three different cities. First stop was Munich. Fresh out of the studio, and with no time to rehearse, The Beatles slapped together a quick set-list which for their entire 1966 tour consisted of 'Rock And Roll Music', 'She's A Woman', 'If I Needed Someone', 'Day Tripper', 'Baby's In Black', 'I Feel Fine', 'Yesterday', 'I Wanna Be Your Man', 'Nowhere Man', 'Paperback Writer' and 'I'm Down'.

Lennon and Harrison used the Epiphone Casinos as their main instruments on the tour. Harrison brought along his Gibson SG Standard as a spare six-sting and his '65 "rounded top" Rickenbacker 360-12 12-string, capo'd at the seventh fret to use on 'If I Needed Someone'. Lennon had his '64 Gibson J-160E as his spare. McCartney preferred to use his signature '63 Hofner violin bass as his main performance instrument, but his Rickenbacker 4001S was brought along as a spare.

The group's new Vox 4120 and 7120 amps, complete with stands, were used for the shows in Germany and later in the Orient. Lennon also had the new Vox Continental dual-manual organ set up on stage, but he never used it, even on the usual organ-fired set-closer, 'I'm Down'. Starr relied on his trusty Ludwig 22-inch-bass set with number-six Beatles drop-T logo. This was the

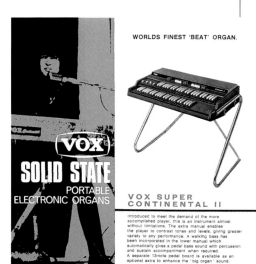

WORLDS FINEST 'BEAT' ORGAN.

VOX SUPER CONTINENTAL II

Introduced to meet the demand of the more accomplished player, this is an instrument almost without limitations. The extra manual enables the player to contrast tones and levels, giving greater variety to any performance. A walking bass has been incorporated in the lower manual which automatically gives a pedal bass sound with percussion and sustain accompaniment when required. A separate 13-note pedal board is available as an optional extra to enhance the 'big organ' sound.

Vox catalogue showing the two-manual Continental organ, as used by the group during the April 1966 Revolver sessions, and then on the road in Germany and Japan.

instrumentation for most of the tour, with only slight deviations. For example, at one of the two opening shows in Munich at the Circus-Krone-Bau, Harrison opted for the Gibson SG Standard in preference to his Casino.

During their brief stay in Munich they were shown a new instrument, the Tubon, by a local keyboard manufacturer. *The Beatles Monthly Book* witnessed the event. "Paul can't resist a new instrument. When somebody gave him [a] Tubon recently, he immediately had to try it out, and … he was most intrigued by the unusual sound that it produced. It's a cylindrical instrument with a small keyboard, and when you play it, it produces different tones, not unlike a small electric organ."[18] It's not known if The Beatles ever used the Tubon on any recording, though it seems unlikely – and anyway, the instrument seemed to be intended for live performance, if anything. After a stop in Essen and the final shows in Hamburg, The Beatles headed for Japan.

Three days of concerts were scheduled at the Nippon Budokan in Tokyo, starting on June 30th. Of the five shows, the first two complete performances were filmed for Japanese NTV (Nippon Television). The footage exists today as the best document of the group's 1966 live stage show, with every angle of the equipment used by the group on display. However, The Beatles seem unrehearsed, even sloppy. Perhaps they didn't care, figuring that they couldn't be heard anyway. For those first two performances they did not have their new Vox 7120 and 4120 amplifiers, but instead used a set of Vox AC-100 amplifiers provided by the Japanese promoter. Later, for the remainder of the Tokyo performances, they switched to the 7120 and 4120 amps. Lennon's Vox Continental dual-manual organ was again set up on stage but was never used as intended on the final song of their set.

Next stop, The Philippines. What started out as two grand concerts on July 4th in front of 80,000 fans at the Rizal Memorial football stadium in Manila quickly turned into a nightmare. The group were not aware of an invitation from Philippine President Ferdinand Marcos and First Lady Imelda Marcos to visit the Royal Palace. When they didn't show, it was taken as a national snub. The band were run out of the country, treated as deviant undesirables. This uncomfortable experience was among the many reasons why they would soon decide never to tour again.

With a few days' stopover in New Delhi, The Beatles eventually made it back to London on July 8th. They had a few weeks to rest before they resumed the tour, switching now to the United States. On August 11th the group flew to Chicago. The relatively brief 14-city American tour was plagued with more unsettling experiences, starting with a press conference on their opening night in Chicago. To combat the negative publicity generated in the States about Lennon's misquoted statement of being "more popular than Jesus", Epstein forced Lennon to explain the comment during the conference and all but apologise to the American press and, thereby, US Beatles fans. This did not exactly get the tour off to a great start.

The first date was at the Chicago International Amphitheater on Friday August 12th. The songs played and instruments used on the tour were the same as in Germany and Japan. Harrison and Lennon used the Epiphone Casinos for their main instruments, Harrison playing his '65 Rickenbacker 12-string on 'If I Needed Someone'. His SG was brought along as a spare, while Lennon had the '64 Gibson J-160E as his backup. McCartney played his '63 Hofner bass and had his Rickenbacker 4001S as a spare, with Starr playing his 22-inch-bass Ludwig set with number-six Beatles logo.

Live in Germany in 1966. John and George are playing their Epiphone Casinos through Vox 7120 amps, while Paul has his '63 Hofner, plugged into a Vox 4120 bass rig. Meanwhile Ringo keeps it all together on his first 22-inch-bass Ludwig set, with Beatle logo number six.

The Vox Super Beatle amp

The Beatles did not bring their new British-made Vox 7120 and 4120 amps to the US. Instead, arrangements were made by Epstein and Vox for the group to use the new American-made Vox amplifiers. Vox had made their deal with Thomas to sell the amps in the US in 1964, and almost immediately had problems supplying enough product to meet the demand. Since that time the American distributor – without Vox's knowledge – had developed plans to manufacture their own line of Vox amps in the States. These plans had now reached their peak with the new Super Beatle amps. California-based Thomas Organ worked feverishly to ready the massive new solid-state amps for The Beatles' summer tour. The company tried to keep the British Vox look and sound, going so far as to enlist the help of Dick Denney to "voice" the amps to achieve the correct Vox tone.

The Super Beatle amp used a similar loudspeaker cabinet design to that of the Vox AC-100, with four 12-inch Vox Bulldog speakers, plus crossovers, and two high-frequency horns. The cabinet was similar too in dimensions, and included the chrome Vox "tilt" roller stand. But the amplifier head was unlike the Vox AC-100. In place of the British Vox's traditional cabinet, the Super Beatle head had sides angled in at the top, providing a unique image. The solid-state amp also had different controls to the British AC-100, including a wah-wah-like "MRB" (mid range boost) effect. (This would later be heard at the end of 'Bungalow Bill', the MRB circuit being subsequently added to British-made Vox amps.)

Thomas Organ had earlier offered a simpler Super Beatle model, the V1124. Now they offered for general sale the new Super Beatle in two varieties, the V1142 and the "fuzz" distortion-equipped V1141. Although the Super Beatle was packed with the latest effects and boasted an impressive 120 watts of power, it lacked the tonal lustre of its British counterparts, the AC-100, AC-50 and even the AC-30. But a Vox Super Beatle did become a required status symbol for many American bands, and was considered one of the best (and certainly the most expensive) amplifiers available in the US in 1966. The V1141 retailed for $1,225 (about £440 then; around $6,650 or £4,700 in today's money) with the fuzz-less V1142 going for $30 less. What more could a band ask for than to play through a Vox amp with the Beatles name on it? It would surely make any group sound better. Thomas Organ thought so, and clearly they were charging accordingly.

Collectively, The Beatles had never endorsed any musical equipment to the point of lending their name to be used on the product itself. According to Vox's Dick Denney, the group knew nothing about their name being used on the Vox Super Beatle, as the arrangement had been made by Brian Epstein. Legend has it that when the group first saw the new Thomas-made Vox Super Beatle amps at the Chicago Amphitheater on August 12th they were not at all pleased by the name. Allegedly, their comment to Brian Epstein was that there was nothing greater than The Beatles – so how could it be a Super Beatle? – and that Thomas Organ should change the name to plain Vox Beatle. Maybe there is some truth to this rumour, because later versions of the Vox Super Beatle were indeed renamed Vox Beatle.

Support acts on the American tour were The Ronettes, The Cyrkle, Bobby Hebb, and The Remains. Barry Tashian, lead guitarist and vocalist of The Remains, who later wrote an engaging first-hand account of the whirlwind two-week tour, recalls that his group intended to use Fender amplifiers on the dates.

"Then word came down that we weren't allowed to use any Fender equipment," says Tashian. "We were disappointed that we would have to use these Vox Super Beatle amps. I was pretty scared, because you get attached to your own sound from your own amp. But it turned out the Vox amp did the job, and at least it was powerful and had two speaker cabinets, one on each side of the stage."

The Remains and The Cyrkle played through some of the seven Super Beatle amps that The Beatles used later in the set, says Tashian. "It was a good thing the Vox representative was travelling

These six live pictures of The Beatles in action were taken on August 21st 1966 by photographer Gordon Baer during the group's final US tour. The photos document Ringo's Ludwig 22-inch-bass kit with logo head number six, John and George with Epiphone Casinos, George with his '65 360-12 for 'If I Needed Someone', and Paul playing his '63 Hofner bass (with pickguard now removed). Note the American-made Vox Super Beatles amps, which were only used for this tour.

with that tour. They were very temperamental amps and there was always stuff going wrong with them." The Remains would go on first to do their set for around 20 minutes, then Bobby Hebb would come out and the group played behind him for another 20 minutes or so. Next on was The Cyrkle, for a 25-minute set, then The Remains were on again to back The Ronettes for another 25 minutes. After a 15-minute break, The Beatles hit the stage.

The Remains used three of the amps: one for electric piano, one for bass and one for guitar. "If I stood in front of my guitar amp," says Tashian, "and looked at the drummer playing 20 feet away from me, I wasn't able to hear him at all. It was like I was watching a silent movie of a drummer. All I could hear was the guitar blasting away. And I'd take a few steps across the stage to be in front of the piano amp and that would be the only thing that I could hear. It was really loud."[19]

Outdoor sound systems

In 1966, staging concerts in very large outdoor arenas was still a new idea. The technicalities of providing good live sound in these places was equally in its infancy. Today, one could consult a list of professional live-sound hire companies and have a wide range of choices. Back in the 1960s, things were very different. Remains guitarist Barry Tashian says that as far as he can remember there was no such thing as a concert-sound company – but there was Bill Hanley. "He was building stuff to use at music concerts," says Tashian. "We hired him for every gig we did, and either he or his brother Terry would bring their gear along. Even if we were only making $400, we'd pay him $250 to come out. From his U-Haul trailer he'd produce Voice Of The Theater speakers, some good mikes and a few powerful amps. As a result, we always had really good vocals which would cut through, even though we cranked up our amps as loud as we did. So when Bill heard we'd got The Beatles gig he just said, 'I'm coming.' We didn't even have to ask him."

At the first date, the Chicago International Amphitheater, Hanley set up his system on the stage. "There were these humungous vacuum tubes [valves] just glowing purple, like a science fiction vision," recalls Tashian. Hours before the show was due to start, word had got around about the Hanley sound system. "Eventually, there was our manager and Brian Epstein standing looking at Bill's gear. Our manager said, 'Well, what do you want to use? This state-of-the-art high powered system this guy brought out, or that puny house thing over there that they use for announcements?' So then and there, Hanley worked out a deal with Epstein to do as much as he could of the tour – which was not all of it, because it was physically impossible to make the distances between dates. They did throw a few extra things on the plane to beef up what they had, and set up some stuff on the stage. He had much better mikes."[20]

Bill Hanley naturally recalls that '66 tour. He claims that Hanley Sound was the first concert-sound company in the US. "We had these big heavy-duty 600-watt tube [valve] amplifiers that would just sit there and cook at full output. We used JBL woofers and Altec Lansing high-frequency drivers. For Shea Stadium, I think I had 16 cabinets. And for mikes I used Shure 546s. We even put mikes on the amps and drums. We had a little mixing board with EQ on the input – we built our own. But

when The Beatles came on and the girls started screaming, you could still hardly hear anything. At Shea Stadium, with 48,000 people facing one direction and screaming, it was just impossible to override that noise level."[21]

The Beatles tour moved on through Detroit, Cleveland, Washington DC, Philadelphia and Toronto. The whole entourage travelled together from city to city by bus or chartered plane. The Beatles would sometimes be taken from an airport in the same bus as the other acts, but more often would move off separately in an armoured car or limo. "After the gig, we would have to wait for the road guys to load all the stuff into the truck," says Tashian, "get out of the stadium, and drive to the airport to load it inside the airplane. I remember standing under the plane helping schlep stuff into the cargo hold myself, all these great big Vox Super Beatles as well as guitars and suitcases."[22]

On August 17th the tour played at Toronto's Maple Leaf Gardens. By this show McCartney had removed or lost the pickguard on his '63 Hofner bass, which has remained pickguard-less ever since. The following night at the Suffolk Downs racetrack in Boston, McCartney almost lost the use of his bass amp as well. Vern Miller, bassist for The Remains, explains: "We all ended up using the same equipment for that tour, and I think it was Suffolk Downs where I blew an amp head. They had a Vox rep on the whole tour, and he managed to fix the amp in time for when The Beatles came on. Later they took us through the plant at the Thomas Organ factory, outside of L.A. They picked us up in limousines and took us out there."[23]

A custom-made Guild Starfire XII electric 12-string guitar originally presented to John, seen here on display at its present home at a Hard Rock Cafe. (inset) Mark Dronge of Guild presents a specially made 12-string electric guitar to John during a press conference in New York City in 1966.

As the tour moved south to Memphis on August 19th, The Beatles faced more opposition and negative publicity. Calls came in making death threats to the group. One such attempt was supposed to occur during a Memphis performance. Touring was no longer a happy-go-lucky experience. Prisoners of their own fame and success, the group were now in fear of their lives.

When the rain comes...

Due to a torrential downpour, the next day's show in Cincinnati was postponed to the 21st, when the group had to play two shows in two different cities: first Cincinnati, and then later at Bush Stadium in St Louis. Evidently Bill Hanley was not providing the sound for this show. Tashian reports a two or three-second delay between singing and hearing the sound coming back. "So there was no way of singing in time! All you could do was to try and shut your ears off and just plough through it – and pay no attention to the sound you were hearing. And the rain … well, I remember getting a few shocks, but I survived."[24]

Roadie for The Remains was Ed Freeman, who also managed to survive. Today, Freeman shrugs at the thought of those unsophisticated days. "That St Louis gig was typical," he says. "The promoter didn't want to pay $200 for a roof over the stage, so the rain poured down on to it. Every time Paul sang he'd bounce up and down, and every time his mouth bounced into the microphone these sparks would fly out.

"My assignment was to sit back with my hands and feet on some monster mains plug, and the first person that went down to the ground, I was supposed to pull the plug for the whole show. That was if someone was totally electrocuted – but no one was. Still, there were sparks flying all over the place and crackles and things going out. It was pretty disgusting. You know, you wouldn't even tolerate it with a garage band. Very unprofessional!"

Freeman explains that he was not in fact a proper roadie at all, but a folk singer from Boston who happened to be a friend of the band. He had no experience of electric instruments. "It was absolutely a new thing for me, and it changed my life. At the time I was still looking down my nose at pop music – I was into old English and Scottish ballads – but I changed then." Later Freeman became a record producer, perhaps his most famous recording being Don McLean's 'American Pie'.

One of the most vivid memories Freeman has of the '66 Beatles tour was that all the gear for all five bands would fit into one stretch van, and was carried in the belly of the plane. "There were no separate equipment trucks," he says. "In fact there was less equipment than one drummer would have on the road now – and fewer roadies than a drummer would have. There were three roadies for five bands for the entire tour, and that was it. Me, Mal Evans, and Mike Owens.

"Mal Evans as far as I could tell was tone deaf. His basic advantage was that he could pick up one of those huge Super Beatle amps, squeeze it between his hands and lift it six feet on to a stage.

He was absolutely stunning that way. He could also pick up half a dozen fans, lift them six feet off the ground and throw them over a fence. Very strong guy – but I don't think he could tune anything.

"Sometimes I'd go out and tune the guitars with the amps full on: I played Shea Stadium and got a round of applause," he laughs. "But I think by the end of the tour, it was obvious that this was a joke as far as actually playing music was concerned. Nobody could hear a damned thing.

"They walked on stage and all you could hear was screaming for the next 20 minutes, and then they walked off stage."[25]

John's Guild Starfire 12-string

The Beatles spent August 22nd and 23rd stowed away at the Warwick Hotel in New York City. For the first day, two press conferences were scheduled at the hotel. It was during one of these that Lennon was given a Guild Starfire XII electric 12-string guitar. Mark Dronge, son of Guild guitar company founder Alfred Dronge, recalls first hearing The Beatles when he was in a record store in London in 1963.

"When they started to come to the States I spoke to our advertising agent at Guild, a guy by the name of Harold Jacobs. He got hold of a photographer that he knew. The guy was going to cover The Beatles at a press conference, and he got me into it. Months before, we'd started working on this deal to make a beautiful guitar that might fit The Beatles. There was nothing in the Guild line that would do the job. We had just started making double-cutaway electric guitars, and we weren't too familiar about electric guitars anyway, but we had a reputation already for our acoustic 12-strings. So we figured we should make an electric 12."

Guild had been set up in New York City by Dronge's father Alfred in 1952, at first making a name for their archtop guitars, and then acoustic flat-tops. Electric guitars began to appear, and the company relocated to New Jersey in 1956. Their Starfire XII 12-string, in a Gibson ES-335 style, first appeared in the line in 1966. For the special guitar to be presented to The Beatles, the factory came up with a body of especially "flamed" or patterned maple, finished in a dark amber stain, with non-standard De Armond pickups, a master volume control, gold-plated hardware and a better bridge and tuners.

"We only made one," says Dronge, "because we wanted to make it special, to really pour our heart into it. My father really didn't know exactly what was going on. He obviously knew that The Beatles were getting big, but he was really funny about giving stuff away. He felt that if someone paid for a guitar, it was because they liked it and they were going to use it. So at the time he took a lot of convincing – and two guitars was just out of the question. But it was an absolutely spectacular guitar for the time."

Once the press conference that Dronge had managed to gatecrash was over, he took the special 12-string guitar out of its case. "I marched up and walked past George, and he'd kind of seen me coming and thought it was for him. I could see his expression getting sour, but I walked right past him and gave it to John. I thought John played the electric 12! I gave it to John ... and George was pissed [off]. I don't even know if the case and the guitar ever got back together until years later, when I saw that guitar in Hawaii, at the Hard Rock Café."[26]

It is unknown if the Guild Starfire XII made it to any Beatle recordings. There is certainly no evidence that it did. Somehow, the guitar did make it into the hands of Tony Cox, Yoko Ono's ex-husband, who years later sold it to the Hard Rock Café and, as Dronge notes, the guitar now hangs on a wall at the fast-food chain's Honolulu branch.

Barry Tashian of The Remains remembers Harrison with the Guild 12-string on the tour plane. "He was plunking around on it and he handed it to me, asking if I wanted to try it. I think I played a few bars of 'Freight Train' and George called me a show-off.

"We usually talked more about music and records [than instruments]. But I did ask Ringo about 'I'm Looking Through You' and that tapping percussion sound on it. He told me that I was privy to a great secret, that he just tapped on a pack of matches with his finger."[27]

Tashian's bassist, Vern Miller, remembers talking to Harrison in particular, primarily about the Indian music he was interested in. "I remember one or two times going up to his room at night after we were done with the shows and listening to these sitar-lesson cassettes by Ravi Shankar that he'd brought with him.

The American-made solid-state Vox Super Beatle (top) allowed Vox's US agent Thomas Organ to capitalise on The Beatles' fame. The close-up of the rear of the head reveals the positioning of the controls, and the US catalogue shows a later version of the amp.

"I also remember that Mal Evans carried a violin-case with a bottle and various other pleasures. He called this violin-case his sin kit," laughs Miller. "Mal was a bit of a character."[28]

Don Dannemann, guitarist of The Cyrkle, recalls how once during a pleasant enough chat he was having with Harrison, someone asked the Beatle about the guitar he'd used on 'And I Love Her'. "George didn't remember," says Dannemann, "and it sort of ruined the conversation actually – because we were having a general conversation and all of a sudden George was being forced to be a Beatle. I had a feeling that we probably knew more about what they used on their records than they did, because we used to study them."[29]

Support band The Remains on-stage in Los Angeles during The Beatles US tour in 1966. All the acts on the tour used Vox Super Beatle amps supplied by Thomas Organ.

Shea Stadium; no to Rickenbackers

On August 23rd the group made their second-ever appearance at Shea Stadium, but this was not a triumphant concert as the first had been. It was certainly successful – over 40,000 fans were in attendance – but the date did not sell out as it had done in 1965, and over 10,000 seats were left unoccupied. The signs were that Beatlemania was beginning to fade a little. No doubt this added yet more strain and disillusionment to The Beatles' touring party.

Immediately after the Shea Stadium show the tour flew to Los Angeles, where The Beatles rented a private home in Beverly Hills and enjoyed a day's rest. On August 25th they flew to Seattle and played two shows at the Coliseum. Returning to LA, they took advantage of a further three days off, hanging out with friends including members of The Byrds, The Beach Boys and The Mamas & The Papas.

During this time, Rickenbacker made another attempt to meet the group and to present them with new guitars. John Hall of Rickenbacker recalls being invited to stop by the house, but not being let in when he arrived. "The guitar I had with me was more of a Roger McGuinn type of 12-string. What was unique about it was the top, which was extremely thin, almost like an acoustic guitar. It was a three-pickup model, but it had a different type of switching, and it had reverse stringing, like an acoustic 12-string. The other one was a prototype, similar to a 325 shape but full-scale, and with a rounded body edge, like our later-style 360."[30]

On Sunday August 28th The Beatles performed at Dodger Stadium in Los Angeles to a capacity crowd of 45,000 fans. One small guitar detail to report: by this show the pickguard on Harrison's Epiphone Casino had been removed.

The following day not only marked the last gig of the group's American tour but The Beatles' final public concert. Touring had taken its toll. As a band they were commercially and financially successful, without doubt, but the negative pressures of touring were making it less and less desirable to travel around playing live. After all, no one could hear much of the performances anyway. The band figured it would be much easier and far more constructive to work on studio recordings. At least that way people would be able to listen to and hear their music. With all this in mind, and without anyone else knowing, The Beatles decided privately never to perform live again after the show on Monday August 29th at San Francisco's Candlestick Park. This concert marked the end of an era. Beatlemania was all but dead.

Returning to Britain, the group knew their contract with EMI was up for renegotiation, so there would presumably be less pressure to go back into the studio to record a new LP or single for an autumn release. Instead, the four Beatles went their own separate ways. Lennon flew to Spain to star in Richard Lester's film *How I Won The War*. McCartney composed the score for the film *The Family Way*. Harrison flew to India to study sitar with Ravi Shankar and absorb Indian culture. Starr spent time at home with his family.

Metamorphosis into a studio band

The Beatles producer, George Martin, later remembered how the group returned to the recording studio in November for the first time since their decision to stop touring in August. "They were fed up with being prisoners of their fame," he said. "We started off with 'Strawberry Fields', and then we recorded 'When I'm Sixty-Four' and 'Penny Lane'. They were all intended for the next album. We didn't know it was *Sgt Pepper* then – they were just going to be tracks on The New Album. But it was

going to be a record created in the studio, and there were going to be songs that couldn't be performed."[31]

The Beatles had barely seen each other for the better part of three months when they reconvened on November 24th at their familiar haunt: Abbey Road's studio 2. They were about to embark on another new album – yet this date marked a new phase in the group's career. Once again exploring new and uncharted ground, this time they would leave behind their duties as a live touring & recording act and reinvent themselves as a studio-only band. At the time, such a move was unheard of. Bands made money by constant touring. Records were the icing on the cake.

But The Beatles knew if they were to remain a functional band and play together, it would have to be in the studio, where they could create music without boundaries, free from external pressures on their time and concentration. They would no longer face deadlines linked to record-release dates. Work would continue on recordings until they were satisfied with the result. This new-found freedom in the studio would uncover yet more of their experimental side, as hinted at on *Revolver*. The result of the new studio sessions would be *Sgt Pepper's Lonely Hearts Club Band*, an album that would change the way in which popular music was made and how it was considered and evaluated.

'Strawberry Fields' and the Mellotron

The first song to be recorded by a band already absorbed by their new role was 'Strawberry Fields Forever', which would be released as a single the following February. The piece would become infused with virtually every studio gimmick that the group and their technical team had learned so far, as well as some new tricks. It would set a new standard for 1967's pop music scene and provide a suitable backdrop for that year's "summer of love" – and yet was recorded entirely within 1966.

The song started out on November 24th with a basic rhythm track of guitars, bass and drums, quickly changing shape with the addition of a Mellotron. As we've learned, Lennon had acquired an early example of the new Mellotron Mark II keyboard back in summer 1965. He'd finally found time to experiment with the tape-replay instrument as he looked for a way to include its distinctive sounds on his latest composition. Ironically, it was McCartney who played the Mellotron on the recordings.

For this first take of 'Strawberry Fields' McCartney played the brass setting on the Mellotron Mark II. The instrument had two keyboards, the right-hand one being the main section for playing melodies, the left split into rhythm parts and accompaniments. Above the right-hand keyboard, pressing the second of six pushbuttons switched to Station 2, which selected the beginning of a particular 42-foot length of pre-recorded tape inside the Mellotron for each key. McCartney – or whoever was working the instrument – would then have moved to a further row of three buttons marked A, B or C, and chosen Track B. This would line up the "brass" portion of the tapes – a recording of close-miked trumpet, trombone and saxophone. Now, pitched single-note lines and chords could be played with this sound on the right-hand keyboard. "Brass" is the Mellotron sound heard throughout take one of 'Strawberry Fields', as released on *Anthology 2*.

The sessions spilled into the following days with new versions being recorded, and various instrumental overdubs added along the way, such as Harrison's slide guitar, a piano, more Mellotron, maracas, and speeded-up vocals treated with Ken Townsend's ADT effect. On the 29th November the song was finalised, take 7 being the favoured version, but by this time the Mellotron sound had been changed. The Mark II's "flute" sound was now used, selected by hitting Station 1 Track A, and most clearly heard at the very start of the official released version. Next, the group started work on another new song, the vaudevillian 'When I'm Sixty-Four', initially featuring McCartney on piano.

The group and George Martin then decided to remake 'Strawberry Fields Forever', starting on December 8th. They went for a different approach, recording a fresh basic track for the song. This new version featured heavy use of backwards hi-hat cymbals, timpani, bongos, tambourine and a wild drum track played by Starr. "All right, calm down Ringo," pleaded Lennon as the drummer created an enormous din.

The following day Harrison added a new Beatle instrument to the developing remake of 'Strawberry Fields', a surmandal (often misspelled as swordmandal). This Indian/Pakistani instrument is similar to a board zither, usually with about 40 metal strings played with a plectrum or plectrums, and provides something like the sound of a high-pitched harp. If the released version of 'Strawberry Fields' is considered as starting with the song's chorus ("Let me take you down…") and having three subsequent verses in between (one: "Living is easy…", two: "No one I think…", and three: 'Always know…") then the surmandal is prominently heard just before the start of verse two (1:18) and verse three (2:04), and also at the end of the song (from 3:06 and prominently from 3:15).

A week later, on December 15th, seven session musicians were hired to overdub trumpets and cellos on to the remake, playing parts that George Martin had written. With this second orchestral/drum version of 'Strawberry Fields' now complete, work turned again to 'When I'm Sixty-Four' with Starr adding orchestral bells. The Beatles were gradually increasing the input of studio musicians to help complement their sound, and on December 21st three more session players were called upon to add clarinets to 'When I'm Sixty-Four'.

Two complete recordings of 'Strawberry Fields Forever' had now been finalised – the take-7 Mellotron/guitar version and the later drum/orchestral version. The story goes that Lennon was still not completely satisfied with either, and that he simply asked George Martin for them to be joined together. According to Martin, the obstacle the producer faced was that the two versions were at different tempos and in different keys. In order to fuse them, tape speeds had to be manipulated using Abbey Road's frequency-control system. Various theories have been put forward based on the official and unofficial releases of 'Strawberry Fields' in its various forms concerning the nature of the tape-speed manipulation. The take-7 Mellotron/guitar version released in its entirety on *Anthology 2* is two semitones higher than the official released version, which implies that it must have been slowed down. Accounts suggest that the drum/orchestral version was also slowed down.

Whatever the technical adjustments, Martin did an apparently remarkable job by bringing the two versions to the same tempo and pitch, and thus was able to satisfy Lennon's request. On the official released recording, about the first minute is the (edited) take-7 Mellotron/guitar version, the rest the drum/orchestral version.[32] To achieve the blend Martin made two edits.[32] The first occurs at 0:55 into the released version, chopping in from elsewhere in the Mellotron/guitar version the "Let me take you down cos I'm…" phrase needed to provide the start of chorus 2. Then at 0:59 comes the main edit, switching to the orchestral/drum version, which kicks in at "…going to Strawberry Fields…". Suddenly there are cellos!

At the very end of the track, coming in around 3:35, is a "re-entry" edit piece with more of the wild Starr drums and some swirling Mellotron. This time, McCartney played the Mark II's left-hand keyboard, selecting a tape of an entire passage of ensemble flutes. The passage was played in a random, repetitive fashion, without necessarily waiting for the internal tape to return to the start after releasing a key. The result sounds something like looped flutes, but is pure Mellotron.

Finally 'Strawberry Fields Forever' was complete, as much a complex studio construction as a new song. Where before the group had been interested in exploring new musical instruments to provide fresh inspiration, the studio itself was now fast becoming an instrument in its own right.

George Martin and his team must have wondered whether every track by the newly-cast recording band was going to be this complicated. The Beatles were clearly taking to their new role in exciting and creative ways, with all four members fully involved and working co-operatively toward a single goal. Whatever next?

More new Vox amps – solid state of the art

When the group had returned to Abbey Road at the end of November in their new guise as a full-time recording band, they were once again bestowed with the latest amp offerings from Vox. In the late summer, Vox had abandoned the 7120 and 4120 amp designs and moved on to a newer line of solid-state (transistor) amplifiers. According to Vox designer Dick Denney the new amps were first shown at the summer 1966 musical instrument trade show in London.

One magazine reporter present at the unveiling became quite excited by the new direction that Vox were taking. "Vox have completely shunned previous concepts this year and introduce their revolutionary range of solid state amplification," he gushed. "These, they say, are lighter, sturdier and do not get so hot as the valve [tube] type."

The principal new amp was "the revised version of the Beatle amp", which Vox called the Supreme. "This has built-in fuzz, treble boost, middle-range boost, reverb, volume and tremolo, all

In 1965 John had been one of the first to acquire a Mellotron Mark II tape-replay keyboard, a kind of early sampler. At the end of 1966 The Beatles finally used the instrument, for the recording of 'Strawberry Fields Forever'. The Mark II pictured above was sold at auction as John's.

CONQUEROR	DEFIANT	SUPREME		DYNAMIC BASS	FOUNDATION BASS	SUPER FOUNDATION BASS

This British Vox catalogue shows the Jennings-made solid-state amplifiers available at the time. Some of these models found their way to The Beatles.

of which are controllable from buttons on a footplate. Each pushbutton has a red light to indicate when the effect it represents is in use. This amp now gives 200 watts."[33]

The reporter went on to itemise the rest of the new line, including four guitars amps – the 100-watt Defiant, 70-watt Conqueror, 40-watt Virtuoso, and 20-watt Traveller – and three bass amps – the 150-watt Super Foundation Bass "with a range of effects to rival the Beatle amp", the 75-watt Foundation Bass, and the 50-watt Dynamic Bass. Prices ranged from the Traveller at 59 guineas (£61.95, about $175 then; around £690 or $965 in today's money) to the Supreme at 259 guineas (£271.95, some $760 then; around £3,020 or $4,230 today). The AC-30 and AC-50 remained, mercifully, as valve (tube) amps.

Dick Denney says that for their late-1966 studio sessions, the group were provided with almost every new Vox amplifier, including prototypes. Denney also points out that The Beatles had requested smaller amplifiers and that they started to mix various Vox amp heads and Vox cabinets. This does not help in trying to determine which Vox amps were used during the *Sgt Pepper* sessions.

Denney mentions a prototype "hybrid" Defiant amp head, mixing valve [tube] and transistor [solid-state] systems, which he built for the group, and goes on to explain the frequent changes made in the Vox line and outlines:

"Vox boss Tom Jennings was always saying that this or that amp was beginning to look stale. He was aware of the fashion aspect of amplifiers. So we would alter the shape or the look, change the knob layout, whatever. That's all it was: to look different and new. We would only make so many of these prototypes, maybe five of this and two of that. Sometimes they were made for the groups and would be given to them to try out – and they would use them up on the stand and get photographed with them. Now nobody can figure out what they were!"[34]

Although Vox did build a larger and louder 200-watt amp in this new series with The Beatles in mind, the reality was of course that the group no longer needed large amps for live concerts. Vox had had no idea, when the 200-watt amps were designed during 1966, that The Beatles were going to stop performing live. But as the group evolved into a recording outfit, the musicians quickly realised that large amps are unnecessary in the studio. This had been evident as long ago as the *Rubber Soul* sessions when their Vox AC-30s were pulled out again for some studio work.

The most likely line-up of Vox amps used during the *Pepper* sessions would be a combination of the newer-style Vox Conqueror or Defiant amps (with controls at the top of the front of the head) along with various prototypes. Some studio photographs show McCartney playing bass through a Vox 4120-style head (controls at the bottom of the front) with a smaller 2x12-style cabinet. In any case, the tone produced by any of these amps would have been very similar. As Denney points out, each had almost identical pre-amp sections.

By the end of 1966 The Beatles were using a range of different Vox amps, including prototypes. Here is a Vox Conqueror similar to those they would have used.

Certainly the cream-coloured Fender Bassman was present throughout the *Sgt Pepper* sessions. As for guitars, Lennon and Harrison both used their Epiphone Casinos and Gibson J-160Es, while McCartney too played his Epiphone Casino, using the Rickenbacker 4001S as his main studio bass. Starr played the same 22-inch-bass Ludwig drum set that he'd used during the final tour, still equipped with number-six Beatles-logo head.

As 1966 came to a close, the year's final sessions were held at Abbey Road's studio 2. On December 29th McCartney introduced a new piece, 'Penny Lane'. As final mixes were made of 'Strawberry Fields Forever' in studio 3, the group were busily delving into this new song, which for now featured piano as its main instrument. It was treated to a number of overdubs, including harmonium and more piano, both run through a Vox amp to create various sound textures. But 'Penny Lane' was not completed this year. The new sessions would spill over into 1967. And what a year it would prove to be.

" ... he's got some crazy stuff on there ... so we were inspired by it. And nicked a few ideas. "

PAUL McCARTNEY, ON HOW THE *SGT PEPPER* SESSIONS WERE INFLUENCED BY BRIAN WILSON'S INSTRUMENTATION ON *PET SOUNDS*

1967

THE BEATLES WOULD EMERGE THIS YEAR AS A MORE SOPHISTICATED UNIT WITH A NEW STUDIO-ORIENTED DIRECTION. EAGER TO LOSE THEIR MOP-TOP IMAGE AND PUT ASIDE BEATLEMANIA, THE GROUP CHANGED THEIR LOOK, NOT LEAST BY GROWING MOUSTACHES AND PAINTING THEIR GUITARS. IT WAS AS IF THEY NO LONGER WANTED TO BE 'THE BEATLES' EVERYONE HAD COME TO KNOW AND LOVE.

A smiling Harrison would even be photographed during the *Sgt Pepper* sessions wearing a Stamp Out The Beatles sweatshirt. Gone was the four-piece rock'n'roll combo using the standard guitars-bass-and-drums format to record their compositions. Now when they came to make basic tracks for their new songs, the group would typically leave behind those familiar instruments and reach for anything but the expected. In many cases the only link to their past would be the use of a bass guitar and a drum kit.

Session musicians, too, were beginning to appear more frequently at Beatle recordings, bringing with them the textures of traditional classical instruments. Almost anything was tried in the studio to make a standard song sound unconventional. It seemed that the more different and unusual the instrument or sound, the better. In the process, the new studio-bound Beatles would change the course of popular music.

McCartney commented later that as far he was concerned, the biggest influence on *Sgt Pepper* was The Beach Boys album *Pet Sounds*, released in the summer of 1966. The American group's creative leader Brian Wilson was, McCartney concluded, a genius. "[That album] is very clever on any level. If you approach it from a writer's point of view it's very cleverly written, the harmonic structures are very clever. If you approach it from an arranger's point of view, the kind of instruments, he's got … some crazy stuff on there. Because of the work that they'd done, it didn't seem too much of a stretch for us to get further out than they'd got."[1]

Work continued almost uninterrupted on 'Penny Lane' when the group reconvened at Abbey Road studio 2 on January 4th. In the following two weeks a swelling number of overdubs were added to the track, including both Lennon and McCartney fitting in some more piano parts, Harrison and Lennon on guitars, and Starr adding his drums while Lennon dubbed conga drums. McCartney tracked on his superb melodic bassline that held the whole song together.

The typical recording procedure elsewhere at the time was to start with drums and bass for a basic rhythm track, but during the *Sgt Pepper* sessions nothing was done conventionally. Adding the bass and drums later to existing instrument tracks worked out just as well – and sometimes better.

McCartney explained recently, "I often used to record without the bass, which George particularly used to get narked at. He'd say, 'Oh, it doesn't sound like a band'. And I knew what he meant. But I'd written it on guitar and I wanted to get the feel of how I'd written it, so I'd often say: do you mind if we don't put the bass on? Pretend it's there, and it'll give me a chance to put it on after."[2] Certainly *Sgt Pepper* is awash with some of McCartney's most melodic and elegant basslines.

Tracking more instruments on to 'Penny Lane' did not stop with bass. A stream of session musicians trooped through the studio carrying flutes, trumpets, piccolos, flugelhorn, oboes, cor anglais (English horn) and double-bass. The memorable B-flat piccolo trumpet section played by David Mason was the last to be added, and after this January 17th session was over 'Penny Lane' was quickly mixed for rush-release as the flip side to 'Strawberry Fields Forever'.

Recording The Beatles

Geoff Emerick, who later won a Grammy award for his engineering work on *Sgt Pepper*, was well aware of the importance of bass to the album's sessions. At first Emerick had used AKG D-20 microphones to capture bass guitar. "When I progressed to *Pepper*, I was using the AKG C-12," he recalls. "If the bass was to be an overdub, I'd use this C-12 up to six feet away from the amp." Emerick says he would sometimes use the C-12 in "figure of eight" format, where the microphone picked up primarily from what was in front of and behind it. The signal from the C-12 would then usually be compressed to tape through an Altec compressor. As we learned in 1966, a compressor generally results in a more punchy, lively sound.

As for McCartney's general playing style, the bass player himself recalls using both plectrum and finger/thumb styles. "I did a bit of both," he explains. "Mainly, if it was an important gig, I'd nearly always resort to a pick because I'd feel safer that way. The engineers used to like to hear the pick, because then they'd get the treble end out as well as the bass and get it to kick right out. I was never trained in any styles, so I just picked it up."[3]

Emerick generally used Neumann microphones for guitar speaker-cabinets. "I used a U47 or U48 about three feet away from the amp, to try to keep the sound a bit cleaner, and the Fairchild 660 or Altec compressor. They played at quite an excessive level. They often ran the guitar through a Leslie cabinet in this period, and when miking the Leslie cabinet we used the old favourite Neumanns again."

Emerick also chose his beloved U47s and U48s for vocals. "There's never been anything better, really, in conjunction with the Fairchild compressor. We always recorded the tracks with the reverb on them. I was looking at some old layout sheets the other day and they reminded me that we used the EMT plate reverb on certain things. But we didn't use a lot of reverb on Beatles stuff. It was minimal. If it was there, it was normally from Abbey Road's live echo chamber."[4]

Richard Lush, second engineer for the *Sgt Pepper* sessions, recalls the pioneering technique of close-miked drums. Close-miking means placing the microphone very near to the instrument or speaker cabinet in question, to get a more intimate sound. "Up to that period everything had mainly been miked at a distance," remembers Lush. "But *Pepper* saw close-miking, especially with the AKG D19s on the drums. That was when Geoff innovated with close miking."[5]

As for tonal changes, Emerick says that they didn't fiddle much with EQ. "That was because the mixing desk at EMI really had very little EQ. The desks just had treble and bass, and I think the top peaked at about 5kHz."[6] Ex-Abbey Road technician Ken Townsend provides more detail on the recording mixer. "At first it was a RED 37, made at EMI's Hayes factory. It had a Siemens amplifier and was used on all the early Beatle sessions. For tone controls, at Abbey Road we had 'classical EQ' or 'pop EQ'. You would physically replace a complete section of the EQ unit underneath the desk by lifting up a cover. The classical EQ was much more gentle, very flat with a gentle fall-off. A pop EQ had a much sharper, harder and higher EQ. And of course on classical recordings you didn't use much EQ anyway. But on pop sessions, and with The Beatles, we put on all sorts of things."[7]

With the multiple overdubs done during the *Sgt Pepper* sessions it's easy to forget that most of the album was recorded on a single four-track tape machine. Richard Lush explains, "When The

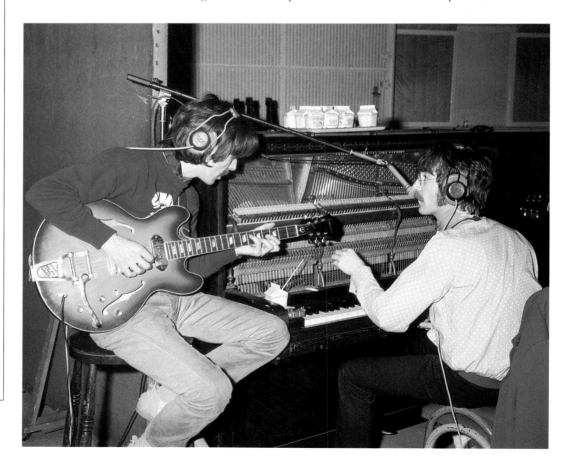

George and John at Abbey Road towards the end of the Sgt Pepper sessions. John plays the studio's "tack" piano that had metal-tipped hammers for a special percussive sound. George meanwhile is using his Epiphone Casino.

Beatles first started they did everything to two-track stereo and mono. When the Studer J-37 four-track machine came along in 1963 they used that straight away, right through to *Sgt Pepper*. Eight-track didn't come along until halfway through *The White Album*."[8]

Because of the inherent quality of the Studer J-37 recorders, tracks could be "bounced" or "reduced" – as the four tracks were filled on one J-37, these were mixed down to one track of another J-37, leaving the other three tracks free for more overdubs. Naturally there was some loss of sound quality, and producer George Martin did not like to go much beyond one bounce. Also, Martin and his team would have to make an artistic decision at this point about the balance of sounds, because the four tracks being mixed down to one would be fixed in the relationship set at this point. Once a "reduction" was made there was no way of going back and remixing the earlier tracks.

A DI In The Life?

The group started work on a new Lennon composition which would become 'A Day In The Life', recording the basic track on January 19th. Lennon sang and played his Gibson J-160E with a basic rhythm track of congas, piano and maracas. There was no middle section worked out for the song at this point, so Mal Evans was enlisted to count to 24, and then an alarm clock rang. The following day McCartney added his Rickenbacker 4001S bass to the track and Starr played his Ludwig drums, listening to the existing track.

The group took a few days out from their recording sessions to film promotional clips for the latest single, soon to be released. The next song was begun on February 1st – and this one prompted the concept that would bind the sessions together. The basic rhythm track for 'Sgt Pepper's Lonely Hearts Club Band' was recorded with a standard arrangement of guitars, bass and drums. McCartney's idea of The Beatles transforming into the Lonely Hearts Club Band was so well received by the group that the song's name became the title of the album. McCartney said later that the idea was to have an album by another band, not The Beatles at all. "[We would] just imagine that it wasn't us playing this album," he explained. "[We imagined that Sergeant Pepper was around] 20 years ago and he taught us to play. We were his protégés – and here we are."[9]

Perhaps it was another way of casting off the Beatle identity with which they had evidently become so bored. This new alter ego would also help them in their bid to re-establish themselves as a studio band. McCartney said that they were quite clearly changing their method of working at the time. "Instead of now looking for catchy singles, catchy singles, catchy singles … [*Sgt Pepper*] was more like writing your novel … It was much more of an overall concept."[10]

During the *Sgt Pepper* sessions a new device designed by EMI engineers at Abbey Road was used for the first time in order to record the bass guitar more clearly. It was called a direct injection transformer, later known as a DI box. McCartney would plug his bass lead (cord) into the unit, which had two outputs: one to feed the bass amp, the other the studio equipment. Although studio documentation shows that a DI box was used on the bass during the *Sgt Pepper* sessions, it should be stressed that the technique was never used exclusively to record the bass tracks. Studio maintenance engineer Ken Townsend emphasises that the bass tone was derived from a mix of the direct signal from the DI box as well as a microphone on the bass amp's speaker. "We used the DI first on a Beatles session,"[11] he says.

But engineer Geoff Emerick's recollection differs. "I never used DI on the bass, always a mike," he remembers. "Keyboards like the Mellotron were miked too – we didn't go direct. We normally ran keyboards through an amplifier to give them natural punch and power. There was very little direct injection. As soon as we tried to record anything direct it sounded so false, probably because we were brought up on real sounds. The DI sound seemed unnatural to us."[12] Whatever the arguments about its use, the invention of the DI box seems to be another new idea connected to The Beatles. Today the DI box has become an industry standard in recording studios as well as for live applications.

Dozens of different studio effects were used throughout the *Sgt Pepper* sessions. Later in the year, when Lennon, McCartney and Starr were interviewed by Kenny Everett for BBC radio's *Where It's At*, Lennon commented on the heavy use of studio effects on the album, using the group's favourite general word that seemed to cover all kinds of effects. "Double flanging, we call it," he enthused. "Flanging is great! They're all doing it. You name the one it isn't on. You name it, you spot it – you get a prize. You get a *Sgt Pepper* badge!"[13]

1967

The basic track for 'Good Morning Good Morning', a new Lennon song, was recorded on February 8th in studio 2. The following day the group held their first documented recording session at an independent studio not affiliated with EMI. 'Fixing A Hole' was started at Regent Sound on central London's Tottenham Court Road. George Martin says the reason for the change of studio was simply down to the group's lack of organisation. "I'm afraid the boys didn't plan very much, and when they wanted to come into a studio they never said to me: keep the next two weeks free, because we're sure we're going to be needing a studio. They would ring me up at 10 in the morning and say: we want to record tonight at 7 o'clock, OK? And I had to find a damned studio."[14] Geoff Emerick thinks that he and George Martin were busy recording Cilla Black at Abbey Road on the 8th.

The recording of 'Fixing A Hole' at Regent featured Paul on harpsichord as the primary instrument. Engineer Richard Lush recalls a later overdub session for the track on February 21st back at Abbey Road. "I do remember that Lennon played the bass on that track, he used a Fender bass on it. If you play the album you can pick it out because it's very simple, and a ploppy sort of sound. It didn't sound as rich as Paul's Rickenbacker bass."[15]

Back at Abbey Road the day after their trip to Regent, the group had a memorable session during the night of February 10th/11th in studio 1 with 40 musicians. The instruments included violins, oboe, cellos, trumpets, tuba and a harp – all there to create the now famous 24-bar glissandos in 'A Day In The Life'. Overdubbing the orchestra on to the existing tracks meant some tough technical problems needed to be solved.

"Some time during the morning before that session George Martin tackled me as I was walking into one of the studio restaurants," remembers Ken Townsend. "He said, 'Oh, Ken, I've got a little problem tonight. I desperately need eight tracks, but of course we only have four-track machines. Couldn't we lock two machines together?' I said I'd think about it."

No doubt finishing his cup of tea first, Townsend went off and tried to find a way of running two four-track tape recorders synchronised to one another ("in sync"). His solution was to put a 50Hz tone on one track of the first machine – the one with the existing piece mixed into stereo on two tracks – and use the tone to drive the capstan motor of the second machine – the one that would record the three or four individual mono takes of the orchestra freaking out. "We marked up the starting points on each tape," explains Townsend, "so that both machines could be started at exactly the same point."

Townsend says the only hitch in the scheme came later, when mixing the song. "I remember George [Martin] getting slightly impatient about the fact that the tape machine in studio 3, where he was mixing, would not lock up exactly in sync. Eventually we had to bring down the same two J-37s that had been used for the recording in studio 1, because they had a slightly different lead-in time as they ran up to the right speed. That was the only problem," says Townsend. "On the session itself, the link-up worked fine. I think it's probably one of the reasons why 'Day In The Life' sounds like it does, because the orchestra tracks are not exactly in sync. They're probably only a millisecond or so out, but that's enough to make it sound stronger."[16]

Strawberry Fields for vinyl

The double-a-side single, with 'Strawberry Fields' and 'Penny Lane', was first issued in the US on February 13th. It's no exaggeration to say that it stunned the music world. By the beginning of 1967 many pop bands thought that they had caught up with The Beatles. But 'Strawberry Fields' quickly changed their minds.

Paul Revere & The Raiders were one of those bands. They were among the most successful US groups during 1966 and 1967. With their own Dick Clark-produced television show, *Where The Action Is*, The Raiders were considered to be the States' own homegrown pop heroes. Despite their own success, they still considered The Beatles as the absolute leaders. Mark Lindsay was the outfit's lead singer. "I remember driving in my car from the studio one day and hearing on the radio the end of 'Strawberry Fields

Forever' for the first time," says Lindsay. "The DJ said it was the latest Beatles single that had just come out. So I went to a store, picked up the 45, and brought it home. At the time I lived with Terry Melcher, our producer. The Raiders had already had a bunch of hits, so we thought we were doing pretty well.

"I came home and told Terry that I had the new Beatles single, so we sat down and I put on 'Strawberry Fields'. When the song ended we both just looked at each other. I said, *'Now* what the fuck are we gonna do?' With that single, The Beatles raised the ante as to what a pop record should be."[17]

Lindsay wanted to share his enthusiasm for this revolutionary record, and promo film-clips for both sides of the new single were screened on *Where The Action Is* on March 14th. Those who listened awe-struck to the new single could hardly have guessed what was to come with the new album, still under construction at Abbey Road.

Back in London, recording progressed, with further overdubs of bass guitar and lead vocals added to 'Good Morning Good Morning'. On February 13th and 14th a new Harrison tune, 'Only A Northern Song', was recorded. Though it failed to make *Sgt Pepper*, the song would surface later on the *Yellow Submarine* film soundtrack.

More keyboards and the Lowrey organ

During the *Sgt Pepper* sessions a number of keyboard instruments were used. The group played Abbey Road's Steinway grand piano, Challen upright piano, "jangle" upright piano, harmonium, and Hammond RT-3 organ with Leslie speaker cabinet – all familiar from previous sessions. They also used their own Mellotron Mark II tape-replay keyboard and Hohner Pianet C electric piano. A new keyboard to the *Pepper* sessions was a Hammond L-100 organ, which was also widely used. The L-100 is a self-contained Hammond console, requiring no external speaker cabinet, and has two manuals (keyboards) of 44 keys each and a 13-note pedal keyboard, plus an "expression" pedal to control volume.

On February 17th the basic track of 'Being For The Benefit Of Mr Kite' was recorded, consisting of drums and bass, plus harmonium played by George Martin and Lennon singing a lead "guide

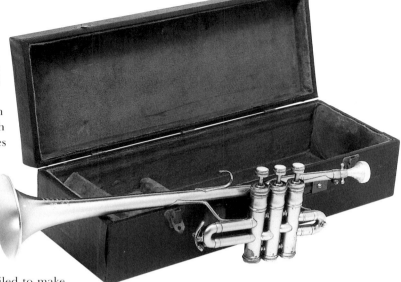

This Couesnon Monopole B-flat piccolo trumpet was the one played by orchestral session player David Mason on 'Penny Lane'. The instrument was later sold at auction.

Studio 1 at Abbey Road, February 10th 1967, and Paul conducts a 40-piece orchestra for the famous glissandos on 'A Day In The Life'.

vocal" (a rough version to help map out the song, to be replaced later). But 'Kite' began to change when Lennon asked Martin to create a circus feel. The producer obliged by finding archive recordings of fairground pipe organs which he transferred to tape. He asked Geoff Emerick to cut up the tapes, which were then mixed around by throwing them in the air. Emerick was further instructed to re-splice the randomly dispersed pieces of tape back together, in the process creating the swirling, disjointed fairground sound that was added to the song.

Intense work for *Sgt Pepper* continued. The dramatic crashing piano chord was added to the end of 'A Day In The Life' on February 22nd. Lennon, Starr, McCartney and Mal Evans sat down at three pianos – probably the Challen, "tack" and Steinway – in studio 2 and simultaneously played an

E-major chord, allowing the decaying sound of the pianos to ring out for almost an entire minute. More new songs followed. 'Lovely Rita' was initially recorded with McCartney on piano, Lennon and Harrison both playing their Gibson J-160Es, and Starr on his Ludwig drums. McCartney added his Rickenbacker 4001S bass after the basic track was down.

Lennon's future classic, 'Lucy In The Sky With Diamonds', was next, started on March 1st. The basic track featured drums, acoustic guitar and piano. Mal Evans and Neil Aspinall wrote a magazine column at the time describing the song's beginning. "[It] starts with McCartney playing Hammond organ," they said, "using a special organ stop which gives a bell-like overchord [sic] effect which makes it sound like a celeste."[18]

Another Abbey Road keyboard, the Hammond L-100 (seen in the catalogue above) was used by the group on many sessions.

Despite this contemporary report, photographic evidence reveals that McCartney in fact used a Lowrey DSO Heritage Deluxe organ to produce the famous opening sound on 'Lucy'. Indeed, neither a Hammond RT-3 nor an L-100 are capable of producing that sound. It was the Lowrey DSO's preset voices of harpsichord, vibraharp, guitar and "music box" that provided the magical tones required. (This same Lowrey organ later ended up at the group's Apple studio and was used during the *Get Back/Let It Be* sessions.)

The drone of a tambura, an Indian lute-like instrument, was also added to the track, helping convey the trippy texture the group had in mind. Later, McCartney added Rickenbacker bass, and Harrison put fuzz guitar on to the song, which was completed on March 3rd. A more traditional line-up of guitars, bass and drums was employed when 'Getting Better' was recorded six days later. Harrison again added a tambura drone to the song.

Adding the sound of brass instruments during the *Pepper* sessions became commonplace, and the title track soon received a French-horn overdub. When it was time to add a brass section to 'Good Morning Good Morning', the group called on their old friends from Sounds Incorporated to help out, and the three saxophone players added baritone, tenor and alto parts to the song, with additional musicians brought in to play trombone and French horn.

The influence of Eastern music

For the opening of 'Lucy In The Sky With Diamonds' The Beatles used a Lowrey Heritage Deluxe (catalogue shot above), one of the many keyboards at Abbey Road used during the recording of the Sgt Pepper album.

Harrison's passion for Indian music had become evident as far back as 1965 during the *Rubber Soul* sessions when he added a simple sitar overdub to 'Norwegian Wood'. By 1966, the Indian influence on the Beatle had become more substantial, clearly heard on the recording of 'Love You To' from *Revolver*. Harrison's interest in Indian music was only enhanced when he travelled to India in late 1966 to study sitar with the instrument's undisputed master, Ravi Shankar. One of the results was Harrison's songwriting contribution to *Sgt Pepper*, 'Within You Without You'.

Shankar explains that sitars have been popular in the northern part of India for almost 800 years, undergoing slight modifications in size and stringing along the way. He speaks of Amir Ksuru, a Persian-born official in India at the end of the 12th century who made some changes to the instrument and named it sihtar. "In Persian that means three strings," says Shankar, "akin to what we had in our old instrument known as the tritantrika vina, the three-string vina. On old vinas all the frets were permanently fixed in wax, making a chromatic scale with all the half tones. Ksuru changed it to movable frets."

The sitar enjoys a similar position and popularity in Indian classical raga music as the violin does in the West. "It takes 10 or 15 years to reach a very good standard. Because it's not just the playing of it," Shankar states. "You have to learn the whole musical system. So what George Harrison did, along with many other people, was to take up the sitar and just start to play it. They produced a sort of sound which to us sounded really ridiculous. It's like if someone in Africa takes the violin and plays

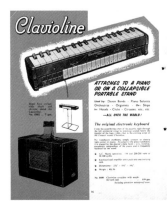

it and says, 'How do you like this scratching sound?' It takes a long time to produce the real sound and play the real music."

Shankar says that Harrison had heard his recordings. "I think it was a student of a student of mine who helped him for 'Norwegian Wood' or some recording. So the sitar was used to play some phrases which he composed. But it was absolutely different and amateurish. Some time after that we met at a party, and at that time unfortunately I knew very little about The Beatles. I knew that they were a very popular group, but I didn't know how famous and how well known they were. So when George showed his interest in sitar and said he would like to learn a little more, I told him very clearly that sitar is not like guitar where you can just learn it on your own. You have to undergo many years of study, like the violin and cello or any of the Western classical instruments."

Harrison told Shankar that he understood this, and still wanted to learn. Shankar gave him a few lessons in Britain, and then Harrison wanted to come to India for a longer period. "Unfortunately that wasn't possible because he had his commitments, and he had to return to England within four or five weeks. And that was the only solid time that he had for beginning the sitar – practising the scales and very simple things. Since then he never could really pursue it as he would have wanted. Along with that is his tremendous interest in Indian philosophy, religion and so on. It was so strong. I gave him a very famous book, *Autobiography Of A Yogi*. That really changed his whole life and mind. That influenced his writing of beautiful songs like 'Within You Without You' and many others."[19]

Harrison's Indian-influenced contribution to *Sgt Pepper* was first recorded on March 15th. He used London-based Indian musicians, some from the Asian Music Circle, to record 'Within You Without You'. It featured tabla (pair of small hand-played drums), surmandal (multi-stringed board zither), dilruba (long-necked fretted fiddle) and three tambura (drone lutes), two of the latter played by Harrison and Neil Aspinall. During later sessions additional musicians were brought in to add Western strings, the section consisting of eight violins and three cellos. Harrison also added sitar and some acoustic guitar, as well as his lead vocal track. He was the only Beatle heard on the piece.

Geoff Emerick miked up the Indian stringed instruments and drums from the front or the back, or a mix of the two, using small condenser microphones, AKG 56s or 54s, and often using a compressor again to keep the volume level up. "Don't forget this is the first time that Indian instruments were used in a pop situation," Emerick points out. "Prior to that they were recorded in a classical fashion. And you certainly didn't compress stuff for classical music. Suddenly we were compressing tabla and limiting sitars to make the sound more poppy. It made it sound a bit more electronic, I think."[20]

As *Sgt Pepper* slowly took shape, more songs were added. As with 'Eleanor Rigby', McCartney's ballad 'She's Leaving Home' featured only a string section, including violins, violas, cello, double-bass and even a harp. No Beatle played any instruments on this song. The only group involvement was McCartney's lead singing accompanied by Lennon's backing vocal.

Paul's Fender Esquire guitar and Selmer Zodiac amp

The sessions continued, with days of overdubs on a number of songs. The group were clearly relishing their new-found role as studio artists. A further magazine piece by Evans and Aspinall[21] mentioned McCartney's electric guitar solos on 'Good Morning Good Morning' and 'Being For The Benefit of Mr Kite'. Photographs taken of McCartney working on the solos at the session on March 28th show him switching between his Epiphone Casino and a Fender Esquire, which he played through a Selmer Zodiac Twin 50 Mark II amplifier.

The sunburst-coloured Fender Esquire was essentially a single-pickup version of the company's classic Telecaster model. The right-handed Esquire that McCartney played was strung left-handed, with the strap-button moved to the body's cutaway horn to facilitate the use of a strap. Selmer's Zodiac was a British-made 50-watt combo amp with two 12-inch speakers. Its second channel featured a series of preset pushbutton tone controls, as well as speed and depth controls for the built-in tremolo. The Esquire guitar and Zodiac amp combination was never seen again afterwards.

John used a Clavioline keyboard instrument, like the one pictured above, during the recording of 'Baby You're A Rich Man' at Olympic Sound studio in west London.

All manner of odd instruments and sounds were used during these sessions in the continuing effort to make the recordings different. There was a glockenspiel and congas, animal sounds and applause, even laughter. Starr recently remembered the lengthy waits between overdubs on these sessions. "The biggest memory I have of *Sgt Pepper* is I learned to play chess."[22]

During the March 28th session more unusual overdubs were made to 'Mr Kite' when a glockenspiel was added and the group happened upon a pair of Hohner bass harmonicas to accentuate the chord changes. McCartney says the influence here was from an old TV programme when he was a child that featured the Morton Fraser Harmonica Gang. But it was *Pet Sounds* again that provided the hint that unusual instruments might find a modern role, as McCartney's ears were pricked by the sound of bass harmonicas on some of those Beach Boy tracks. "It's very cleverly done … So we were inspired by it," he said later. "And nicked a few ideas."[23]

There had not yet been the traditional song for Starr to sing on the new album, so Lennon and McCartney obliged by writing 'Bad Finger Boogie' – which quickly became 'With A Little Help From My Friends'. The basic track was recorded on March 29th in studio 2 and started with Starr on his Ludwig drums, McCartney on piano, Harrison on electric guitar and Lennon playing cowbell.

The following day Michael Cooper photographed the group within artist Peter Blake's now famous *Sgt Pepper* cover setting, at the Chelsea Manor studios in London. Later that evening in studio 2 McCartney and Lennon's backing vocals were added to 'With A Little Help From My Friends' while Harrison overdubbed additional guitar parts.

McCartney added his Rickenbacker bass to the track, as Richard Lush, second engineer at the session, recalls. "Ninety-nine per cent of the time he used a Fender amp," says Lush, "but on this track Paul used an Altec loudspeaker. We had his bass going through a speaker in the studio … I think that was the best bass sound on the album. I'm pretty sure he played the Rickenbacker in the control room and we sent the signal down into the studio through the Altec speaker, which we miked."

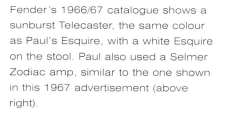

Fender's 1966/67 catalogue shows a sunburst Telecaster, the same colour as Paul's Esquire, with a white Esquire on the stool. Paul also used a Selmer Zodiac amp, similar to the one shown in this 1967 advertisement (above right).

Lush, who played guitar himself at the time, also remembers that the group used tortoiseshell plectrums that were about half an inch square with a little point at the bottom. "There'd always be hundreds of them left on the floor after the sessions, so I used to take them home and use them for playing guitar myself."[24]

The last session for the *Pepper* album with all four Beatles present took place on April 1st when 'Sgt Pepper's Lonely Hearts Club Band (Reprise)' was recorded in studio 1 with the traditional line-up of drums, bass and two guitars. Later that day percussion and Hammond organ were added. Two days later McCartney flew to the US while the *Pepper* album was mixed and edited for a June 1st release.

It had been suggested that the group should produce a *Sgt Pepper* television special, with film clips of each song on the album. A production schedule was even drawn up, but the project never happened. In the second week of April, during McCartney's flight back from the US, he came up with a song and the idea for a new TV feature, *Magical Mystery Tour*. Upon his return, McCartney met with the other Beatles about the scheme and plans were made immediately.

The scheduled release of *Pepper* was more than a month away and The Beatles were already back in Abbey Road's studio 3 to record the title song for this new project. The basic track of 'Magical Mystery Tour' was recorded on April 25th, with Starr on drums, Lennon and Harrison playing acoustic and electric guitars and McCartney playing piano and singing. A considerable amount of overdubs were made to the song in the days that followed. McCartney put down a bass track using his Rickenbacker 4001S, and tambourines, maracas and a cowbell were added. The group also devised the infectious "roll up …" backing vocals, once more using the technique of recording at a slower speed so that when played back the result would be faster and at a higher pitch. The final overdub was the addition of a four-piece trumpet section. By May 4th the song was being mixed.

John and the Clavioline

Another project that the group agreed to during the early part of May was a full-length animated feature film to be produced by King Features – *Yellow Submarine*. It would contain some older Beatle songs as well as a few new originals. With this in mind The Beatles didn't wait before jumping back into the studio to record a new composition, intended for the film. Instead of using Abbey Road, they ventured out to a studio that The Rolling Stones regularly used. On May 11th 'Baby You're A Rich Man' was recorded at Olympic Sound in London. Second engineer at the session was Eddie Kramer, who would later produce Jimi Hendrix and Kiss. According to Kramer the intention was to impress the group with the set-up at Olympic, which was independent of record company control.

"We wanted to make sure that they walked out of there being completely blown away," says Kramer. "Which they were. 'Baby You're A Rich Man' was recorded, overdubbed and mixed in one night. There was a Clavioline that happened to be in the studio, and John played it. This was a French electronic instrument with a small keyboard. It had a little strip which you put your thumb on and moved it up and down the length of the keyboard as you played, to get vibrato. George played his guitar and Ringo his kit, and McCartney played bass and then piano. So the only thing different was the Clavioline."[25]

The Clavioline was a monophonic keyboard – meaning only one note sounded at a time, precluding chords. It was in effect a predecessor of modern synthesisers, and had been designed in 1947 by Constant Martin in Versailles, France. The instrument consisted of two units: the keyboard, with built-in valve (tube) sound generator; and the separate amplifier-and-speaker box. The two pieces were connected by a power lead (cord), and the keyboard could be fitted into the back of the amplifier unit for convenient carrying. A built-in octave transposer switch gave the keyboard's single oscillator a five-octave range. The overall volume was controlled by a knee-operated lever. The Clavioline's unusual sound, heard whirling intermittently through 'Baby You're A Rich Man', had also been evident on 'Telstar', a big hit for the British group The Tornados on both sides of the Atlantic in 1962. Several different models of the Clavioline were sold in Britain over the years by Selmer, and by Jennings using the Univox brand.

The Beatles experience

Work on songs for *Yellow Submarine* continued the day after the Olympic visit. The group, back at Abbey Road's studio 2, turned to the primarily acoustic tune 'All Together Now', a loose party-style song featuring Lennon and Harrison on their Gibson J-160E electric-acoustic guitars and McCartney on bass, with Starr throwing in sporadic drum parts. The song featured harmonica, a barrage of sound effects – and even a triangle. More experimentation continued in studio 2 on May 17th when they recorded what is arguably their oddest song, 'You Know My Name (Look Up The Number)'. In fact it would not be released until 1970. Three more full evening sessions were spent on this peculiar song, one of which featured Brian Jones of The Rolling Stones on alto saxophone.

On May 25th, leaving Abbey Road again to try yet another London studio, the group landed at De Lane Lea, where groups such as The Yardbirds and The Jimi Hendrix Experience recorded. Another track for the *Yellow Submarine* film was cut, Harrison's 'It's All Too Much', with an arrangement of drums, bass guitar, Hammond organ and lead guitar for the basic track. The blistering guitar intro to the song with its feedback and detuning tremolo-arm work is certainly reminiscent of Hendrix's style. The young American guitarist was gaining a good deal of attention from his fellow musicians at the time, and clearly had an effect on The Beatles. The group would frequently check him out at clubs like the Bag O'Nails, the Speakeasy and the Roundhouse.

Of course, The Beatles also had a profound influence on Hendrix. When *Pepper* was released in Britain on Thursday June 1st, Hendrix reacted quickly. Experience bassist Noel Redding recalls that their first album, *Are You Experienced*, had come out only weeks before *Sgt Pepper*. "So it was only The Beatles that stopped us from being number one in Britain," he says. "*Pepper* came out on a Thursday, and we were playing on the Sunday at the Saville Theatre, which was owned by Brian Epstein. We always used to meet at [manager] Chas Chandler's flat before the gig and get a taxi around there, or we'd meet in a pub near the theatre. Hendrix said, 'Let's play "Sgt. Pepper".' So there in the dressing room we learned the intro, which is A, C and G. We didn't do the middle part, because we didn't

Paul in Abbey Road studio 2 on March 28th 1967, the day on which he recorded the guitar solos for 'Good Morning Good Morning' and 'Being For The Benefit Of Mr Kite'. He's using his Fender Esquire through a Selmer Zodiac amp. His Epiphone Casino is also close to hand.

know it. So we played the intro a couple of times, there'd be a couple of guitar solos, finish ... and then go into our set. I found out later that all The Beatles were in the audience and it freaked them out. After the show they invited us to a party at Brian Epstein's house. Hendrix loved The Beatles – we all did – and it was nice to become friends with them."[26]

All you need is a song

The next great undertaking after the release of *Sgt Pepper* came when The Beatles agreed to represent Great Britain for the BBC-inspired *Our World*, the first televised satellite-linked programme, intended to join together 18 countries and over 400 million viewers worldwide. The broadcast was scheduled for June 25th, but less than two weeks prior to the event the group had not yet recorded any special song for it.

On June 14th they set out to start work on their contribution and returned to Olympic Sound. Eddie Kramer, chief engineer on this session, thinks the main reason for this and the May visit to Olympic was because Abbey Road was busy. "They came in and it was, 'Well, what are we going to do now?' John had the idea for 'All You Need Is Love' and he sat next to me in the control room. We rigged the talkback mike so that it could be used for vocals, and he sang through that. There was a bunch of instruments left over in the studio from previous sessions, including a double-bass that Paul played, and George Martin played harpsichord. Ringo was on drums."

A report made by Mal Evans and Neil Aspinall in a contemporary magazine says, "Lennon played the harpsichord – sounds like a very tinny piano sound on the record. Paul used an arco [bowed] string bass ... and Ringo on drums as usual. Plus George played the violin for the first time in his life." [27] Kramer has no recollection of the violin. "They did the song from beginning to end for a good half-hour," he remembers. "They'd get to the end of the song and John would count it off again without stopping, doing it again and again until they got the one that they liked."[28]

A few days later, back at Abbey Road's studio 3, the group continued work on 'All You Need Is Love', overdubbing piano and vocals, as well as banjo, apparently played by Lennon. Second engineer for this session was Richard Lush, who recalls the Olympic tape that came to Abbey Road as a basic backing track with harpsichord, drums and backing vocals. "Then

John shows off the back of his Casino, sprayed white or grey during The Beatles' psychedelic phase in 1967.

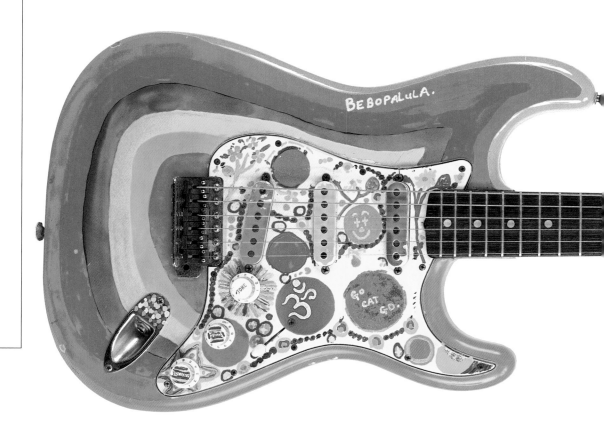

we put some more backing vocals on it, Paul played bass, John sang the vocal and George did the electric guitar. After it was all done I think Ringo did a little drum roll on the beginning. And then on the actual day, of course, we had the orchestra."[29]

Painting guitars

Somewhere between the tail end of the *Pepper* sessions and the 'All You Need Is Love' broadcast, The Beatles decided to try a new look for their guitars. By the spring the psychedelic movement in London was in full swing and minds were being expanded. Keeping in step with the psychedelic mood, the group decided to paint their instruments. "The Beatles have so many guitars (yes, Ringo included) that they can well afford to experiment with a few," ran a contemporary report. "They now have a craze for covering them in paint, not just haphazardly, of course, but carefully with spray guns. The results are weird but attractive. Most of the guitars they spray themselves, but others they leave to a motley crew of artists who drift in and out of their circle of friends."[30]

Lennon and Harrison both used their Fender Stratocasters during the *Pepper* sessions. Lennon's Strat remained in its original sonic blue finish, but Harrison's underwent a major cosmetic change, receiving a splendid psychedelic treatment. He recently described how this happened. In that period, he said, everything was more colourful. "Colourful clothes, colourful houses and cars, and it was just logical to have a coloured guitar. So I got some dayglo paint out of a tin and just painted [the Strat] with a brush. And it's not so much a great paint job, but that's the way it came out – there's some of [Harrison's then wife] Pattie Boyd's nail varnish on the top, green glittery stuff. And the guitar's called Rocky."[31] In another interview, in the late 1980s, Harrison said, "When we all took certain substances, I decided to paint [my Strat] in dayglo colours. And that [guitar was on] 'I Am The Walrus' and 'All You Need Is Love'. Now I've got it set up for slide."[32]

McCartney's Rickenbacker 4001S bass also received a psychedelic treatment, of white, silver and red paint in a "dripping" pattern. As McCartney remembers, "We did the cars too. If you did the cars, you might as well do your guitars. It looked great, and it was just because we were tripping. That's what it was, man. Look at your guitar and you'd trip even more."[33]

Lennon's experimental paint job was directed at his Epiphone Casino, but he limited the effect by simply spraying a white or grey finish on to the rear of the guitar's body and neck. A more stunning psychedelic paint job was applied to his Gibson J-160E. Lennon had met a group of Dutch artists, Marijke Koger, Simon Posthuma and Josje Leeger, better known as The Fool, who befriended The Beatles. Embracing psychedelia, Lennon commissioned The Fool to paint his Rolls Royce, his upright

(left) A set of recent Gibson John Lennon limited-edition reissue guitars illustrates the three stages in the life of John's J-160E: original sunburst; painted psychedelic by The Fool; and later sanded down to natural wood, with John's caricatures of himself and Yoko Ono which he added in 1969.

The group filming the 'I Am The Walrus' segment for their Magical Mystery Tour TV special in September 1967. George uses his psychedelic Strat, John is at the piano, Paul plays his painted Rickenbacker 4001S bass, and Ringo has his first 22-inch-bass Ludwig kit with a newly-painted "Love/The Beatles" drum-head.

George's Fender Stratocaster. George took the group's psychedelic guitar-painting mood to its extreme with this fantastic piece of artwork, applied on top of the guitar's original sonic blue finish. He first used it for the 'All You Need Is Love' worldwide broadcast. George still owns this guitar today.

IF YOU DID THE CARS, YOU MIGHT AS WELL DO YOUR GUITARS. IT LOOKED GREAT...

Paul McCartney, on the psychedelic

paint-jobs given to The Beatles

instruments

piano and his Gibson J-160E. Marijke Koger of The Fool remembers, "John had asked us to paint his car and piano. We did all kinds of things. He would just tell us to do what we wanted."[34]

Lennon had The Fool paint his J-160E especially for The Beatles' upcoming live worldwide satellite broadcast of 'All You Need Is Love'. The symmetrical waves of paint that covered the guitar in two shades of blue were accented with red outlines. Lennon unveiled his newly finished psychedelic J-160E at the June 24th rehearsals at Abbey Road with the intention of playing the guitar during the broadcast. Photos taken that day in studio 1 confirm that the psychedelic J-160E was present. Unfortunately, Lennon did not use the coloured guitar on camera. Engineer Richard Lush says, "They were playing to a track, and I think John wanted to play guitar. Then he was told that he would have to sing live on the air, and that's why he opted not to play guitar – just to sing. He was very nervous."[35]

During the rehearsals for the group's all-important satellite broadcast, Starr played his standard 22-inch-bass Ludwig kit, which still had number-six Beatles drop-T logo. McCartney used his Rickenbacker 4001S bass with its psychedelic paint job. Harrison rehearsed playing Lennon's Epiphone Casino, which by this time was without its pickguard. (Oddly enough, the pickguard's mounting bracket was left on the guitar. The instrument also by now had a black knob replacing one of the original gold-coloured controls.) Lennon sang but did not play anything.

The following day saw the *Our World* event. The afternoon began with more rehearsals of 'All You Need Is Love'. Set up in Abbey Road's large studio one, McCartney played his psychedelic Rick 4001S bass through a Vox Defiant amp, while Harrison chose to use his psychedelic-painted Strat through the cream-coloured Fender Bassman amp and speaker. Lennon had his newly painted psychedelic Gibson J-160E lying on the ground at his feet, which again he did not play, opting to concentrate on singing. Starr was on his Ludwig set.

Photos taken during the afternoon rehearsals for *Our World* show a new feature on Starr's drum kit. A drum-head for the front of the bass drum was specially made for the broadcast. This head was painted orange with the word "Love" hand-painted at an angle across the head in yellow, with a spiralled O and a heart-shaped V. Toward the bottom of the head and in smaller hand-painted letters "The Beatles" appears, also in yellow. For the rehearsals the new head was simply placed in front of the bass drum to cover the existing Beatles drop-T logo. Prior to the event, however, the Love drum-head was properly fixed to the Ludwig kit. Pictures taken at a gathering in studio 1 before the broadcast show the number-six Beatles-logo head discarded and left under a grand piano.

The group's live satellite-broadcasted performance later that night went off smoothly, beamed worldwide without a hitch. 'All You Need Is Love' was a huge success, and EMI decided to rush-release the song as a new Beatles' single. On July 7th, less than two weeks after the *Our World* programme, 'All You Need Is Love' backed with 'Baby You're A Rich Man' was released in Britain and shot to the top of many pop charts. The Beatles had defined the mood of the times and 'All You Need Is Love' became an anthem for 1967's glorious summer of love. Relishing their success and triumphs, the group took the better part of the next two months off, only to regroup on August 22nd at yet another London recording studio. This time the chosen spot was the Chappell studio on Maddox Street where they continued work on their next endeavour, *Magical Mystery Tour*. That evening and again the following day they recorded the basic track for 'Your Mother Should Know'.

Brian Epstein dies – the beginning of the end

The second Chappell session, on the 23rd August, was the last Beatle recording session that Brian Epstein attended. Two days later the group travelled to Bangor, north Wales, to study transcendental meditation under the Maharishi Mahesh Yogi. While there they were told that Brian Epstein had been found dead. "I was stunned. We all were, I suppose," Lennon said later. "The Maharishi, we went in to him … and he was sort of saying oh, forget it, be happy – like an idiot, like parents. Smile. That's what Maharishi said. And we did. I knew we were in trouble then. I didn't really have any misconceptions about our ability to do anything other than play music, and I was scared. I thought, we've fucking had it."[36]

The four Beatles met days after Epstein's death at McCartney's home to plot their future and to work out their next moves. The decision was made to continue with the *Magical Mystery Tour* TV special, already scheduled to air in Britain. They would produce the film themselves. It seemed so simple: record a few more new songs, film a bunch of wacky people on a trippy bus ride, edit the footage with some new songs into an entertaining hour, and you have a film. But soon the group's lack of experience in film production became evident, as well as their poor grasp of organisation – for which they had depended on Epstein.

The group pressed on. As scheduled, they re-entered Abbey Road's studio 1 on September 5th to record Lennon's fabulous 'I Am The Walrus'. The basic track was recorded with Starr on his Ludwig drums, McCartney playing Rickenbacker bass, Harrison on electric guitar and Lennon playing Hohner Pianet electric piano. A Mellotron was reportedly added, though it does not seem to have made the released version. The next day more overdubs were made to 'Walrus' and then two new songs were recorded. First was McCartney's vocal/piano demo of 'The Fool On The Hill' and then a complete basic track of Harrison's 'Blue Jay Way' featuring a good deal of Hammond organ. More work on the song spilled into the next day.

On September 8th yet another new piece was recorded for *Magical Mystery Tour*. 'Flying', an instrumental credited to the entire band as writers, featured standard guitar, bass and drums plus an array of keyboards, including prominent Mellotron played by Lennon. The main theme used the instrument's "trombone" pre-recorded sound.

Next on the schedule was filming. On September 11th the group set out on a hired bus freshly painted with the Magical Mystery Tour logo, loaded with a film crew, The Beatles and an odd cast of characters. It became a surrealistic trip – and it was all put on film. As the company headed for England's west country they soon ran into unforeseen logistical problems. It quickly transpired that making a film involved rather more work than they had planned for. The group did the best they could, and filming continued on the road until September 15th when they returned to London. The following day they hopped back into Abbey Road's studio 3 to continue work, and made a mix of 'I Am The Walrus' to be used during filming.

Electric sitar

Guitar manufacturers were looking closely at The Beatles and their music, trying to figure out ways of profiting from the group's success. Hofner used the popularity of the 500/1 violin bass and adapted the style into a six-string guitar. The Danelectro company, founded by Nat Daniel in New Jersey in the 1950s, originally as an amp maker but moving into guitar production, had guessed that some guitarists wanted the sitar sound made famous by The Beatles, but in an easily playable form.

Danelectro designed a way to capture a sitar-like sound from an electric guitar in a new instrument called the Coral Electric Sitar. It had 13 drone strings in addition to the regular six, plus a curved "Sitarmatic" bridge that produced something like the characteristic twang of a sitar. Danelectro had introduced its new Coral brand at the beginning of 1967 and the Sitar was the first in a series of new products. Two of the first Coral Sitars made were given to Harrison and Lennon. Unfortunately, the instruments were never used on Beatle recordings.

Commenting on his guitar collection for a magazine feature in the 1980s, Harrison pointed to an instrument and said: "There's the [Coral] electric sitar they gave me because of the Ravi [Shankar] thing. It's supposedly the very first one; it's got a strip on the back saying 'Patent Pending'. Spencer Davis saw it once and said, 'Oh, can I borrow that for a night?' And he hijacked it. I never saw it for about two years – by which time everybody had used one. So I never actually used it."[37]

The Spencer Davis Group first brought Steve Winwood to the record-buying public's attention with mid-1960s hits such as 'Gimme Some Loving' and 'Keep On Running'. Davis recalls hanging out with The Beatles in London nightspots such as the Ad Lib and the Scotch of St James. He planned to use a sitar on a Spencer Davis Group song called 'After Tea' and so asked George's advice. "He said he'd got this Coral Sitar, and that I could borrow it, which I did. But we ended up using Dave Mason to play a real sitar on 'After Tea' so we didn't need the Coral. In between all the travels and stuff it sort of got stuck in my house. Then George's office called and said, 'We understand you've got Mr Harrison's sitar.' And I said yes, as a matter of fact I have. So I put it in the Mini, drove off and returned it."[38]

Harrison still owns his Coral Sitar, and Lennon's is now on display at the Rock & Roll Hall Of Fame in Cleveland, Ohio, on loan from Yoko Ono. One can only wonder what Harrison might have done with the Coral Sitar on record had the guitar not been "hijacked".

The Vox display at an instrument trade fair in England, with a prototype of the unusually-shaped Kensington model (far right). John and George used one that was given to them by Vox man Dick Denney.

Vox prototype guitar

Filming for *Magical Mystery Tour* continued from September 18th to the 24th, during which time a memorable performance of 'I Am The Walrus' was filmed at the West Malling Air Station in Kent. This was one of the only performance pieces in the resulting film, where McCartney can be seen playing his psychedelic-painted Rickenbacker 4001S bass, John at a white grand piano, and Starr on his Ludwig kit with the Love/Beatles-logo drum-head. On the final film version, Harrison is seen with his painted Fender Strat, but during some earlier rehearsals he'd used a different guitar.

John's Coral Sitar (right). The New Jersey-based Danelectro company produced an electric sitar model, and gave John and George two of the first ones made. The instrument was designed by New York session man Vinnie Bell, pictured in the ad below. John's Coral Sitar is today owned by Yoko Ono.

You don't have to be HINDU to play the CORAL® ELECTRIC SITAR

Danelectro CORPORATION
A SUBSIDIARY OF MCA INC.
211 West Sylvania Avenue, Neptune City, New Jersey 07753

Coral PRESTIGE GUITARS AND AMPLIFIERS   *Vincent Bell* SIGNATURE DESIGNS

Beat Instrumental journalists were on hand to report on the West Malling filming. Their photographs reveal Harrison playing a Vox prototype guitar instead of his Strat. The guitar had first been seen when Vox's parent company Jennings showed one at the '66 British music-trade fair. Vox intended to call the guitar the Kensington model. As always, Jennings would show The Beatles their latest Vox gear and prototypes. Vox designer Dick Denney suggests that they probably made two of the Vox Kensington guitar. Each had a dark brown mahogany hollow body with a scroll shape inspired by an old piano Denney had seen.[39] One of the prototypes – the one tried by The Beatles – had white pushbuttons for effects similar to those fitted to Vox's Marauder guitar.

Back in the studio on September 25th the group recorded a proper version of 'Fool On The Hill' for their TV film. Photographs of the session in Abbey Road's studio 2 show Lennon playing his Spanish-made classical guitar and McCartney playing a recorder as the group huddles around the studio's Steinway grand piano, working out ideas for the song. 'Fool On The Hill' also featured the return of bass harmonicas, this time played by Lennon and Harrison. The photographs document the first time that Lennon brought his new friend Yoko Ono into the studio.

During the following four days final work was done to some songs for the *Magical Mystery Tour* film. 'I Am The Walrus' received an elaborate overdub of 16 orchestral instruments played by session musicians: eight violins, four cellos, a contrabass clarinet and three horns. Then a 16-piece choir was added, singing the odd lines: "Ho-ho-ho, hee-hee-hee, ha-ha-ha" and "Oom-pah, oom-pah, stick it up your jumper".

A magazine feature on Lennon's home studio at the time revealed his newly-painted psychedelic

Gibson J-160E – the last known photographs of the guitar in its psychedelic state. Also on view is Lennon's fireglo (red sunburst) Rickenbacker 1996 model guitar – again the last photographs of Lennon with this instrument.[40] Lennon later gave this Rickenbacker to Starr, who still owns the instrument today.

With autumn approaching, a new single was needed for Christmas sales, so on October 2nd the group recorded 'Hello Goodbye' in studio 2. The basic track featured drums, piano, organ and assorted percussion, but on the 19th guitars and vocals were added and six days later McCartney put down his bass guitar track. 'Hello Goodbye' was finished on November 2nd.

John's Martin D-28 acoustic guitar

With the new 45 scheduled for release on November 24th the group again needed to film a promotional clip, so they spent the 10th at the Saville Theatre filming mimed performances of

The Beatles in their Sgt Pepper uniforms at the Saville Theatre, London, on November 10th 1967, filming promos for the 'Hello Goodbye' single. John plays his new Martin D-28, George his Epiphone Casino, Paul uses his psychedelic-painted Rickenbacker bass, and Ringo is playing a miniature drum set. To the left is a prototype Vox 4120 amp, and then two Vox Defiants with matching 2x12 cabinets.

'Hello Goodbye'. Three clips were filmed, all with a backline of Vox amps that was set up but not actually played through. There were two Vox Defiant amps with matching 2x12 cabinets, and a Vox prototype 4120 with a similar cabinet.

The first clip filmed saw the group dressed in their *Sgt Pepper* uniforms. McCartney played his psychedelic Rickenbacker 4001S bass, Harrison used his Epiphone Casino, while Lennon played a Martin D-28 flat-top acoustic guitar. He most likely needed a new acoustic because the paint on his psychedelic J-160E muted its sound. The CF Martin company was America's finest producer of flat-top guitars. Lennon's D-28, first seen at this shoot, quickly became his main acoustic. Starr used a small child-size kit in white pearl finish for one of the film clips. Gerry Evans, then manager of London's Drum City store, was asked to supply two kits for the filming. He thinks the child-size kit may have been a Trixon-brand outfit. "They also wanted an oversized kit, a Ludwig."[41]

For the second film clip the group wore everyday clothes. Harrison and McCartney played the same instruments as the first clip; photographs show Lennon using the Vox Kensington prototype guitar Harrison had tried during the 'I Am The Walrus' shoot, but the prototype guitar is not seen in any of the 'Hello Goodbye' promo footage – Lennon switched back to the Martin D-28. Starr used his standard 22-inch-bass Ludwig – the number-six Beatles head back to replace the Love-logo head.

The third promotional sequence filmed on November 10th showed the group dancing about the stage without instruments, but the kit in the background had been changed again, to a larger 24-inch-bass silver-sparkle Ludwig four-piece set, without a Beatles logo. This was the only time this kit was seen with The Beatles as it was soon returned to Drum City.

The final song recorded by the group in 1967 was for their fifth fan-club Christmas record, the infectious 'Christmas Time (Is Here Again)'. It was made on November 28th and featured McCartney on piano, Harrison on acoustic guitar, Starr on drums and Lennon playing tympani.

As the year wound down, The Beatles unveiled a new business venture. They decided to open a clothing store at 94 Baker Street in central London. The Fool were commissioned to paint a psychedelic mural on the side of the building, and on December 7th the Apple boutique was opened to the public. Thus began the group's own company, Apple Corps. Finally in 1967, BBC television aired the group's new film, *Magical Mystery Tour*, on Boxing Day, December 26th, to mixed criticism.

It was the first time the press did not unanimously praise The Beatles for their work.

I DIDN'T REALLY HAVE ANY MISCONCEPTIONS ABOUT OUR ABILITY TO DO ANYTHING OTHER THAN PLAY MUSIC, AND I WAS SCARED.

John Lennon, on Brian Epstein's death – despite the band's huge success, he worried what the future might hold

" **This is my song, we'll do it this way. That's your song, you do it that way.** "

JOHN LENNON, ON THE WAY THINGS WERE DURING THE MAKING OF *THE WHITE ALBUM*

1968

THE PSYCHEDELIC FREE-FORM PARTY OF THE PREVIOUS YEAR SEEMED TO BE DISINTEGRATING ALMOST THE MOMENT 1968 BEGAN. THE LESS THAN ECSTATIC REVIEWS OF THE *MAGICAL MYSTERY TOUR* TV SPECIAL WERE SOBERING FOR THE GROUP. CLEARLY THEY WERE NOT INVINCIBLE. WITHOUT BRIAN EPSTEIN'S MANAGEMENT AND DIRECTION, THE GROUP WERE NOW TAKING CARE OF THEIR OWN BUSINESS AND REACHING OUT TO INDIA FOR SPIRITUAL GUIDANCE.

Both were questionable endeavours. For these and other reasons, this would be the year in which The Beatles started to drift apart, both musically and personally. Work on independent projects would inevitably dilute the whole.

George Harrison had started the year busily, making the soundtrack for Wonderwall, a film directed by his friend Joe Massot. Recording initially at Abbey Road's studio 2, Harrison called on his old friend from Liverpool, Colin Manley, to help. Harrison had "all kinds of instruments" in the studio, says Manley. "He started to mess around with a Fender double-neck pedal-steel guitar, which he seemed to like. Gear would be delivered every day! And I remember [Peter Tork] from The Monkees played banjo on a session. Peter was so nervous that his hands were shaking."[1]

Further *Wonderwall* sessions continued when on January 7th Harrison travelled to India where he enlisted the help of local musicians to complete the recordings at EMI's Bombay studio. While there, with the aid of over a dozen Indian musicians, Harrison recorded the basic tracks for 'The Inner Light', which would end up as the flip-side of The Beatles' next single. The song featured harmonium and flutes and sitars, plus a plethora of Indian instruments including dholak and pakhavaj (double-headed drums), sahnai (conical oboe), santur (box zither), sarod (a lute-like instrument with double soundbox), surbahar (bass sitar), tabla (pair of hand-drums), and tar sahnai (a fiddle with an amplifying horn).

Back in England, The Beatles fulfilled an obligation to make a cameo appearance in their upcoming animated film, shooting a small section for the end of *Yellow Submarine* on January 25th at Twickenham film studios. The group had planned a lengthy trip to Rishikesh in India to study transcendental meditation again with The Maharishi, but before leaving they decided to record a new single for release while they were away.

So it was that work started on McCartney's 'Lady Madonna' on February 3rd at Abbey Road. The basic track consisted of piano played by McCartney, with Starr providing great brush-work on the drums. Later that evening McCartney added a bass overdub while Lennon and Harrison both added fuzz guitar played through the same amplifier.

The next day, work started on a new Lennon song intended for the forthcoming single. The basic tracks for 'Across The Universe' included Lennon playing his Martin D-28 and Harrison on tambura. Harrison then added sitar, and many experiments were made on the tape of the song. At one stage Lennon's vocal and all the instruments were put through a Leslie speaker-cabinet and then flanged for effect. More overdubs were added when McCartney invited two Beatle fans who were hanging around outside the studio to come in and sing falsetto harmonies for the "nothing's gonna change my world" section.

Harrison's vocal was added to the Bombay tape of 'The Inner Light' on February 6th, Lennon and McCartney slipping in a brief harmony to complete the song. 'The Inner Light' marked the last time that Indian instruments would be used on a Beatle recording. Later that evening, overdubs were made to 'Lady Madonna'. Lennon, McCartney and Harrison sang backing vocals and recorded their voices to mimic a brass section in the middle of the song. Then session musicians were called in to add a section of alto, tenor and baritone saxophones.

Vox wah-wah pedal

More work on 'Across The Universe' continued in studio two on the 8th. It was decided then to issue 'Lady Madonna' backed with 'The Inner Light' as the new single. 'Across The Universe' was instead given up for inclusion on a charity album for the World Wildlife Fund organised by comedian Spike Milligan, who was at the studio that day. (The LP, *No One's Gonna Change Our World*, would not be released until December 1969.)

Lennon was not yet happy with his 'Across The Universe', so recording continued as he looked for the right combination of instruments and effects to convey his ideas. Various overdubs were tried and then erased, including backwards bass, guitar and drum parts, a Mellotron played by Lennon, as well as a Hammond organ passage. Finally, Lennon decided to use a Vox Wah-Wah pedal on his guitar as an overdub. The wah-wah had become a popular effect for guitar players. Eric Clapton had first used it on record in 1967. While he was on tour with Cream in the US in April of that year, Clapton had picked up a Vox wah and used it on his group's 'Tales Of Brave Ulysses', which was recorded that spring at Atlantic studios in New York. Jimi Hendrix also used the device soon afterward to great effect.

Ads for the Vox Wah-Wah appeared in British trade magazines as early as June '67. Ex-Vox man Dick Denney says that the company's US distributor, Thomas Organ – who by now had a controlling interest in Vox UK – came up with the wah-wah and the associated MRB (mid-range boost) effect at the same time in the mid 1960s. Joe Benaron and/or Stan Cutler at Thomas had developed the wah-wah with brass instruments in mind, naming the first model the "Clyde McCoy" after a trumpet-player who would make a wah-wah sound by moving his hand in and out of his instrument's bell. The new wah-wah pedal boosted the harmonic peaks of the signal passing through it as the pedal was rocked up and down by foot control, emulating the trumpet effect – but, as musicians discovered, it was very effective on electric guitar.

The Vox V846 Wah Wah was fitted in the same casing used for the Vox Continental's V838 Volume Foot Control. In Britain a Vox Wah Wah cost £16/10/- (£16.50, about $40 then; around £170

John, George and Paul in studio 3 at Abbey Road in February 1968, working on vocal takes.

or $240 in today's money). Lennon used the Vox Wah-Wah at the February 8th overdub session for 'Across The Universe', the first time a wah-wah appeared on a Beatles song. Other instruments and gear in the studio on the 8th included the Hammond RT-3 organ with Leslie speaker-cabinet, Fender "blackface" Dual Showman amp, Vox Conqueror guitar amp, Harrison's Gibson SG, the Steinway grand piano, Lennon's Martin D-28, and Starr's Ludwig drum set. McCartney played his Rickenbacker 4001S bass through what appears from photographic evidence to be a Vox Foundation bass amp.

The last recording session before the group left for India took place on February 11th in studio 3. A basic rhythm track for 'Hey Bulldog', a song Lennon had written specifically for the *Yellow Submarine* soundtrack, was recorded with piano, drums, electric guitar and bass. Overdubs of vocals, fuzz bass, lead guitar, tambourine and drums were added, and the song was mixed.

A promotional film was needed for the forthcoming single, 'Lady Madonna', so during the ten-hour recording session on the 11th the group were filmed at work and the footage assembled into a useable clip. As a promo for the 1999 reissue of *Yellow Submarine* Apple Corps would re-edit and issue the clip with music from 'Hey Bulldog'. Lennon's Epiphone Casino, Harrison's SG and a Vox Defiant amp are all glimpsed during the film. Starr's Ludwig set once again has the Love/Beatles psychedelic drum-head.

Brian Gibson, then a technical engineer at Abbey Road, recalls today that there was a storeroom in an annexe to studio 3 where unused instruments, cases and other odds and ends could be kept. "Ringo's drum with the Beatles skin on it was left in there, and I remember thinking how attractive to a collector that particular item would be. Strangely enough – and I plead not guilty on this – we came in one day and someone had neatly trimmed the skin out of the drum frame. "So someone somewhere has got the original Beatles skin that came out of Starr's drum kit. After that they used the red-painted skin with 'Love' in yellow, rather than bother to get another Beatles skin, because they obviously weren't going to be appearing on stage any more."[2]

Meditation in India

In just a two-week period the group had made a new single, which was ready for release, filmed a promotional clip for the a-side, 'Lady Madonna', recorded a song and given it to charity, and fulfilled their commitments for their animated film. Finished with their immediate musical obligations, The Beatles headed off to Rishikesh in India to study transcendental meditation with The Maharishi. Mia Farrow, Mike Love of The Beach Boys, Donovan Leitch and other celebrities joined them.

Wah-Wah PEDAL

The idea was to stay some months and study the teachings. While there they would write songs, relax and meditate at the foot of the Himalayas. Donovan had met The Maharishi in California, and once initiated was invited to India for further instruction.

"But it was unprecedented for stars such as we all were to just stop the merry-go-round and leave for the East," Donovan says of the gathering. "It was natural to try anything we wanted. We were privileged and wanted to bring the philosophy from the bohemian circles into pop music. We knew it would change millions of youths who were searching for the new consciousness."

Donovan says that a typical day in Rishikesh at first seemed like a typical day at home, with hundreds of media folk at the door. But the intruders soon went home. The routine then became meditation all day, with meals passed under doors. The inmates stopped for dinner and an evening gathering, where sometimes they would discuss their deep experiences. "Lennon would play a song he'd written," recalls Donovan. "We all would be writing. George and I worked up a couple. The Beatles' roadie Mal Evans and I worked on 'The Sun Is A Very Magic Fellow'. We had brought acoustics, I remember John and Paul had Martin D-28s, and George had ordered in a sitar and a tambura, plus tabla for Ringo."

Intrigued by Donovan's playing style on the little Gibson J-45 that the Scottish musician had brought along, Lennon asked if he'd teach him this fingerstyle or claw-hammer method. "I explained it would take three days at least to get the basics," says Donovan. "He was a good student. It's a difficult style that requires perseverance. When John had it down, he was so pleased to find a whole new way of songwriting emerge. That's what happens to a natural songwriter when you get a new set of performing skills. He immediately wrote 'Dear Prudence' and 'Julia'. Maybe 'Crippled Inside' too. John wrote lots of songs for *The White Album* based on this new style.

"Paul was not interested in study, though he did pick up bits of the fingerstyle from watching me teach John. Paul got a less accomplished set of moves from me, like he plays on 'Blackbird' perhaps … George was happy to stick with his Chet Atkins-inspired fingerstyle. He was more into sitar that year, anyway."[3]

Starr left India after only a few weeks and McCartney stayed a little over a month. Lennon and Harrison remained for almost two months before returning to England in disgust, a little disillusioned by The Maharishi's behaviour when he allegedly made a pass at one of the female guests. From that point on The Maharishi, transcendental meditation and India were never again a focus for Beatle attention.

New relationships

Back in London, The Beatles regrouped to make plans for their new Apple Corps business venture. Lennon and McCartney even flew to the United States on May 11th to hold press conferences to unveil the new schemes. In concept, Apple was a great idea. A record label, music-publishing operation, recording studio, film unit, management and promotion companies – what more could an artist or musician want? The Beatles thought they had plenty of money available to run and sustain such an organisation. But they were artists with great ideas, not businessmen. Harrison said later of this manifestation of Apple, "There were a lot of ideas, but when it came down to it, the only thing we could do successfully was write songs, make records and be Beatles."[4]

Lennon had first met avant-garde artist Yoko Ono back in November 1966 at her art exhibition at the Indica Gallery in London. They kept in contact. But when Lennon came back from India, he and Ono became soul-mates. On May 19th, while Lennon's wife Cynthia was away on holiday, he and Ono made experimental recordings at his Kenwood home. Ono reported, "It was midnight when we started and it was dawn when we finished, and then we made love."[5] Cynthia returned to find Ono wearing her dressing-gown. This prompted John and Cynthia to split. From then on, Lennon and Ono were inseparable. The recordings made that night were released on Apple on November 29th as *Unfinished Music No 1: Two Virgins*. The album cover featured a picture of a nude Lennon and Ono.

John used a Vox Wah Wah like the one illustrated in this catalogue (left) on early versions of 'Across The Universe'.

John in Rishikesh, India, in 1968. While there, Donovan taught John fingerstyle guitar-playing, and John is seen here working on the new technique using Donovan's Gibson J-45.

John, Paul, George and friends – including Mike Love and Donovan – surround The Maharishi in India during their time spent learning from the guru. While there, The Beatles wrote the bulk of the songs that would become The White Album.

Back in the studio for The White Album

The songs written in India were plentiful and the group were once again ready to record a new LP. They started the process in the latter part of May by recording demos of over 20 new songs at Harrison's Esher home (some of which would be released in 1996 on *Anthology 3*). Most would be re-recorded for the next album, which would be simply titled *The Beatles* but has become better known as *The White Album*.

Harrison said recently, "The experience of India and everything since *Sgt Pepper* was all embodied in the new album. Most of the songs that were written in Rishikesh were the result of what The Maharishi had said. When we came back, it became apparent that there were more songs than would make up a single album, and so [it] became a double album.

"What else do you do when you've got so many songs and you want to get rid of them so that you can write more? There was a lot of ego in the band, and there were a lot of songs that maybe should have been elbowed or made into b-sides."[6]

Although The Beatles had set out to record another group album, the sessions never really became a communal effort, but more or less four solo projects. Lennon said, "[*The White Album*] was just saying, 'This is my song, we'll do it this way. That's your song, you do it that way.' It's pretty hard trying to fit three guys' music on to one album. That's why we did a double."[7]

Lennon later admitted that The Beatles had effectively broken up after Epstein's death. "[That album] was just me and a backing group, Paul and a backing group … and I enjoyed it. We broke up then."[8] Harrison said: "I remember it [was like] having three studios operating at the same time. You know: Paul was doing some overdubs in one, and John was doing something in another one, and I was doing horns or something else in another studio."[9]

The White Album would become one of The Beatles' most highly acclaimed records, yet it was made amid much tension within the group. Each member now had personal outside interests, side projects, business and other pressures – any number of things that seemed to be pulling the band apart. McCartney said later that they always used to be asked at American press conferences about what they would do when the bubble burst – mainly because they'd planted someone to ask that each time. "It was never a serious question to us. Of course … the bubble did start to burst about a year before The Beatles broke … It just did. Friction came in, business things came in, relationships between each other. We were all looking for people in our lives. John had found Yoko. It made it very difficult, he wanted a very strong intimate life with her. At the same time, we'd always reserved the intimacy for the group … With Yoko, you can understand he had to have time with her. But [it was]: 'Does he have to have that much time with her?' … [that] was the sort of feeling in the group. So these things just started to create immovable objects and pressures that were just too big."[10]

Ono was Lennon's new constant companion, by his side it seemed at almost every minute of every recording session. This added to the general unease. Never had The Beatles been so distracted and less focused as a group while working on a recording project. Looking back, McCartney later characterised *The White Album* as "the tension album".[11]

The project got underway on May 30th at Abbey Road's studio 2 with the recording of the first track intended for the new album. Lengthy versions of Lennon's new song 'Revolution 1' were recorded with a basic track of piano, drums and acoustic guitar. The session continued the next day with Lennon delivering his lead vocal and McCartney adding his Rickenbacker bass, resuming on June 4th as Lennon re-recorded his lead vocal while lying flat on the floor in studio three. Also added were more drum parts, McCartney's organ and Lennon playing fuzzed-out guitar riffs on his Epiphone Casino.

Stripping guitars for the natural look

Back in the studio for *The White Album* sessions was Lennon's newly transformed Gibson J-160E. Around this time he had the psychedelic paint job stripped off to reveal the instrument's plain wooden body from under the various finishes. He thought the guitar would sound better as a result. Donovan remembers telling The Beatles while in India that a guitar would sound better without a heavy finish on it.[12]

Along with the Gibson J-160E, Lennon and Harrison sanded down their Epiphone Casinos. Harrison said that once they'd removed the finish they became much better guitars. "I think that works on a lot of guitars," he explained. "If you take the paint and varnish off, and get the bare wood, it seems to sort of breathe."[13] A recent examination of Lennon's Gibson J-160E and Epiphone Casino shows that the guitars were professionally sanded down to the wood and finished with a very thin, dull, unpolished protective coat of varnish. Closer examination of the inside soundhole of the J-160E reveals remnants of the blue paint applied during the guitar's psychedelic period.

When the J-160E underwent its refinishing to bare wood the guitar's pickup was moved back to its original neck position, where it still remains today. At the same time a new pickguard was put on the guitar. Photographs taken during *The White Album* sessions show that after Lennon's Casino was refinished to natural wood the original pickguard-mounting hardware was put back on the guitar – but without the pickguard. This served no function and indicates that the refinishing job may not have been done at a music store or instrument repair shop.

McCartney would join the natural-wood club with his Rickenbacker 4001S at the beginning of next year. A magazine report contemporary to that adds weight to the idea that the sanding-down of the psychedelic paint-jobs was done by someone outside the musical instrument business. "Here's a sure sign that the psychedelic *Sgt Pepper* era is well and truly ended," trumpeted the piece. "Paul recently took his Rickenbacker bass to an elderly craftsman in a Soho backstreet to have a two-year-old coat of psychedelic painting removed. McCartney chatted to the old man throughout the hour it took to strip off the bright colours and smooth the guitar's woodwork to a plain, unpainted finish."[14]

Back in summer 1968, work continued on the tracks for the *White Album*, with a new song written

THAT'S WHAT HAPPENS TO A NATURAL SONGWRITER WHEN YOU GET A NEW SET OF PERFORMING SKILLS.

Donovan Leitch, who taught John Lennon fingerstyle guitar-playing while in India, prompting a new range of Lennon compositions

1968

by Starr, 'Don't Pass Me By', recorded on June 5th. Its basic track was recorded with just McCartney on keyboards and Starr on drums and sleigh-bells. The next day the song was almost completed as Starr sang his lead vocal and McCartney added bass. While Starr finished work on 'Don't Pass Me By', Lennon and Ono began 'Revolution 9', without doubt The Beatles' most bizarre released recording. Harking back to the tape-loop experiments that worked so effectively on *Revolver*'s 'Tomorrow Never Knows', 'Revolution 9' was entirely comprised of such loops, with no conventional instruments. The "song" had odd tape-loops mixed in and out of the main track, creating a montage of sound that was not at all musical … but very deep. Lennon spent many hours and days in the studio seriously working on this experimental piece.

Harrison and Starr left the studio and flew to the US on June 7th where Harrison was filmed with Ravi Shankar for the film *Raga*. Back at Abbey Road, Lennon worked in studio 3 on 'Revolution 9' and McCartney recorded 'Blackbird' in studio 2, a simple acoustic ballad featuring his new right-handed Martin D-28 strung upside-down and played to the simple accompaniment of a metronome. The song was completed and mixed that night. On June 20th McCartney also flew to the US, on business for Apple. Harrison and Starr had returned to England a few days earlier.

John's Epiphone Casino ES-230TD. After returning from India in 1968, The Beatles stripped the painted finish off many of their instruments, including John's Casino, pictured here (plus back, below). The guitar, now owned by Yoko Ono, has stayed in this condition, and is currently on display at the John Lennon Museum in Tokyo, Japan. The headstock of the instrument (right) reveals the fixing holes for the original tuners. At one stage Lennon had replaced a missing volume knob with this black one (below left), but at present the Casino is back to four gold knobs.

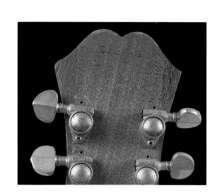

IF YOU TAKE THE PAINT AND VARNISH OFF, AND GET TO THE BARE WOOD, IT SEEMS TO SORT OF BREATHE.

George Harrison, who, along with the other Beatles, stripped off the psychedelic paintwork in 1968

Lennon, Ono and Harrison attended a studio session in studio 2 on the 21st when session musicians added two trumpets and four trombones to 'Revolution 1'. When McCartney returned to London a week later, the four Beatles started on another new song, a rocker in true Lennon style titled 'Everybody's Got Something To Hide Except Me And My Monkey'. A few days later 'Good Night', a simple bedtime song that Lennon had written for his son Julian, was recorded, the basic track featuring Lennon playing his Epiphone Casino and Starr singing lead vocal. Lennon's guitar track was later replaced by piano, and finally an orchestra was added consisting of 12 violins, three violas, three cellos, three flutes, a harp, clarinet, horn, vibes and double-bass, plus a choir of four girls and four boys.

The Apple grows

In June the group bought a building at 3 Savile Row in central London for their new Apple headquarters. The basement of the building was converted into their own Apple recording studio while the top floors housed their offices. Apple business and commitments would increasingly distract The Beatles, and instead of concentrating on being musicians and making records they found themselves entangled in the business of the music industry.

While *The White Album* sessions were underway, Lennon worked with Ono on avant-garde projects. McCartney spent time producing Welsh singer Mary Hopkin, and Harrison was producing an album for Jackie Lomax, former frontman for Liverpool group The Undertakers. Both projects would be released on Apple Records.

Lomax explains that he'd known Harrison since the Hamburg days. During 1967 he'd been trying to form a new band with ex-Searchers drummer Chris Curtis. "We went to see John and Paul when they were still in the NEMS offices, after Brian was gone. John pulled me aside in the middle

John pictured with his Casino back in 1966, showing how the guitar looked with its original sunburst finish, before the paint was stripped off.

of this kind of interview and said, 'You know, you don't need a band.' I asked what he meant, and he said, 'You write songs, don't you? Well we're looking for writers, so why don't you go and see Terry Doran who's running the publishing?' Which I did, and Terry signed me.

"I was signed to Apple as a writer before there was Apple Records," says Lomax. "I used to go to the office in Baker Street above the shop where they were selling the Fool-designed clothes. Above Terry's office there was an attic room where they had a Revox two-track recorder and I would put down all the songs I was writing. Then George heard them and said he'd like to take it into the studio and do an album. But I had to wait for them to come back from India."[15] Lomax's Apple album *Is This What You Want?* would be released in March 1969. Meanwhile, in July of 1968 a new band, The Iveys, were signed to Apple Records, and later changed their name to Badfinger. They would record 'Come And Get It', a song McCartney had written and produced for the band which became a number-four UK hit in January 1970.

As the businessmen in charge of Apple, The Beatles made themselves accessible to almost anyone with an idea. Lennon said he tried to see them all. "And there wasn't anybody with anything to offer to society or me. There was just 'I want, I want' and 'why not?' Terrible scenes [were] going on in the office, with hippies and all different people getting very wild with me." Lennon also concluded that spending all his time listening to other people's songs probably had a negative effect on his own output.[16]

Fender tries again

The Beatles were no longer committed to the gentleman's agreement that Epstein had made for them with Jennings, who made Vox amps. Epstein's promise that "as long as I am their manager The Beatles will use Vox amplifiers" had effectively expired. And the group were, of course, always looking for new ways of creating sounds. During July of 1968, when they were more accessible than they had been for some time, Fender boss Don Randall took the opportunity to meet the group himself and try to persuade them to use Fender guitars and amplifiers.

Randall's persistence paid off. Today he recalls his meeting with McCartney, Lennon and Ono at Apple. "Paul was outgoing and enthusiastic, a great guy to talk to, very upbeat. John and Yoko were not all that great. Yoko didn't talk, period. And John said, 'What the hell are we doing here?' After he got us to explain, they took two of our Fender Rhodes pianos. They used them later in the *Let It Be* picture."

Randall says that Fender eventually supplied The Beatles with various amps, the Rhodes pianos, a VI six-string bass, a Rosewood Telecaster, and even a Fender PA system. Some were supplied through the British distributor, Arbiter, but the pianos came direct from the US. "We never had a formal agreement with them at all," explains Randall, "but naturally we would sing the praises of who was using our product and why they were using it."[17]

The White Album sessions were relatively poorly documented photographically, but it seems the group started out essentially using the same equipment as in 1967. In general, McCartney used his still psychedelic-painted Rickenbacker 4001S bass through the cream-coloured Fender Bassman or one of many Vox prototype amps, such as the Conqueror head with a 2x12 cabinet. Other guitar amps to hand included the blackface Fender Showman head and cabinet. McCartney also favoured his Martin D-28 flat-top acoustic during these sessions.

Lennon primarily played his newly stripped Epiphone Casino and Gibson J-160E guitars. Harrison used his psychedelic Fender Strat and his Gibson SG until some further instruments came along (about which more later). Starr played his trusty oyster black pearl-coloured four-piece Ludwig kit, now with the front head of the bass drum removed and left off for a better recording tone. Also present was the Hohner Pianet electric piano, as well as Abbey Road's acoustic pianos, Hammond organs and harmonium. But new equipment would begin to appear as the sessions progressed, and thanks to Don Randall's efforts a good deal of it was made by Fender.

> THERE WAS A LOT OF EGO IN THE BAND, AND THERE WERE A LOT OF SONGS THAT MAYBE SHOULD HAVE BEEN ELBOWED OR MADE INTO B-SIDES.
>
> George Harrison, on the *White Album* sessions

Studio life goes on

Technical engineer Brian Gibson had come to work at Abbey Road at the end of 1967. "I was in and out of the studio quite a lot during *The White Album* sessions, and Paul more often than not used the Rickenbacker bass with the paint splashes over it. John used his Epiphone stripped down to the wood quite a lot – that seemed to be his favourite guitar. With the front skin off the bass drum they would stuff blankets and all kinds of things in to dampen it. Sometimes they'd fold up one of the canvas covers from the grand piano and stuff that inside. That was usually done by Mal Evans, because he would set up the drums and tune them. He'd fill the shell of the bass drum about half full and then, with the sound engineer, shove the microphone inside the drum itself.

"A lot of time was spent tuning the kit. They would regularly dampen the snare drum, which

John and Paul each acquired a Martin D-28 flat-top acoustic guitar, similar to the 1967 example shown here. They used them extensively while writing and recording The White Album. Paul played his – adapted for left-handed use – on the recording of 'Blackbird'.

involved taking an empty cigarette carton and taping it to the top skin of the snare. They also used to put a light towel over the toms and sometimes the snare."[18]

As work continued through the beginning of July, McCartney's new song 'Ob-La-Di Ob-La-Da' was recorded, the original track consisting of Starr on drums and McCartney on acoustic guitar. Second engineer Richard Lush remembers McCartney using his Martin D-28 for this work.[19] Various versions of the song were recorded in the days that followed with Lennon on piano, Harrison playing acoustic guitar, McCartney on bass and Starr on drums. McCartney recalls a moment when Lennon arrived late at the studio, keen to do some work, only to find some rather stale fellow Beatles running through yet another take of 'Ob-La-Di Ob-La-Da'. Lennon did not pick up a guitar, but strode over to the piano and instantly played what we now recognise as the song's opening notes.

"And we all went, 'Fucking hell!'" recalls McCartney, laughing. "I thought we were gonna hit the roof – and that became the total vibe of [the song]. Then I put the bass on … and double-tracked it with an acoustic guitar, which is a cool idea: an octave up from the bass, playing exactly the same on acoustic. We used to drive the meters right into the red – and in those days you could defeat machines. So [in that way] you could make acoustics sound like electrics by overdriving the machines. It toughened up the sound."[20]

By July 9th "proper" vocals and some more overdubs were added to 'Ob-La-Di' and the song was finished. Lennon wanted 'Revolution 1' to be the group's next 45 release, but Harrison and McCartney felt the song was too slow for a single. Lennon then decided they should re-record the song faster – and this livelier version, recorded on July 10th, became the 'Revolution' single. It was the heaviest song The Beatles ever recorded, featuring both Lennon and Harrison playing heavily overdriven guitars. Engineer Geoff Emerick says that the guitar fuzz effect for 'Revolution' was done at the mixing desk. "You had a full spectrum of frequencies distorted. So that's why the 'Revolution' guitars sound the way they do. Today, you'd just have 5kHz distorting, or maybe 60Hz distorting." Technical engineer Brian Gibson's recollection, however, is that the distorted guitars on 'Revolution' came mostly by overdriving the amps.

Overdubs added on July 11th included saxophones to 'Ob-La-Di Ob-La-Da' and piano to 'Revolution', the latter played by legendary session man Nicky Hopkins who at various times contributed to records by The Kinks, The Who, The Rolling Stones and many others. Another studio player was brought in the following day to add a country-style violin to 'Don't Pass Me By'. By mid-July, engineer Geoff Emerick had stopped working with The Beatles. He has since explained[21] that he'd had enough of the arguments and the generally tense atmosphere that surrounded the sessions. Emerick would not work with The Beatles again until the following year.

The Beatles attended the world premiere of their animated feature film *Yellow Submarine* on the 17th at the London Pavilion cinema, and the following day continued work in the studio on Lennon's new 'Cry Baby Cry', laying down acoustic guitar, organ, drums and bass, plus harmonium played by producer George Martin. Later that evening all four Beatles played together, recording extended versions of McCartney's song 'Helter Skelter'. It was a return to their old way of recording live as a band with a drum kit, a bass guitar, and rhythm and lead guitars. McCartney took the lead vocal.

McCartney had read a piece in the musicians' newspaper *Melody Maker* where The Who were claiming to have made the loudest, most raucous rock'n'roll record, the dirtiest thing they'd ever done. "That made me think, 'Ooh! Got to do it! I really see that.' And I totally got off on that one little sentence in the paper. I said, we've got to do the most loudest, most raucous … and that was 'Helter Skelter'."[22] An edited out-take of 'Helter Skelter' from this July 18th session is on *Anthology 3*.

Lennon and Harrison's recent abrupt departure from India had prompted Lennon to write a sarcastic song about their guru. Originally called 'Maharishi', by the time it got to the studio on July 19th the song had been renamed 'Sexy Sadie'. Later remakes and overdubs meant that it would not be completed until late August.

More classic tracks – and George's Gibson J-200

One of Harrison's greatest songs, 'While My Guitar Gently Weeps', was started next. Technical engineer Brian Gibson remembers that it was destined to go through a number of transformations. "I recorded the original acoustic demo with George in studio 1. The other guys were doing something else in 2, and he wanted to record the demo so that the others could hear it and learn it. George used a big sunburst Gibson acoustic guitar with flowers on the pickguard, and I miked it with a Neumann KM56.

"Over the course of several weeks the song changed a lot, and I remember George wanted to get

This Gibson catalogue illustrates a J-200 acoustic guitar similar to the one George began to play during The White Album sessions.

IT WAS A BIT OF A
NUMBER FOR ME TO
DARE TO TELL
GEORGE HARRISON –
ONE OF THE
GREATEST, I THINK –
TO NOT PLAY. IT WAS
LIKE AN INSULT...

Paul McCartney, recalling an
awkward incident during the
recording of 'Hey Jude'

a different guitar sound. One of the things we tried was recording backwards, overdubbing the solo line with the tape playing backwards. I remember we spent a whole evening, maybe even longer, experimenting with that idea, and in the end he just gave up. It wasn't working out."[23] Harrison's new guitar with the flowery pickguard was a Gibson J-200 that he'd acquired while in America. Legend has it the guitar is the same one that Bob Dylan is seen holding on the cover of his 1969 album *Nashville Skyline*.

The Beatles were due for another new single. The "faster" version of 'Revolution' had been cut with that in mind, but a flip-side was needed. One day on the way to visit Lennon's wife Cynthia and son Julian, McCartney came up with the idea for 'Hey Jude'. As he was driving out to Lennon's house, soon after John and Cynthia had been divorced, he began to come up with things he might say to Julian. McCartney later recalled his initial thoughts: "[It was:] 'Hey Jules, don't take it bad, take a sad song and make it better.' You know, it'll be all right. So I got the first idea on the way out there with this 'Hey Jules', as I thought it was going to be called. It seemed a little bit of a mouthful, so I changed it to Jude. And then I liked the song a lot and I played it to John and Yoko."[24]

The first session for 'Hey Jude' took place on July 29th at Abbey Road's studio 2. The song was never intended for *The White Album*, but was specifically designed as the group's next single. These initial recordings featured McCartney on the studio's Steinway grand, and also on lead vocal, Starr on his Ludwig drums, Lennon playing his Gibson J-160E, and Harrison on electric guitar.

McCartney explained later that an incident during this session probably contributed to the group's ill-defined unease. "I told George not to play guitar," McCartney recalled, "[but] he wanted to play … I really didn't see it [the way he did] and it was a bit of a number for me to dare to tell George Harrison – one of the greatest, I think – to not play. It was like an insult, almost."[25]

The next day, work continued in studio 2 on 'Hey Jude'. This session was filmed by The National Music Council Of Great Britain for a feature titled *Music!*. The colour footage shows McCartney singing and playing piano, Lennon using his stripped-down Gibson J-160E, and Starr playing the four-piece Ludwig oyster-black-pearl kit. The bass-drum head has been removed and towels are draped over the toms and snare. Harrison was nowhere to be seen. Reportedly, he stayed in the control room with George Martin. The Abbey Road recordings of 'Hey Jude' were more or less rehearsals, because the "proper" recording was planned for the following day at London's new independent Trident studio.

The big attraction of Trident was that it had one of London's first functional eight-track recorders. EMI was behind the times, still using only four-track machines. The Beatles were familiar with Trident as they had hired the studio for sessions for various Apple recording artists, McCartney and Harrison having visited when working on Apple projects with Mary Hopkin, Jackie Lomax and James Taylor.

On Wednesday July 31st at Trident the basic track for 'Hey Jude' was recorded with McCartney on piano, Lennon on acoustic guitar and Starr on drums. This session did include Harrison, who played some melodic electric guitar lines at the end of each long "verse". The following day McCartney added his lead vocal and bass guitar, while the other Beatles dubbed on backing vocals. Later on the Thursday, 36 studio musicians piled into Trident to overdub the song's outro. The instruments included ten violins, three violas, three cellos, two flutes, a contra bassoon, a bassoon, two clarinets, a contrabass clarinet, four trumpets, four trombones, two horns, two double-basses, and a percussionist. Quite a sound. In the following days, mixes of 'Hey Jude' would be made at Trident studio.

George's Lucy, the Gibson Les Paul

By the summer of 1968 more new guitars and other gear had crept into The Beatles camp. In August, Harrison acquired a guitar with a unique history, his now famous Gibson Les Paul, known as Lucy. Later, as we shall see, Harrison would have to chase Lucy half way around the world in order to bring her back from hiding. But the first public indication of the new arrival in the guitar collection had come in Mal Evans's monthly column for *The Beatles Monthly Book*.

Evans, discussing the recording of Harrison's new song 'Not Guilty', wrote: "This is one of two August recordings you won't hear on the new album because they were dropped at the last minute in favour of more recent numbers … Interesting note – he used Lucy for the first time on this session.

Lucy is the fantastic solid red Gibson guitar that was given to George at the beginning of August by Eric Clapton. Recording began on August 7th at EMI Studios."[26] The Beatle roadie's report puts to rest the myth that Clapton ceremoniously gave the Les Paul to Harrison after Clapton had played the lead guitar on 'While My Guitar Gently Weeps'. Clapton would not record his celebrated solo on that track until September 6th.

Gibson had first offered a solidbody Les Paul model for sale in 1952, just two years after Fender's shock introduction of the brand new solidbody-style electric guitar. Gibson's instrument was typically well crafted, offering fine playability and good workmanship, and was soon being offered with a pair of the company's powerful noise-cancelling humbucking pickups. By 1968 many guitarists, particularly those playing in a blues-rock or similar style, were alert to the Les Paul's ability to provide a fat, sustaining sound well suited to their musical requirements, and the instruments – older 1950s models as well as new "reissues" – were enjoying a fresh burst of popularity.

When Harrison received his Les Paul it had a red finish. The serial number on the back of the instrument's headstock is not in the correct original typeface and style, but reads 7-8789 which would date the guitar's manufacture to late 1957. Gibson's records indicate that a gold-finished Les Paul with this number was shipped by the company on December 19th 1957. All Gibson Les Pauls of this type made in 1957 were finished with gold-painted body faces, now known as "gold-tops". So how is it that Harrison's guitar has a red finish? Tracing the instrument's history takes us to guitar legend Rick Derringer, best known for his work with Edgar Winter and Steely Dan. Derringer was one of Lucy's former owners.

Around 1966, when Derringer was in The McCoys, he had a Les Paul gold-top that originally had a Bigsby vibrato fitted, and which had previously been owned by The Lovin' Spoonful's John Sebastian. "I loved playing it, but my dad – who always loved a guitar looking real good – used to comment on how it was kind of beat up," recalls Derringer. "It was a very, very used guitar, even when I got it. But it played great. So I figured that since we didn't live so far from Gibson's factory in Kalamazoo, the next time the group went there I'd give it to Gibson and have it refinished."

Such an opportunity soon arose, and Derringer considered his options for the refinish. "Did I want it to be a gold-top again? I decided no, let's do something interesting and different. So I had it done at the factory in the SG-style clear red finish that was popular at the time. However, after that work had been done the guitar just never played as good again. I couldn't keep that sucker in tune any more, and it just didn't feel the same. I loved it before the refinish, but it had changed into an altogether different guitar that I didn't love any more. So I traded it on a sunburst Les Paul at Dan Armstrong's guitar shop in Manhattan, New York. And then Eric Clapton bought it at that store."[27]

Harrison started to use his Gibson Les Paul almost exclusively throughout the remainder of 1968 and well into 1969. With a dual-humbucker Les Paul now in his possession, Harrison rarely played his similar Gibson SG. He eventually gave the SG to Pete Ham, lead guitarist for Badfinger. Joey Molland, the group's rhythm guitarist, says it was during the time Badfinger were signed to Apple that Harrison gave the guitar to Ham. "I guess Pete liked it, so George gave it to him," Molland says. "The sad thing about that guitar is that after Pete's death in the 1970s his wife sold it at a garage sale, not knowing what it was. So that guitar is floating around somewhere in the middle of the United States, and whoever got it doesn't even know what they have. It would be impossible to trace now." Ham can be seen playing the ex-Harrison Gibson SG in a promotional clip for Badfinger's 1970 hit, 'No Matter What'.

Back to summer 1968, and Abbey Road's studio 2. Work continued on Harrison's song 'Not Guilty', with lengthy sessions between August 8th and 12th producing over 100 takes of a basic rhythm track of drums, bass, guitar and electric piano (later replaced by harpsichord). Unfortunately, after all the work put into the song, 'Not Guilty' did not make the final version of *The White Album* and was only officially released on *Anthology 3* in 1996.

Trying new ideas in the studio was now, of course, standard procedure for The Beatles, so for the session on August 13th Lennon suggested the band set up in a small, cramped room adjacent to studio 2 and record playing live. This is exactly what they did. The result was 'Yer Blues', made with a basic track of bass, drums, and lead and rhythm guitars. The following day, Lennon overdubbed a lead vocal. Later that evening, another bizarre Lennon composition, 'What's The New Mary Jane', was recorded by Lennon and Harrison with the help of Yoko Ono and Mal Evans. This piece too failed to make it to *The White Album* and also had to wait until *Anthology 3* for an official airing.

I LOVED IT BEFORE THE REFINISH, BUT IT HAD CHANGED INTO AN ALTOGETHER DIFFERENT GUITAR.

Rick Derringer, the former owner who was responsible for the paint-job on Lucy, George's red Les Paul

Fender six-string bass and more amps

As we've learned, Fender had now offered The Beatles more or less any equipment they asked for. In most cases it was Ivor Arbiter, UK distributor for Fender, who would provide the gear. Arbiter had been at the Beatle meeting with Fender boss Don Randall. "After that we gave them whatever they wanted, without question,"[28] says Arbiter. One of the new Fender pieces that came to the group during *The White Album* sessions was a Fender VI.

The VI had first been produced by Fender in 1961 and was in effect a six-string baritone guitar. Its heavier strings were tuned like a bass guitar, an octave below a regular guitar, and the body shape was similar to a Fender Jaguar, although the instrument had a slightly longer neck than regular Fender six-strings. The VI was set up with guitar players in mind rather than bassists, and included a Fender vibrato system and three pickups. Both Lennon and Harrison used the group's right-handed VI for some of the bass parts on *White Album* songs.

Other new arrivals included a pair of Fender combo amps. ("Combo" means an amplifier plus speaker or speakers in a single box.) One was a Fender blackface Deluxe, the other a silverface Deluxe Reverb. They were virtually identical 20-watt vibrato-equipped amps with a 12-inch speaker, except for the reverb circuit on the Reverb model, controlled by an extra knob on the second channel (making a total of nine control knobs on the front panel).

Some photos of Lennon in the studio recording for *The White Album* show him using the blackface Deluxe. Given that he could have chosen anything from a vast line of Fender amplifiers, perhaps it was his fond memories of his first Fender Deluxe "tweed" amp in Hamburg that drew him to this new version.

'Rocky Raccoon' was recorded on August 15th in studio 2 with McCartney singing and playing his Martin D-28, Starr on his trusty Ludwig four-piece kit, and Lennon playing bass with the Fender VI. It was one of the only songs for *The White Album* that was fully completed after just one night's

George's Gibson Les Paul. Eric Clapton gave this guitar to George in 1968. The guitar originally had a gold top, but was refinished to its red colour by Gibson in the early 1960s. The guitar, nicknamed Lucy, is still owned by George today. Gibson's archive reveals this log entry for George's Les Paul, serial 7-8789, shipped on December 19th 1957.

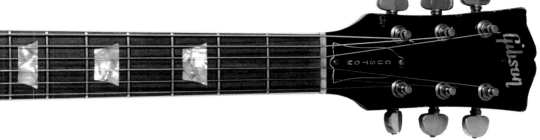

THE MIXING DESK WE WERE USING AT THE TIME WAS LAUGHABLE BY TODAY'S STANDARDS.

Richard Lush, second engineer on the *White Album* sessions

work. Harrison was unhappy with the acoustic feel of 'While My Guitar Gently Weeps', so the song was re-recorded on August 16th with Starr on drums, McCartney on bass, Lennon on organ and Harrison on electric guitar. The song would continue to receive a treatment of overdubs in the sessions that followed.

By now it was apparent that even though The Beatles were still a group, they no longer thought as one – at least not in the way they had in the past. By design, their Apple company would be the cohesive link between the four members. Signs that Apple was starting to develop some soft spots were evident when in the summer the Apple Boutique was closed down. On July 31st the contents of the shop were given away to the public. The group had recognised that the shop was failing and made the smart decision to call a halt. This was one of the first signs that not all their plans for Apple were working.

Tension was continuing to build in the studio, with Starr apparently the first to snap. He left the group and on August 22nd flew to the Mediterranean to spend time on the yacht of his friend Peter Sellers. Ironically, that same day, with Starr gone, Lennon, McCartney and Harrison recorded one of the group's most rocking songs, 'Back In The USSR'. The song was recorded in studio 2 with the ever-versatile McCartney taking over on drums, Harrison playing electric guitar and Lennon using the Fender VI. The following day overdubs were added, with more bass parts played by Harrison and McCartney, electric guitar also added by McCartney, a piano, backing vocals and handclaps tacked on, and McCartney also finding the energy for a lead vocal.

Back at Trident studio on August 28th, and still without Starr, the trio recorded 'Dear Prudence' with Lennon and Harrison playing guitars and McCartney continuing to fill in on drums. During the following few days, still at Trident, work continued on the song with overdubs by McCartney on bass, piano and even flugelhorn, while Lennon double-tracked his lead vocal, creating the by-this-time familiar Lennon vocal sound.

Starr returned to the group on September 3rd and the restored Beatles gathered at Abbey Road's studio 2. This same day was also the first occasion at Abbey Road when the group recorded to an eight-track machine. Richard Lush, second engineer on the sessions, says that *The White Album* was started on four-track but moved to eight-track as soon as the new 3M machine was available. "Some of the existing tapes were dubbed across to eight-track. But the mixing desk we were using at the time was laughable by today's standards. It only had ten channels, though by adding small passive mixers we could get up to 16 inputs. So you were still limited with the amount of mikes you could use on a session."[29] EMI's technical department did manage to come up with an improved 24-channel mixer during 1968.

One of the pieces shifted from its original four-track form to the new eight-track recorder was

The Beatles had a Fender VI six-string bass guitar, like the one pictured in this catalogue. The instrument was like a regular six-string guitar but tuned an octave lower.

The Beatles' Apple boutique in London had a psychedelic mural painted by The Fool (top), but later, by unpopular demand, it was painted over in white.

'While My Guitar Gently Weeps', leaving four tracks free for overdubs. It was on the night of the 3rd September that Harrison experimented with the backwards lead-guitar parts for 'Gently Weeps', but the idea was later abandoned.

It was a tricky job in any circumstances. The backing tape would need to be played backwards while Harrison familiarised himself with the new geography of the piece. He would then have to rehearse and try a few phrases, bearing in mind the way the "shape" of the notes change when reversed. Harrison would then record a part against the backwards-running tape, which would afterwards be played back in the standard direction. The new guitar part just added would now sound "backwards" against the regular track. (The master of the backwards guitar solo then was Jimi Hendrix: listen to his 1967 track 'Are You Experienced' for a prime example.)

The Beatles' new single, 'Hey Jude' and 'Revolution', was released on August 30th in Britain, the group's first on their own Apple record label. On September 4th, the day after Starr had rejoined, the all-important promotional clips for the new 45 were filmed at Twickenham studios.

The promo for 'Revolution' features the group performing in a familiar live stage setting. McCartney plays his original '61 Hofner bass (with something stuck under the strings by the bridge), Harrison has his new red Gibson Les Paul, and Lennon uses his natural-wood Epiphone Casino.

The Beatles did not actually play, but mimed to a music track, with only Lennon's lead vocal and Harrison and McCartney's backing-vocal tracks live. To fool the powerful Musicians' Union which insisted on and promoted live music, The Beatles had amplifiers set up behind them with pilot lights on, implying that the performance was for real. The all-Fender backline included Lennon's blackface Deluxe and Harrison playing through the silverface Deluxe Reverb, while McCartney had only a Fender Showman cabinet set up behind him – with no matching amp head to be seen. How could McCartney be playing a bass through just a speaker? Apparently the Union wasn't so sharp after all.

Starr was equipped with his famous Ludwig four-piece oyster black pearl drum set, but without a Beatles drop-T logo on the front head. Instead, Mal Evans had painted over the yellow lettering of the existing Love/Beatles head to give a solid reddish-orange coloured head. Probably the group had figured that it would be odd for them to stand there singing about Revolution with a drum-head that proclaimed Love.

The second clip filmed that day was for 'Hey Jude'. This has McCartney playing an upright piano, adding a live vocal to his pre-recorded vocal track. Lennon again plays his Epiphone Casino plugged into the Fender blackface Deluxe. Harrison uses the Fender VI seemingly "plugged into" the Fender Showman speaker cabinet upon which he is sitting. The Beatles' amps were active during the filming of TV presenter David Frost's introduction, as Lennon and Harrison can be heard goofing around on their guitars as they sing about their host. Starr again played his Ludwig oyster-black-pearl set – and this was the last time he would be filmed using it.

A 36-piece tuxedo-clad orchestra helped fill the scene as they too mimed to the music track of 'Hey Jude'. Adding yet another dimension, more than 300 extras were recruited to hang out with The Beatles and help sing the long anthem-like chorus at the end of the song. 'Hey Jude' became The Beatles' best-selling single.

Les Paul weeps

The protracted, laborious *White Album* sessions at Abbey Road dragged on. Another remake of 'While My Guitar Gently Weeps' was recorded on Thursday September 5th because Harrison was still dissatisfied, the main difference to this final version being a change of key. (Compare this *White Album* version to the demo on *Anthology 3*.) The remake featured Starr on drums, Harrison singing lead vocal and playing acoustic guitar, Lennon on electric guitar and McCartney playing piano. Mal Evans's magazine column suggested that Lennon also played organ on this session.[30]

The following evening Harrison brought in his old pal Eric Clapton to play the now-legendary lead guitar part on 'While My Guitar Gently Weeps'. Clapton used Harrison's "Lucy" Les Paul to overdub the blistering lead. Later, more overdubs were added to the song including fuzz bass played by McCartney, Starr's handy percussion and a vocal overdub by Harrison. Chris Thomas, studio assistant to George Martin, recalls the mixing of the song. "I was given the grand job of waggling the oscillator on the 'Gently Weeps' mixes," he says. "Apparently Eric Clapton insisted to George [Harrison] that he didn't want the guitar solo so typically Clapton. He said the sound wasn't enough of 'a Beatle sound'. So we did this flanging thing, really wobbling the oscillator in the mix. I did that for hours. What a boring job!"[31]

Starting afresh on already-recorded songs during *The White Album* sessions was becoming commonplace, and on September 9th a new attempt was made on 'Helter Skelter'. With The Who's "most raucous and dirtiest ever" quote still in mind, McCartney took 'Helter Skelter' over the edge. The final version recorded on the 9th featured very heavily distorted electric guitars, drums and piano. The song comes to a halt amid much chaos and feedback, appropriately ending with Starr screaming, "I got blisters on my fingers!" The next day Lennon added bass using the Fender VI. He also overdubbed saxophone, while Mal Evans apparently played trumpet.

Evans used his magazine column to describe the 'Helter Skelter' session. "The first version of this one played for 24 minutes, but the finished one you'll hear on the LP is no longer than average. Paul sings this in his screaming rock voice and the backing features The Two Harrys on brass. That's Mal Evans on trumpet and John Lennon on saxophone! When we did the final version of this in the second week of September, I made a note in my diary that The Beatles were the first people to use a brand-new eight-track recording machine just installed at EMI Studios. Theme of the song's lyrics? Boy to girl: 'Do you don't you want me to love you?' John plays bass, which is unusual."[32]

Happiness is a cool studio

'Glass Onion' was recorded and worked on from September 11th through to the 16th, the basic track consisting of McCartney on bass, Harrison on electric guitar, with Lennon singing and playing his Gibson J-160E guitar. Evans's column explained that Starr used "two drum kits instead of one".[33] This experimentation with two kits may have been the spur for Starr to acquire a five-piece outfit a few months later. Meanwhile, in a composition loaded with references to earlier Beatle songs, McCartney overdubbed a brief recorder part in the section about 'The Fool On The Hill'.

On September 16th in studio 2 McCartney recorded his simple acoustic tune 'I Will' on which he sang and played his Martin D-28, keeping the beat with a wood block as Starr played maracas. The next day McCartney added an unusual but effective hummed vocal-bass part as well as another acoustic guitar track, while on the 18th the group recorded 'Birthday', a song partly inspired by watching the rock'n'roll movie *The Girl Can't Help It*. 'Birthday' featured drums, bass, guitar and piano, but there was also an odd keyboard-type sound added to the final track. Mal Evans mentioned it in his column, explaining, "[The] curious sound which someone suggested was like an electric harpsichord is, in fact, a carefully prepared upright piano played by Paul – 'prepared' to give it a very special sound with reverberation, wow-wow and technical things like that."[34] The effect – heard most clearly at the very end of the song – may in fact have been produced by the three settings of the MRB (mid-range boost) control that was fitted to some Vox amplifiers of the period.

Harrison's brilliant 'Piggies' was cut on September 19th in studio 1. He sang and played acoustic guitar, McCartney played bass and Starr was on tambourine. George Martin's assistant Chris Thomas, who produced this session in Martin's absence, played harpsichord. Lennon's contribution to the song was a set of tape loops of pigs snorting. His own 'Happiness Is A Warm Gun' took shape next. On the 23rd the basic track was cut using drums, bass, electric guitars, then piano, organ and even a tuba.

ERIC CLAPTON INSISTED ... THE SOUND WASN'T ENOUGH OF 'A BEATLES SOUND'. SO WE DID THIS FLANGING THING, REALLY WOBBLING THE OSCILLATOR IN THE MIX. I DID THAT FOR HOURS...

Chris Thomas, George Martin's assistant, on recording Clapton's solo in 'When My Guitar Gently Weeps'

1968

A change of scenery landed The Beatles back at Trident on October 1st where they recorded 'Honey Pie'. The Roaring 20s-style tune was led by McCartney on piano and vocal, Starr on drums, Lennon playing his Casino and Harrison on the Fender VI. An arrangement was later scored by George Martin to add brass, sax and woodwinds played by 15 session musicians. As work continued at Trident, Harrison's 'Savoy Truffle' and McCartney's 'Martha My Dear' were also recorded.

Back at studio 2 in Abbey Road, 'Long Long Long' was recorded on the 7th with Harrison playing acoustic guitar and singing, Starr on drums, and McCartney playing Hammond organ and later overdubbing bass. The sound heard at the end of the song (starting around 2:32) is of a bottle of wine rattling on the top of the organ's Leslie speaker-cabinet. Two Lennon songs followed on the 8th: 'I'm So Tired' and 'The Continuing Story Of Bungalow Bill'. The opening classical-guitar phrase for 'Bungalow Bill' was not played by one of the group but was one of the complete taped passages that could be reproduced from a key on the left-hand keyboard of the Mellotron Mark II. The "mandolin" in the verses and the "trombone" heard on the outro (from about 2:09) are also Mellotron, played on this session by Chris Thomas.

It was now well into the autumn, and the pressure was on to finish the album. As the sessions started to wind down, some last-minute songs were recorded. McCartney taped 'Why Don't We Do It In The Road' over just two days, October 9th and 10th. Playing all the instruments himself, McCartney started out on guitar and vocals, then added piano, bass and finally drums. Except for a small drum overdub by Starr, the song was recorded without the help of the other Beatles.

Session musicians were brought in to play the string arrangements of violins, violas and cellos for 'Piggies' and 'Glass Onion'. Then a brass section of six saxophones – four tenors and two baritones – was added to 'Savoy Truffle'. Frantic mixing had been going on to finalise the double-album for release, and on October 13th Lennon recorded the last song for *The White Album*. 'Julia' was made in studio 2 with just Lennon playing his Gibson J-160E and singing. His guitar and voice were double-tracked and the song was mixed and ready for release the same day.

George Martin later characterised some of the songs on *The White Album* as coming from a basic idea that was then expanded with a jam session. "Which sometimes didn't sound too good. I complained a little about their writing during [that] album," the producer remembered, "but it was fairly small criticism. I thought we should probably have made a very, very good single album out of it rather than making a double album. But they insisted. I think it could have been made fantastically good if it had been … condensed. A lot of people I know think it's still the best album they made. It's not my view; horses for courses. I later learned that by recording all those songs they were getting rid of their contract with EMI more quickly."[35]

Released on November 22nd, *The White Album* (or, officially, *The Beatles*) sold nearly two million copies in two weeks. The album's look was the antithesis of last year's ornate packaging. Where 1967 had been psychedelic, with wild clothes, colourful record covers and painted guitars, 1968 offered a stripped-down Beatles. The group had taken their guitars down to bare wood. Lennon and Ono even shed their clothes, stripping naked for the sleeve of their *Two Virgins* album. And the new record came in a plain white album cover without colour, bearing a simple embossed title.

The White Album received critical acclaim, but the tensions that had become apparent while the group were making the record had done nothing but drive The Beatles further apart. The desire to pursue their individual interests was evident as Harrison's *Wonderwall Music*, the first Apple LP, was released on November 1st. Lennon put out his solo Apple project with Yoko Ono, *Unfinished Music No 1: Two Virgins*, on November 29th.

Lennon took the idea of working without The Beatles a step further. On December 11th he appeared with Ono as special guest for the filming of The Rolling Stones' television special, *Rock'n'Roll Circus*. A memorable performance in the film, only recently released, was by the supergroup Dirty Mac whose members included Eric Clapton on guitar, Keith Richards on bass, Mitch Mitchell on drums and Lennon playing his Epiphone Casino guitar.

Dirty Mac's legendary performance of the *White Album* song 'Yer Blues' was one of the highlights. Ono then joined Dirty Mac on stage, adding a wailing vocal to the song named 'Her Blues'.

(opposite) Making a promotional clip for 'Hey Jude' at Twickenham film studios. George, sitting on a Fender Showman cabinet, holds the Fender VI; John has his stripped Epiphone Casino, plugged into a "blackface" Fender Deluxe amp (behind George); Paul is on piano; and Ringo uses his first 22-inch-bass Ludwig kit with the "Love" head overpainted to a reddish-orange colour.

Fender's 1966/67 catalogue shows a "blackface" Fender Deluxe amplifier similar to the one used by John.

"**We stopped being a band when we stopped going into record stores and stopped trying to improve on our favourite singles.**"

JOHN LENNON, ON THE BEATLES GRADUAL DISINTEGRATION

1969.

THE PREVIOUS YEAR HAD ENDED DISMALLY FOR THE BEATLES, AND 1969 STARTED
IN MUCH THE SAME MOOD. THE BAND LACKED DIRECTION. THERE WAS NOTHING
THEY HADN'T DONE BEFORE, NOTHING LEFT TO CONQUER. THEY WERE ALREADY
THE WORLD'S BIGGEST BAND. AND AS THEIR OWN MANAGERS, THEY HAD NO ONE
TO MOTIVATE AND GUIDE THEM, NO ONE TO PROVIDE A CRITICAL OUTSIDE VIEW.

All the same, McCartney tried to push the band forward by suggesting a new project. Because
The Beatles no longer played concerts, he proposed to get back to what they had always done best:
playing together as a performing group. McCartney said later that he always considered The Beatles
as a great little band. "Nothing more, nothing less. You know, for all our success, when we sat down
to play we played good, from the very beginning – from when we first got Ringo into the band, and
before. [And] when we got Ringo into the band it really gelled. We played good! We never had too
many of those times where it's just not working. We had them like any other band, but often we were
just a great little rock'n'roll band that played any blues and rock'n'roll things. And it seemed to work.
It seemed to gel."[1]

The idea was to do another television special, this time showing the group rehearsing and
preparing new songs for a special live concert. The finale to the programme would be The Beatles
performing at some grand place such as a Roman amphitheatre or a stage in the middle of the
Sahara desert – or even a relatively small London club such as the Roundhouse. It seemed a good
idea, but never achieved a consensus within the group. Discussions about the project became so
heated that Lennon suggested the group just call it quits. Harrison was not at all keen on the idea of
performing live, and Starr reminded the group that he would be busy filming *The Magic Christian*
from the beginning of February. This left only a month to complete the project.

Despite all the disagreements and tension, McCartney did manage to persuade the others at
least to move the idea forward, and perhaps change it into something else. "The original idea was
that you'd see The Beatles rehearsing, jamming, making up stuff, getting their act together," he
explained later, "and finally we'd perform somewhere [at a big] concert."[2]

Filming of rehearsal sessions started on January 2nd at Twickenham film studios. Although the
idea was at first to make a television documentary, the material from the Twickenham shoots was later
used and assembled with other footage of the group and finally released more than a year later as
the *Let It Be* film.

Michael Lindsay-Hogg was recruited as director and assigned the task of capturing on film the
group getting it together. Unfortunately, what was committed to celluloid during this two-week
ordeal at Twickenham was four miserable-looking Beatles drudging through songs as if they really
wished they were somewhere else. Years later, McCartney commented that these filmed sessions in
fact portrayed how a group comes apart. "We didn't realise that we were actually breaking up as it
was happening,"[3] he said. Lennon's sentiments were similar. "When it came to *Let It Be*, we couldn't
play the game any more, we couldn't do it any more," was his assessment. "We'd come to the point
where it was no longer creating magic – and the camera being in the room with us made us aware
[that it was] a phoney situation."[4]

Putting all that to one side, the film shot at Twickenham does at least provide us with an accurate
document of the instruments and gear that the group were using at the time. The final version of
the *Let It Be* film opens with a new Beatles-logo drum-head. This is number seven in our scheme,
and the last of the Beatles drop-T heads. The new logo was painted on a 22-inch Ludwig Weather
Master head. It was similar to the previous logos, the main difference coming in the longer, narrower
lettering, with a very thin S, pointed at the end of its lower curve.

A non-pearl Ludwig for Ringo, and new Fender amps

The new Beatles-logo head was intended for Starr's new Ludwig five-piece drum kit, but was never
used on it. In late 1968 Starr had received the new kit, but did not unveil it until these sessions. The
Ludwig Hollywood maple-finish kit came with a standard 22-inch by 14-inch bass drum, 12x8 and
13x9 rack tom toms, 16x16 floor tom, and a 14x5 all-metal Supra-Phonic 400 snare drum. It was
equipped with two Ludwig cymbal stands, a snare stand, a hi-hat stand, and a Ludwig Speed King
bass pedal. Retail price would have been £484 (about $1,160 then; around £4,750 or $6,650 today).

1969

Paul's Rickenbacker 4001S bass guitar. Paul was given this bass in 1965 by Rickenbacker, at which time it was in the original "fireglo" (red sunburst) finish. Later he had it sanded down to natural wood, which is how it remains today. Paul still owns the bass.

Starr did not use the regular retracting double tom tom holder, but instead chose a free-standing double tom stand that he used set up in front of the kit. The front drum-head was removed from the bass drum – which was standard practice when recording The Beatles at the time. This explains why the new Beatles-logo head never appeared on the five-piece kit.

Starr preferred not to use the metal snare drum that came with the Hollywood kit, reverting to his trusty wooden Ludwig oyster-black-pearl Jazz Festival snare drum. As with the sessions during 1968, the snare was covered with a light towel to dampen its sound. Each tom tom on Starr's new Ludwig kit had Drum City stickers fixed to the shell, remnants of which are still there today. This would be the Ludwig kit that Starr used for the remainder of 1969 with The Beatles.

During the filming at Twickenham a makeshift rehearsal area was marked out, complete with a wash of coloured lighting as a backdrop. Starr's kit was set up on a drum riser with the group's other equipment casually arranged around it. A new set of Fender amplifiers was brought in for the sessions. A pair of Fender Twin Reverb amps were set up for Lennon and Harrison to play through, while McCartney used a new Fender Bassman. The Twin Reverb was an 85-watt amp with two 12-inch speakers, featuring a vibrato circuit, and a reverb section that operated a large two-spring reverb tank inside the amp's box. The Bassman head was a 50-watt amp, with Fender's tall redesigned Bassman cabinet containing two 12-inch speakers (the model later switched to two 15s).

The amps, manufactured in 1968, were covered in Fender's black Tolex material and came with the new "silverface" look. This meant a silver-coloured control panel replacing the traditional black one, and a new silver grille cloth with a distinct blue-sparkle sheen. The grille had an aluminium trim around its edge and was labelled with a raised, underlined Fender logo.

Photographs taken during the early sessions at Twickenham show the side of McCartney's new cabinet with Fender's identifying "Bassman" sticker still in place. At some point at Twickenham McCartney saw this and presumably liked the idea of clarifying his role. So he removed the sticker from the cabinet and fixed it to the face of his '63 Hofner bass, where it stayed during most of the filming. McCartney was the Bassman.

As for guitars, McCartney's Rickenbacker 4001S bass, newly stripped to natural wood, was available at Twickenham but never used. Also present was his '61 Hofner bass. Out-take footage from the sessions – later used in the promotional clip for 'The Ballad Of John And Yoko' – shows McCartney playing this original Hofner. But the Twickenham sessions would be one of the last occasions when McCartney used the '61 bass, which was stolen shortly afterward. For the bulk of his bass playing during the filming, McCartney preferred to play his '63 Hofner, which was now fitted with a set of black nylon-tapewound strings.

Lennon almost exclusively used his stripped Epiphone Casino and Harrison his Gibson "Lucy" Les Paul. McCartney often switched to a Blüthner grand piano, and then Lennon or Harrison would take over on bass, using the Fender VI through the Bassman amp. Other instruments around at the Twickenham sessions included Harrison's Gibson J-200 and the Lowrey DSO Heritage Deluxe organ.

Photographs in *The Beatles Get Back* book that originally accompanied the *Let It Be* album show Harrison at Twickenham with a Vox Wah-Wah pedal (complete with carrying bag) and a silver-

This is how the Hollywood kit was offered in Ludwig's catalogue.

THE CAMERA BEING
IN THE ROOM WITH
US MADE US AWARE
IT WAS A PHONEY
SITUATION.

John Lennon, on the filmed sessions

that became the *Let It Be* movie

coloured Arbiter Fuzz Face distortion pedal. "I am the inventor of the Fuzz Face," laughs Ivor Arbiter today. "That's my claim to fame. Jimi Hendrix was the Fuzz Face man. It's not something that we promoted, it was just that fuzz was hip. Most of the effects footpedals in those days used to slide all over the place, but I got the idea from the base of a microphone stand to use a case that was heavy-duty. Then we put a volume control and a tone control on and they looked like two eyes, and the footswitch looked like the mouth. So it became the Fuzz Face. Big deal!"[5]

The footage of the Twickenham rehearsals mainly shows the group trying out ideas for new songs as well as jamming old standards. When some of this film was finally released in the movie, the sometimes awkward, often uninspired performances gave the impression that The Beatles were only playing together because they had to. Eventually, on January 10th, the sessions broke down when Harrison walked out. He parted with the off-hand remark that he would see them around the clubs.[6]

Making *Get Back* at Apple

Harrison agreed to come back to the group on the condition that the television-show idea was dropped and that the "get back to being a band" concept would be switched to the recording of a new album. The filming could continue, but now it would document the making of a new record. Last of all, The Beatles would abandon the unpleasant atmosphere at Twickenham and move the sessions into their own newly-built Apple recording studio at 3 Savile Row in London.

The new *Get Back* recording sessions were due to start at Apple on January 20th, but more problems arose. Alex Mardas was an eccentric friend of the group who had some wild ideas for electronic gadgets and inventions. Nicknamed Magic Alex, Mardas headed The Beatles' Apple Electronics company and was in charge of installing a state-of-the-art multi-track recording studio in

Ringo's Ludwig Hollywood kit. Ringo acquired this five-piece set and began to use it at the beginning of 1969 during the filming for the Get Back/Let It Be project at Twickenham. He still owns the kit today.

the basement at Savile Row. The group had faith in Magic Alex's promises. The origins of the group's intention to have their own recording studio can be traced to *The White Album* sessions. Peter Bown, a stand-in engineer, had been at the session for 'Revolution' on June 4th 1968 when one of Abbey Road's tape machines broke down.

Bown said: "I remember Lennon coming into the control room saying, 'The fucking machine has broken down *again*? It won't be the same when we get our own studio down at Apple…' I replied, 'Won't it?'"[7]

Bown's reply was prescient. Although The Beatles had acquired their own 3M eight-track tape recorder for the new Apple studio, Magic Alex had his own ideas about multi-track recording and decided to build a special mixing desk and playback monitors of his own devising. This proved to be disastrous. Engineer Alan Parsons, who was brought in to the Apple studio from Abbey Road to help sort out the mess, recalls the sight that greeted him. "It was unbelievable," sighs Parsons. "Alex had a speaker for every track, each speaker about a foot-and-a-half tall. The mixing desk looked like it had been built with a hammer and chisel. None of the switches fitted properly, and you could almost see the metal filings. It was rough, all right, and it was all very embarrassing, because it just didn't do anything. It was clear within a day that nothing was going to be achieved on this stuff. We certainly never managed to get anything on tape through his mixing desk. So then the Abbey Road guys came in with a couple of four-track desks – and off we went to work."[8]

Apple artist Jackie Lomax remembers his record label's new studio. "The room where you played was nice, with a fireplace and reversible panels on the wall with one side carpet and the other side metal – it could be changed depending on the sound you wanted. The studio itself had a good sound." Lomax would visit Savile Row virtually every day during this period, and so could hardly have avoided noticing Magic Alex. "He was full of these advanced ideas that he could never quite pull off," says Lomax. "It all sounded so good. But every time anything went wrong, old Magic used to faint, faking a heart attack, and go into hospital to recuperate. I never saw anything of his working, and I don't think The Beatles did either."[9]

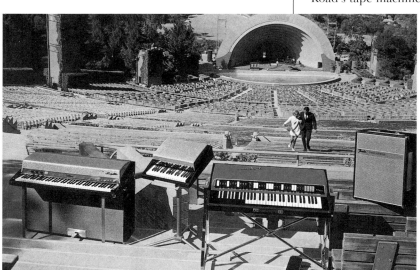

A Fender Rhodes Seventy-Three "sparkle top" electric piano, similar to the one used by The Beatles, is pictured (left) at the Hollywood Bowl in Fender's 1969 catalogue.

Billy Preston: the last fifth Beatle – and a Fender Rhodes piano

Now that the recording equipment had been straightened out at Apple, on January 23rd the recording sessions for the new album started. A new face was added to the group's recording line-up when Harrison asked their old friend, keyboard player Billy Preston, to sit in on the sessions.

Preston had first met the group back in 1962 when he was playing in Hamburg as a member of the Little Richard band. The Beatles were the opening act for Richard. "They were my favourites," Preston remembers. "I always used to watch them from the wings. One night George asked me to come out and play with them, because my organ was sitting there. But I said no – because Richard would have gone mad!"

Come 1969, and Preston was playing with Ray Charles at the Festival Hall in London. Harrison was in the audience, spotted a familiar face at the keys, and got a message to Preston to phone him. "The next day I called George," says Preston, "and he invited me over to see the guys. I went over to Apple, and there they all were recording. We started jamming. What you see in the film is basically how it happened: I walked in and we started jamming the old songs. It was like a reunion. At the end of the day they asked would I stay over and help them finish the record? And of course I told them yes. I was there with them every day after that. We would meet and have breakfast and then go down and play all day, stop and have lunch, and go back down and play. I mostly stayed with George, at his house. But we were just working all the time."[10]

A brighter outlook for the Apple studio sessions, which were now about to start, seemed to rekindle the group's interest in new sounds and equipment. They decided they'd like a Fender-Rhodes electric piano – or two. Mal Evans was deputised to acquire some of the Californian keyboards, and so he put in a call from the studio to Fender's UK agent, Ivor Arbiter. "He told me they were going to be in the studio for the next two days, that Paul desperately wanted the sound of a Rhodes, and they were going crazy to try and get hold of this piano," Arbiter remembers. He had

The Beatles used an Arbiter Fuzz Face during the Get Back/Let It Be sessions, like the one pictured here.

no stock of Rhodes pianos at the time, but Evans pleaded with him to find some. "I said I'd get on to Fender in the States right away. And I clearly heard John say in the background, 'Well, if they're gonna send one, send two because I'd like one as well.'"

Fender sent the pianos to Britain urgently by air, because it was regularly emphasised that The Beatles needed them immediately. Foggy weather in London meant the plane was diverted to Sweden. "Meanwhile, they were like kids wanting a new toy," says Arbiter. "They were going mad for these pianos. So we chartered a special plane. I remember going down to Apple and helping to unpack one of them outside the studio with Mal Evans. We took in this Rhodes, plugged it in, and Paul came over and played three chords. He looked up at me and said, 'No, that's not the sound I meant.' And that little episode cost around $8,000 as far as I remember. I think they were actually looking for the sound of a Wurlitzer electric piano."[11]

The Fender-Rhodes that ended up at Apple Studios was a silver-sparkle-top Seventy-Three model, a 73-key electric piano that incorporated a loudspeaker, amplifier and stand. The instrument's inventor, Harold Rhodes, had devised the first electric piano, his Pre-Piano, in the late 1940s. After he teamed up with the Fender company a series of Fender-Rhodes electric pianos was launched, beginning in 1963. The unique bell-like tone of the Rhodes derives from its unusual mechanism where rubber-tipped hammers strike tuning-fork-shaped metal "tines" that vibrate and are amplified. Despite McCartney's initial misgivings, the Rhodes was used on a number of the *Get Back* sessions. You can best hear its rich, percussive sound on Billy Preston's solo on 'Get Back'.

The Rhodes piano wasn't the only keyboard available at the Apple studio. Preston remembers a number of instruments set up and ready to go. "They had the Hammond, an acoustic piano, the Fender-Rhodes, and a Hohner electric piano. I would pick whichever I thought would fit the song. We always used the Hammond with the Leslie speaker. George loved the Leslie so much that he'd use it for his guitar." Photographic evidence confirms Preston's recollection, although both a Lowrey DSO Heritage Deluxe and a Hammond organ were present, and there were two acoustic pianos, an unidentified upright and the Blüthner grand.

George's Rosewood Telecaster, and a Leslie speaker

More new equipment appeared at the Apple recording sessions. Mal Evans detailed some of the new arrivals in a magazine column. "George had a pair of interesting presents to bring into the studio for the first session. One was a splendid Rosewood Telecaster guitar from Fender of America. The other was a Leslie speaker from Eric Clapton. It's a speaker with two revolving horns and a revolving drum. You can put a guitar or organ through it and ... it gives a terrific swirling effect."[12]

The Leslie speaker cabinet Harrison was given was a model 147RV, similar to the company's 147 but with the addition of a reverb control. To connect his guitar to the Leslie, Harrison had first to plug it into a Leslie combo pre-amp which accepted any "line level" instrument and thus enabled his guitar to benefit from the Leslie's wonderful churning sound. Clapton's gift to Harrison provided a useful new tone colour for the guitar sound on these *Get Back* recordings, and the Leslie would be used on a number of takes of various songs.

Harrison's new guitar was a Fender Rosewood Telecaster, custom-made for the Beatle. Phillip Kubicki, an inspired young guitar maker, worked for Fender for ten years from 1964 in the company's research and development department, at first under the watchful eye of master builder Roger Rossmeisl. (Rossmeisl had worked for Rickenbacker where he designed the models that Lennon and Harrison used.) Fender's marketing department wanted to add a new solid-rosewood Telecaster and Stratocaster to their line, and decided that a good way to publicise them would be to give a prototype of the Tele to George Harrison and of the Strat to Jimi Hendrix.

"In the autumn of 1968, Roger Rossmeisl told me we would be making these two special guitars," recalls Kubicki. "For me this was about as exciting as things could get. The Beatles and Hendrix were at their peak and were a big part of the times." Rossmeisl decided that a safe course would be to produce two prototypes each of the Rosewood Telecaster and Rosewood Stratocaster and then select the best to give to the star musicians. The bodies for the guitars were made with a thin layer of maple sandwiched between a solid rosewood top and back. "I spent hours sanding the bodies to perfection," recalls a misty-eyed Kubicki. "Eventually, a clear polyurethane finish was applied and allowed to dry, and we selected the two best bodies and necks for Harrison and Hendrix."

> WELL IF THEY'RE GONNA SEND ONE, SEND TWO BECAUSE I'D LIKE ONE AS WELL.
>
> John Lennon, ordering a Fender
>
> Rhodes on the spur of the moment

"Silverface" Fender Twin amp.

"Silverface" Fender Bassman.

John and George both used silverface Fender Twin amps during 1969, while Paul had a matching silverface Fender Bassman. Similar examples are pictured above.

He says that Harrison's Telecaster became a priority, because Fender knew it was required for an album that The Beatles were working on. "George's guitar was to have a particular hand-done satin finish," Kubicki remembers. "To achieve this, the body and neck were hard-block sanded with 500-grit paper, following the grain, until the surface was smooth, flat and fine. Then the surface was carefully rubbed with a fine cloth until it became highlighted. The guitar was set up, checked and rechecked to Roger's satisfaction, placed in a black hardshell case, and delivered to marketing. I never saw the guitar again – not in person, at least."

The second body and neck were stored in Fender's R&D department. Kubicki has since documented the story of the guitar precisely, and reports that Harrison's guitar was flown to England – in its own seat – accompanied by a courier, and hand-delivered to the Apple offices in December 1968. "I remember when I saw the guitar for the first time in the *Let It Be* film," smiles Kubicki. "I was so thrilled I almost jumped out of my seat."[13] The Hendrix Rosewood Stratocaster would not be completed until about April 1970, but for some reason was never sent to the guitarist – who died that August. Kubicki has no idea what happened to the instrument.

A myth that has circulated for years insists that Harrison and Lennon each received a Rosewood Telecaster, but Lennon certainly never had one. Harrison's Fender Rosewood Telecaster bore serial number 235594. Largely due to his use of the instrument in the *Let It Be* film, Fender introduced a production model later in 1969 which remained available for the next few years. The Rosewood Stratocaster, however, went no further than the two prototypes. Harrison used his Rosewood Tele almost exclusively for the *Get Back* recording sessions, although at times he did move to his Gibson "Lucy" Les Paul or J-200 acoustic. If McCartney was playing piano, Harrison would sometimes hold down the job of bass player and use the Fender VI.

Another new instrument that turned up at this time was a right-handed Fender Jazz Bass, with its distinctive offset body shape. The Beatles' example was in traditional sunburst finish. The band needed a decent right-handed bass because the sessions for *Get Back* were to be recorded live in the studio with virtually no overdubs. Many of McCartney's originals featured him playing piano, so the new Jazz Bass would in theory provide Harrison or Lennon with the ability to play a more suitable regular four-string bass, rather than the VI which had a less traditional bass sound. Nonetheless, even though the Jazz was present at the sessions, Lennon and Harrison still favoured the Fender VI.

This is the Rosewood Telecaster that was custom-made for George Harrison by Fender in 1969, and which George subsequently gave as a gift to Delaney Bramlett, who still owns it today. George used it on Beatles recordings in 1969 – including the group's final live performance on the Apple roof-top.

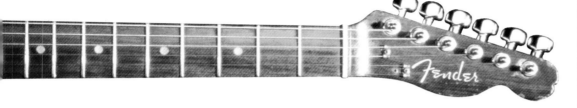

Lap of luxury

The Beatles had naturally set up their Apple studio to be as convenient and comfortable as possible. Their EMI-enhanced Vox PA system was brought in for playback, but Fender supplied a new PA system as well. The Fender rig was the company's new Solid-State series PA, consisting of a simple four-channel head and a pair of Fender "Solid-State" speaker columns. The Fender system was used in the studio recording room for live monitoring of vocals.

McCartney played his '63 Hofner bass almost without exception at the Apple sessions, although his stripped Rickenbacker 4001S was present as a backup. For 'Two Of Us' he used his right-handed Martin D-28, strung upside-down as ever to accommodate his left-handedness. Some photographs taken at the time also show McCartney's Epiphone Casino lying around in the Apple studio.

Lennon again preferred to use his stripped Epiphone Casino when he played guitar, but he too would sometimes fill in as bass-player with the Fender VI – for example on 'Let It Be'. Lennon is also seen in the film playing the VI on 'Dig It'. But here he is not using it as a single-note bass instrument. Instead, Lennon pounds out full chords on the VI, in the process providing the song with its thick, hard edge.

As he had done with his Epiphone Casino and Gibson J-160E, Lennon had his Martin D-28 sanded down, and removed its pickguard. The "new" D-28 was present at the Apple sessions, but Lennon was more often seen playing Harrison's Gibson J-200 when acoustic work was needed.

Lennon was also filmed using a Hofner lap-steel slide guitar on 'For You Blue'. Distributed in the UK by Selmer, these German-made Hofner instruments were advertised as Electric Hawaiian Guitars and available in two models: the Hawaiian Artist and – Lennon's choice – the Hawaiian Standard. A "table top" Fender slide guitar also showed up at Apple, and although there are pictures of McCartney playing the instrument in the studio, it is unclear if it was ever used on any of the recordings.

Starr used his new Ludwig Hollywood five-piece maple finish kit. It was set up more or less the same way he'd used it at Twickenham, except that he now added a cymbal and stand near his floor tom, giving Starr a total of three cymbals on which to improvise.

The eight days of sessions from January 22nd to the 29th had more or less fulfilled the group's plan to record an album live in the studio and to document on film how, as a band, they were getting back to their roots.

George joined Delaney & Bonnie And Friends during their 1969 British shows. This picture shows them on-stage with Delaney Bramlett playing George's Rosewood Telecaster, which the Beatle had given to him as a gift.

I THINK IT WAS
BECAUSE IT WAS
SUCH A LITTLE
LIGHT GUITAR THAT
IT LED YOU TO PLAY
ANYWHERE ON IT,
LED YOU TO BE A
BIT FREER.

Paul McCartney, on his famous

Hofner bass, which he could still be

seen using with The Beatles in the

Let It Be film.

Another instrument used by the group
at the time was a Fender Jazz Bass, as
in this 1968 Arbiter flyer.

The roof-top final performance

A grand finale was needed to end the film. The idea of playing a gig in front of a real live audience was now evidently out of the question, so with only days left before Starr would have to leave to begin filming *The Magic Christian* the group opted for Plan B. They would play on the roof of their Apple headquarters in central London.

Billy Preston remembers the idea coming up during one of the studio sessions. "It was Lennon's witty idea to play on the roof," he says. "They were worrying about where they could play and how to fit everyone into a concert hall. They didn't want to tour, they wanted to do one concert where everybody could come. So Lennon said, 'Let's just go on the roof and play for everybody.' I said, 'That's cool. Let's go!'"[14] Mal Evans's diary column reported the birth of the idea more specifically. "[It] came after we'd taken a breath of fresh air on the roof after lunch the previous Sunday [January 26th]. Anyway, it's certainly the first time The Beatles have recorded an album track on a roof in the middle of London!"[15]

Second engineer Alan Parsons says the decision appears to have been made on the spur of the moment, and was in keeping with the theme of the record – that they were trying to record themselves as if they were playing live rather than set up in a studio. "But although they were performing live in the studio they still had the screens and everything configured for optimum recording quality," says Parsons. "So they said they'd just all go up on the roof and play, and we'd send lines down and record it all here in the basement studio.

"It was a long night trying to get it all ready," Parsons remembers. "On the day, [engineer] Glyn Johns thought that there was going to be a problem with wind going into the mikes. So he sent me out to buy some stockings, or pantyhose. There I was in this local ladies-wear shop saying, 'Give me a pair of ladies stockings.' The clerk said, 'Yes sir. What size?' I said, 'It doesn't matter.' I think she thought I was going to rob a bank or dress up as a transvestite or something."[16]

On Thursday January 30th the filming climaxed with The Beatles' celebrated performance on the rooftop of their Apple Corps office building in Savile Row in London. It was the last public performance given by The Beatles as a band. Fortunately, this magical event was well documented by a slew of film cameras and still photographers – and an eight-track tape recorder rolling in the Apple basement.

Mal Evans made sure that The Beatles were set up correctly. Their backline largely consisted of the same equipment used during the previous few weeks. McCartney played his '63 Hofner bass through the silverface Fender Bassman rig. Today, he remembers playing his Hofner on the roof. "One thing I've noticed when I've seen old films [is that because the Hofner] is so light, you play it a bit like a guitar. All this sort of high stuff I used to do, I think it was because of the Hofner. A heavier bass – like when I now play a Fender and stuff – sits me down a bit and I play just bass. But I noticed in the *Let It Be* film, I play it right up there in 'Get Back' … And I think it was just because it was such a light little guitar that it led you to play anywhere on it, it led you to be a bit freer."[17]

Lennon played his stripped Epiphone Casino through the silverface Fender Twin Reverb, while Harrison chose to use his Fender Rosewood Telecaster, also playing through a silverface Twin. Billy Preston was perched to the side of McCartney, playing the group's Fender-Rhodes Seventy-Three electric piano, which had its own built-in amplification. A third silverface Twin was set up to amplify a Hohner Pianet N electric piano situated to the side of Harrison. Preston says the Pianet was there as a backup keyboard, but it was not used. Starr had his new Ludwig Hollywood five-piece maple-coloured kit, still with the three-cymbal set-up instead of his standard two.

To amplify their voices the group used their new Fender Solid-State PA system, with the speaker columns tilted slightly downward to face the perplexed pedestrians in the streets below. Vox speaker columns were set up on the ground in front of the group, facing their feet, effectively providing an early form of PA monitor. The group played 'Get Back', 'Don't Let Me Down', 'I've Got A Feeling', 'The One After 909' and 'Dig A Pony', with some treated to more than one take.

The following day another "live" performance was staged. This time it was in the privacy of their Apple basement studio, where the group set up to play and record the piano-based and acoustic guitar-based songs that would not have worked on the roof. In front of the film cameras they performed 'The Long And Winding Road' and 'Let It Be' featuring McCartney on piano and vocal, Lennon on Fender VI and Harrison on his Rosewood Telecaster. An acoustic version of 'Two Of Us' was also filmed and recorded, with McCartney singing and playing his Martin D-28, Lennon also singing and playing acoustic, while Harrison used his Rosewood Tele for lower-register guitar riffs that resembled basslines (there was no real bass guitar on the song). Starr used his new Ludwig Hollywood kit for the entire session.

This January 31st filming and recording session marked the end of the *Get Back* project. As a marked contrast to *The White Album* or for that matter *Sgt Pepper*, both of which took months to record and perfect, the songs for *Get Back* were all recorded in just ten days. The group had achieved their objective. They had captured The Beatles live and raw, without overdubs, studio musicians, polish or recording gimmicks. It was just the band as they sounded at that moment. And virtually all of it – good, bad or indifferent – had been captured on film and recorded on tape.

Get Back: the album that never was

The laborious job of editing and mixing-down the hours of tapes into a cohesive album was left to Glyn Johns. A new Beatles album was slated for a late-summer release. "*The Beatles Get Back is The Beatles with their socks off*," wrote Mal Evans of the proposed new LP, "human Beatles kicking out their jams, getting rid of their inhibitions, facing their problems and working them out with their music."[18] Evans's track-by-track run-down of *Get Back* described the recordings as interesting and down to earth. The album's cover was to be a parody of the group's first LP sleeve, *Please Please Me*, shot in exactly the same location at EMI's London headquarters and by the same photographer, Angus McBean.

But the group rejected Glyn Johns's final mix of the album. The record's release date was regularly postponed, and eventually dragged into January 1970. Johns was enlisted to mix the record for a second time. This new version of the album was also rejected. Perhaps the group genuinely disliked both attempts by Johns to mix *Get Back*, or maybe they simply became less enchanted with their own raw performances.

The idea for the album had clearly been to show The Beatles getting back to basics, live in the studio. But maybe what the group heard now was something they did not want to be or to go back to. It was easier to blame Glyn Johns's mixes than themselves. The *Get Back* project can be seen now as a key factor in the group's loss of identity and eventual break-up. When contacted by this author, Glyn Johns responded quite simply and concisely: "I have nothing to say about The Beatles."[19] It's easy to see why he might be bitter. Nonetheless, Johns went on to a very successful career as a respected and talented producer, making records with Eric Clapton, Bob Dylan, The Eagles, The Rolling Stones, The Who and many others.

Producer Phil Spector, widely admired for his superb "wall of sound" records of the early 1960s, was later brought in with the idea of salvaging the project. In March 1970 he would take the raw tapes and polish them with overdubs, in the process turning the *Get Back* tapes into the released *Let It Be* album. Bootlegs of Glyn Johns's *Get Back* album reveal The Beatles as a rock'n'roll band, just as they had apparently intended. By comparison, Spector's job sounds over-produced and heavy-handed. It seems a pity that with all the recent official releases of unheard Beatles material the *Get Back* album has still not been commercially issued.

Peace at last

Back at the end of January 1969, with the *Get Back* sessions finished, each Beatle went off in a different direction. As planned, Starr immediately started work on the *The Magic Christian* film, with Peter Sellers. Harrison worked alone at home on an experimental album, later released as *Electronic Sounds* on The Beatles' new Zapple label designed for left-field music. Spending some of his birthday at Abbey Road studios, Harrison also worked on demo recordings of his new songs 'All Things Must Pass', 'Old Brown Shoe' and 'Something'. McCartney took some time out with his girlfriend Linda Eastman, and on March 12th they were married at London's Marylebone Register Office.

Lennon started work on more avant-garde recordings with Yoko Ono, and eventually performed live with her at Cambridge University on March 2nd. This abstract performance was recorded and later released on Zapple as *Unfinished Music No 2: Life With The Lions*. Lennon and Ono were married on March 20th and spent their honeymoon at the Amsterdam Hilton where they held their first Bed

During 1969 The Beatles used a Fender Solid State PA system like the one pictured here, for vocal monitoring.

1969

> I REMEMBER WHEN I SAW THE GUITAR FOR THE FIRST TIME IN THE *LET IT BE* FILM, I WAS SO THRILLED I ALMOST JUMPED OUT OF MY SEAT.
>
> Phillip Kubicki, who built George's Rosewood Telecaster while working at Fender

In for peace. Lennon had clearly turned his focus and attention on the collaborative work he was enjoying with his wife, and they would turn out experimental albums faster than The Beatles could record a single. Lennon and Ono even formed a new musical unit, The Plastic Ono Band.

On May 26th they held their second week-long Bed In, this time at a hotel in Montreal, Canada. During that week they recorded their anti-war anthem 'Give Peace A Chance', released on Apple as a single by The Plastic Ono Band on July 4th. For this recording Lennon used his Gibson J-160E to help convey his message of peace. Lennon etched two sets of caricatures of Ono and himself on the front of the guitar, marking and commemorating their Amsterdam and Montreal Bed-Ins. Ono says today of the drawings, "They were done on the spur of the moment, full of love for what we were doing."[20]

The Beatles' new single, 'Get Back' and 'Don't Let Me Down', was released on Apple on April 11th, credited to The Beatles With Billy Preston. Celebrating his marriage to Ono, Lennon wrote 'The Ballad Of John And Yoko' and decided to record the song on April 14th as The Beatles' next single release – even though 'Get Back' had come out only days earlier. Just Lennon and McCartney played on the record. Making good use of Abbey Road's eight-track tape recorder, they overdubbed all the instruments themselves. The recording started with Lennon on acoustic guitar and vocal while McCartney played the drums. With the basic track done, McCartney then added bass, with Lennon tracking some electric guitar, then another overdub of McCartney on piano and Lennon laying down a further electric guitar part. A backing vocal by McCartney was then put on, followed by maracas, and Lennon thumped out the beat on the back of his acoustic guitar.

On April 16th & 18th The Beatles recorded the flip-side for the new single. Harrison's 'Old Brown Shoe' was cut in studio 3 with Starr on drums, McCartney playing jangle piano, Lennon on rhythm guitar and Harrison playing lead guitar and singing. Later, bass, organ, backing vocals and an additional lead guitar part played through a Leslie speaker were tracked on. 'The Ballad of John And Yoko' backed with 'Old Brown Shoe' was released on May 30th, on the heels of the 'Get Back' 45.

Another Abbey Road photo opportunity

A young American band called The AeroVons were working at Abbey Road at the same time as The Beatles. The previous year, the young St Louis group had landed a recording test with Capitol Records. Their leader, frontman and guitarist was Tom Hartman. "I was only 17 at the time and I just loved the Beatles," he remembers. "All I wanted to do was record where The Beatles recorded in England."

As it turned out, Hartman's dream came true. The AeroVons did record at EMI's Abbey Road. During their April 1969 recording sessions at the London studios they kept their equipment in the same room in which The Beatles' gear was stored. Hartman says they were directed to a small storeroom. It had once been a control room and thus had a window that looked into studio 3. "But now it was filled with guitar and drum cases, and a drum set," says Hartman. "It was tight quarters, but it all fitted. One night, while rummaging among our equipment, Mike our drummer said, 'I think you should come here.' We found ourselves standing over a drum case that had 'Ringo Starr' stencilled on the outside. We opened it, only to find a ton of Fender light-gauge Rock'n'Roll strings, and the famed Beatles drumhead. We pulled out the head, and quickly and nervously snapped a bunch of pictures of each of us holding it. With trembling hands we replaced it and began looking around for more.

"We found John's Rickenbacker 325 12-string and George's 'Revolution' Les Paul," continues Hartman. "We took some more shots – and then forever stayed away from their side of the room.

Playing in public for the last time, The Beatles perform on the roof of their Apple headquarters in central London on January 30th 1969.

This was plainly something that could have got us booted out of the studio." Hartman, looking back to an event some 30 years ago that clearly had a great effect on him, remembers around 15 guitar cases, Starr's maple drum set, and an Epiphone bass on top of a Hofner case.

One afternoon while in the room, the American musicians heard The Beatles recording 'Old Brown Shoe' next door in studio 3, and could not help but take a peek through the curtained window. They saw the group around a microphone, repeatedly singing "Who knows baby, you may comfort me…", trying for the perfect take.

Soon afterward Hartman ran into George Harrison in one of the studio's corridors, and asked him about a particular guitar sound he was having trouble with. "He was very gracious," says Hartman, "and impressed me with his empathy for my problem. 'Have you tried playing it backwards and reversing it?' he said. This led to a discussion of how sometimes one just has to try different things. We spoke for a few more minutes, then he excused himself. But at least I'd had the terrific experience of talking shop with George Harrison."[21]

Meanwhile, business struggles at Apple plagued Lennon, McCartney, Harrison and Starr, causing a good deal of tension among them. Lennon remarked, "I got a note from accounting saying, 'You're broke and if you go on it's going to all go, whatever you've got left.' [The accountant] laid it out to all of us, but I think I was the only one that read it. And then I announced it in the press and said, 'We're going to be broke if they don't stop this game, this Apple business.'"[22] Being a Beatle did not look like that much fun any more. They each wanted to get on with their personal lives, and the future of The Beatles as a band seemed bleak at best. An attempt to save Apple was made, however, when Lennon, Harrison and Starr outvoted McCartney and hired The Rolling Stones' manager Allen Klein to step in and manage the business. The friction within the band only grew.

One last album – *Abbey Road*

George Martin said later that he really thought The Beatles were going to break up after the *Get Back* sessions. "I thought I would never work with them again. I thought, what a shame to go out that way. So I was quite surprised when Paul rang me up and said, 'We're going to make another record, would you like to produce it?' And my immediate answer was, 'Only if you let me produce it the way we used to.' And he said to me, 'We do want to do that.' And I said, 'John included?' He said, 'Yes, honestly.' So I said, 'If you really want to do that, let's do it and get together again.' And it was a very happy record. I guess it was happy because everybody knew it was going to be the last."[23]

On July 1st work started on The Beatles' last studio album, untitled as yet but soon to be named *Abbey Road*. Almost two solid months – from July 1st to August 29th – were booked at the studio for the project. Although songs like 'Something', 'I Want You', 'Oh! Darling' and 'You Never Give Me Your Money' had already been started, the *Abbey Road* sessions officially started at the beginning of July when the group came up with the idea of making a final Beatles album. As Harrison put it recently, "Everybody decided, well, we've got to do one better album."[24]

The sessions started without Lennon as he and Ono had been on holiday in Scotland and while there were involved in a car accident that resulted in a stay in hospital. With Lennon incapacitated, McCartney, Harrison and Starr worked on numbers like 'Golden Slumbers', 'Carry That Weight' and 'Here Comes The Sun'. Engineer Alan Parsons says he got the feeling that the record was already less than a group effort. "It was really an album of four individuals – a compilation of each of them. McCartney was literally working alone, Harrison was working alone, Lennon was working alone. All with George Martin of course. They were avoiding each other, really."[25]

'Here Comes The Sun' was a great new song written by Harrison, first recorded on July 8th in studio 2. Parsons says that the demo track was predominantly acoustic, and remembers the handclaps taking a long time to get right. "Glyn Johns was out there trying to do it – and he dropped out because he kept screwing up."[26]

Lennon returned from hospital to the sessions the following day and worked with the other three Beatles on 'Maxwell's Silver Hammer'. Ono had been ordered to total bed-rest, so Lennon arranged to have a double bed set up in studio 2 so that he could be with her. Fender's UK agent Ivor Arbiter remembers this non-standard piece of studio equipment. "I was at Abbey Road and there was Yoko lying on the bed in the studio and then walking around in a see-through nightdress. That stuck in my mind. I thought, now that's a bit unusual. But that was how it had to be."[27]

IT WAS REALLY AN ALBUM OF FOUR INDIVIDUALS – A COMPILATION OF EACH OF THEM.

Alan Parsons, engineer on the *Abbey Road* album sessions

It's almost impossible to account accurately for all the instruments used on the *Abbey Road* sessions as there have been very few photographs published of the work in progress. It is likely that the instruments and amps were virtually the same as for the *Get Back* sessions. This would mean that Starr used his five-piece Ludwig Hollywood maple-finish kit, the amps were the silverface Fender Twin Reverbs and the Bassman, McCartney used his '63 Hofner bass, Rickenbacker 4001S, Martin D-28 and Casino, Lennon his Casino and Martin D-28, and Harrison his Gibson Les Paul, Fender Strat and Fender Rosewood Telecaster.

The Fender VI and Jazz Bass were also used during the *Abbey Road* sessions. And Lennon's new number 'Come Together', a highlight of the resulting album, featured overdubs of the group's Fender-Rhodes electric piano.

The Beatles and the Moog synthesiser

The only really new instrument that would grace *Abbey Road* was a significant one: a Moog synthesiser that Harrison had purchased in November 1968 while in Los Angeles producing Jackie Lomax's Apple album. Harrison brought back the Moog to the UK and used it at his home to record that experimental *Electronic Sounds* LP in February 1969 (released on Zapple on May 9th).

Lomax remembers making seven of the tracks for his *Is This What You Want?* record in LA, and says that Harrison, ever intrigued by new instruments and sounds, wanted to investigate the relatively new sonic world of the synthesiser. "He hired the guys that worked on the Moog, Bernie Krause and Paul Beaver," says Lomax. "They came down to the studio where we were recording and brought a synthesiser. We'd discuss what kind of sound we wanted, and they'd twiddle and fiddle around with the knobs – and then we would kick them off the machine and start playing it ourselves. George had a particular thing in mind and he took over the keyboard."[28]

Robert Moog is the acknowledged inventor of the first synthesiser – although as is so often the case, others were working along similar lines at the time. In 1968 Moog's new instrument received an enormously important publicity boost when Walter Carlos released *Switched On Bach*, a commercially successful album of the classical composer's best-known works played entirely on Moog synthesisers. From that time on the word Moog became virtually synonymous with synthesiser.

Moog's pioneering early voltage-controlled keyboard synthesisers used electrical currents deployed in various ways to simulate the vibrations which create musical sounds. As with the Bach record, there was a potential to emulate electronically the sounds of existing instruments, but just as exciting and stimulating for some musicians was the possibility of creating a whole new array of electronic sounds and tones and effects. The synthesiser could have been custom-made for a group that had just gone through its "roots" period and was keen once more to hunt for the newest, most modern sounds available.

Harrison bought one of the earliest "modular" Moog systems, a model IIIp that had first hit the market in 1967. This came with a separate keyboard unit and "ribbon" controller, along with a series of cases. The basic model had two cases, but more could be added to customise the instrument. The cases contained dozens of controls organised into various sections, including the basic building blocks that are used in voltage-controlled synthesis: oscillators, filters, amplifiers, generators and so on. Connections were made as required by the user with some of the 43 patch cords (leads) supplied with the synthesiser, which as a result often ended up looking something like a musical telephone exchange.

"We had the I, the II and the III models then," says Robert Moog, "and George's IIIp was the largest – the 'p' stood for portable. That's the one most musicians wound up buying. Paul Beaver and Bernie Krause were sort of partners of mine at the time – Paul was our representative and salesman in Los Angeles – and they sold that Moog to George."

A myth that has grown up around the story of Harrison and his Moog has The Beatles liking the sound of the synthesiser so much that they wanted to invest in Robert Moog's company and make it part of Apple Electronics. Today, Moog laughs at the suggestion. "We looked high and low for people who would want to invest in us," he says, "and finally, long after I got desperate, I found some guy to buy us out. If The Beatles had wanted to invest in us, we would have been there in a second! In those early days in Trumansburg, New York, we were running on fumes."[29]

When Harrison brought his new Moog synthesiser back to London and the *Abbey Road* sessions,

> IT WAS A VERY HAPPY RECORD ... I GUESS BECAUSE EVERYBODY KNEW IT WAS GOING TO BE THE LAST ONE.
>
> George Martin

THE BEATLES WERE ALWAYS LOOKING FOR SOMETHING NEW, ANYTHING TO DISGUISE THE SOUND OF THEIR VOICES OR THE INSTRUMENTATION.

Alan Parsons

it quickly became the must-have sound on many of the tracks that the group were working on. Always keen to be ahead of the pack, The Beatles were among the first to make good musical use of a synthesiser on record. Almost everyone who worked at Abbey Road at the time clearly remembers the new toy. Engineer Richard Lush recalls Harrison bringing the new instrument into the building. "He set it up in room 43, which was at the back of studio 3. George spent hours in there playing around with it, plugged through a little Fender speaker. I'd never heard anything like it before. The sound was something like that odd [theremin] on The Beach Boys 'Good Vibrations'."[30]

Maintenance engineer Ken Townsend recalls the Moog's first use on a Beatles track. "It was 'Because', and the Moog was a bit of a marvel instrument. To get that French horn sound it took a whole set of flightcases full of jack plugs and filters."[31]

Engineer Alan Parsons, who'd worked on some of the recordings made at Apple earlier in the year, came to *Abbey Road* after most of the basic tracks were down, as second engineer on the overdub sessions. "We were working in studio 2, and the reason the Moog was set up in 43 – a sort of overdub room for studio 3 – was because they wanted it to be reasonably accessible but they didn't want it to be so far away. It was a lot of work to get anything out of it, and you could only sound one note at a time, which was a disadvantage."

Parsons especially remembers McCartney's work on the Moog on 'Maxwell's Silver Hammer'. The IIIp included a "ribbon" controller, a long strip which induces changes in the sound being played depending on where it is touched and how the player's finger is then moved. "Paul did 'Maxwell' using the ribbon," says Parsons, "playing it like a violin and having to find every note – which is a credit to Paul's musical ability."

The Moog was certainly novel for the time, emphasises Parsons. "The Beatles were always looking for something new, anything to disguise the sound of their voices or disguise the

John's Gibson J-160E. In 1968 John had stripped the psychedelic finish from this guitar, revealing the natural wood. During John and Yoko's second Bed In for peace in Montreal, Canada, John drew the caricatures of himself and Yoko. This guitar is owned today by Yoko Ono.

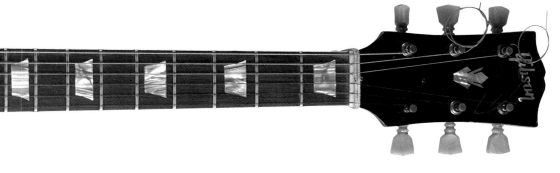

> PAUL DID 'MAXWELL' USING THE RIBBON [CONTROLLER ON THE MOOG], PLAYING IT LIKE A VIOLIN ... WHICH IS A CREDIT TO PAUL'S MUSICAL ABILITY.
>
> Alan Parsons

instrumentation. I think they were aware that they relied so much on experimentation. They also leaned very heavily on George Martin and the engineers to come up with innovative ideas and new sounds that would make them different. John in particular hated the sound of his own voice and was always looking for some new effect to put on it."[32]

The distinctive sounds of the Moog IIIp modular synthesiser are spread over a good deal of the resulting *Abbey Road* album. Overdubs of the instrument started at the beginning of August, and there are some notable occurrences to be heard on the released LP. 'Maxwell's Silver Hammer' has synth following the vocal in the second and third verses, and a fine outro solo from 3:03. 'Because' features a well-defined synth solo sound from 2:12. 'I Want You (She's So Heavy)' sees Lennon using the Moog as a "white noise" generator to create the swirling wind effect at the close. And 'Here Comes The Sun' has a lovely ribbon-assisted downward slide on the intro, and glorious synth sounds filling the "sun, sun, sun" middle section. Orders for Moog synthesisers must have soared as soon as musicians worked out what was making these intriguing sounds on the new Beatles record.

Another new keyboard sound introduced during the *Abbey Road* sessions came from a Baldwin Combo electric harpsichord which George Martin played on 'Because' – it's particularly evident on the striking arpeggios at the very start of the track. And who could forget the anvil that Starr played on 'Maxwell's Silver Hammer'? As with the *Get Back* sessions, Harrison often relied on the Leslie speaker cabinet to add a gentle effect to his guitar sound, though it's more marked on 'Sun King', especially noticeable on the intro.

On the morning of August 8th, photographer Iain Macmillan shot the famed zebra-crossing shot outside the studio that provided the album's cover. Later that day work continued in the studio. 'The End' was intended to be the last song on *Abbey Road*, and gives the listener an all-too-brief glimpse of a great three-way guitar duel. McCartney, Harrison and Lennon, in that order, each take a two-bar solo, cycling around three times. McCartney probably used his Casino, Harrison's work is pure wailing Les Paul, and Lennon makes an aggressive, distorted howl with his Casino.

John gives peace a chance while playing his Gibson J-160E at the Hotel Reine-Elizabeth in Montreal.

The same song features Starr playing his first and last drum solo on a Beatles record. Some fellow drummers at the time noticed its similarity to the solo heard on Iron Butterfly's summer 1968 top-30 US hit, 'In-A-Gadda-Da-Vida'. Butterfly's drummer Ron Bushy was also aware of the similarities. "We played London back in '71," he recalls now, "and Ringo and Paul came to see us.

Ringo sent up his man backstage and invited me out to a private club called Tramps. We had dinner and drinks and were up all night shooting the shit. He told me then that he kind of copped my solo for their song 'The End' on *Abbey Road*. And I just thought that was cool. It was the biggest compliment that I could ever get."[33]

The message of the song was clear. The end of The Beatles was near. *Abbey Road* was completed by the end of August and was released on September 26th.

Plastic Ono Band – nervous in Toronto

Effectively finished with The Beatles, Lennon sprang into action with his new Plastic Ono Band. He was invited to perform at a Toronto concert to be held on September 13th that would also feature Chuck Berry, Bo Diddley, Little Richard, Jerry Lee Lewis, Fats Domino, The Doors and Alice Cooper.

The Plastic Ono Band was quickly transformed into a "real" band, with Lennon on vocals and guitar (his Epiphone Casino), Yoko Ono on vocals, Eric Clapton on lead guitar, Klaus Voormann on bass, and Alan White on drums. The musicians jumped on a plane bound for Toronto – and only thought about rehearsing once they were in the air.

Alan White, later a member of Yes, was in a band called Griffin at the time. Lennon happened to see him playing at a London club. "The next day I got a call from him," recalls White. "He said he'd like me to go to Canada tomorrow to play in his new band – and by the way Eric Clapton is on guitar and Klaus Voormann is on bass, and the whole thing is called The Plastic Ono Band. First of all I thought it was a crank call, but it turned out to be true. He called back later and said, 'If you want to do it, there'll be a limo along in the morning to pick you up and take you to the VIP lounge at Heathrow airport.'"[34]

The limo did indeed arrive at White's place the following morning, and rehearsals took place on the plane. "I had a pair of sticks and played on the back of the seats," White laughs, "and they had some guitars that they'd carried on. They sang and we went through some of the numbers – and then we did the gig. It was one of the biggest breaks of my career, and the beginning of my relationship with The Plastic Ono Band. Every time they went into the studio, I got invited to play the drums. Jim Keltner played on some things, but John used me for quite a few songs including 'Imagine' and 'Instant Karma'. And that led to me playing with George on *All Things Must Pass*."

Los Angeles-based producer, songwriter and musician Kim Fowley was the MC for the Canadian concert, from which The Plastic Ono Band's *Live Peace In Toronto 1969* album was drawn. Fowley reports that Lennon threw up before going on stage. "He was terrified, almost in tears," Fowley remembers. "He was very ashen and pale. I asked him if he was sick, and he told me he didn't feel well. I asked why. He said, 'Imagine if you were in The Beatles from the beginning and you were never in any other band. Then all of a sudden you're going on stage with this group who've never played live together, anywhere. We formed on the plane coming over here, practising acoustically, and now we're gonna play in front of 20,000 people. Please do something so people don't know how frightened I am!'"

Fowley's response was to dredge up a memory of the movie *Miracle Of Our Lady Of Fatima* from Catholic grade school in the 1950s. "The Blessed Virgin came out and all these pilgrims lit candles," says Fowley. "So I had the genius – and John Lennon was supposed to be Jesus Christ anyway – of having everyone light matches and lighters. You can hear it at the beginning of the live album, when I say, 'Get your matches ready.' So when John came out on to the stage, all of a sudden 20,000 matches and cigarette lighters lit up, which cast a psycho quasi-religious glow to the festivity. Everybody was so astounded with it that they didn't notice the nervousness."

These pictures were snapped in 1969 by The AeroVons, a group recording at Abbey Road who stored their gear in the same room as The Beatles' equipment. Left to right: Beatles number-seven drum-head logo; Ringo's trap case; George's Les Paul; various cases and amps; AeroVons and Beatles drum-heads; Beatle guitar cases; AeroVons guitarist posing with John's Rickenbacker 325 12-string; and Ringo's Ludwig Hollywood set.

The next day the promoters took Fowley over to see Lennon and Ono. "I went to a mansion that had been rented for them," says Fowley. "We sat around, and John was very quiet. Everyone was sitting there, the entire Plastic Ono Band, and so I came up with a great question. 'John,' I said, 'what was the secret of The Beatles, how did it work, and then why did you break up?' All in one question! Well, the room went even more quiet. I don't think John had ever been asked this question before. But he answered it.

"John said, 'When we didn't have any money, we used to go into record stores and listen to singles. We'd memorise the techniques. And then we'd take those techniques back and write songs. We'd have a band based on techniques that inspired us. We stopped being a band when we stopped going into record stores and stopped trying to improve on our favourite singles.' After that, he thanked me for being helpful to him at the concert last night. I said well, thank you for selling tickets so we could all get paid."[35]

Back in the UK, Lennon took his new band into Abbey Road's studio 3. On September 25th Lennon, Ono, Clapton, Voormann and Starr recorded his haunting 'Cold Turkey'. Quickly released on October 24th as an Apple single by The Plastic Ono Band, the song was credited only to John Lennon. This was the first time that Lennon had been credited on his own as a songwriter – without the familiar addition of "and McCartney". It was a bold move that further distanced Lennon from The Beatles.

By the end of 1969, each Beatle had ideas for solo projects. Starr started his studio album, *Sentimental Journey*, at Abbey Road's studio three on October 27th, with George Martin producing. McCartney and Harrison would start work on their own solo records soon afterward.

Eric Clapton & Friends

Work with other bands for the group's Apple record label continued. By September 1969, The Beatles had purchased a new 16-track recorder for their own Apple studio. "The man in charge is, of course, ginger-haired Geoffrey Emerick," said a contemporary report, "who [has] left EMI to work with the boys. A 16-track machine will enable The Beatles to record 16 separate sounds or instruments and then mix them afterwards. So it does appear that they are not going to 'get back' in their recording activities in future, but will produce more progressive and advanced-type Beatle music, which will please the majority of their fans."[36]

On December 1st, Harrison and Starr attended a performance by the American act Delaney & Bonnie at the Albert Hall in London. The duo's backing band was billed as Eric Clapton & Friends. After the show, Clapton asked Harrison to become a member of the group for a number of shows throughout Britain and Denmark. Harrison agreed, joining the troupe the day after their Albert Hall show, and presented Delaney Bramlett with a generous gift – his Fender Rosewood Telecaster. Handing over the Tele, he told Bramlett that it was "for what you did for me last night". The guitar has since remained in Bramlett's possession.

During the shows in the UK and the three concerts in Denmark, Harrison used his red Gibson "Lucy" Les Paul and his psychedelic-painted Fender Stratocaster, now nicknamed "Rocky". By this time Harrison had added to the psychedelic artwork of his Strat. The name "Rocky" was applied to the guitar's headstock, "Bebopalula" to the upper body of the guitar, and "Go Cat Go" on the pickguard (see photo on page 206).

Bramlett remembers using mainly his newly acquired Rosewood Telecaster during the tour. "But we all used to switch guitars. It was like whatever was there you'd pick up. Sometimes I would use Eric's guitar and he would use mine. We had a lot of fun!"[37]

IMAGINE IF YOU WERE IN THE BEATLES FROM THE BEGINNING AND NEVER IN ANY OTHER BAND. THEN ALL OF A SUDDEN YOU'RE GOING ON STAGE WITH THIS GROUP WHO'VE NEVER PLAYED LIVE TOGETHER...

John Lennon, explaining his terror before the first Plastic Ono Band gig

1970

A missing Les Paul

Giving or receiving an instrument as a gift seems almost sacred to Harrison, and he frequently gave away guitars to his close friends as a token of friendship. In the same way, Harrison held in high esteem the gift that Eric Clapton had given to him – his Gibson "Lucy" Les Paul. It was obviously more than just another guitar. So it was particularly shocking to Harrison when in the early 1970s his beloved Les Paul was stolen. "It got kidnapped and taken to Guadalajara," he explained later. "I had to buy this Mexican guy a Les Paul to get it back."[38]

To help him find Lucy, Harrison enlisted the help of musician Mark Havey, who at the time – around 1973 – was living in California, but had also lived in Mexico. "I had a musician friend, Miguel Ochoa, who came up from Mexico to buy some instruments," Havey remembers. "He walked into a Guitar Center store in Hollywood and saw hanging on the wall a cherry-red Les Paul, which he bought for $650."

The only similar guitar Ochoa had seen was pictured on the inside cover of *Let it Be*. He gave the store Havey's address and phone number for the receipt. The following day the guitar store called Havey, asking for Ochoa. They told Havey that they owed his friend some money because they had overcharged for the Les Paul.

"I said that didn't sound very likely," recalls Havey. "So then the store explained to me that Miguel had bought a guitar that they had only recently acquired, and by law they were supposed to keep it for 30 days to see if it clears any 'hot' stolen-property lists. 'As it turns out,' they said to me, 'the guitar belongs to George Harrison. So we're in deep shit here.'"

Thinking that this must be some kind of joke, Havey told the store that if the guitar really belonged to Harrison, they ought to have the Beatle guitarist call him and sort it out.

"About 30 minutes later the phone rang," says Havey, "and a nice gentleman with a very British accent said, 'This is George Harrison.' He told me the guitar had been stolen from under his bed over the holiday. His home in Beverly Hills had been burglarised, and among the things that were taken was the cherry-red Les Paul. So I called my friend Tony Baker, and we met with George." Harrison explained to them that the guitar wasn't really his – it belonged to Eric Clapton and was effectively on loan to him. "So he had to get the guitar back. He asked if we could help get it back from Miguel. We said sure."

A Moog IIIp modular synthesiser similar to the one George bought and which was subsequently used by The Beatles in the studio in 1969 for the Abbey Road album.

Havey then spoke to Ochoa, who was somewhat surprised by the news. He said he needed some time to think. "We grew up learning how to play Beatle stuff, and this was George Harrison's guitar!" says Havey. "So Miguel gets off the phone and we don't hear from him for two days. In the meantime we're in constant contact with George, who wants to know what's going on. We told him what was happening, and he thought it didn't sound very good. George said that he wouldn't have a problem paying Miguel at least what he paid for the guitar, so that he wouldn't be out on any money."

Two days later Ochoa called Havey and said that he might want to keep the guitar – and promptly went back home with it to Guadalajara, Mexico. By this time Harrison was, understandably, growing impatient. He asked Havey to contact his friend and find out what he wanted to return the guitar. Eventually, says Havey, Ochoa came up with his requirements.

"He proceeded to give us a wish list," Havey remembers, itemising a couple of desirable and expensive collector's items. "He wanted a 1958 sunburst Les Paul, an early Fender Precision Bass, and about four other instruments. We told him that he was being totally unreasonable and that he should consider the reality of the situation. So we got him down to a guitar and a bass. We told this to George, and we all got together to go looking for a '58 sunburst Les Paul. What was interesting was that every time we went into a store they would quickly pull off all the guitars' price-tags once they realised it was George Harrison.

This went on for a week. Eventually we found a guy called Norm Harris who had the right guitar. It was bought, and George flew my friend Tony and I down to Mexico. We made the trade: the guitar and bass for the cherry-red Les Paul. Then we came back and gave it to George."[39]

And all for the love of a guitar. This demonstrates once more that Harrison was the true guitar fan among the Beatles – and indicates just how much certain instruments came to mean to him.

The end of the Sixties, the end of The Beatles

When the Delaney & Bonnie tour ended, Lennon recruited the duo plus George Harrison, Keith Moon, Eric Clapton, Billy Preston, Bobby Keys, Klaus Voormann, Alan White and Jim Gordon to join him and Ono for a Plastic Ono Band supergroup performance at the Lyceum in London on December 15th 1969. The charity concert was organised to benefit UNICEF.

During the show, Clapton used Harrison's psychedelic "Rocky" Strat, while Lennon played his favoured Epiphone Casino. (By now the Casino's tuning pegs had been changed from the original Kluson models to a standard set of gold-coloured Grover tuners, which is how the guitar remains today.) Harrison played his "Lucy" Les Paul.

A new decade had come around, and the early 1970s would see a number of Beatle solo projects. In spirit, The Beatles ended at the same time as the 1960s. But officially they were still a band, and there were some matters that had still to be finished. By the beginning of 1970 the objective seemed to be to tie up any loose Beatle ends and move on to solo careers.

Looming large was the necessity to bring the *Get Back* project to some kind of amenable conclusion. Postponed numerous times during 1969, an album drawn from the sessions needed to be released. The decision was made to add a Harrison song to the album, so on January 3rd 1970 Harrison, McCartney and Starr – without Lennon – worked in Abbey Road's studio 2 on 'I Me Mine'. This would turn out to be one of the last occasions that the majority of The Beatles were present at a recording session. The basic track was recorded with Starr on drums, McCartney on bass and Harrison singing and playing acoustic guitar.

On January 27th Lennon and his new Plastic Ono Band visited Abbey Road's studio 2 and recorded 'Instant Karma!', with Phil Spector producing the session. On February 11th the Plastic Ono Band appeared on BBC TV's *Top Of The Pops* performing the new single. Unofficially at least, Lennon and The Beatles were no more.

McCartney began 1970 working on his own solo album. Recording in the privacy of his home on a four-track Studer machine, McCartney put down the songs that would end up as *McCartney*, released on Apple on April 17th 1970.

A week prior to his album's release, McCartney made it known to the British press that he was leaving The Beatles and that the group had essentially split up.

Let It Be

As we've seen, The Beatles had twice rejected the live, raw sound of Glyn Johns's final mixes of *Get Back*. So, as we've said, the idea was put forward to bring in Phil Spector as producer in order to salvage the tapes for what would be deemed a proper release.

On March 23rd Spector started flooding the *Get Back* tapes with his lavish wall-of-sound production. He added a 50-piece orchestra – 18 violins, four violas, four cellos, a harp, three trumpets, three trombones, two guitarists, 14 singers and Starr on drums – to tracks including 'Across The Universe', 'The Long And Winding Road' and 'I Me Mine'. The loose rock'n'roll *Get Back* concept was gone, and the orchestrated *Let It Be* album was in place.

Film footage from the January 1969 *Get Back* sessions was edited for a *Let It Be* motion picture that would be put out to coincide with the album. On May 5th 1970 came the release of The Beatles' swansong, the *Let It Be* album. It was of course issued by the group's own record company, the LP's centre label bearing a red-coloured apple, as opposed to the fresh green fruit that normally appeared there. A ripe apple is past its best.

"It's just natural, it's not a great disaster," said John Lennon of the group's break-up. "People keep talking about it as if it's the end of the earth. It's only a rock group that split up – it's nothing important. You know, you have all the old records there if you want to reminisce."[40]

WE'D COME TO THE POINT WHERE IT WAS NO LONGER CREATING MAGIC.

John Lennon

WE WERE JUST A GREAT LITTLE ROCK'N'ROLL BAND.

John Lennon

FOOTNOTES
Footnote references are arranged here by chapter.

Chapter 1: 1956-7 pp6-15
1 (Barry) Miles *John Lennon In His Own Words* (Omnibus 1980)
2 (Barry) Miles *John Lennon In His Own Words* (Omnibus 1980)
3 Ray Coleman *Lennon* (McGraw-Hill 1984)
4 *Beat Instrumental* December 1964
5 (Barry) Miles *John Lennon In His Own Words* (Omnibus 1980)
6 Author's interview December 7th 1995
7 *Liverpool Echo* December 7th 1981
8 Author's interview November 1st 1996
9 Hunter Davies *The Quarrymen* appendix (Omnibus 2001)
10 Author's interview May 3rd 1996
11 (Barry) Miles *John Lennon In His Own Words* (Omnibus 1980)
12 Author's interview December 7th 1995
13 Author's interview May 3rd 1996
14 *Beat Instrumental* December 1964
15 Author's interview December 7th 1995
16 Author's interview June 7th 1996
17 (Barry) Miles *John Lennon In His Own Words* (Omnibus 1980)
18 *The Beatles Anthology* video box-set (Apple 1996)
19 *The Beatles Anthology* video box-set (Apple 1996)
20 Author's interview December 7th 1995
21 Len Garry *John, Paul & Me Before The Beatles* (CG 1997) interview CD *Len Garry & Pete Shotton Tour Liverpool And Mendips*
22 Author's interview May 3rd 1996
23 BBC Radio 2, December 1999
24 Len Garry *John, Paul & Me Before The Beatles* (CG 1997)
25 (Barry) Miles *John Lennon In His Own Words* (Omnibus 1980)
26 Author's interview September 3rd 1996
27 *Musician* August 1980
28 Interview with Tony Bacon November 30th 1994
29 *Beat Instrumental* December 1964
30 Interview with Tony Bacon November 30th 1994

Chapter 2: 1958-9 pp16-27
1 Author's interview May 31st 1996
2 *Guitar Player* November 1987
3 *Beat Instrumental* November 1964
4 Interview with Tony Bacon November 30th 1994
5 Author's interview June 7th 1996
6 *The Beatles Anthology* video box-set (Apple 1996)
7 (Barry) Miles *Beatles In Their Own Words* (Omnibus 1978)
8 *Guitar Player* November 1987
9 Author's interview May 31st 1996
10 *The Paul McCartney World Tour* (MPL/Emap Metro 1989)
11 Author's interview May 31st 1996
12 *Musician* interview, August 1980
13 Author's interview January 8th 2001
14 Ray Coleman *Lennon* (McGraw-Hill 1984)
15 *Beat Instrumental* November 1964
16 Author's interview March 29th 2001
17 *Beat Instrumental* December 1964
18 Sotheby's "Collectors' Carousel" sale catalogue (Sotheby's New York, June 26th 1992)
19 *All About Us* (publisher unknown c1965)
20 Author's interview March 7th 1998
21 *The Beatles Anthology* video box-set (Apple 1996)
22 Author's interview May 1st 1998
23 Interview with Tony Bacon November 30th 1994
24 Ray Minhinnett & Bob Young *The Story of The Fender Stratocaster* (Miller Freeman)
25 *Guitar Player* November 1987

Chapter 3: 1960 pp28-43
1 Interview with Tony Bacon November 30th 1994
2 Author's interview July 25th 1996
3 Author's interview September 3rd 1996
4 Author's interview January 8th 2001
5 Pete Best & Patrick Doncaster *Beatle! The Pete Best Story* (Plexus 1985)
6 Author's interview January 8th 2001
7 Pete Best & Patrick Doncaster *Beatle! The Pete Best Story* (Plexus 1985)
8 *The Beatles Anthology* video box-set (Apple 1996)
9 Author's interview January 8th 2001
10 *A Concise History Of the Frying Pan* BBC Radio 1, 1987
11 Ray Coleman *Lennon* (McGraw-Hill 1984)
12 Author's interview November 29th 1995
13 *Musician* July 1996
14 *A Concise History Of the Frying Pan* BBC Radio 1, 1987
15 Author's interview January 8th 2001
16 Interview with Heinz Rebellius April 18th 1994
17 Interview with Heinz Rebellius May 3rd 2001
18 *Beat Instrumental* December 1964
19 Pete Best & Patrick Doncaster *Beatle! The Pete Best Story* (Plexus 1985)
20 Pete Best & Patrick Doncaster *Beatle! The Pete Best Story* (Plexus 1985)
21 Author's interview January 8th 2001
22 Author's interview January 8th 2001

Chapter 4: 1961 pp44-59
1 Bill Harry *Ultimate Beatles Encyclopedia* (Hyperion 1992)
2 *The Beatles Anthology* video box-set (Apple 1996)
3 Interview with Tony Bacon November 30th 1994
4 Interview with Tony Bacon November 30th 1994
5 *Guitar Player* July 1990
6 Mo Foster *Seventeen Watts?* (Sanctuary 1997)
7 (Barry) Miles *Beatles In Their Own Words* (Omnibus 1978)
8 Author's interview March 28th 1997
9 *Musician* August 1980
10 Pete Best with Bill Harry *The Best Years Of The Beatles* (Headline 1996)
11 *Guitar Player* July 1990
12 *Beat Instrumental* October 1964
13 Author's interview January 8th 2001
14 Interview with Tony Bacon November 30th 1994
15 Interview with Tony Bacon November 30th 1994
16 Interview with Heinz Rebellius April 18th 1994
17 *The Paul McCartney World Tour* (MPL/Emap 1989)
18 Author's interview April 25th 1997
19 *Beat Instrumental* August 1963
20 Author's interview January 8th 2001
21 Author's interview April 25th 1997
22 Pete Best & Patrick Doncaster *Beatle! The Pete Best Story* (Plexus 1985)
23 *Guitar Player* November 1987
24 Ray Minhinnett & Bob Young *The Story Of The Fender Stratocaster* (Miller Freeman 1995)
25 Hans Olof Gottfridsson *The Beatles From Cavern To Star Club* (Premium 1997)
26 *Guitar Player* November 1987
27 Jay Scott *The Guitars Of The Fred Gretsch Company* (Centerstream 1992)
28 Author's interview June 28th 1996
29 Yoko Ono & Sarah Lazin *Imagine John Lennon* (Macmillan 1988)
30 Author's interview January 8th 2001
31 Author's interview January 8th 2001
32 Author's interview June 28th 1996
33 Author's interview April 7th 1997
34 Author's interview June 28th 1996
35 Author's interview July 22nd 1996
36 Brian Epstein *A Cellar Full Of Noise* (Doubleday 1964)
37 Author's interview July 25th 1996
38 *Guitar Player* July 1990
39 Author's interview January 8th 2001
40 Author's interview April 7th 1997
41 Yoko Ono & Sarah Lazin *Imagine John Lennon* (Macmillan 1988)
42 Barry Miles *The Beatles: A Diary* (Omnibus 1998)
43 Barry Miles *The Beatles: A Diary* (Omnibus 1998)

Chapter 5: 1962 pp60-79
1 Barry Miles *The Beatles: A Diary* (Omnibus 1998)
2 Barry Miles *The Beatles: A Diary* (Omnibus 1998)
3 (Barry) Miles *John Lennon In His Own Words* (Omnibus 1980)
4 Author's interview January 8th 2001
5 Author's interview January 8th 2001
6 Author's interview January 8th 2001
7 Author's interview September 8th 1999
8 Author's interview September 8th 1999
9 Brian Epstein *A Cellar Full Of Noise* (Doubleday 1964)
10 Mark Lewisohn *The Beatles Recording Sessions* (Harmony/Crown 1988)
11 Author's interview October 21st 1996
12 Mark Lewisohn *The Beatles Recording Sessions* (Harmony/Crown 1988)
13 *The Beatles Anthology* video box-set (Apple 1996)
14 *A Concise History Of The Frying Pan* BBC Radio 1, 1987
15 Author's interview October 14th 1996
16 *Beat Instrumental* August 1963
17 Author's interview February 7th 1997
18 Author's interview September 26th 1996
19 Author's interview July 25th 1996
20 Author's interview June 2nd 1998
21 Author's interview June 21st 1996
22 Author's interview September 8th 1999
23 *Mersey Beat* October 4th-18th 1962
24 Author's interview July 22nd 1996
25 Author's interview July 25th 1996
26 Author's interview April 7th 1997
27 Author's interview April 11th 1997
28 Author's interview April 11th 1997
29 Author's interview July 25th 1996

Chapter 6: 1963 pp80-103
1 Author's interview April 7th 1997
2 Author's interview August 19th 1996
3 To Tony Bacon August 3rd 1995
4 Barry Miles *The Beatles: A Diary* (Omnibus 1996)
5 Barry Miles *The Beatles: A Diary* (Omnibus 1996)
6 Author's interview July 6th 1998
7 Author's interview March 22nd 1996
8 Author's interview April 10th 1996
9 Author's interview December 1st 1995
10 Author's interview January 8th 2001
11 *Beat Instrumental* July 1963
12 Author's interview April 10th 1996
13 Author's interview January 3rd 1997
14 *Beat Instrumental* July 1967
15 Interview with Tony Bacon October 1st 1993
16 Author's interview April 5th 1997
17 Author's interview February 7th 1997
18 *Beat Instrumental* August 1965
19 *The Beatles Monthly Book* April 1967
20 Author's interview April 2nd 1996
21 Author's interview April 6th 1997
22 *Melody Maker* September 28th 1963
23 Author's interview October 16th 1996
24 Interview with Tony Bacon February 22nd 2001
25 *Beat Instrumental* October 1964
26 *Press & Journal* October 25th 1963
27 *Beat Instrumental* May 1964
28 Author's interview January 3rd 1997
29 *The Beatles Monthly Book* January 1966
30 *Musician* July 1996

Chapter 7: 1964 pp104-155
1 Author's interview July 2nd 1996
2 *Beat Instrumental* April 1967
3 *The Beatles Monthly Book* March 1964
4 Author's interview May 31st 1996
5 Keith Badman *The Beatles Off The Record* (Omnibus 2000)
6 *The Music Trades* February 1964
7 Author's interview July 7th 2000
8 Author's interview May 3rd 1996
9 Author's interview November 29th 1995
10 Author's interview October 16th 1996
11 *A Concise History Of The Frying Pan* BBC Radio-1 1987
12 *Melody Maker* April 4th 1963
13 *The Music Trades* January 1965
14 Interview with Tony Bacon November 30th 1994
15 Author's interview December 1st 1995
16 *The Music Trades* March 1964
17 Author's interview November 29th 1995
18 Author's interview May 10th 1996
19 Author's interview November 5th 1996
20 Author's interview March 22nd 1996
21 *Beat Instrumental* November 1964
22 *Melody Maker* April 18th 1964
23 Author's interview March 22nd 1996
24 Author's interview July 26th 1996
25 Author's interview February 12th 1997
26 Letter dated July 26th 1994
27 Author's interview October 4th 1996
28 *Beat Instrumental* October 1964
29 *Beat instrumental* August 1964
30 *Beat Instrumental* July 1967
31 Author's interview November 5th 1996
32 Bonhams sale catalogue (Bonhams Tokyo, March 22nd 1997)
33 Author's interview March 14th 1997
34 *Leighton Buzzard Observer* September 7th 1965
35 Author's interview May 3rd 1996
36 Author's interview September 3rd 1996
37 *Record Mirror* June 6th 1964
38 Author's interview April 10th 1996
39 Author's interview September 8th 1999
40 Author's interview September 3rd 1996
41 *Beat Instrumental* November 1964
42 Author's interview March 28th 1997
43 Interview with Tony Bacon November 30th 1994
44 Author's interview March 22nd 1996
45 Author's interview February 7th 1997
46 *Beat Instrumental* June 1965
47 Author's interview February 7th 1997
48 *Beat Instrumental* July 1964
49 Author's interview January 3rd 1997
50 *Beat instrumental* October 1964
51 *Beat Instrumental* November 1964
52 Author's interview February 7th 1997
53 Author's interview February 7th 1997
54 *Guitar Player* November 1987
55 Author's interview May 10th 1996
56 *The Music Trades* April 1964
57 *Beat instrumental* November 1964
58 Author's interview December 11th 1995
59 Author's interview December 1st 1995
60 *The Music Trades* November 1964
61 Author's interview April 9th 2000
62 *Beat Instrumental* November 1964
63 *Beat Instrumental* June 1965
64 *The Music Trades* May 1964
65 *Beat Instrumental* December 1964
66 Author's interview October 23rd 1996
67 *Melody Maker* November 7th 1964
68 Ian MacDonald *Revolution In The Head* (Fourth Estate 1994)
69 *The Beatles Anthology* video box-set (Apple 1996)
70 Author's interview February 7th 1997
71 Author's interview March 28th 1997
72 Author's interview September 27th 1996
73 *The Beatles Monthly Book* September 1964
74 *Beat Instrumental* July 1965
75 Author's interview September 27th 1996
76 *Beat Instrumental* February 1967
77 *Beat Instrumental* October 1964
78 Author's interview July 14th 1997
79 Author's interview March 28th 1997
80 *Guitar Player* July 1990
81 Author's interview March 6th 1997
82 BBC Radio 2, 1996
83 BBC Radio 2, 1996
84 Author's interview April 5th 1997
85 Author's interview February 7th 1997
86 Letter dated October 26th 1982 (AEI Music Legends)
87 *Melody Maker* April 18th 1964
88 *Beat Instrumental* February 1965

Chapter 8: 1965 pp156-175
1 Ray Minhinnett & Bob Young *The Story Of The Fender Stratocaster* (Miller Freeman 1995)
2 *Melody Maker* February 27th 1965
3 *A Concise History Of The Frying Pan* BBC Radio-1 1987
4 *A Concise History Of The Frying Pan* BBC Radio-1 1987
5 Interview with Tony Bacon November 30th 1994
6 *The Beatles Monthly Book* August 1965
7 Author's interview June 3rd 1996
8 *Beat Instrumental* September 1965
9 Author's interview September 27th 1996
10 *Musician* July 1996
11 *Musical Merchandise Review* September 1965
12 Author's interview November 29th 1995
13 Interview with Tony Bacon November 30th 1994
14 The Byrds Turn! Turn! Turn! December 1965
15 Barry Miles *The Beatles: A Diary* (Omnibus 1998)
16 *The Beatles Anthology* video box-set (Apple 1996)
17 *Sounds Of The Sixties* BBC Radio-2 c1990
18 Author's interview June 27th 1997
19 Interview with Tony Bacon November 30th 1994
20 Interview with Tony Bacon November 30th 1994
21 Author's interview October 21st 1996
22 Author's interview February 7th 1997
23 *Beat Instrumental* November 1965
24 *The Beatles Anthology* video box-set (Apple 1996)
25 *The Beatles Monthly Book* November 1965
26 *Beat Instrumental* January 1966

Chapter 9: 1966 pp176-195
1 *The Beatles Monthly Book* February 1966
2 *The Beatles Monthly Book* November 1964
3 *The Beatles Monthly Book* December 1964
4 *The Beatles Monthly Book* January 1965
5 *The Beatles Monthly Book* April 1966
6 *Beat Instrumental* April 1966
7 *The Beatles Monthly Book* April 1966
8 Author's interview October 23rd 1996
9 Author's interview February 7th 1997
10 *Musician* August 1980
11 Author's interview October 23rd 1996
12 Author's interview October 23rd 1996
13 Author's interview October 21st 1996
14 Author's interview October 23rd 1996
15 Author's interview October 21st 1996
16 Author's interview October 21st 1996
17 Author's interview October 23rd 1996
18 *The Beatles Monthly Book* December 1966
19 Author's interview January 23rd 1996
20 Author's interview January 23rd 1996
21 Author's interview November 21st 1996
22 Author's interview January 23rd 1996
23 Author's interview January 26th 1996
24 Author's interview January 23rd 1996
25 Author's interview January 26th 1996
26 Author's interview December 5th 1995
27 Author's interview January 23rd 1996
28 Author's interview January 26th 1996
29 Author's interview September 26th 1996
30 Author's interview November 29th 1995
31 *The Beatles Anthology* video box-set (Apple 1996)
32 Joseph Brennan *Strawberry Fields Forever: Putting Together The Pieces* (website only)
33 *Beat Instrumental* October 1966
34 Author's interview February 7th 1997

Chapter 10: 1967 pp196-211
1 *The Making Of Sgt Pepper* film (Really Useful/Walt Disney 1992)
2 Interview with Tony Bacon November 30th 1994

3 Interview with Tony Bacon November 30th 1994
4 Author's interview October 23rd 1996
5 Author's interview December 20th 1996
6 Author's interview October 23rd 1996
7 Author's interview October 21st 1996
8 Author's interview December 20th 1996
9 *Musician* August 1980
10 *The Making Of Sgt Pepper* film (Really Useful/Walt Disney 1992)
11 Author's interview October 21st 1996
12 Author's interview October 23rd 1996
13 BBC Radio-1 1967
14 Interview with Tony Bacon May 1987
15 Author's interview December 20th 1996
16 Author's interview October 21st 1996
17 Author's interview August 13th 1996
18 *The Beatles Monthly Book* June 1967
19 Author's interview April 30th 1997
20 Author's interview October 23rd 1996
21 *The Beatles Monthly Book* June 1967
22 *The Making Of Sgt Pepper* film (Really Useful/Walt Disney 1992)
23 *The Making Of Sgt Pepper* film (Really Useful/Walt Disney 1992)
24 Author's interview December 20th 1996
25 Author's interview June 7th 1996
26 Author's interview March 19th 1997
27 *The Beatles Monthly Book* August 1967
28 Author's interview June 7th 1996
29 Author's interview December 20th 1996
30 *Beat Instrumental* June 1967
31 Ray Minhinnett & Bob Young *The Story of The Fender Stratocaster* (Miller Freeman 1995)
32 *Guitar Player* November 1987
33 Interview with Tony Bacon November 30th 1994
34 Author's interview December 22nd 1997
35 Author's interview December 20th 1996
36 Barry Miles *The Beatles: A Diary* (Omnibus 1998)
37 *Guitar Player* November 1987
38 Author's interview July 12th 1996
39 Author's interview February 7th 1997
40 *Beat Instrumental* October 1967
41 Author's interview March 22nd 1996

Chapter 11: 1968 pp212-231

1 Author's interview March 28th 1997
2 Author's interview June 25th 1996
3 Author's interview March 21st 1998
4 *The Beatles Anthology* (Cassell 2000)
5 Bill Harry *The Ultimate Beatles Encyclopedia* (Virgin 1992)
6 *The Beatles Anthology* (Cassell 2000)
7 *The Beatles Anthology* (Cassell 2000)
8 (Barry) Miles *John Lennon In His Own Words* (Omnibus 1980)
9 *The Beatles Anthology* video box-set (Apple 1996)
10 *Musician* August 1980
11 *Musician* August 1980
12 Author's interview March 21st 1998
13 *Guitar Player* November 1987
14 *The Beatles Monthly Book* April 1969
15 Author's interview August 30th 1996
16 *The Beatles Anthology* (Cassell 2000)
17 Author's interview December 11th 1995
18 Author's interview June 25th 1996
19 Author's interview December 20th 1996
20 Interview with Tony Bacon November 30th 1994
21 Mark Lewisohn *The Complete Beatles Recording Sessions* (Hamlyn/Crown 1988)
22 *Musician* August 1980
23 Author's interview June 25th 1996
24 *The Beatles Anthology* video box-set (Apple 1996)
25 *Musician* August 1980
26 *The Beatles Monthly Book* November 1968
27 Author's interview February 23rd 1996
28 Author's interview April 10th 1996
29 Author's interview December 20th 1996
30 *The Beatles Monthly Book* November 1968
31 Mark Lewisohn *The Complete Beatles Recording Sessions* (Hamlyn 1988)
32 *The Beatles Monthly Book* November 1968
33 *The Beatles Monthly Book* November 1968
34 *The Beatles Monthly Book* November 1968
35 *The Beatles Anthology* (Cassell 2000)

Chapter 12: 1969-70 pp232-251

1 *The Beatles Anthology* video box-set (Apple 1996)
2 *The Beatles Anthology* video box-set (Apple 1996)
3 *The Beatles Anthology* (Cassell 2000)
4 *The Beatles Anthology* video box-set (Apple 1996)
5 Author's interview April 10th 1996
6 Mark Lewisohn *The Complete Beatles Chronicle* (Pyramid 1992)
7 Mark Lewisohn *The Complete Beatles Recording Sessions* (Hamlyn/Crown 1988)
8 Author's interview July 4th 1998
9 Author's interview August 30th 1996
10 Author's interview May 12th 2000
11 Author's interview April 10th 1996
12 *The Beatles Monthly Book* March 1969
13 Author's interview January 16th 2001
14 Author's interview May 12th 2000
15 *The Beatles Monthly Book* March 1969
16 Author's interview July 4th 1998
17 Interview with Tony Bacon November 30th 1994
18 *The Beatles Monthly Book* July 1969
19 Author's interview August 16th 1996
20 Author's interview May 21st 1998
21 Author's interview May 14th 1996
22 *The Beatles Anthology* (Cassell 2000)
23 *The Beatles Anthology* video box-set (Apple 1996)
24 *The Beatles Anthology* video box-set (Apple 1996)
25 Author's interview July 4th 1998
26 Author's interview July 4th 1998
27 Author's interview April 10th 1996
28 Author's interview August 30th 1996
29 Author's interview November 22nd 1995
30 Author's interview December 20th 1996
31 Author's interview October 21st 1996
32 Author's interview July 4th 1998
33 Author's interview January 3rd 1997
34 Author's interview December 13th 1996
35 Author's interview February 23rd 2001
36 *The Beatles Monthly Book* October 1969
37 Author's interview February 2nd 1997
38 *Guitar Player* November 1987
39 Author's interview April 26th 2000
40 *The Beatles Anthology* video box-set (Apple 1996)

KEY TO PHOTOGRAPHS

After the relevant page number we list the illustration, followed usually by its owner or the picture's owner and/or photographer (sometimes plus the agency or other supplier, in brackets). In the case of instruments, the owner of the item is listed first, with the photographer and agency or other supplier in brackets. Principal instrument photography is by Miki Slingsby. Frequently-occurring names are represented by initials: AB Andy Babiuk; LW Larry Wassgren; MS Miki Slingsby; PD Paul Day; TB Tony Bacon.

Jacket front: Ludwig kit Ringo Starr (MS, Balafon); Hofner bass Paul McCartney (MS, Balafon); Rickenbacker guitar George Harrison (MS, Balafon); Vox ad Balafon. **Jacket rear**: Live on-stage Hulton Archive/Central Press; drum-head Russ Lease & Ron Wine (MS, Balafon); George seated Jurgen Vollmer (Redfern's); colour studio Hulton Deutsch/Apple Corps Ltd; Paul studio © Sean O'Mahony; Cavern sign Sotheby's. **2/3**: Hulton Deutsch/Apple Corps. **5**: Jurgen Vollmer (Redfern's).

Chapter 1: 1956-7 pp6-15
10: string pack Rod Davis; magazine LW. **10/11**: Gallotone guitar LW (MS, Balafon). **11**: Gallotone guitar Sotheby's; Gallotone flyers Gallo Africa Archive. **12**: fete Hulton Getty. **13**: fete programme AB. **14**: Whitman ad TB. **14/15**: Zenith guitar LW (MS, Balafon). **15**: Broadway kit Colin Hanton; banjo and tea-chest Rod Davis (Jonathan Davis); Egmond guitar LW (MS, Balafon); Zenith catalogue PD.

Chapter 2: 1958-9 pp16-27
18/19: Hofner guitar LW (MS, Balafon). **19**: George and guitar Hulton/Keystone; Egmond guitar LW (MS, Balafon); Hofner catalogue PD; Egmond catalogue PD. **21**: Mimi LW; Hessy receipt AB; card AB. **22**: pic Ray Ennis. **22/23**: Hofner guitar LW (MS, Balafon). **23**: Hofner guitar LW (MS, Balafon); Hofner catalogues PD. **24**: LW. **25**: Jurgen Vollmer (Redfern's). **26**: Hessy receipt AB; Futurama ad TB. **26/27**: Futurama guitar LW (MS, Balafon). **27**: guitar/case LW (MS, Balafon).

Chapter 3: 1960 pp28-43
30: Hessy receipt AB; Hofner catalogue PD. **30/31**: Hofner bass Sotheby's. **31**: Selmer amp LW (MS, Balafon); Hessy receipt AB. **33**: Rosetti catalogue PD; HP book Sotheby's. **34**: Hulton Deutsch/Keystone. **35**: Premier catalogues Rob Cook; Watkins amp LW (MS, Balafon); Elpico amp LW (MS, Balafon). **36**: Jurgen Vollmer (Redfern's). **37**: catalogue Don Randall. **38**: poster Sotheby's. **39**: Gibson catalogue TB; Gibson amp LW (MS, Balafon); Fender amp LW (MS, Balafon). **40/41**: Astrid Kirchherr (Redfern's). **42**: picture Rickenbacker archive. **42/43**: Rickenbacker guitar and details Yoko Ono (MS, Balafon). **43**: document Rickenbacker archive.

Chapter 4: 1961 pp44-59
46: Sheridan pic Redfern's; Cavern sign Sotheby's. **47**: Jurgen Vollmer (Redfern's). **48**: K&K Studios (Redfern's). **49**: Peter Bruchmann (Redfern's). **50**: Hulton Getty/Keystone. **51**: card AB. **52**: catalogue TB. **53**: Reslo mike LW (MS, Balafon); Martin catalogue Balafon. **54**: Cavern pic Bill Harry. **54/55**: Gretsch guitar George Harrison (MS, Balafon). **55**: Bigsby catalogue TB; John pic Hulton Archive/Evening Standard. **56**: Hessy ad LW. **57**: Glenn A Baker Archives (Redfern's). **58**: K&K Studios (Redfern's). **59**: both Adrian Barber.

Chapter 5: 1962 pp60-79
62: Roy Young. **66**: Dick Denney. **67**: Quad catalogue TB; Coffin rig AB; Vox amp Martin Kelly (MS, Balafon). **68**: catalogue TB. **70**: catalogue Balafon. **71**: Premier kit Sotheby's. **72**: Rushworth's ad LW. **74**: poster AB. **74/75**: Gibson guitar George Harrison (MS, Balafon). **75**: receipt Sotheby's; log Gibson archive (Walter Carter); catalogue TB; group pic Hulton Getty/Keystone. **76/77**: Peter Bussey (Redfern's). **78**: club receipts Bruce Mineroff. **78/79**: pic K&K Ulf Kruger OHG (Redfern's).

Chapter 6: 1963 pp80-103
82: Hulton Getty/Keystone. **83**: logos Tex O'Hara; pic Hulton Getty. **84**: © Sean O'Mahony. **85**: Michael Ochs Archives (Redfern's). **86**: Vox ad TB; drums Ringo Starr (MS, Balafon); Ludwig finishes Rob Cook. **87**: Ludwig kit Ringo Starr (MS, Balafon). **88**: ad AB. **89**: Best pic Bill Harry. **90**: poster AB. **90/91**: Gretsch guitar Gary Dick (MS, Balafon). **91**: Gretsch guitar Gary Dick (MS, Balafon); George pic Jennifer Cohen. **92**: Paul pic © Sean O'Mahony; Vox top boost Michael Gagliano (MS, Balafon); Vox ad TB. **93**: David Redfern (Redfern's). **94**: backstage pic © Sean O'Mahony; document Rickenbacker archive. **94/95**: Rickenbacker guitar Bruce Mineroff (MS, Balafon). **95**: Maton catalogue TB; Maton pic Steven Stevlor (National Centre for Popular Music); group pic David Redfern (Redfern's). **98**: Maestro Fuzz-Tone Greg Prevost (MS, Balafon); Maestro ad Balafon. **98/99**: Hofner bass and detail Paul McCartney (MS, Balafon). **99**: group pic Tom Hanley (Redfern's). **100**: David Farrell (Redfern's). **102**: David Redfern (Redfern's). **103**: poster AB.

Chapter 7: 1964 pp104-155
106/107: Gretsch guitar AB (MS, Balafon). **107**: George pic © Sean O'Mahony. **108**: letter & message Rickenbacker archive. **109**: © Sean O'Mahony. **110**: ad Balafon. **110/111**: Rickenbacker guitar George Harrison (MS, Balafon). **111**: George pic © Sean O'Mahony. **113**: document Rickenbacker archive. **114**: drum-head Russ Lease & Ron Wine (MS, Balafon). **115**: © Sean O'Mahony. **116**: Hulton Archive/Central Press. **118**: document Rickenbacker archive. **118/119**: Rickenbacker guitar and detail Yoko Ono (MS, Balafon). **119**: guitar snap Ron DeMarino; group pic Hulton/Keystone. **121**: Max Scheler K&K (Redfern's). **122**: label AB. **123**: drum-mount Ringo Starr (MS, Balafon); Rogers catalogue Rob Cook. **124/125**: Max Scheler K&K (Redfern's). **126**: swing-ticket Balafon. **126/127**: Hofner bass and details Sotheby's. **127**: Clifftops pic John Bunning. **128**: letter Rickenbacker archive. **130/131**: Rickenbacker guitar Yoko Ono (MS, Balafon). **131**: group pic Hulton Deutsch; strap Martin Kelly (MS, Balafon). **133**: David Redfern (Redfern's). **134**: strings AB; group pic Glenn A Baker (Redfern's). **135**: Ludwig kit Ringo Starr (MS, Balafon). **137**: © Sean O'Mahony. **138**: Vox ad Balafon; Vox amp Michael Gagliano (MS, Balafon); handshake pic Dick Denney. **139**: group pic Michael Ochs (Redfern's); tour programme AB. **140/141**: Hulton Getty/Evening Standard. **142**: log Gibson archive (Walter Carter); gold drum & case Ringo Starr (MS, Balafon); presentation pic Ludwig Industries. **143**: Hohner pack AB. **144**: © Sean O'Mahony. **145**: Roadrunners pic Charles Lytle. **146**: Paul/George pic © Sean O'Mahony; Texan ad TB. **146/147**: Epiphone guitar Gary Dick (MS, Balafon). **148**: Casino ad TB. **149**: © Sean O'Mahony. **150**: Gretsch guitar & case & detail John Gillard (P J Cullen); Epiphone log Gibson archive (Walter Carter). **150/151**: Epiphone guitar Paul McCartney (MS, Balafon). **152**: ad TB. **154/155**: Rickenbacker guitar Nick Rowlands (MS, Balafon). **155**: ad TB.

Chapter 8: 1965 pp156-175
158: label AB. **158/159**: Fender guitar Gary Winterflood (Matthew Chattle, Balafon). **159**: John pic © Sean O'Mahony; ticket AB. **162**: Hulton Deutsch/Apple Corps Ltd. **163**: Hohner keyboard AB (MS, Balafon); magazine cover pic © Sean O'Mahony. **164**: George/John pic © Sean O'Mahony; Framus catalogue AB. **166**: Vox keyboard AB; Vox catalogue TB; Paul pic Hulton Deutsch. **167**: main pic Hulton/Apple Corps Ltd; Vox keyboard Bonhams. **168**: Vox ad TB. 170: George pic © Sean O'Mahony. **170/171**: Rickenbacker guitar AB (MS, Balafon). **171**: Rickenbacker catalogue TB; presentation pic Don Johnson (*Musical Merchandise Review*); Hammond catalogue Joe Barone. **173**: Vox fx box Michael Gagliano (MS, Balafon). **174**: Ludwig kit Ringo Starr (MS, Balafon). **175**: Gibson ad TB; George pic © Sean O'Mahony.

Chapter 9: 1966 pp176-195
178: Fender catalogue TB. **178/179**: Gibson guitar Gary Dick (MS, Balafon). **179**: Gibson catalogue TB; Gretsch guitar John Reynolds; John pic © Sean O'Mahony. **181**: © Sean O'Mahony. **182**: Burns catalogue PD. **183**: Hulton Deutsch/Apple Corps. **186**: Vox catalogue TB. **187**: Friedhelm von Estorff/K&K (Redfern's). **188/189**: 6 live pics © 1966 Gordon Baer. **190**: Guild main shot David Franzen, inset Mark Dronge. **191**: Vox amp/cab Will Houde-Walter (MS, Balafon), amp (rear) House Of Guitars (MS, Balafon); Vox catalogue AB. **192**: pic Barry Tashian. **193**: ticket AB. **194**: Mellotron Sotheby's. **195**: Vox catalogue TB; Vox amp Michael Gagliano (MS, Balafon).

Chapter 10: 1967 pp196-211
198: © Sean O'Mahony. **201**: trumpet & case Sotheby's; Paul & orchestra Hulton. **202**: Hammond catalogue TB; Lowrey catalogue Joe Barone. **203**: Clavioline catalogue TB; Clavioline keyboard/amp AB (MS, Balafon). **204**: Fender catalogue/Selmer ad TB. **205**: © Sean O'Mahony. **206**: John pic © Sean O'Mahony. **206/207**: Fender guitar George Harrison (MS, Balafon). **207**: 3 guitars Gibson Montana Division; group pic Hulton Deutsch/Apple Corps. **209**: pic Balafon. **210**: Sitar ad PD. **210/211**: Coral sitar Yoko Ono (MS, Balafon). **211**: group pic: Hulton Getty.

Chapter 11: 1968 pp212-231
214: Hulton Getty/Keystone. **215**: Vox catalogue TB; John pic Hulton Deutsch. **216**: Hulton Getty/Keystone. **218/219**: Epiphone guitar & details Yoko Ono (MS, Balafon). **220**: Apple/Hulton Deutsch/ Keystone. **222/223**: Martin guitar Acoustic Centre (MS, Balafon). **223**: Gibson catalogue PD. **226/227**: Gibson guitar George Harrison (MS, Balafon). **227**: log Gibson archive (Walter Carter); Fender catalogue TB. **228**: Apple store, top: Hulton Deutsch; bottom: Redfern's. **230**: © Sean O'Mahony. **231**: Fender catalogue TB.

Chapter 12: 1969-70 pp232-251
234: Ludwig catalogue Rob Cook. **234/235**: Rickenbacker bass Paul McCartney (MS, Balafon). **235**: Ludwig kit Ringo Starr (MS, Balafon). **236**: Fender catalogue TB. **237**: Arbiter fx box Robin Guthrie (MS, Balafon). **238**: Fender Twin amp Rod Phelps (MS, Balafon); Fender Bassman amp House Of Guitars (MS, Balafon). **238/239**: Fender guitar Delaney Bramlett (Bonhams). **239**: Delaney & Bonnie pic Kim & Delaney Bramlett. **240 & 241**: Fender catalogues TB. **243**: Hulton Archive. **246/247**: Gibson guitar and detail Yoko Ono (MS, Balafon). **247**: John pic Hulton Getty. **248/249**: 8 pics Tom Hartman. **250**: Moog synthesiser Martin Newcomb (MS, Balafon).

ACKNOWLEDGEMENTS

The author and publisher would like to thank The Beatles and their associates who helped with this book:

George Harrison, Harry Harrison, Alan Rogan.

The Lennon Estate, Yoko Ono, Karla Merrifield, Studio One.

Sir Paul McCartney, John Hammel, MPL Communications Ltd.

Ringo Starr, Bruce Grakal, Bill Harrison.

Sir George Martin; Geoff Emerick.

The author sends very special thanks to the following whose help and encouragement made this book possible: Tony Bacon, Nigel Osborne, and everyone at Backbeat UK; Kevin Walsh; Larry "I only collect pre-Ringo instruments" Wassgren; Russ Lease; Miki Slingsby; Bob Martin. Dick Denney became a good friend during the making of this book, and went out of his way to help, so it was with deep regret I learned of his death during 2001. I'll miss Dick – but every time I play my AC-30 I'll think of him.

This book would not have been possible without the existence of three key Beatle books. They are The Complete Beatles Recording Sessions (Hamlyn/Crown 1988) and The Complete Beatles Chronicle (Pyramid 1992) by Mark Lewisohn, and The Beatles Anthology (Cassell 2000). Mark's painstaking work on researching and cataloguing The Beatles' recordings and other activities is unequalled and his definitive books are a must. This book would also have been considerably more difficult to put together had it not been for Sean O'Mahony and the reports and photographs he published in the 1960s in his Beat Instrumental and Beatles Monthly Book magazines, which helped unravel the puzzle. Grateful thanks to Mark and Sean.

The author would like to thank: Bob Adams, Phil Alexander, Kent Allen, Sidney Amsellem, Dave Anderson, Ivor Arbiter, John Arbiter, Arbiter Group, Chet Atkins, Avedis Zildjian Co, Randy Bachman, Gordon Baer (Cincinnati), Ginger Baker, Vic Baltusis, Rick Bandoni, Adrian Barber, Joe Barone, John Barrelli, Peter Barton (Rothery Artist Management International),
Johnny Bee Badanjek, Tom Bender, Christian Benker, Peter Bennett, Jay Bertalan, Pete Best, Roag Best, Bev Bevan, Alf Bicknell, Roger Binette, Micheal Blum, Colin Blunstone, Dick Boak, Mike Boise, Bonhams, Boosey & Hawkes, Hank Borchers, John Borrelli, Mike Boyack, Gloria Boyce, Les Braid, Delaney Bramlett, Kim Bramlett, Rich Briere, Harold Bronson, Lee Brovits, Joe Brown, Ken Brown, Michael Brown, Pat Brown, Jack Bruce, Wally Bryson, John Bunning, Jim Burdett, Eric Burdon, Danny Burgauer, Ron Bushy, Terry M Butz, John Sean Byrne, Johnny Guitar Byrne, Joe Carducci, Bun E. Carlos, Walter Carter, Jeff Cary, Peppy Castro, Jim Catalano, Sam Catalona, Cheap Trick, Neil Cherian, The Chesterfield Kings, Jeff Chonis, Christie's, Mike Cidoni, Allan Clarke, Reg Clarke, Mitch Colby, Rob Cook (Rebeats), Gene Cornish, Fred Coyner, Inciardi Craig, Tony Crane, Kenny Daniel, Don Dannemann, Jonathan Davis, Rod Davis, Spencer Davis, Paul Day, John De Christopher, Dave Dean, Ron DeMarino, Dera & Associates, Rick Derringer, Gary Dick (Gary's Classic Guitars), Bo Diddley, Dennis Diken, DJ Printing, Dick Dodd, Lee Dorman, Chris Dreja, Mark Dronge, Aynsley Dunbar, Jamie Duquette, Allison Dutch, Eager Bros Music, Elliot Easton, Ian Edwards, EMI International, Kris Engelhardt, Dresden Engle, Ray Ennis, John Entwistle, Epiphone, EPL Pictures Ltd, Gerry Evans, Fender Musical Instruments, Ren Ferguson, Bill Flores, Kim Fowley, Darik Franks, Ed Freeman, David Fricke, George Fullerton, Mike Galia, Freddie Garritty, George Eastman House, Brian Gibson, Gibson Montana, Gibson USA, John "St John" Gillard, Doug Gould, Lou Gram, Phil Grant, Rick Greenstein, Fred Gretsch, Fred Gretsch Enterprises Ltd, Eric Griffiths, Henry Gross, Guitar Salon International, Mick Guzauski, Randy Haecker, F.C. Hall, John Hall, Tom Hamilton, Bill Hanley, Garth Hannie, Hansal, Colin Hanton, Hard Rock Hotel, Justin Harrison, Louise Harrison, Richard Harrison, Bill Harry, Tom Hartman, Bruce Hastell, Brian Hatt, Bob Havalack, Mark Havey, Justin Hayward, Lenny Helsing, Tony Hicks, Rick Hock, Karl Hofner GmbH, Barry Hood, Daryl Hooper, Jamie Hoover, Matt Horwitz, Will Houde-Water, House Of Guitars, Chris Huston,
Bob Irwin, Jeff Jarema, Stan Jay (Mandolin Bros), Glyn Johns, Robi Johns, Don Johnson (Musical Merchandise Review), Bruce Johnston, Davy Jones, Mick Jones, Laurence Juber, Jorma Kaukonen, JD King, Billy Kinsley, Marijke Koger, Korg USA, Billy J Kramer, Duke Kramer, Eddie Kramer, Howard Kramer, Paul Kreft, Carl Labate, Denny Laine, Greg Lake, Glen Lambert, Mark Lapidos, Rob LaVaque, Carol Lawrence, Pearl Leaberman, Donovan Leitch, Tony Levin, Rick Levy, Ace Ray Lichtenstein, Deb Lindsay, Mark Lindsay, Miriam Linna (Norton Records Archives), Richard Lipack, Tim Livingston, Jackie Lomax, Jim Lopes (B-Sharp Music), Brett Louden, James Lowe, John Duff Lowe, William Ludwig Jr, The Ludwig/Selmer Company, Richard Lush, Charle Lytel, Robert Malvasi, Colin Manley, Jim Marince, Gerry Marsden, Chris Martin IV, C.F. Martin Guitar Company, Mike Maxfield, Brian May, John Mayall, Stephen Maycock, Gabe McCarty, Delbert McClinton, Eric McDow, Jerry McGeorge, Roger McGuinn, Scott MacKenzie, John McNally, Scotty Meade (EPL Pictures Ltd), Terry Melcher, Dale Menten, Ron Mesh, Tim Miklaucic, Billy Miller, Vern Miller, Bruce Mineroff, Joey Molland, Zoot Money, Bill Monot, Dr Bob Moog, Malcolm Moore, Paul Morabito, Graham Nash, The National Centre For Popular Music (Sheffield), Rick Nielsen, Paul Nunes, Brian O'Hara, Mark O'Hara, Tex O'Hara, The Old Hippie, Rob Olsen, John Oram, Brian Ormand, Ted Owen, Wally Palmar, May Pang, Alan Parsons, Siobhan Pascoe, Tom Passamonte, Alby Paynter, Les Paul, Mike Pender, Carl Perkins, Rick Perrotta, Tom Petersson, Rod Phelps, John Phillips, Nick Phillips, Bruce Pilato (Pilato Entertainment Group), Ethan Porter, Simmon Posthuma, Don Potter, Greg Prevost, Amalia Ramírez (José Ramírez Guitarras Musica SL), Don Randall, Noel Redding, Retro/Active Music Memorabilia, Rickenbacker International Corporation, Rock & Roll Hall of Fame & Museum, Betty Rodrigues, Tommy Roe, Wayne Rogers, Hari Rogulj, Jim Rosenberg, Chris Roslan, Rothery Artist Management International , John Ryan, Bob Sabellico, Mark Sampson, Jim Sawyers, Bruce & Armand Schaubroeck, Jay Scott, Mike Selby, Ravi Shankar, Tony
Sheridan, Kim Simmonds (Savoy Brown), Richard Smith, Jim Sohns, Sotheby's, David Soule, Jim Spencer, David Spero, Warwick Stone, Alan Stratton, Sundazed Music, Art Swartele, Barry Tashian, Dick Taylor, Doug Taylor, Steve Taylor, Jean Toots Thielemans, Brad Townsend, Ken Townsend, Mark Tulin, Sal Valentino, Scott Van Dusen, Vox Amplification Ltd, Keith Wechsler, Jeff & Brad Wheat, Alan White, Silagh White, Steve "It'll only take you a weekend" (six years later!) White, Barry Whitwam, Chris Whorton, Carl Wilson, Zal Yanovsky, Carol Young, Roy Young, Robin Zander.

The publisher would like to thank the following in addition to those named in the Key To Photographs: Junichi Akutsu (John Lennon Museum), Rob Allingham (Gallo Africa Archive), Walter Carter, Paul Day, Gary S Dick (Gary's Classic Guitars), Lyn Edwards, Suzanne Elston (Abbey Road), Alexander Crum Ewing (Bonhams), Lee Gagliano, Dave Gregory, Ben Hall, John Hall (Rickenbacker), Tetsuo Hamada (Produce Centre), John Hammel, Bill Harrison, Rick Hock, Sanae Ito (Produce Centre), Donald James, David Kean, Howard Kramer (Rock & Roll Hall Of Fame), Russ Lease, Mark Lewisohn, Christie Lucco (Rock & Roll Hall Of Fame), Brian Majeski (The Music Trades), Bob Martin, Barry Mason, Stephen Maycock (Sotheby's), Karla Merrifield (Studio One), Barry Moorhouse (Acoustic Centre), David Nathan (National Jazz Foundation Archive), Geoff Nicholls, Em Parkinson (Hulton Archives), Greg Prevost, Heinz Rebellius, John Reynolds (Golden Age Guitars), Phil Richardson, Chris Roberts, Alan Rogan, Lisa Savage (Rock & Roll Hall Of Fame), Dave Seville, Mark Vail, Jaap van Eik, Larry Wassgren, Masatoshi Watanabe (John Lennon Museum), Jon Wilton (Redfern's).

Trademarks: Throughout this book a number of registered trademark names are used. Rather than put a symbol next to every occurrence of a trademarked name, we state here that we are using the names only in an editorial fashion and that we do not intend to infringe any trademarks.

Currency in the UK in the 1950s and 1960s was pounds/shillings/pence (£/s/d) expressed like this: £230/15/6. Twelve pence equalled a shilling, 20 shillings equalled a pound. Some luxury goods were priced in guineas; one guinea equalled one pound and one shilling. In this book original UK and US retail prices are sometimes expressed in today's buying power based on formulas devised by the British Government Statistics Office and the US Department Of Labor.

Chart positions quoted come from the Guinness compilations which, for the period covered by this book, are drawn from material originally published in NME and Record Retailer.

Updates? The author and publisher welcome any new information for future editions. Write to Andy Babiuk c/o Backbeat UK, 115J Cleveland Street, London W1T 6PU, England. Or email Andy at beatlesgear@att.net, or visit www.beatlesfabgear.com

This book is dedicated to my wife Monica and my children Elizabeth, Victoria, Catherine, Andrew and Laura.

"John loved his guitar collection, all of the guitars. However, his favourite guitar was always the one he'd just bought."
Yoko Ono AUTHOR'S INTERVIEW MAY 1998